*The New Connoisseurs' Guidebook
to California Wine and Wineries*

The New Connoisseurs' Guidebook
to California Wine and Wineries

Charles E. Olken
Joseph Furstenthal

UNIVERSITY OF CALIFORNIA PRESS

BERKELEY   LOS ANGELES   LONDON

University of California Press, one of the most distinguished university presses in the United States, enriches
lives around the world by advancing scholarship in the
humanities, social sciences, and natural sciences. Its activities are supported by the UC Press Foundation and by
philanthropic contributions from individuals and institu-
tions. For more information, visit www.ucpress.edu.

University of California Press
Berkeley and Los Angeles, California

University of California Press, Ltd.
London, England

Library of Congress Cataloging-in-Publication Data

Olken, Charles E.
    The new connoisseurs' guidebook to California wine
and wineries / Charles E. Olken, Joseph Furstenthal.
        p. cm.
    Includes bibliographical references and index.
    ISBN 978-0-520-25313-1 (pbk. : alk. paper)
    1. Wine and wine making—California. 2. Wineries—
California—Guidebooks. I. Furstenthal, Joseph. II. Title.
III. Title: California wine and wineries.
    TP557.O438 2010
    641.2'209794—dc22   2010010390

Manufactured in the United States of America
16   15   14   13   12   11   10
10   9   8   7   6   5   4   3   2   1

The paper used in this publication meets the minimum
requirements of ANSI/NISO Z39.48-1992 (R 1997)
(*Permanence of Paper*). ♾

CONTENTS

LIST OF WINE REGIONS

LIST OF MAPS

PREFACE

IT IS NOW THREE DECADES SINCE MY FIRST BOOK, *The Connoisseurs'
Handbook of California Wines*, appeared in print. In that era, it was easy
to cover virtually every winery and to extend the book's reach to Oregon
and Washington. There was nothing comprehensive in print covering West
Coast wines, and those books that had earlier described the California wine
scene had been made obsolete by the industry's rapid expansion in the early
1970s. At the same time, the extraordinary quality improvements being made
by new and existing producers alike because of new understandings about
winemaking and improving technology also altered the landscape. In short,
California and the West Coast had changed, and the *Handbook* was able to
capture those changes for a growing wine-buying world.

The *Handbook* held on gamely through four major revisions and many
reprintings, and in one form or another, stayed in print for over twenty-
five years. But, like all attempts to take a snapshot of a moving target, it
became increasingly a captive of past scenes and could not adapt to the
new reality of thousands of labels, greatly expanded growing areas, and
the changes in information exchange brought about by the emergence of
the Internet.

When my writing partners, Norman Roby and Earl Singer, and I finally
put the *Handbook* to bed almost a decade ago, it had outlived its usefulness
in its existing form. Today, one can get more information via the Internet

than any basic reference book can provide. When it came time to produce another broadly written look at the California wine industry, it was clear that a new approach was needed, and this book, rather than trying to out-produce the Internet, takes full advantage of the extensive resources available at everyone's fingertips by providing Web addresses for every winery and for many other valuable sources of information.

Virtually every winery Web site is more extensive than anything we or any other author could put into written form. In this book, then, the basic introductory matter for each winery sets the scene for the detailed background information that follows—data not generally available such as production level and vineyard acreage, examinations of house winemaking styles, and ratings for thousands of wines. This book has one other advantage, too: it combines in one place information on almost five hundred wineries, on some 130 or more places that grapes are grown, and about virtually every important grape and wine type made in California. No single Web site does all that as comprehensively as this book.

Another aspect of this book that separates it from winery Web sites is the provision of critical evaluations of wine quality based on the independent, blind tastings conducted by my newsletter, *Connoisseurs' Guide to California Wine*, at www.cgcw.com. Every year, the guide publishes thousands of wine reviews for its subscribers, and it is only through sources like *Connoisseurs' Guide* that wine lovers are able to keep up with the very latest releases from the wineries included in this book.

This book owes its existence first to my partners in the earlier *Connoisseurs' Handbook*, Messrs. Roby and Singer, and now to my friend and partner in this latest opus, the redoubtable Joe Furstenthal, whose enthusiasm and vision have caused this new project to take wing.

In putting this new book together, we focused the chapters on the turf from which California wines come. Rather than providing one encyclopedic alphabetical list, this book takes the reader into every identifiable appellation from which wine is made. Then it identifies the key producers in each of those wine regions. The accompanying maps will show the locations of each area and the general location of each winery mentioned in the text.

The suggestions and comments that follow in the next pages describe more fully how the book is constructed and guides you through the most thorough, comprehensive set of information about California wineries in print today. It is a ready reference of tremendous value, but it is also a snapshot of available information at the time of its writing.

The Reading List section of this book cites books, periodicals, and Internet sources for day-to-day information. Up-to-date reviews of the most recently released wines can be accessed to some extent from newspapers and Internet blogs. For more comprehensive sets of wine evaluations and recommendations, wine lovers often subscribe to wine review publications whose thousands of critical evaluations are the standards of reference used substantially throughout the wine industry.

I invite readers of the book to visit the *Connoisseurs' Guide* site at www.cgcw.com, to read our daily blog covering subjects of interest, latest news, and daily wine recommendations and to sample our monthly subscriber newsletter. You can also request a complimentary look at the Subscriber Only portion of the *Connoisseurs' Guide* Web site and can leave comments about this book or any other topic of wine interest through the Web site or by direct e-mail to cgcw@aol.com. Periodic updates to the book will be available only to you and to our newsletter subscribers at www.cgcw.com/book. Please register with the password "guidebook."

Charles E. Olken

USING THIS BOOK AND ITS WINE RATINGS

ANYONE CAN WRITE A CALIFORNIA WINE BOOK with a few basic facts. That's the easy part. The facts are out there on the Internet and in other books. What is not so readily available, however, is judgment and analysis. In this book, the authors set the stage with the basic facts about each of the almost five hundred wineries included.

What comes next is a framework for those facts and explanations, analysis and recommendations that provide depth and understanding. In one sense, this is a complex book. But it is also easy to read when you want to track from one set of facts to another. It takes lots of information to understand wine. History, grapes, winemaking, terminology, geography, and critical review all come into play in the wine choices we make. And so do a variety of information sources. This book does all of that and more for California wine.

A BRIEF HISTORY OF WINE IN CALIFORNIA

California wine history is short compared with Europe's, but it has moved very quickly over time, and it is helpful to know how California got to the point of being a world power in the international wine scene. This chapter traces its wine history in a brief, easily read manner. Other books share longer history sections, and whole books are available that relate to California wine history. You will find the best of those works recommended in the Reading List at the end of this book.

HOW WINE IS MADE

This section will not turn you into a winemaker, but it does explain the basics of the winemaking process together with brief discussions of the major choices that wineries face in producing the wines we see in bottles.

GRAPES AND WINE TYPES

Almost every wine made in California, and indeed, in most parts of the New World, contains either the name of the grape or a reference to a wine type. In most parts of Europe, the system is quite different. There, wines are very often labeled only with the name of the area from which they come, and wine drinkers are expected to know that those place names are related to very strict rules about which grapes can be used.

Happily, we do it differently, and the result is that California growers and wineries have much more flexibility in what they grow and what they make. The result is a system in which grape and wine type names are the most important designation of what is in the bottle.

GEOGRAPHY AND WINERIES

Because this book has been organized to group wineries with geographic area, the Winery Index in the back of the book helps you easily find both the places and wineries in the book.

These two elements of geography and winery are next most important label designations. Each of the nine central chapters in the book is identified by geographic region, and each of those chapters contains (1) a description of the smaller areas within those regions and (2) an entry for the most important wineries in each of those regions.

THE GEOGRAPHY ENTRIES

The chapters start with a discussion of geography because "place" is important. The soils and climate of each place are the key elements in the kind of wine that comes from those places. Wineries can and do modify what the geography gives them, but no winery can make better wine than the grapes allow them to make. You will also find Web site references in these entries for the organizations that function within the various geographic areas. Depending on the size and complexity of the information provided, these sites provide information about terrain, wineries located there, visiting hours, grapes grown there, maps of the area (often interactive), and more general information than a book of this size and portability can contain.

THE WINERY ENTRIES

When you read a winery entry, you will see that its first lines tell you where it is located both by city and also by appellation. By reading the geography descriptions at the front of each chapter, you will get an idea of how place plays into the winery's production and style. The basic facts that follow for each winery will tell you where each gets its grapes, how large its production is, what vineyards it owns, what its house style is, and how well its wines are regarded qualitatively.

WINE QUALITY RATINGS EXPLAINED

Within winery entries, usually as the concluding remarks, you will find an assessment of the wine quality that those wineries are producing. Those assessments are based on the blind tastings of tens of thousands of wines that the authors have conducted and then described in the monthly newsletter, *Connoisseurs' Guide to California Wine.* You can see a detailed explanation of our tasting methodology and symbolic notation scale on our Web site at www.cgcw.com. You can also view a sample of our monthly newsletter, and you may request complimentary, month-long access to the newsletter complete with our extensive data base of past reviews. Sign up on the Web site for monthly updates to this book at www.cgcw.com/book. These updates are available only to our subscribers and to readers of this book who sign up for the updates.

The qualitative ratings in this book are expressed in what is called the "100-point scale," which is modeled after the standard school grading systems. Ratings are often expressed as ranges of scores because wines vary by vintage. As used here, the ratings have the following meanings:

Mid-90 points and above. These ratings are for superlative wines only. They are simply the best of the best, and they are few and far between—typically the top 1 to 2 percent of all wines we have reviewed.

Lower 90 points. Wine ratings in this range are excellent wines by almost any standard. Historically, such wines have accounted for about 10 to 15 percent of all wines reviewed. The wineries in this book have been chosen, in large part, because of the quality of wines they produce, but also because you are more likely to find them or to hear of them.

Upper 80 points. These are recommended wines of their type. They are well-made, enjoyable wines of above-average quality.

Mid- to upper 80 points. Wines of average to slightly above average quality are found at this level. They are often very Good Values when priced accordingly and typically are free from winemaking flaws. Wines in this ratings range represent the greater portion of wines mentioned this book.

Mid- to lower 80 points. Not many wines in this book rate below the mid-80s, but some wines inevitably fall into that category in lesser vintages. At this rating level, price is a major factor in any buying decision.

Wines identified as Good Value. Many producers overachieve at their chosen price levels. When they do, their wines are identified as offering "Good Value."

PART ONE

A California Wine Primer

A Brief History of Wine in California

MORE THAN TWO HUNDRED YEARS after Spanish missionaries brought vine cuttings with them from Mexico's Baja California and established the first of the California missions in San Diego, researchers at Madrid's National Biotechnical Center, using DNA techniques, have traced those first vines back to a black grape that seems to be a dark-colored relative of the Palomino grape still in use for the production of Sherry. That humble beginning may not seem like it would have much to do with today's burgeoning wine industry, but the fact is that the Mission variety became the vine of choice in California as its population grew first through the arrival of trappers and wealthy landowners, then with the small but steady stream of wagon trains that came west out of the country's heartland and the establishment in the 1840s of the clipper ship trade. By the time the transcontinental railroad was completed in 1869, California's wine economy had become established, and despite world wars and periods in which the sale of alcohol was banned, the industry hung on and finally exploded into its current shape with the wine boom of the 1970s. Today, the Mission grape is gone, but the wine industry it helped spawn now boasts over a half million acres of wine grapes from one end of the state to the other.

In 1769, Father Junípero Serra established the first of the Spanish missions at San Juan Capistrano in Orange County south of Los Angeles. Despite the supposed two hundredth anniversary of California wine that was celebrated in 1969, it is believed today that Father Serra did not plant vines and make wines until a decade later. During the last fifteen years of his life, Serra established eight more missions and associated vineyards. Serra planted a grape variety from Mexico that became known as the Mission grape and later thrived as the leading grape in California until the wave of settlers in the 1850s and 1860s would bring more noble varieties to California. What became a total of twenty-one missions would sustain the production of more wine, but it was all for the members of the church and not a wine "industry" per se.

During this period, the only ways to get to California were overland, mostly by wagon train, or by clipper ship around the southern tip of South America. Because the continental railroad was still two decades away, California might have resisted population growth had it not been for the discovery of gold and the resulting Gold Rush. Indeed, in the early 1800s, there was almost no nonnative population in existence in the region. By the 1830s, though, Mexican land grants led to the establishment of farms and then to the development of villages. One such landowner was George Yount, who settled in the Napa Valley in 1836 and soon after planted the first vines there. It wasn't long until he attached his name to history by establishing Yountville in the Napa Valley.

Also during the 1830s, an aptly named Frenchman, Jean Louis Vignes, brought the first substantial stock of French vines to Los Angeles. While his contribution did not spark the first California wine expansion, his vines did find their way into the plantings in Southern California. And while Vignes may have been the first, his influence did not spread. Rather, it took a completely different circumstance to change California forever—the discovery of gold in the Sierra mountains east of San Francisco.

Back east, prior to the Gold Rush, a small wine industry developed in the Midwest, focused substantially in Ohio, while, at the same time, horticulturalists along the East Coast were growing grapes in hothouses and entering them in the competitions of the day. We know that one such person was a clipper ship captain named James Macondray. His prize-winning Zinfandel grapes were honored in Boston as early as the 1830s. Macondray would, by 1850 or so, settle in San Francisco. The records of his journey do not specifically list Zinfandel as part of his cargo, but it is very likely that Macondray is a primary source of the grape that for so long was known as California's own. His cuttings found their way to Napa and then to Sonoma.

Also during this period, Spanish land grants gave over-large blocks of what was thought to be unproductive dirt to California farmers. The shape and location of these holdings would influence later development, and even today the land grant known as Los Carneros still finds its name prominently attached to the Napa and Sonoma wine country. Still, by all accounts, the population of California at the end of this period was something like fifteen thousand, with about 40 percent immigrants and 60 percent native inhabitants. By 1850, that total would grow to almost one hundred thousand, boosted by statehood and the Gold Rush.

1850 TO 1870

This era was the first explosive period of California wine growth. With the discovery of gold in the Sierras, the population of California grew enormously and wine production along with it. While historians may differ on the impact of the Gold Rush, it is clear that the population of California grew from fifteen thousand in 1848 to almost six hundred thousand by 1870 and that the great majority of that population was centered in the swath from San Francisco to Sacramento and up into the Sierras. During the height of the Gold Rush, local agriculture in the Sierras and Sierra Foothills flourished. El Dorado County alone reported that six thousand acres were devoted to agriculture to feed the miners and camp followers who quickly filled the hills. Approximately half of that was vineyard land, and there were substantial holdings in the other foothill counties as well.

At the same time, the urban population was growing apace. About half of the newcomers arrived by boat in San Francisco, many of whom settled there and elsewhere in Northern California. Many of the settlers were of European ancestry, including notable wine pioneers such as "Count" Agoston Haraszthy (Sonoma County), Charles LeFranc and his future son-in-law, Paul Masson (Santa Clara County), and Charles Krug (Napa County). Hungarian Count Haraszthy, for one, imported some hundred thousand cuttings from many European vineyards and planted them in California. Haraszthy pioneered numerous winemaking techniques now thought commonplace, including hillside planting, and caves dug for aging. He founded the Buena Vista Winery in the Sonoma Valley, considered the birthplace of winemaking in California. Less well-known but also important were the exploits of folks like Sam Brannan who set up camp near the hot springs in Calistoga, thinking that he would re-create the atmosphere around New York state's Saratoga, and who, in 1860, realizing the potential for grape growing in the Napa Valley, would go to Europe, where he also arranged for thousands and thousands of noble grape vines to be sent back. At the same time, New Englanders other than Macondray began to import their prized grapes from home, and Zinfandel was prime among them—albeit as both table grape and wine grape.

The recognizable potential in California and in the West generally sparked interest in the construction of a transcontinental railroad as early as the mid-1840s. Statehood in California and Oregon and the subsequent discoveries of precious metals intensified that interest, not to mention that thousands of people were heading west by wagon train and long ocean journey. By the 1850s, a plan was realized, but the railroad was not completed until 1869. Until that time, the booming wine industry in Ohio and elsewhere supplied most of the wine for thirsty easterners. The establishment of the railroad would help change that equation forever.

By 1870, the basis for a California wine industry had been established. Grape varieties far more suited to fine table wine production had been introduced, and many of the areas that today are world famous for wine quality had seen their first plantings go in. Wine had very quickly progressed from religious use to thirst slaker for the mining community to commodity for sale first to a growing urban population and then to the rest of the country. California winemakers were able to compete with the established midwestern and eastern makers, and California very soon became the single largest wine-producing state—a status that has remained unchallenged to this day.

1870 TO 1919

With its base established, the California wine industry entered a long period of expansion. The Napa Valley slowly became the center for fine wine production. With Krug and Jacob Schram opening wineries in the 1860s and others planting grapes, Napa's place in history began to emerge. Among

MAP 1

California

names we still recognize today, Beringer was started by the brothers Jacob and Frederick in 1875 and was followed by Captain Gustave Niebaum, who founded Inglenook in 1880, and by Georges de Latour with Beaulieu in 1900. At the same time, new regions were emerging. Spring Mountain was first planted about 1880, and the very significant grape-growing operations in the Livermore Valley were started by the likes of Karl Wente and James Concannon in the 1880s. Grapes were also planted in the Santa Cruz Mountains, and the Montebello Wine Company came into being in the 1880s as well. Today, Ridge Vineyards is the most important winery on Monte Bello Ridge. Grape growing and winemaking found homes all around the San Francisco Bay and in almost every friendly agricultural valley and flatlands from the southern reaches of Santa Clara Valley up to Santa Rosa and beyond. Mendocino County was not really opened up to grape growing until the 1900s despite limited attempts prior to that time.

California's population grew from 600,000 to 3,500,000, and San Francisco and Los Angeles each rushed past 500,000 in population as they became important financial and commercial centers in their own right. But there was trouble brewing as well, and the scourge of phylloxera, a root louse found in the East, reared its ugly head. During the 1870s, various native American grape varieties were taken to England for study, with the unintended consequence that phylloxera went along for the ride and became introduced to Europe, where it quickly attacked European grape varieties that had no built-in defense and thus died off. The disease waited a decade or so before it also decimated many of the fledgling vineyards of California. It wasn't until the closing years of the nineteenth century that scientists and growers learned that by grafting European vine material onto native American rootstock, the disease could be thwarted. It was then, and into the early decades of the twentieth century, that wine production flourished in America, and in California in particular. The growth of the California wine industry presaged the developments of a hundred years later, but it took many a twist and turn before the California industry would mature. California growers brought in disease-free vines and made wines similar to the ancient and prestigious offerings of France and elsewhere in Europe. In the early decades of the new century, California vintners were in the enviable position of exporting their product to Europe and Asia. In the period leading up to Prohibition, California wines were winning tasting competitions in Europe, a feat that would not be repeated for sixty years—because everything would change thanks to the moral imperatives of Prohibition.

In 1920, the United States went dry—by law. What happened in reality is another story, but the ratification of the Eighteenth Amendment one year earlier meant that as of January 17, 1920, the "manufacture, sale or transportation of intoxicating liquors" was prohibited. To the wine industry, and indeed every sector of the economy that was involved in the prohibited activities, it mattered not that a third of the states has always been dry and that several others had joined their ranks during World War I for "patriotic reasons." The forces of the Anti-Saloon League, the Women's Christian Temperance Union, and a host of social and industrial reformers had banded together and brought about the outlawing of alcohol. There were attempts after the ratification process had run its course to define the amendment as not applying to beer or wine, but Congress passed the Volstead Act, which said that the amendment specifically limited the level of alcohol in any potion to 0.5 percent.

In addition to providing Eliot Ness with a stream of cases, Prohibition created new levels of subterfuge among winemakers and average citizens, the former making medicinal and sacramental wines and the latter becoming expert garage winemakers. Bootlegging flourished. Bathtub gin became a popular drink, and the Roaring Twenties, with its uproarious ways, made the cocktail more popular than ever before. Grape prices went through the roof for varieties that could be shipped, but other varieties fell out of favor. Working within the provisions of the law that allowed home winemakers to produce up to two hundred gallons a year for home consumption, large businesses sprung up to ship and distribute grapes across the country. Crowds lining up to receive boxcars full of grapes in the fall became the order of the day. In the world of unintended consequences, grape acreage increased during Prohibition by almost 100 percent.

Despite the many ways in which people skirted the law, both legally and illegally, Prohibition all but destroyed the production side of California's wine industry. Production in wineries fell dramatically—some measures suggest by as much as 95 percent. Businesses closed, and tanks went empty, rotted, or dried out. By the time the country recognized that a monster of illegality and violence had been created and allowed the industry to open its doors again, both the wine industry and the public had changed. And it did not help that Repeal came in the midst of the Great Depression of the 1930s.

Repeal arrived at the end of 1933, the result of a recognition that consumers did indeed want to use alcoholic beverages without a criminal stigma.

But the industry was unready for the impact of Repeal. Demand for wine grew but failed to reach the levels of two decades earlier, and home winemakers remained a major buyer of wine grapes for decades. Much of the wine that was produced turned out to be inferior, and the industry went through a period of readjustment. The sales of fortified wines exceeded the sales of tables wine in the post-Prohibition era, and it took thirty-five years for varietal table wines to outsell fortified wines again. Prohibition had shaken the winemaking industry to its roots, and it would take another revolution to turn it back in the direction with which it had flirted at the turn of the century—namely, as an industry that could produce wines of high quality.

1933 TO 1966

During the middle years of the twentieth century, winemaking grew first in quantity and then in quality. In the late 1930s, Beaulieu Vineyards' George de Latour had introduced—with the help of noted winemaker André Tchelistcheff—new techniques such as cold fermentation, malolactic fermentation, and aging wine in small French oak barrels. Brother Timothy built the Christian Brothers into a leading winemaker after Prohibition. Wineries like Krug, Martini, Inglenook, Simi, and Sebastiani all survived, and they and others frequently produced wines of great quality. However, quality was not really in vogue except among a small band of dedicated collectors. The most intriguing figure during this era was the iconoclast Martin Ray, who got his start at Paul Masson and later went on to found his own winery. Insisting on using the techniques of the best Old World wineries, but not always able to find consistency, Ray made some of the legendary wines of the era as well as some of the most expensive vinegar. Still, it was Martin Ray, as much as anybody else working in the post-Prohibition era, who made it possible for others to imagine a fine wine world in California.

In the 1950s, with winemaking still mostly done in old wood vats, without temperature control, and almost never using small barrels for aging, the industry saw the emergence of a few pioneers who would set the stage for the wine boom that would follow. James Zellerbach, a San Francisco financier with a taste for the wines of Burgundy, bought land high in the eastern hills of the Sonoma Valley and began to produce both Pinot Noir and Chardonnay using modern techniques, including fermentation in stainless steel and aging in oak barrels imported from France. At the same time, advertising executive Fred McCrea bought land in the Napa Valley hills for a summer retreat. He soon added grapes, and over the years, Stony Hill Chardonnay became one of the most sought-after wines made in California. Lee Stewart was yet another 1950s pioneer. His Souverain winery evolved over time to become a producer of very high-quality Cabernet Sauvignon—so much so that by the time the wine boom hit, his winery was already a household name to collectors.

By 1960 and the years that followed, things began to heat up in the winery formation business. Joe Heitz, who had been instrumental in opening up Beaulieu to the world, left and founded his own label. David Bennion and a bunch of Stanford friends founded Ridge Vineyards. And in 1966, Robert Mondavi, son of Cesare Mondavi who had purchased Charles Krug in the 1940s and moved his wine business to Napa from Lodi, left the family business in a huff and, with the help of investors, built the first new winery in Napa Valley in decades. But it was not just the newness of the winery that made it instantly successful. Mondavi had chafed under old winemaking regimes at Krug and felt that there was a better, more modern way to make wine. When so many of his competitors, even successful competitors such as Beaulieu and Inglenook, were still following the practices of years gone by, he adopted new techniques, recast wine in new styles, and, more than anyone else, set the tone for the modern California wine industry as it exists today.

The Gallo brothers, Ernest and Julio, might have argued that they, not Robert Mondavi, were the driving force in the reemergence of table wine as the focus of the industry. And it would be hard to argue. Aggressive in marketing and driven to bring wine to the masses, the Gallo brothers built a jug wine empire that, at its peak, was reputed to be selling one-third of all the wine produced in California. In fact, the Gallos and Mondavi were great friends who understood that they were looking at the wine industry through opposite ends of the telescope. Now, in an industry that has matured, it is unlikely that we will ever again see titans like Robert Mondavi and Ernest and Julio Gallo.

1966 TO 1980

By the late 1960s, great wines were already being made with the modern techniques of the day. California fine wine had become a collectible for more than a few, but it was still only a larger few. Yet, in truth, despite the many fine wines available, the modern industry was still in its infancy. Consider just these three sets of facts. First, in 1964, there was not enough acreage of

Chardonnay to have it be listed among the grapes planted in California. It was instead listed among other "red" varieties and was outnumbered by the likes of Green Hungarian, Grey Riesling, Burger, and, yes, even the long-ignored Mission. Second, by 1970, its standing acreage had increased to three thousand; by 1980, it had reached twenty thousand. Finally, it took until 1968 for the sales of table wine to exceed the sales of fortified wines. Prohibition ended in 1933, yet the industry, once having a table wine focus, took thirty-five years just to get back to parity with fortified wines. Today, the ratio is 30 to 1 in table wine sales versus those of fortified wines. Winery expansion is significant as well. From the beginning of the period to the end (i.e., 1966 to 1980), the number of wineries doubled to something just over five hundred. The 1970s were the years of the Great Wine Boom. No longer was the industry building a platform. It was maturing, growing, and expanding into new vineyard areas. By this time, California wine had begun to play on the world stage again. But how to rebuild the reputation of an industry not long removed from fortified wines made in enormous quantities? By deciding that it was time for table wine to become world-class at the top end and to lose its "cheap, soft, mawkish" character at the low end. The jug wine orientation of Sonoma and other areas changed to a varietal focus. Whole new regions, such as Monterey, San Luis Obispo, and Santa Barbara counties, emerged as major players; at the beginning of this period, only San Luis Obispo with five hundred acres of Zinfandel rates a mention in the grape acreage charts, but by the end of 1980, these three counties are nearing fifty thousand acres total and have become integral parts of the California wine scene.

The recognition that California had a special set of circumstances capable of making world-class wine meant that wine styles changed forever. Old tanks made of overused redwood and cement were replaced by stainless steel. Fermentation temperatures were controlled; grapes were crushed with an eye toward producing tighter structures, more tannin, and greater age worthiness capable of matching the best from Europe. At the same time, Zinfandel emerged from the background, first with encouragement from folks like Darrell Corti, the Sacramento-area wine merchant and rising star in the wine firmament, and helped along by wineries like Sutter Home with its early production of Amador County wines, by the now-legendary Joe Swan and the bunch at Ridge who recognized the inherent potential of old-vine Zinfandel grown in coastal counties. By the end of the period, Ravenswood, Rosenblum, Seghesio, and others were making Zinfandels that capture the palates of millions. Sauvignon Blanc, in the hands of Robert Mondavi, became a dry wine with recognizable varietal character and bracing acidity. And Cabernet Sauvignon, long considered California's best red grape, leads the charge as the number of collectable wines grows from two dozen at best to hundreds with the establishment of a long, long line of makers including Mondavi, Heitz, Ridge, Chappellet, Caymus, Stag's Leap Wine Cellars, Chateau Montelena, Conn Creek, Mount Eden, Clos Du Val, and Cuvaison, to name just a few of the more obvious players at the time. In the mid-1970s, California also recognizes that Cabernet Sauvignon in Bordeaux is regularly blended with other varieties; and starting with Louis Martini in 1968, Merlot, so long absent from California, makes an appearance. By the end of the period, Merlot has become a staple, and wineries like Duckhorn emerge and make a career with this newly accepted grape.

Along the way, the French unwittingly helped—much to their chagrin. In 1976, to celebrate America's bicentennial and to introduce California wine as a much-improved product, Paris wine seller Steven Spurrier organized a blind tasting in which top California wines were evaluated alongside their French equivalents. The tasters were all members of French wine nobility, and after concluding that the highest-rated wines in the tasting were all French, they were amazed to find out that the winners were from California. In the Chardonnay category, Chateau Montelena was ranked highest by the judges. Stag's Leap Wine Cellars had won among the reds for its Cabernet Sauvignon. The world knew then what many fans of California wines had already concluded: California could make and sell wines of great quality. The Paris tasting may not have started the wine boom, but it certainly confirmed its validity and boosted it further.

Journalistic coverage of the California wine scene also changed in the 1970s and paralleled the growth of the industry. By 1974, both the *California Grapevine* and *Connoisseurs' Guide to California Wine* gained very quick popularity for their concentration on California wine. A few years later, the *Wine Spectator* emerged in a brief newsprint format. All three of those publications, and Robert Parker's *Wine Advocate* with its worldwide focus, became the new voices in wine writing and still exist today as major forces. Others have joined them over time, of course, but these pioneers of the 1970s changed the face of wine journalism in the United States for decades to come.

1980 TO PRESENT

By 1980, the California wine industry had begun to enter into a period of "dynamic maturity." Large-scale changes continued to appear, but so did a series of events that were intended to bring even greater levels of "fineness" in the ways that grapes were grown, wine was made, labels were expressed, and the land was tended. Grapes continued to be planted across the entire three decades with the result that 270,000 producing acres grew to approximately 450,000. Cabernet Sauvignon jumped from 20,000 to 75,000; Chardonnay vines in production increased from 13,000 to 92,000; Pinot Noir grew from 9,000 to 26,000; Merlot expanded from 2,000 to 47,000. At the same time, less well-appreciated grapes were pulled out at astonishing rates, and the once ubiquitous Mission is now about to disappear—its few hundred acres of grapes barely register.

Rhône varieties, so long ignored, finally arrived in earnest by the mid- to late 1980s. Pinot Noir, 125 years in the doldrums, found new homes in the 1980s in Carneros, the Russian River Valley, the Anderson Valley, and Santa Barbara County and fell in love with its new cool-climate homes. By 1990, Pinot Noir displayed a new, more vibrant, more keenly focused personality and became world-class. Even the world's leading wine writer, Jancis Robinson, commented that Russian River Valley Pinot Noir now stands second in the world only to its native Burgundy.

Beginning in 1980, the regulatory arm of the federal government, then known as the Bureau of Alcohol, Tobacco, and Firearms (BATF) and now morphed into the Alcohol and Tobacco Tax and Trade Bureau (TTB), began to allow a new form of geographic identification on wine labels. This system, called American Viticultural Area (AVA), is more fully explained in the later chapter The Language of Wine. Its existence has given rise to a series of geographic definitions that, in most cases, more accurately describe where the grapes in the bottle were grown than the old system of counties and states. In California, the Napa Valley AVA was the first to be recognized, and there are now over a dozen smaller AVAs within the larger boundaries of the Napa Valley designation. Today there are well over one hundred such AVAs, each of which is described in this book, ranging in size from tiny, one-grower areas to multicounty designations. The intent, not always realized by the areas approved, was to improve the accuracy of wine labels by encouraging area definitions that offered common characteristics.

Along with the AVA system, other aspects of a mature industry also arose even as the final decades of the twentieth century continued to see enormous production growth in California in both high-volume and low-volume sectors of the industry. On the one hand, there was great consolidation within the industry, creating a handful of megaproducers with worldwide distribution and substantial marketing resources. On the other hand, many, many small, "boutique" winemakers turned loose a raft of superior wines that could compete with any in the world. Prices at the high end of the industry increased exponentially at the same time as customers sought out values such as those offered by the negotiant Bronco Wines, essentially a broker looking to buy or sell the surplus wines found in the market. Its "Two Buck Chuck," sold exclusively by Trader Joe's markets for $1.99 a bottle, demonstrated to the industry that there were truly two ends of the California wine spectrum and that even incredibly low-priced, cork-finished wines would sell and not give one a bellyache.

New areas continued to emerge with potential for great wines. Hillsides once thought far too steep to cultivate now became home to row upon row of vines, their planting and management made economically feasible by consumer demand and wine quality. Even today, relatively unheard-of varieties for Californians continue to find their ways here, and if grapes like Marsanne, Roussanne, and Tempranillo are far from household words, they are being planted in the hopes that they, too, will find the same happy homes that their European predecessors have enjoyed. By 2010, the number of bonded wineries in California rushed past three thousand, despite the economic downtown, and California continues to produce nearly 90 percent of all wine made in America, even though this proportion has slipped a point or two over the past decade due to the dramatic growth of winemaking across the country.

By the twenty-first century, the California wine industry had reached a semimature stage. Wine styles and grapes have become established, and, if the rate of growth has slowed, it has not come close to stopping. With nearly half a million acres of wine grapes and most areas of the state now participating in the wine industry, it is issues like wine characteristics, explorations into new clones, attempts to define small patches, and the care and stewardship of the land that now occupy center-stage attention. Concern for the environment, on the one hand, and concern for the most natural way to grow grapes, on the other, is today leading winery after winery into the development of sustainable agriculture practices. Organic grape growing is becoming commonplace despite the lack of evidence that it improves wine quality because, at the very least, practitioners believe it is good for the planet. And a few wineries, some with high reputations earned decades ago, have adopted the biodynamic teachings of the German mystic Rudolf Steiner. At the same time, the choice of grape clones has become a major focus for many wineries—so much so, in fact, that it is not unusual to pick up a bottle and find references to various clones by number or source shown on the label as an indication of the winery's pride in its proprietary mix of intended grape characteristics.

The clash between natural winemaking and extensive intervention in the process of turning grape juice into wine is going to become increasingly public. The naturalists will make it so by proclaiming their use of native yeasts, noninterventionist farming, reduced reliance on high ripeness, and oak barrel characteristics. And they will charge you accordingly for the privilege of the hands-off policy—which, by the way, requires far more diligence and hard work than relying on chemicals and over-the-top ripeness to achieve attractive characteristics. The level of alcohol in California wine, already dropping by the middle to the end of the 2000s decade, will retreat further as more and more wineries gain acceptance for a brisk, sturdier, but less forceful style of wine. There will be attempts to bring back some of the grape varieties that have been abandoned over the years like Riesling and Chenin Blanc, as well as new attempts to make something special from Grenache, Tempranillo, Nebbiolo, and Malbec—all grapes that produce wines with interesting personalities in other parts of the world.

California winemaking may have matured, but it will not rest. There is more history to be made here, and the combination of climate, soils, creativity, and imagination that have built a world-class wine industry over the last century and a half remains as much in place as ever. Together these factors assure that maturity does not mean complacency.

How Wine Is Made

IT IS A TRUISM THAT WINE IS MADE IN THE VINEYARD, and that other truism—it takes great grapes to make great wine—is also beyond dispute. Yet, when one sees professional winemakers coming up with dramatically different results from the same vineyard sources, it also becomes true and patently obvious that the hand of the winemaker is the key ingredient in bringing out the personality that is hidden in the fruit. Winemaking is part craft and part art, and it is only when the two are combined to very good effect that great wine can be made. It is easy to make wine. It is not so easy to make great wine.

In California, winemaking has also taken on a distinctly technical quality. Whereas traditional methods meant crushing the grapes and throwing them in a big container to ferment at whatever temperature nature achieved, today's winemakers coddle their grapes and the wines they produce from field to crusher, from fermenter to barrel to bottle. By using different techniques, producers can affect the style of wine from one vintage to the next, or experiment in subtle ways in hopes of finding something different or better. With such flexibility, California winemakers have advanced the quality curve at a rate not matched anywhere in the world; indeed, they are, more often than not, determining the shape and pace of experimentation and advancement. One need only look to Argentina and southern Italy, for example, to see how the acceptance of new technology and more advanced technique has spread to places where wine had not changed for decades and more.

To help understand the influence of winemaking on the finished product, this chapter looks at the primary functions of winemaking in the same sequence as actual winemaking.

IN THE VINEYARD

The many geographic entries in this book address how the soils and climates of the various regions and areas affect grape quality and characteristics, but, regardless of region, the grapes are the start of the process. A typical yearly cycle begins in midwinter when the vines have gone dormant. That is when crews are dispatched to remove the previous year's growth and to prepare each vine for the next year. There are many shapes and sizes, strategies and tactics for shaping the vine, but each has the common denominator of cutting back old growth and leaving a certain number of "buds" intact for the next growing cycle.

Most vines today are trained on wire systems called trellises. There are many variations of trellises, and one would need a technical book on grape growing to understand them all. Nevertheless, the general idea is that a trellis helps guide the growth of the vine and allows the grower to more efficiently choose how much fruit is allowed to mature on the vine and what the leaf pattern for each vine will be. The old-fashioned system of having each vine be free-standing and cutting it back each winter to its basic "head," thus producing a new "bushy" look each year, is not especially efficient, but some wineries believe the old-fashioned systems produced better fruit.

During the growing cycle, the buds start to appear with the arrival of warm weather, and soon leaves and shoots follow. The makings for grapes then appear in midspring, and they need to be pollinated to produce what is called the "set," or the actual formation of grape bunches. In spring, especially in trellised vineyards, one can see vineyard workers tying vines in place and generally getting the shape of the vines as desired. Later in the summer, many vineyardists send crews through the rows of vines to adjust the growth patterns of both the leaves and the grape bunches. Often, at this stage, some fruit will be cut off, or "dropped," from the vine so that the vine's energy can be concentrated in the remaining grapes. This process of thinning the crop is called "green harvest."

Most vineyards in California are irrigated. Vineyardists measure humidity in the soil and also examine the health of the leaves to help determine what water amounts or nutrients might be needed in the vineyard. Some wineries adhere to a practice of not adding any water to the vineyard in the belief that the vine will search for enough moisture to survive and that the more natural the process, the better the grapes. This procedure, called "dry farming," is far from universal, especially in parts of California where the annual rainfall patterns are light. Today, most water applications are provided through the drip irrigation system, both because of better control of how much and where the water goes and also because "drip" uses less water than other methods.

Late in the summer, from mid- to late August for the first grapes, until deep into the fall, the grapes will reach the level of maturity desired by the wineries and will be picked. Grape maturity is measured in a number of ways, most often by the extent to which sugar has become concentrated in grapes. The level of acidity and the balance between sugar and acidity are also important considerations, as are flavor development as determined by old-fashioned tasting of the grapes and the color of the grape seeds. The term *physiological maturity* is often spoken at wineries and refers generally to the point at which the grape seeds turn from green to brown. The potential onset of bad weather also can play a role in picking decisions, and it is not unusual in wet years for some wineries to brag that they got their grapes in before the rains. See also our discussion of the term *Brix* in The Language of Wine for an explanation of how vineyardists measure sugar in grapes.

THE SORTING TABLE

Once the grapes are picked, they are brought into the winery, weighed, and inspected in a gross way for visible defects. Most loads of grapes are acceptable, it turns out, and then the process of winemaking begins. The step may not be universal, but many wineries will pass their grapes across a sorting table where the staff tries to pick out anything that does not belong in the fermentation. Loads of grapes typically carry leaves, twigs, the occasional moldy bunch of grapes, or even an unripe bunch of grapes. The sorters pick out the MOG (matter other than grapes) and any grapes not meeting their standards. A few wineries will also pass the grapes through a chilling process to ensure that fermentation starts at a lower temperature and thus does not roar out of control and reach temperatures higher than the winemakers prefer. A number of producers also try to pick before or at first light so that the grapes have cooled down overnight.

After the grape harvest and the inspection of the grapes, the first step in the winemaking process is the extraction of the juice from the grapes. In the typical operation today, grapes are lightly crushed to allow the juice to run out without breaking the seeds or causing excessive extraction from the skins. Whites are typically sent to the fermenter without the skins, while reds will go with the skins because the color in red wines is almost entirely derived from the skins, not from the juice. Crushing is the most common method to extract the juice without breaking the bitter seeds, or "pips." Contemporary machinery can separate the grapes from the stems and break the grape skins without damaging the seeds. In California, most winemakers use a combination of crushing and pressing.

The old-fashioned grape press where grapes had the very essence squeezed out of them is no longer in use, but pressing does release more juice, albeit sometimes with higher tannins as the result of the extra pressure put on the skins. Juice derived without crushing is often referred to as "free run," while the rest is thought of as press wine. Some wineries, especially those making big-bodied, bold reds, will either not worry about making a smooth "free run" or will use the press juice in some percentage to give the "grip" that we associate with reds of that style. Where pressing was formerly used to maximize the amount of juice derived from the grapes, improved technology permits more control of the pressure used in a winepress, particularly those used to make top-quality wines.

FERMENTATION

Once the juice has been extracted, it is moved to various containers ranging from oak barrels to very large tanks where it is stored and begins to ferment. Some fermentations are intentionally delayed to allow the juice to stay in contact with the skins. Color and tannin are often extracted in this process called "cold soaking," and some winemakers believe that this is a more gentle way of getting those elements into their wines. At some point, whether immediately after the juice has been moved to the fermentation vessels or hours or days thereafter, the alcoholic fermentation (also called the "first fermentation") begins. In this process, the sugars of the grape juice are converted into alcohol, carbon dioxide, and heat through the actions of yeast and other microflora and enzymes. Most fermentations are started through the additions of chosen yeast strains to the unfermented must, as the juice is called, but fermentation can also happen with reliance on native yeasts that come into the winery on the grapes themselves. In such cases, the wild yeasts carry out what is called "natural fermentation." Some winemakers believe that such fermentations make more complex wines; others believe that wild yeast fermentations lead to unexpected results.

When the sugar has been consumed by the fermentation process, the yeast stops working, and the grape juice has been converted into wine. However, winemakers are also able to stop the fermentation and leave a desired level of residual sugar in the wine. The so-called aromatic whites of Riesling, Gewürztraminer, Chenin Blanc, and Pinot Gris have long contained a bit of sweetening. We rarely think of them as sweet wines, however, because the amount of sugar is often not high, and the wine is kept in balance by flavor depth and acidity.

Winemakers make many choices during fermentation in order to achieve a desired style of wine. Choices of containers, yeasts, acid additions, alcohol reduction, and fermentation temperature all have a direct bearing on the final wine style. Many Chardonnays, for example, and some other wines are fermented in small oak barrels because those wineries expect richer or smoother wines to be produced by this costly, hands-on method. Some fermenters are open topped to facilitate a particular flow of oxygen to the fermentation, while other fermentations are done in closed containers and are intentionally as anaerobic as possible. Ultimately, the alcoholic fermentation stops on its own or by the actions of the winemaker, and the wine is given a specific aging regimen consistent with the style of wine being made.

CLARIFICATION

After fermentation is completed, particles such as yeast cells, protein, tannins, and grape skins remain in the wine. Clarification removes these particles, leaving the wine bright and clear. Many processes are commonly used to clarify wine, of which racking, fining, and filtration are the most common. Other process such as cold stabilization (i.e., chilling wine to cause materials to precipitate out of solution) and centrifugation are also in use.

Racking is a natural system of clarification in which wine is moved from one container to another so that only clear wine moves, leaving sediment behind in the original vessel. Most wines are racked at least once, usually immediately after fermentation. Racking can be accomplished by pumping, use of an inert gas, or gravity. A fair number of Chardonnays are now not racked but left in contact with the detritus of fermentation, including the dead yeast cells. The idea is to pick up additional character from this process of "aging on the lees" (*sur lie* in French). In this case, the wine in the barrel is typically stirred or the barrel rolled to move the lees into the liquid for a period of time. Wineries will also use the French term *battonage* to describe the process of lees stirring. Most wineries will then clarify the wine through filtration, but there is a handful of hazy Chardonnays and even the intentionally hazy Sauvignon Blanc on the market these days, and although they look less than polished, they can often be full of flavor.

Fining uses an agent such as egg whites, a powdery clay called Bentonite, gelatin, or other substances, depending on the type of wine being clarified or otherwise modified. The fining agent is dropped into the wine and spread across the surface. It drops through the wine to the bottom of the container taking the solids with it. Fining with eggs whites, for example, is a process that also helps remove excess tannin from wine. Because the fining process works by attracting the unwanted elements to the fining agent, it can be used, as in tannin fining, to remove elements of the wine that are not in suspension.

Filtration, in contrast, because it relies on a process of pumping the wine through a series of screens or pads of varying degrees of porosity, is used to remove particulate matter from wine, including dead yeast cells and grape solids. The process is typically used very late in the process and is done with care so as not to strip the wine of its character in the bargain. A late filtration before bottling, often called a "polish filtration," is done to ensure the visual clarity of the wine.

BLENDING

Blending occurs at some stage for virtually every wine. It may only be the blending of barrels into a finished wine, but before those barrels are selected for the blend, it is typical for the winery to sample each barrel to be sure that it is clean and has the desired character. Blending also occurs in wines with multiple grapes such as the many Cabernet Sauvignon–based wines that carry varying percentage of other grapes, most notably the grapes with which it has traditionally been blended in its native Bordeaux, but, in fact, anything that the winemaker decides to put together. Producers can combine wines by region, by vineyard, by grape variety, and even by vintage—as is the case for wines that carry no vintage, including a large percentage of the Sparkling Wine made here and around the world, including in Champagne. The purpose of blending often is to create a wine that is better than the sum of its parts, but it is also true of price-competitive wines that blending can help achieve a better wine for the money by the inclusion of less expensive grapes. Many wineries have very large tanks, sometimes referred to as "blending tanks," into which are put the several lots of blended wine in order to create the whole blend.

AGING

Some wines reach market within months of harvest, primarily those intended for early consumption in their juicy, fruity youth. Some Rosé wine will follow this course, as will a very limited number of early-drinking reds, but, for the most part, the early release of wine is oriented toward inexpensive whites. Most wines, however, are aged for several months to several years in the winery. Here again, the more ready to drink the wine, the more likely it is to be released young. Fresh, fruity whites are therefore more likely to see retail shelves earlier than heavier whites or most red wines.

Fermentation and aging containers (vessels) range from very large stainless steel tanks to large wood vats, mostly of oak but some of redwood, although these have been mostly phased out in modern winemaking, to cement tanks (an old-fashioned container making a modest comeback) to small oak barrels. In typical practice, wines that spend their lives in stainless steel tanks tend to be bottled in the first year of their lives and released early. It is not unheard of, and thus not that unusual, for wine in other containers to also be bottled before the next harvest. Still, a very high percentage of wine aged in small oak casks, typically of fifty to sixty gallons in size, will stay in the barrel for over a year. Some wineries that specialize in expensive, full-bodied reds will keep their wines in barrel for two years and sometime a bit more. While not unheard of, it is the rare winery that ages its reds in barrel much beyond that period of time.

Wine can also be aged in the bottle, and it is often the case that long-aging red wines, especially Cabernet Sauvignon from some producers, will not be released to market until it is three or four years old. A few producers wait even longer, but that practice tends to be the exception rather than the rule. And once many of these wines have been purchased, they are put into storage ranging from the bottom of a central closet to a full-blown wine cellar for many more years of aging. The best of the full-bodied reds like Cabernet Sauvignon, but also some Syrah, can age well for two decades in cool cellar conditions. Chardonnay and Sauvignon Blanc, when well made and firmly balanced, will often age up to a decade in the cellar, and the same is true for other high-acid whites like Sparkling Wine and some Rieslings.

Stainless steel tanks, which are almost always equipped with temperature control mechanisms, are nearly airtight, and while wine will change in them, the rate of change is typically slower than in barrel and can be slowed even further by dropping the temperature of the wine. Very few wines are stored in stainless for extended periods, however. The idea is to sell young-tasting wine when it is young.

Wine is aged in wood barrels, mostly oak from France or the United States, for several purposes. Not only do small wood containers tend to soften and round out the wines stored within, but also the wood can add extra dimension to the wine. Most wine barrels are still crafted by hand, and, as a result, winemakers are able to specify the sources of the wood, the tightness of the grain, and the amount of charring that occurs when heat is applied to bend the straight staves into the rounded form of wine barrels. The making of the barrel contributes to the personality it imparts to the wine; although the grapes are still the most important item, the added notes of caramel, spice, bacon, toast, or coffee that will appear in some wines are typically contributed from the wood.

It is rare, but there are references to 200 percent new oak in some winery literature. In this instance, the wine has been stored for a period of time in new barrels, and then when it has extracted a fair bit of character, it is moved to another set of new barrels. It takes a very characterful wine to be able to emerge from this treatment and still have its fruit personality intact. A more complete discussion of oak aging and its impacts on wine character is provided in The Language of Wine section at the end of the book.

STABILIZING AND BOTTLING

Filling bottles with wine is the final step in the winemaking process. After the wine has been aged and blended to the winemaker's approval, the wine is typically cold stabilized to prevent reactions to chilling once the wine is out in the real world. When complete, the wine is introduced to the final blending tank, where different batches and lots of the same wine are stored for a few days, making the entire batch homogeneous.

The wine is now ready for bottling on a sophisticated bottling line or, very occasionally at the smallest wineries, by hand. The principal objective of either method is to retain a clean environment so that no bacteria can be introduced into the final product. Bottling is more than just filling the bottles, since this is the stage at which decisions are made regarding bottle types (size, shape, and color), corks (real cork, plastic, or screw tops), dressing (what sort of capsule to use), and labeling (shape of the label, front only, front and back, neck labels, side labels, and what information to provide).

There is a minimum amount of required information on a wine label, and a few wineries provide nothing more than that which is called for by regulation. But wineries are allowed to put a great deal more on their labels. For full definitions of labeling terms, please see the several related entries in the Wine Terminology section of this book. Many terms are not required on labels and have no legal meaning, including *Reserve* and all other designations that suggest special status, *Old Vines*, cuvée names, designations related to Sparkling Wine such as brut, proprietary names like Meritage, *late harvest*, and several others.

At a very minimum, the label must contain the following:

The name of the company offering the wine. More often than not, the name is that of a real winery, but there are many variations from those names that are merely second labels or additional names of a real winery to names that are made in someone else's winery but were made from scratch, to names that are nothing more than covers for wines bought and bottled.

A reference to the alcohol level of the wine. For wines under 14 percent alcohol, the percentage on the label must be within 1½ percent of the actual alcohol level but may not state above 14 percent unless the wine is above 14 percent. For wines above 14 percent, the leeway is 1 percent from the actual level, but the label may not say below 14 percent.

An appellation, a place name that tells where the grapes were grown. When the name is a small area, it can have significance, but names that are as large as several counties or an entire state are not especially helpful.

A statement indicating the level of involvement of the selling entity in the wine's making. Terms like *produced* and *bottled by, made and bottled by,* and *vinted and bottled by* have meaning but have little significance as regards wine quality. See The Language of Wine for extensive discussions of these label terms.

The location of the company offering the wine. This site is actually the location of the winery where the wine was bottled.

Grape and Wine Types

THERE WAS A TIME WHEN WINE LABELS did not focus on grape varieties, but that was when Chardonnay was grown almost exclusively in Burgundy, Chenin Blanc almost exclusively in the Loire, Syrah almost exclusively in the northern Rhône, and nothing of note in the United States, Australia, Argentina, South Africa, New Zealand, or anywhere else except so-called native varieties. The change came about slowly at first. Winegrowing expanded to new places without history and without rules, and the wines had to be called something. At first, they were identified with names that reflected the European territory of the grapes used. Names like Sauterne (we somehow lost the *s*), Chianti, Burgundy, Claret, Hock, and Rhine were employed, and varietal monikers were rarely to be seen.

But the change did come, and whether one traces the turning point to the post-Prohibition era in this country or to something else, it is clear that names like Cabernet Sauvignon, Pinot Noir, Sauvignon Blanc, Johannisberg (to use the name of days past), Riesling, and others became the currency in which wines were traded. Today, no one would think of calling Pinot Noir by the name Burgundy or Sauvignon Blanc by Sauterne. In today's world, outside of the most fabled European winemaking regions, the wines of the world are first differentiated by grape variety. Chardonnay in Argentina or Chile sounds the same to wine lovers everywhere as Chardonnay in

Australia or France or California. Syrah, even in its occasional disguise as Shiraz, is still Syrah.

When winemaking came to California not long after the Gold Rush, the first wines were probably not labeled by variety but by color. But, soon enough, a grape-growing industry took hold, and varieties like Zinfandel, Cabernet Sauvignon, Sauvignon Blanc and Semillon jumped to the upper-quality echelons and, over time, became the names by which wines were to be known. The period following Prohibition, from the late 1930s through to the 1960s, saw the greatest shift from the generic naming of wines into varietal identification, but it was not until two decades later that European place names like Burgundy, Sauternes, and Chianti were finally removed from California wine-labeling practice.

The beauty of varietal labeling, of course, is that it instantly tells us what is in the bottle. But there is more to the argument for varietal labeling than "truthfulness." It is the grape variety, more than any other single factor, that determines the potential character of the wine. Everything else is a modifier. The soil in which the grapes are grown, the exposure to sun and wind, the temperatures that affect how the grapes ripen, the attention paid to the vineyard practice, amount of crop left on the vine as the grapes ripen, the ripeness and balance at picking, and the skill of the winemaker are all major players in the production drama that culminates when we pull the cork on our favorite tipple.

Not only does each variety have its own unique flavor characteristics, structure, and longevity, and thus potential for greatness, but, once matched to site, raised with care, and made into wine by a practiced hand, the variety and blends of varieties chosen ultimately come to define the wine when it is sent to market.

In parts of Europe, varietal names do not appear as part of the labeling system, but variety actually rates even more importantly. In specific geographic regions like Burgundy and Bordeaux, Vouvray, Sancerre, and Châteauneuf du Pape, Côte Rotie and Cornas, the wines produced there are strictly limited to certain varieties that have proven over hundreds of years to be successful in those regions. California has no such restrictions, and while Chardonnay is found almost exclusively in Burgundy in France, it is grown in forty-five of the forty-seven California counties in which grapes are found, and its turf extends from San Diego to the Oregon border.

In that sense, California is the land of opportunity for grapes. Any grape can be grown anywhere a vineyardist or farmer cares to put vines in the ground. It is only half a century ago when significant varieties like

TABLE I

Grape Acreage Standing in California by Variety

	2010	2000	1990	1980	1970
Alicante Bouschet	1,100	1,600	2,100	5,000	7,500
Barbera	6,900	11,500	10,700	19,300	3,300
Cabernet Franc	3,500	3,500	1,600	200	200
Cabernet Sauvignon	75,800	69,700	33,200	22,800	6,100
Carignane	3,600	7,200	11,000	25,300	27,100
Chardonnay	95,000	103,500	52,200	17,000	2,700
Chenin Blanc	7,700	19,400	33,000	32,300	5,300
French Colombard	25,500	42,100	58,900	44,300	13,600
Gewürztraminer	1,800	1,600	1,900	3,600	700
Grenache	6,600	11,500	13,600	17,600	13,000
Malbec	1,500	800	100	100	100
Marsanne	100	100			
Merlot	46,200	50,000	7,400	2,700	300
Mourvèdre	900	600	300	900	1,900
Petit Verdot	1,800	700	100		
Petite Sirah	7,600	3,700	3,100	11,200	4,500
Pinot Blanc	500	1,000	1,800	1,900	500
Pinot Gris/Grigio	12,700	1,600			
Pinot Noir	36,400	19,400	9,500	9,400	3,200
Riesling (White Riesling)	3,700	2,000	5,000	10,200	1,700
Roussanne	300	200			
Sangiovese	1,900	3,300	200	100	100
Sauvignon Blanc	15,400	13,600	13,400	7,300	1,200
Sauvignon Musqué	200	100			
Semillon	900	1,400	2,200	2,800	1,300
Syrah	19,200	12,700	300	100	
Tempranillo	900	700			
Viognier	3,000	1,800	100		
Zinfandel	49,900	50,200	34,200	29,100	21,500
California Wine Grape Total	473,300	480,700	330,400	336,800	146,000

NOTE: Excerpted from *The California Grape Acreage Report* dated April 2010 and past reports, published by the U.S. Department of Agriculture in cooperation with the California Department of Food and Agriculture.

Chardonnay and Syrah were nowhere to be found in California. And it is only within the last decade and a half that significant new and very successful growing areas for Pinot Noir were planted extensively. France may think it knows where Syrah can and cannot be planted, and thus has laws that protect the successful areas from intrusions of other grapes, but it is those very laws that prevent old habits established centuries ago from changing and adapting to modern conditions and new understandings of how to choose plant materials and how best to farm those plants.

Still, those century-old teachings have established a certain pecking order of grapes, and that hierarchy has produced California's leading varieties as well. While California has not succeeded with all the so-called noble varieties, its most highly regarded grapes, which also produce its most expensive wines, are Cabernet Sauvignon, Pinot Noir, and Chardonnay, followed by Zinfandel, Merlot, Syrah, and Sauvignon Blanc. All told, there are over sixty wine grape varieties planted in California, and this chapter provides details on virtually all whose names appear somewhat regularly on wine labels. You will also find entries that address recognized blend categories and also wine types for which style and intent are as important as variety.

Absent from this chapter are important grape varieties that have never managed to establish a significant foothold in California and a handful of grapes whose standing was significant in the past but have now been largely abandoned by California wineries in favor of varieties that have turned out to have greater success as wine and consequently with the public. It is only within the last several decades that varieties like Burger, Green Hungarian, Grey Riesling, and Sylvaner among the whites and Charbono and Pinot St. George among the reds have virtually disappeared from California vineyards. Table 1 looks at the varieties present today, not the varieties that are gone and nearly forgotten.

ALICANTE BOUSCHET

The day will come when Alicante Bouschet will join the list of forgotten varieties. Virtually all of its planted acreage is a remnant from the past, and almost none has been put into California vineyards over the last decade. But there was a time when Alicante Bouschet had great importance in three significant areas of wine production. During Prohibition, when home winemaking took the place of winery production, Alicante Bouschet was widely prized for its ability to ship well across country and to make heady, deeply colored, fairly tannic wine that was then often cut with water and had its natural sugars enhanced by table sugar in fermentation. The resulting wine, often drunk young, may not have rated highly on the quality scale, but it was immensely popular. At its peak, during those sometimes dark years, planted acreage reached upward of thirty thousand acres. And, not unexpectedly, with the end of Prohibition, that acreage began to drop.

Still, Alicante Bouschet had two other lives of some importance. Its juice is a deep red, unlike most so-called black varieties whose fresh juice runs white to very pale pink. For some varieties low in color, Alicante Bouschet became the coloring agent, and it did not hurt that the grape also produced full-bodied wines with sturdy tannins. The grape's most lasting mark has been its role in the production of jug wines from the hot Central Valley of California where, despite an occasional sprinkle of older vines in cool, coastal vineyards, Alicante Bouschet's remaining plantings are now confined. It occasionally also pops up as a minor blending agent in Zinfandel from the North Coast, and then almost exclusively because the very oldest vineyards there were frequently planted to field blends intended to cover all bases in terms of fruit, body, color, and longevity. Today only 1,100 acres of Alicante Bouschet remain in California, most of which stand in the very hot southern end of the Central Valley.

BARBERA

Not unlike Alicante Bouschet, Barbera is losing its toehold in the New World and is hanging on longer because it has value as a provider of acidity and backbone to inexpensive red wines that otherwise might be even more dull, soft, and lacking in vitality. Barbera's fall from grace is paralleled to some extent in its native Italy where the grape, famous for its role in the Piedmont region under the guise Barbera d'Alba, is now diminishing in favor of plantings in the hotter regions farther south.

It was not always thus, of course. Not much more than three decades ago, there was enough Barbera planted in coastal areas to encourage several dozen versions of the grape; and, with important names like Martini and Sebastiani as its chief supporters, Barbera enjoyed a modicum of staying power and presence for its tightly structured, somewhat tangy, food-friendly wines. As late as 1980, there were some twenty thousand acres of Barbera vines, albeit the majority were in the hot regions of the Central Valley. That total has been dropping more or less steadily, and today the grape claims some 6,900 acres of vineyard, 90 percent of which are in the southern end of the Central Valley.

CABERNET FRANC

Cabernet Franc leads a three-way life in its native France. Its split personality in Bordeaux sees it perform as a blending agent for Cabernet Sauvignon–based wines grown on the left bank of the river in such famous appellations as Pauillac and Margaux. On the right bank, it combines with Merlot to form the basis of the wines grown in Pomerol and St. Emilion. Cabernet Franc is also an important grape in the Loire Valley, where it assumes a lighter, fruitier personality in wines labeled as Chinon.

In California, it is seen mostly as a blending agent for Cabernet Sauvignon; not surprisingly, it is planted most heavily in the Napa Valley, where Cabernet Sauvignon rules the roost. In the three-plus decades since its arrival in California vineyards, a few wineries have attempted to make the wine on its own, and most have failed. Napa's Lang and Reed winery has succeeded better than most, but few others have found happiness with the grape.

Most efforts have tended to be heavy, tannic, and not especially fruity, and fewer still have come close to the comfortable style that the grape has shown in the Loire Valley. Its severe styling has led some producers to cut back on its use, and there is a shift of minor but significant proportion away from Cabernet Franc and into Petit Verdot as a blending grape. Recent DNA testing has established that a Cabernet Franc–Sauvignon Blanc cross produced Cabernet Sauvignon. Three decades ago, there were only 200 acres standing in all of California. That number has grown to some 3,500 today. Napa leads the way with some 1,200 acres, followed by Sonoma at 600 and San Luis Obispo near 400.

CABERNET SAUVIGNON

Setting aside arguments about whether Cabernet Sauvignon or Pinot Noir is the more admired red grape than any other in the wine world, it is true that Cabernet Sauvignon does remarkably well in a broader variety of places and that it is the grape most likely to make a big percentage of the most highly regarded reds in Australia, Chile, and California. In Argentina, where Malbec wants to reign supreme, there are also Cabernets of surpassing beauty; in Italy, there is a small but significant industry growing up around the notion that Cabernet Sauvignon makes the most desirable and price-worthy reds from that country as well. We will leave it to the French to decide whether the red wines of Bordeaux surpass those of Burgundy, and we need not even debate whether California Cabernet makes superior wine to the best of our Pinots.

What we know instead is that considerably more Cabernet Sauvignon is being grown in California, and the prices for the grape and for its wines are higher than for comparable Pinot Noirs. Some might argue that Pinot Noir can be the better value. Given the ease with which so many Napa and Sonoma Cabernets now slip through the $100 price barrier, it may be that Pinot's greatest advantage in this intramural rivalry is that of price—because, whether measured by acreage or by dollar value, Cabernet is king in California.

If Cabernet is king, then the Napa Valley is the seat of its power. Long considered the leading local combination of grape and place, Napa Cabernet Sauvignon has been winning prizes around the world for a century and more. When the wine boom of the 1970s hit in earnest, Cabernet Sauvignon plantings led the way; and while there may have been challengers for acreage growth among jug wine varieties like Barbera, it was Cabernet Sauvignon that stood at the top of the growth charts in coastal counties from Napa to Santa Barbara. Indeed, the rush to plant Cabernet Sauvignon was so exaggerated in those heady days that one grower put in some 1,500 acres in one giant stand in Monterey County. Few grapes of that planting survive today, having been replaced by varieties more suited to the area, but the loss of inappropriately sited plantings all over California has not prevented Cabernet from becoming our number two grape behind only Chardonnay.

Cabernet Sauvignon's ability to adjust to and thrive in a variety of growing conditions around the world is part and parcel of its desirability in California. Even in the Napa Valley, where Cabernet from the West Rutherford benchlands is arguably the grape's gold standard, Cabernet grows not just in those moderated, east-facing soils with their long sunshine but shaded late afternoons, but all over the valley in microclimates ranging from quite cool to fairly warm. Whether it is the chilly settings of Carneros or the somewhat steamy pockets near Calistoga, up on the hills both east and west of the valley floor, or in the adjoining Chiles and Pope valleys where the growing season is shorter and more intense, Cabernet Sauvignon can, in many vintages, make wines that earn their spurs as the best of the variety.

Napa Valley Cabernets are frequently described as curranty with nuances of rich soils and tea leaves; yet in the more exposed locations and up on the hillsides, the character of the wines will shift toward a black cherry type of fruitiness. The best of the breed always seems to have little whiffs of cola and sometimes of root beer, hints of graphite and even of black walnuts. The valley floor wines tend to be rounder in structure, while the wine from hillside locations like Mount Veeder, Howell Mountain, and Diamond Mountain tend to be more tannic and at times can be blunt and direct.

Those kinds of generalizations can help us understand Cabernet, but the influence of the leading examples of the winemaker's hand is also not to be ignored. The bold, deep, and very ripe Cabernets from Shafer in the Stags Leap District are very different from the refined, almost reserved style that shows up in the wines of its near neighbor at Stag's Leap Wine Cellar. There are similarities in the fruit profile, but the great differences in structure and directness come from the winemaker. And similar contrasts can be seen all over the Napa Valley and, indeed, throughout California. Cabernet Sauvignon makes good wine in a variety of styles and from a variety of sites.

Cabernets from Sonoma and from Mendocino, in general, are a more direct, less long-aging lot. There are very good wines coming from isolated pockets in those counties, but Cabernet is not king in those places regardless of the many attractive versions under labels ranging from Sebastiani to Verité. Fewer grandly scaled Cabernets are coming from south of San Francisco, yet the second only to Napa Cabernets and rivaling the best of that group on its best vintages is Ridge Montebello, a wine grown in the hills above San Jose. Over the years, this wine has been consistently rated near the top of the Cabernet sweepstakes, and it has had occasional company from neighbors at Mount Eden and Gemello. Yet, as those other wines have faded, Ridge has stood the test of time and reminds us of an earlier era when there were many more outstanding reds coming from those hillside locations.

Two other locations in California bear watching. The first of these is located in the cooler, west side vineyards of San Luis Obispo County in the Paso Robles AVA. Wineries like Adelaida and Justin have found sites that yield tasty, reasonably well-balanced wines. There is Cabernet Sauvignon in other parts of Paso Robles, of course, but the warmer the site as one heads east across the AVA, the more likely that the wines will be riper and more suited to early drinking.

A second area that is beginning to show great potential is the Happy Canyon area of Santa Barbara County. Folks have been trying to grow Cabernet in this county for several decades with mixed results at best because so much of the growing area is simply too cool for the variety. But, back away from the coast in areas protected from fog intrusion, one finds wines in their first vintages from Dierberg under the Star Lane label and Napa's Screaming Eagle connections with their Jonata bottling.

Table 1 earlier in this chapter lays out the steady-growing Cabernet Sauvignon acreage here in California. Whether one ascribes to the theory that high prices for Cabernet have encouraged much of this expansion or one sees wine quality as driving the continuing interest in the grape, it is clear that Cabernet Sauvignon has simply jumped ahead of every other red grape in importance, both for the prices its wines bring and for total acreage. The total planted acreage of 75,800 is led by Napa County with 19,000, followed by Sonoma (10,900), San Joaquin (10,900), and San Luis Obispo (9,300).

CARIGNANE

Once the workhorse of the California wine industry, Carignane was the most widely planted red wine grape in California vineyards as little as thirty years ago. It came by its high standing for the same reason that it is so widely planted in France and Spain. It is productive and has good color and reasonable structure. It is also a late-blooming variety and thus seemed to avoid the early spring frosts that were once so prevalent in winegrowing areas everywhere.

Today, Carignane is diminishing in importance, and its last stand seems to be a heavily producing grape for jug wine production. But even that role is being lost as vineyards age and more interesting varieties take over. One still sees occasional mention of Carignane from wines from coastal vineyards, mainly because Carignane had been interplanted in old red blend vineyards whose prime focus was either Zinfandel or Petite Sirah. Carignane topped the list of red varieties in California in the 1950s to the 1970s with a more or less steady total of 25,000 to 27,000 acres, but then began to drift; by the mid-1980s, it was down to 12,000 and now covers just 3,600, with almost no new plantings over the last decade. Major plantings include 1,300 acres in Madera County and 1,200 in San Joaquin County. Mendocino at 400 acres and Sonoma at 200 represent the last stands of old plantings. It is not uncommon for Carignane to show up as a small percentage of Zinfandels and Syrahs from those locations, and there has even been the occasional Carignane Rosé, including a superb example from Zinfandel specialist Carol Shelton.

CHARDONNAY

Where, oh, where did all the Chardonnay come from? A little over forty years ago, just before the California wine boom of the 1970s took flight, Chardonnay was almost nowhere to be seen. A few of the more famous groundbreakers in those days put the grape in, aged it in imported French oak (a winemaking tactic not seen previously), and sold their limited production to the few California collectors of the day. The grape acreage report of 1961 amazingly lumps Chardonnay into the Other Red Varieties category of "red grapes" having fewer than five hundred acres. It took until the latter 1960s for Chardonnay's acreage to creep up to one thousand and for the grape to emerge on its own. By then, it had become a staple for the top wineries; and when the important wine writers of the day began to compare the local product with its French brethren from Burgundy, a new controversy was born.

The early 1970s saw almost every newcomer to the industry jumping onto the Chardonnay bandwagon. Although its acreage of several thousand still trailed varieties like Chenin Blanc and Riesling, its importance to wine drinkers was underscored by the fact that the price for well-made, oak-aged Chardonnay soon eclipsed that of all other white wines.

In 1976, a blind tasting sponsored by a Parisian wine merchant who wanted to do something to celebrate the United States bicentennial found a panel of French wine professionals picking out California wines over their own. The story, which has assumed near-mythological status, gained instant fame when *Time* magazine picked it up under the headline "Judgment of Paris." Three of the top four Chardonnays came from California, with Chateau Montelena 1973 taking top honors, Chalone 1974 finishing third, and Spring Mountain Vineyards 1973 coming in fourth. In fairness, two California wines also finished last. But it was first, not last, that mattered, and California Chardonnay instantly acquired world-class status.

There were two very good reasons why California Chardonnay won that tasting and continues to win tastings today. The better California versions of the grape are deep in character, rich in flavor, and very well balanced with a clean and specific ripe apple, sweet citrus character that mimics the French wines but goes beyond them. Moreover, California wines can be more luscious and ripe than their Gallic counterparts, and therein lies one of the great debates that has now raged over three decades and more.

It is easier for California wines to be full-bodied and intense with plenty of obvious fruit. It is a blessing that lovers of the local style admire, and it is why Chardonnay has become the most widely planted grape in California. The propensity of Chardonnay to deliver deep and attractive character in a dry white wine also explains why it has taken off all over the world.

In California vineyards, just as in places like Australia and Chile, Chardonnay readily adapts to the site and finds a way to reward those who plant it. In cooler locations in the North Coast, Chardonnay is fruity, lively, full of ripe apple juiciness, and it can pick up a little of the rock candy edge that is also a part of many Australian efforts. Wines from California's Central Coast tend to have more of a tropical fruit edge in their makeup, but the best examples from that area retain a ripe apple quality at their very hearts. The key to success in these coastal locations is the winegrower's ability to choose sites and growing techniques that deliver ripe fruit with plenty of zesty acidity and minerality.

Indeed, the most important trend in Chardonnay making today is the pursuit of balanced ripeness rather than extreme intensity. The better California Chardonnays will never lack for depth, but they have often lacked for vitality and balance. Today, wineries like Ramey, HDV, Chasseur, Talley, and many, many others are demonstrating that depth and balance are not mutually exclusive. Even when the very ripe, highly oaked versions of the grape emerge these days, producers like Paul Hobbs and Pahlmeyer are able to capture both great intensity and sufficient underlying solidity to be useful wines with rich foods.

Today, Chardonnay's 95,000 acres dwarf every other grape. It is planted in virtually every county in which grapes are grown, including Monterey (16,500), Sonoma (15,100), San Joaquin (14,300), Napa (7,200), and Santa Barbara (6,800).

CHENIN BLANC

This honeysuckle-perfumed grape has had a long run here in California, but it has lost standing and now is made by only a dozen or so wineries in spite of its great potential to produce attractive, bright, and balanced wines either in totally dry styles or with a touch of residual sugar as it does so successfully in France's Loire Valley. From time to time, it is also turned into a late-harvest beauty, and there remain patches of the grape that continue to perform well, albeit in relative obscurity.

It was not always this way, of course. Back in the days when Chardonnay was merely a blip on the radar screen, Chenin Blanc (which was also called White Pinot by some producers despite the fact that it is not a member of the Pinot family) consistently outpointed Chardonnay in acreage counts. Even in the late 1970s, when Chardonnay had been discovered by every winery from one end of the state to the other, Chenin Blanc had more than twice as much acreage to its credit while reaching its peak plantings of nearly thirty thousand acres. Now, with the exception of a few hundred acres in each of Monterey, San Luis Obispo, and Santa Barbara counties, the grape clings to some 7,500 acres in the Central Valley, mostly for jug wine production and a handful of inexpensive table wine bottlings.

FORTIFIED WINES (INCLUDING PORT AND SHERRY)

In years past, generic names related to European places of origin (Burgundy, Champagne, Chianti) have been banned from use on American labels. Port and Sherry, the two most commonly seen fortified wines coming from California wineries avoided the "chop" because they are themselves generic names for wines produced in Portugal's Douro River valley east of the city of Opporto and in Spain's Jerez district. But, no more. Only labels in existence may further use those names.

Thus, Sherry, which is an aged, somewhat nutty-charactered wine, and Port, usually sweet and somewhat grapey, still survive as allowed names. Their making involves the addition of high-proof alcohol, usually brandy, in a process known as "fortification." This strengthening helps preserve the wines to some degree and, when those wines are sweet, the brandy is added before fermentation is complete in order to kill the yeasts and retain some of the natural grape sugars.

There are also wines to which brandy is added for the same purpose but are not labeled as Port or Sherry. Grapes that ripen to very high levels of sugar and have interestingly fragrant personalities like the Muscats, Black Malvoisie, and others can be given the fortification treatment and serve as after-dinner sippers. A few dry Sherries can be enjoyed before the meal, but most California Sherries are sweet and not very well suited to predinner service. And whether dry or sweet, fortified wines in the United States fall under the legal definition of dessert wines.

GAMAY NOIR

Among the many grapes misidentified in California, Gamay Noir stands near the top. Not so long ago, perhaps as recently as the 1970s, there were two grapes in California bearing the name Beaujolais. The grape called Gamay Beaujolais turned out to be nothing more than a light clone of Pinot Noir, and the grape called Napa Gamay is, in reality, that old French workhorse, Valdigué, grown in the southwestern area of France and being phased out there just as it has been phased out here.

Gamay Noir—or Gamay Noir Au Jus Blanc as it is known in France's Beaujolais region, where it is responsible for the fruit-driven wines of that district—seems to exist in small pockets in California but not in enough quantity (fifty acres or more) to be included in the lists compiled by the Department of Agriculture. A few wineries are using the name on wine labels. Gamay Noir may yet have a future here, but if it does, it has yet to take root.

GEWÜRZTRAMINER

Gewürztraminer is grown all over the world, but only in its adopted home in France's Alsace region does it perform with consistency. There, and occasionally on North America's West Coast, in New Zealand, and on rare occasions in Australia, the grape will yield floral, perfumed wines that are typically described as rose petals and lychee. Growing Gewürz can be an exercise in frustration because its aromas do not develop until the grapes get quite ripe, but its acidities tend to fall off quickly when that happens, and the resulting wines lose their vitality.

It is not unusual to see the grape described as a "dry" wine, and certainly many of its best examples are made in that style, but increasingly it is seen with a touch of residual sugar that helps smooth out a slight tendency to finishing bitterness. There was an attempt to popularize a soft, rounded version of Gewürztraminer in the late 1970s and early 1980s, but it soon joined the march into obscurity along with almost every other white grape. Now only a handful of wineries pay much attention to the grape, and the very best versions, some of which are extremely good, come from Mendocino's ocean-cooled Anderson Valley. From its peak of approximately 4,000 acres in the early to mid-1980s, the grape began to lose its place in California vineyards and now stands in just 1,800 acres statewide. The counties of Monterey (600), Mendocino (200), and Santa Barbara (200) are the acreage leaders.

GRENACHE

Grapes like Nebbiolo and Sangiovese, Gewürztraminer, and even Riesling have worldwide followings but seem to work best in only one or two specific locations. And then there is Grenache, widely reported to be the most heavily planted variety in the world with bountiful crops in France, Spain, and Australia. True, there are not many Grenache-based wines that have captured the mantle of greatness. But when one realizes that the rich Châteauneuf du Papes, and indeed red wines from all over the southern

Rhône region as well, almost always carry majority portions of Grenache, and that the grape under the name Garnacha in its native Spain is used extensively in Spain where it is the most widely planted red variety, one has to wonder: Why does it not perform in California?

Frankly, no one really knows the answer, but some of what ails Grenache lies in the confluence of its siting in vineyards in the hottest parts of California and in its tendency to lose acid and to oxidize. Neither trait makes it a top-notch candidate for local vineyardists, and even those who are trying to plant it alongside Syrah in cooler locations are meeting with mixed results. It boasted almost twenty thousand acres of planted vines by the 1980s but has now dropped back to six thousand six hundred at latest count. Jug wine makers are now eschewing it for their products, as continuing acreage drops in Fresno (2,200) and Madera (2,100) counties show. San Luis Obispo County, the outright leader in Syrah plantings, is tops among coastal counties with almost three hundred acres of Grenache, and San Joaquin now sports four hundred acres, both slight increases as Grenache grows in its use in Rhône blends.

MALBEC

In the United States, until a few years ago when Argentinean reds finally came into their own, Malbec was viewed as only a minor blending grape in Bordeaux and a maker of stolid reds somewhere down there near the Pampas. Now, it turns out that Malbec is still viewed as a minor blending grape to Cabernet Sauvignon, but its rather amazing success under the modernized techniques now holding sway in Argentina, primarily in the high plains of the Mendoza region at the foot of the Andes, has brought the grape new prominence and put yet another frown on the faces of those who try to succeed with it here and in France. Even the French, who seem to have footholds all over the world these days, admit that Malbec in Argentina may look like Malbec in France, but it does not taste like the same grape. Malbec plantings in California, never very high, have grown in the last decade from less than 500 acres to a reported 1,500 but still represent less than 2 percent of Cabernet's total. There are those who believe that great Malbec is possible in California. But for every true believer, there is a vintner who is turning to Petit Verdot as the better supporter for Cabernet Sauvignon. Napa, Sonoma, and San Joaquin counties each possess about three hundred acres of Malbec.

Marasanne's place in California is not especially secure; indeed, it is not especially secure in its native France, where, at least it is only one of two white varieties allowed to be grown in the Rhône region of St. Joseph. With but one hundred reported acres and only a handful of adventurous wineries producing it in limited quantities, it makes highly aromatic wines often smelling of honey, honeysuckle, and almonds. It is often blended here with Roussanne, as it is in France, to impart a lighter, brighter side to its personality. The most interesting Marsanne/Roussanne blend seen so far has been JC Cellars' First Date.

MERITAGE

As little as three decades ago, California wines bearing the name of a grape were allowed to contain only 51 percent of the named variety. But, as the wines became more collectible, and thus more expensive, the laws were changed to require 75 percent content in order to use a grape name on the label. This requirement, adopted into labeling regulations at the behest of consumer activists and producers of fancy wine, meant only good things for most varieties. But it did create a problem for wines whose blends emulated several European wines, most prominently both red and white bottlings from Bordeaux that are identified only by the maker's name and the place where the grapes are grown. In those appellations, the use of the place name also limits grapes that can be contained in such wines. The Bordeaux region is split by the Gironde River, and the red wines from its left bank are typically built on Cabernet Sauvignon with varying, often substantial portions of Merlot, Cabernet Franc, Malbec, and Petit Verdot. Wines from the right bank of the Gironde typically contain a blend of Merlot and Cabernet Franc, with only a very few wines, Chateau Figeac being the most notable example, having even a smidgen of Cabernet Sauvignon in their makeup.

California has no such limits on where grapes can be planted, and thus the use of place names on the local wines would have absolutely no meaning or definition. Yet, there are very compelling reasons why wineries might wish to produce blends of Cabernet Sauvignon, Merlot, and the other Bordelais varieties in which no grape reaches the 75 percent varietal content requirement. And, into that breach came a group of vintners who literally invented a new category of wine which they called "Meritage" (pronounced as "heritage" but with an *m*). Red Meritage can contain any combination of the red grapes from Bordeaux, and white Meritage is limited, as are the dry whites of Bordeaux, to Sauvignon Blanc, Semillon, and Muscadelle de Bordolais (not much seen in these parts). The only fly in this new ointment is that a winery cannot use the name *Meritage*, unless it joins the Meritage Alliance. That is why one sees many Bordeaux-styled blends with proprietary names such as Joseph Phelps Insignia.

MERLOT

It was only in 1968 when the Louis Martini winery produced what is generally regarded as the first of the modern-day Merlots in California. At the time, there was not enough Merlot planted here to register on the annual grape acreage reports of that year. At the time, the wine industry was just emerging into the first stages of maturity with new techniques and new money coming onstream to start a process that literally revolutionized the industry. As part of that new maturity came an interest in the grapes that were blended with Cabernet Sauvignon in Bordeaux. California, after all, had a century of success with Cabernet, but it was fairly widely recognized that the wines of the time were not of the same quality as those of their French counterparts. The impetus for Merlot, in addition to the search for greater complexity, was its tendency to produce more supple and earlier-maturing wines than Cabernet.

The Martini interest in Merlot was part of that maturation process, but as Martini found out, along with almost everyone else who planted Merlot in the top locations for Cabernet Sauvignon, it was making a quite good and uniquely rich and drinkable wine on its own. At the same time, many wineries were discovering how to tame the rough side of Cabernet, and it soon became clear that Cabernet Sauvignon could be made into a more supple wine on its own. Thus was the Merlot craze as its own varietally identified wine born. In its first decade, Merlot acreage grew from nothing to almost 4,000 by 1978, and it has climbed steadily since then to the point where it now adds up to an astounding 46,200 acres, second only to Cabernet Sauvignon among red grapes.

Coastal counties contain the greater portion of Merlot plantings, but, despite the grape's penchant for softness, it is also grown extensively in warmer inland locations where it struggles for fruit and for structure. Among the cooler locations, Napa (6,700 acres), Sonoma (6,300), Monterey (4,900), and San Luis Obispo (4,100) counties lead the way, while the warm but not brutally hot San Joaquin County (7,700) is a supplier of more moderately priced Merlots.

MOURVÈDRE

California wine enthusiasts could come to love Mourvèdre, but chances are that they never will, and it is not Mourvèdre's fault. True, Mourvèdre is not one of the great grapes of the world by itself, and its most useful role in the wine world is as a willing supporter to the thinner but fruitier Grenache in the red wines of Provence, including both the expensive, age-worthy, and justifiably popular wines from Châteauneuf du Pape and the less pricey but popular Côte du Rhônes. Absent a Grenache-based wine category in California, however, Mourvèdre is destined to remain an outsider. Back in the days when vineyards were composed of field blends, the grape enjoyed a kind of unrecognized popularity; but with the greater emphasis on varietal labeling and the rather heavy, thick wines that it produces on its own, it is now planted to only nine hundred acres despite having boasted almost three times that much in 1968. It is also known as Mataro, and a few wineries continue to use that name mainly for historical reasons having nothing to do with grape or wine quality.

PETIT VERDOT

Long looked down upon as one of the minor blending varieties to the far more majestic Cabernet Sauvignon in Bordeaux's left bank vineyards, Petit Verdot is experiencing a minor "boomlet" in California where some producers have decided that it adds both a bold berryish edge and a bit of backbone to Cabernet. And while it is true that that grape needs no help in finding a tannic spine, it is the added complexity delivered by Petit Verdot that has recently captured added attention. In truth, it is the last of the Bordeaux blending grapes to get a look, and the results, while far from final, are encouraging. As a result, Petit Verdot acreage has grown from 400 ten years ago to 1,800 today. Acreage leaders include Napa (600), San Luis Obispo (300), Sonoma (200), and San Joaquin (200) counties.

PETITE SIRAH

It is the fate of Petite Sirah, for better or for worse, that it is blessed with the potential to produce the biggest, toughest, brawniest red wines made in California. Its creator, a French vineyardist named Durif, had no such intentions, of course. He was simply looking for a way to craft a new grape based on Syrah that would not have Syrah's tendency toward powdery mildew when it gets wet in the vineyard. Durif was working a century and a half ago at a time when vineyard practices were primitive by today's standards and when all grape varieties had difficulty getting ripe.

In his pursuit of something better, Durif crossed Syrah with a lesser-known variety, Peloursin, and came up with what we, on this side of the Atlantic, call Petite Sirah. He, on the other hand, in a congratulatory flash of self-expression, named his new creation "Durif." Turns out that Durif's Durif never really caught on in France because its tight bunches tended to rot when they got wet. But, somehow, the grape made its way to our world where it mistakenly became identified as the true Syrah. And, because we have so little moisture during the growing season, the grape's rotting problems were not the instant disqualifiers here that they were in France.

There was always a suspicion that Petite Syrah was not Syrah, and as early as the 1940s, the Louis Martini Winery was bottling it as Durif. But, in the absence of the true Syrah, the Petite Sirah moniker took over; and, together with the unmistakably bold wines it produced, a legend of sorts was born. In the early 1970s, when California vineyardists started to enjoy wide-scale success and saw many of their wines take on the style and aging characteristics of European wines, Petite Sirah came into prominence. There were those who, based solely on the aggressive tannins in the wine, claimed that our "Syrah" would live even longer in the bottle than those grown in France.

It turns out that they were right and wrong at the same time. Some of the Petite Sirah tannic monsters of that era have, indeed, shown the ability to age forever. However, those old wines do not begin to grow into the beauty and "complex power" that the real Syrah can deliver. And as that recognition grew, along with the notion that we were not growing the real Syrah, Petite Sirah's popularity plummeted. Over the last thirty years, while California's grape acreage has more than doubled, Petite Sirah plantings have dropped by over half. What remains are patches that go into blends to give them more structure and a small but steady stream of bold wines whose convinced followers have elevated the grape to "cult" status. By comparison to the leading red varieties, Petite Sirah is just a blip on the radar, but to the true believers, the search for Petite Sirah greatness is like the search for the Holy Grail.

As a child of Rhône-area varieties, it is not surprising that Petite Sirah grows in protected vineyards along the coast and in fairly warm but not brutally hot locations inland. A total of 7,600 acres now stand in California, with the greatest concentrations in San Joaquin (1,800 acres) and San Luis Obispo (1,300) counties. The cooler coastal counties are also well represented by Napa (700), Sonoma (500), and Mendocino (500).

PINOT BLANC

This white variant of Pinot Noir has never had much of a following in California, just as it does not have a large fan base in its native France. Despite being a grape of Burgundy, where Chardonnay dominates white varietal plantings, it finds a small but continuing base in Alsace, where it toils alongside but in the shadows of Gewürztraminer, Riesling, and Pinot Gris. To add to the confusion, it is now thought that most of what growers have been calling Pinot Blanc is actually Melon, the grape of the thin, high-acid Muscadet wines grown in vineyards at the very mouth of the Loire Valley as it empties into the Atlantic Ocean. In California, the grape, regardless of its true identity, is used mostly as a minor blending addition to sparkling wines. Pinot Blanc acreage reached a peak of some two thousand acres in the late 1980s but has plummeted since then and now adds up to only four hundred acres. No county has so much as one hundred acres of Pinot Blanc.

PINOT GRIS/PINOT GRIGIO

This Johnny-come-lately to California, and the West Coast, has found almost immediate acceptance and has gone from nonexistent to third place, behind Chardonnay and Sauvignon Blanc, in the white wine sweepstakes. At the same time, it has become the number one white variety in Oregon vineyards. California wineries have the option of using the Italian designation, Pinot Grigio, or the French moniker, Pinot Gris, and there is no use trying to divine the style of wine from its name.

There are versions of Pinot Grigio that are much closer to the French (Alsatian) version of the grape in which body and a honeyed, slightly floral character dominates, and there are thin, wiry versions of Pinot Gris that are much closer to the narrow and neutral style that is most often found in the Italian versions. Because Pinot Gris has a tendency to lose acidity as it ripens, many California types of Pinot Gris, especially those from warmer growing regions, tend to rely on succulence rather than raciness for their direct charms. Pinot Gris from cooler coastal locations can be higher in acidity and have a brighter style, but even wines from those locales can reach high levels of ripeness and sport a full and rich personality.

Just twenty years ago, there was no recorded Pinot Gris acreage in California, and even ten years ago, there were just nine hundred acres standing in local vineyards. Today, the California plantings have risen to 12,600 acres, and there has been no let-up in the rush to the variety. Fairly sizable plantings in medium-warm inland locations like San Joaquin (4,100), Sacramento (1,200), and Yolo (1,000) counties total somewhat more than those from coastal counties, including Monterey (1,400), Santa Barbara (900), Sonoma (500), and Napa (300).

PINOT MEUNIER

The reason why there are some two hundred acres of Pinot Meunier in California is its importance in the making of Champagne. Although the most expensive bubblies from the Champagne region are made exclusively from Pinot Noir and Chardonnay, Pinot Meunier is a component in medium-priced Champagnes. It matures earlier than those other grapes and has a softer, rounder character, and for that reason, it finds its way into Champagnes that are not aged for years and years before being brought to market.

In California, it is not necessary to use Pinot Meunier to make a more open Sparkling Wine, and, of course, the local vintners are not limited in their choice of grapes, thereby inviting many other varieties into lower-priced Sparkling Wine. It is also worth noting that Sparkling Wines from other regions of France, even those that may be brands based in the Champagne region, are also not limited to a few specific varieties. The few hundred acres of Pinot Meunier in California are not likely to find their numbers increasing.

PINOT NOIR

Of all the so-called noble varieties, those grapes that make wines of surpassing beauty, Pinot Noir may be the most fickle. It teases us with subtlety and nuance, with fruit and whiffs of smoke and earth, with a velvet texture more silky than any other red grape, and with a sturdy underpinning of acidity and tannin that brings it both balance and a measure of age worthiness. It is no wonder that some have applied the description "an iron fist in a velvet glove" to its character.

In its native Burgundy, Pinot Noir can deliver wines that are at once both deep and complex, solid and refined, and the most famous of those wines, the Romanee-Contis, are among the most expensive red wines on the market. Even lesser Burgundies can have a subtlety that is simply not found in all but a few outstanding Cabernets, Merlots, and Syrahs. But Pinot Noir can also be thin and unlovely when not grown in the hospitable sites, and it becomes soft, flabby, and dull when the temperatures rise.

For almost all of recorded wine history, its glories have been confined to France, and to just one small part of France at that. Virtually every other Pinot Noir simply did not measure up—at least until recently. As wine plantings have expanded in the New World, both on the West Coast and down under in New Zealand's South Island and a few good patches in Australia as well, the grape has found homes with the right soils, and the appropriate levels of heat and length of growing season; and now Pinot Noir, still as fickle as ever, does have new homes in which superb wines are being grown.

In its early days in California, Pinot Noir suffered not only from being planted in areas that were often too warm to produce exceptional wine but also from old-fashioned winemaking techniques such as, again, in large, old tanks. The wine boom of the 1970s and the need to replant old vineyards together with the recognition that Pinot Noir needed to move to cooler winegrowing regions sowed the seeds of its rehabilitation in these parts. Growing areas like Carneros became a welcoming home, and so did the Russian River Valley. The opening up of San Luis Obispo County in the Edna and Arroyo Grande valleys and the Santa Barbara in the Santa Maria and Santa Ynez valleys resulted in a change for the better. These developments together with a long list of dedicated Pinot Noir–loving winemakers whose willingness to adopt better winemaking approaches set Pinot Noir on a path that has seen the grape prosper.

It is true, of course, that Pinot Noir acreage is still a fraction of Cabernet Sauvignon's; it is also true, regardless of the escalation in price for the top Pinots, that prices for Cabernet still outdistance Pinot Noir substantially. Pinot Noir aficionados have no complaint in that regard. The best California Pinots are often recognized as the best outside France, and they can be had for what appear to be relative bargains by comparison both to their French counterparts and to their Cabernet competition.

The leading areas for Pinot Noir are all in coastal locations. The Russian River Valley, especially in its cooler location near Sebastopol and just north and west of Santa Rosa leading up the Westside Road, the often agreed-on home of California's most outstanding, world-class Pinots, is easily the dominant area in terms of prestige and planted acreage. Sonoma County, including both the Russian River Valley and Carneros along the edge of San Francisco Bay, accounts for nearly 30 percent of all the Pinot acreage standing in California. Monterey County is a distant second, and much of its acreage, although in cool growing districts, generally rates somewhat lower on the quality charts. However, both the Santa Lucia Highlands to the west of the Salinas Valley floor and the Chalone area in the limestone-studded hills to the east have made outstanding Pinots. The various Santa Barbara locations, including the newly minted Sta. Rita Hills AVA, come next in importance. Mendocino County, based substantially on the Pinot Noirs of the Anderson Valley, also deserves a place on any listing of favorable locations for the grape.

Pinot Noir is not just useful as a very special red wine, however. It is a major player in the making of Champagne in its native France, and it enjoys that role here as well. It is an honor it shares, as it does in France, with Chardonnay. If one judges by the quantity of midpriced and higher-priced Sparkling Wine produced here, it is possible that one-quarter or more of all Pinot Noir acreage is devoted to the production of our top bubblies.

Today, there are some 36,400 acres of Pinot Noir standing in California. Sonoma County tops the list at 11,000, with Monterey at 8,000, Santa Barbara at 4,500, Napa at 2,800, and Mendocino at 2,400 acres next in line.

PRIMITIVO

Not seen on many labels and barely showing up in grape acreage surveys, Primitivo is none other than Zinfandel in sheep's clothing. It is found in vineyards in southern Italy where it produces a wine that tastes very much like Zinfandel when first made but is a bit cruder and grapier as it ages. Because Primitivo, with its increased numbers of smaller bunches, is identical to Zinfandel in DNA, it must be viewed as a clone of Zinfandel and not its own variety. To date, several producers have made both Zinfandel and its Primitivo clone, and it is an open argument as to which is better when grown side by side. Reported acreage nears two hundred.

Once almost universally called Johannisberg Riesling in California after a top producer, Schloss Johannisberg, in its native Germany, Riesling produces wines boasting exquisitely floral perfume, great depth, and racy, brisk balance, especially in Germany and also to some lesser but still significant extent in France's Alsace region and in parts of Australia. Riesling also has the ability to yield dessert wines that are arguably the finest examples of richness and beauty in the world. Although California versions of the grape can imitate the noble characteristics of the world-class table wine and the dessert wine styles, it has never really come close enough to earn a substantial following among wine drinkers and thus to warrant a continuing commitment by the growers and wineries.

The result is that the eight thousand acres standing in vineyards three decades ago have dwindled today to three thousand seven hundred. Every few years, the wine establishment tries to foster a comeback for this potentially exceptional variety, but none of those efforts has ever taken hold. In California, the best Rieslings have come from cool coastal locales such as Monterey County (2,200 acres planted mostly in the northern part of the county), Santa Barbara County (300), and Mendocino (100).

Some labels still use the name White Riesling, once used to differentiate the grape from the innocuous Trousseau Gris variety but now long gone from California vineyards, which was inappropriately identified as Gray Riesling. Emerald Riesling, a name no longer seen on wine labels, was created by crossing Riesling with Muscadelle in the hope of creating a wine of noble personality that could be grown in California's hot Central Valley.

ROSÉ AND VIN GRIS

Ranging in color from the palest gray-pink to bright copper-orange and hitting most of the hues of pink in between, these wines are meant to be light and easy to drink. Many are outright sweet in their making, but the more expensive versions are more likely to be dry and brightly fruity than having been helped along their ways with a figurative spoonful of sugar.

Rosé wines can be made from the juice of red grapes kept from more than minimal contact with the grape skins from which they extract both color and tannin during the days after crush. The juice, called "must" before it has been turned into wine, is light in color at the time of crush. When Rosé is made from red grapes, the pink color is achieved typically from a brief bit of contact with the skins or from the addition of a red wine or red must. It is also legal to make Rosé from white grapes into which a bit of red wine is introduced after fermentation.

Despite the occasional success, very few pink wines have been made over time with anything in mind but sweet, soft character meant for unceremonious drinking. And things got decidedly worse when White Zinfandel, a pink wine despite its name, ruled the roost. But, within the last five years or so, "Rosé" is in, and wineries large and small have jumped on the bandwagon. It was as if vinous manna had all of a sudden begun to fall from the heavens on a category that has been essentially bankrupt for years.

So what is all the fuss about? In part, it is because over the last three decades, all wines have become cleaner, fresher, and more rewarding. And in part, it is because there are surpluses in grape supply that invite the production of inexpensive Syrahs and Merlots and Sangioveses with little color. But mostly it is because a $17 Rosé can be released six months or so after crush, cost virtually nothing for oak barrels, and make more money for the winery than its $20 wines that are so much more demanding in terms of time, attention, and finances.

Sparkling Wine Rosé is the one category where pink translates into extra dollars at the pump. And in these wines, the added color is typically achieved by adding about 5 percent red wine to the base cuvée. Lately, a few producers are pushing sparkling Rosé into drier and more tannin directions with the hope that these more structured bottlings will turn out to be fan favorites for uses alongside the same dishes for which a light, zesty Pinot Noir might be suited.

Vin Gris is, in reality, another name for "Rosé" in that wines by this moniker are made with the white juice of red grapes. With Vin Gris, the color is intended to be as pale as possible, and, for the few so labeled in California, the wines are dry and crisp in style.

RHÔNE BLENDS

France's Rhône district is divided into two sections, north and south. Because wines from the southern Rhône may contain over a dozen varieties for red and at least five for the occasional whites from the area, the term *Rhône blend* is intended to signify California wines that mimic the wines of the south. For reds, the dominant grape tends to be Grenache, and the famous wines of the area, such as Châteauneuf du Pape, Gigondas, and

Vacqueyras, almost always contain over 50 percent of that variety with lesser additions of Mourvèdre, Syrah, and a raft of lesser-known grapes.

It is not unusual, however, for California wines meant to be in the style of the southern Rhône to carry higher levels of Syrah and to contain other related or similar varieties such as Petite Sirah, Carignane, and Zinfandel. The intention is to create rich and somewhat open, tasty wines like those of the southern Rhône. Given the relative lack of success shown by Grenache and Mourvèdre here, it is not unusual that the California versions would look to highest-quality grapes likely to make similar wines.

The red wines of the northern Rhône are either wholly made from Syrah or made from Syrah with minor additions of Viognier, Marsanne, or Roussanne. The whites of the northern Rhône are entirely made from Viognier in the commune of Condrieu and are blends of Marsanne and Roussanne elsewhere in the northern Rhône.

ROUSSANNE

Most often seen as a partner to Marsanne, with which it is blended in the northern Rhône district of France, Roussanne totals just about four hundred acres locally, mostly in the hands of those who would try their luck with the many variations of Rhône wines, both white and red. It is fragrant but not especially fruity in character and can come with good acidity. Still, its lot here would seem to parallel its place in France where it is a rare but occasionally admired variety. The Central Coast counties of Monterey, San Luis Obispo, and Santa Barbara dominate the small but growing population of Roussanne vines.

SANGIOVESE

This red grape of Tuscany, responsible for an ocean of Chianti ranging from thin and innocuous to ripe and rich, has been found in California vineyards for decades but has shown very little. Nonetheless, starting in the early 1990s, and helped along by a desire to find the next new hot wine, the grape was planted widely and had a momentary burst of fame only to fall back into California's vinous nether reaches within a decade or so.

With but 200 acres under vine by 1990, Sangiovese acreage exploded to some 3,400 acres near the turn of the century but then began receding, and now it stands at 1,900 and continues to fall as wineries remove it from their lists of offerings.

In a white-wine world increasingly dominated by Chardonnay, it is hard to believe that Sauvignon Blanc is grown successfully in more locales around the globe than Chardonnay and produces exceptional wines in a greater variety of styles. Whether one is partial to the wiry, melon, and grass versions that have made New Zealand one of the darlings of the Sauvignon Blanc world or the smoky, flinty versions from France's Loire Valley, the sweet, late-harvest delights from Sauternes, or the more fleshy and complex stylings of some New World growing regions, Sauvignon Blanc seems happy to render them all.

Not surprisingly, given the range of growing conditions, California vineyards are producing Sauvignon Blanc in virtually every fashion, and it is often a question of winery preference rather than vineyard location or historical custom that dictates whether the predominant dry versions of the grape will be brisk and grassy or fleshy and melony or even fat and oaky. Sweet versions are also produced in vineyards in many coastal locations, and while those wines may not challenge the best of Sauternes, they do demonstrate the grape's ability to become incredibly lush and concentrated when the grape mold, *Botrytis cinerea,* is allowed to work its magic on the grapes by simultaneously reducing water levels in the grapes while concentrating sugar and acidity.

Today, the leading versions of Sauvignon Blanc take advantage of California's sunny climate and tend to be fairly full in body yet also carry brightening acidity and are lightly to moderately rich from short-term oak aging. Yet, it was only a few decades ago when Robert Mondavi almost single-handedly changed the character of Sauvignon Blanc from soft and round to rich and brisk. At the time, he labeled his new wine as Fumé Blanc to differentiate it from the style of the day. Today, the Fumé Blanc name is less seen because it is the accepted custom that Sauvignon Blanc, whether ripe and oaky or firmer and bristling with acidity, will be a dry wine designed to go with food.

Current planted acreage of Sauvignon Blanc now stands at 15,400, a total that has been more or less stable for some twenty years. Plantings are spread between the medium-warm locations near the Sacramento River Delta and cooler coastal vineyards. Sonoma (2,400 acres), Napa (2,500), Lake (1,900), Monterey (1,000), and San Luis Obispo (800) counties set the pace among the locales with direct ocean influence, while the breezy but warmer locations in San Joaquin (2,000), Sacramento (1,600), and Yolo (600) sport substantial plantings.

SAUVIGNON MUSQUÉ

Some wineries use the term *Sauvignon Musqué* for wines made from a clone of Sauvignon Blanc believed to have muscatty overtones to its fruit. In fact, Sauvignon Musqué is listed as a separate variety in the annual count of planted vines even though DNA testing has shown that it is, in fact, only a variant of Sauvignon Blanc. Its listed total of some two hundred acres is not entirely accurate since many growers will more correctly report the clone as Sauvignon Blanc.

SEMILLON

Far more important to California's early vinous history than it is today, Semillon was often blended with generous amounts of Sauvignon Blanc into slightly to moderately sweet white wines labeled generically as "Sauterne." With the introduction and great acceptance of dry-styled Sauvignon Blanc, and the resulting loss of standing of the sweeter, softer version, Semillon lost its role and has not found one since.

It is today used to flesh out the occasional Sauvignon Blanc, and it infrequently is made into a very sweet, late-harvest dessert wine, but its remaining nine hundred acres result in very few wines called Semillon. No county has as much as two hundred acres of Semillon, and very little has been planted in the last couple of decades.

SPARKLING WINE

Often referred to as Champagne, although that name is legally reserved for wines with bubbles from France's Champagne district, California Sparkling Wine comes in many forms, from world class and expensive to jug wine quality.

Both the choice of grapes and the method of manufacture tend to separate Sparkling Wines. The top brands are made from grapes grown in very cool regions such as Carneros, the Anderson Valley, Sonoma Coast, and cool areas of Monterey and San Luis Obispo counties. Even coastal Marin gets into the act with its high-acid grapes. Less expensive wines, especially those selling for a few dollars, rely on less costly warmer-weather grapes and on less costly production methods.

World-class Sparkling Wine, and anything but the most inexpensive bubblies, are made by what is called the "*méthode champenoise,*" a process by which still wine is placed in the bottle together with a bit of sugar and yeast and then all the pieces sit there together for years on end. The lower end of the price range for these Sparkling Wines may stay in contact with the resulting bubbles and dead yeasts for a year or so, while the upper end may rest "*en tirage*" for five to ten years.

The longer the wine stays in its developmental (autolysis) stage, the smaller its bubbles become and the richer and deeper becomes the toasty, roasted nut and soy character imparted by the dead yeast. Most Sparkling Wine made by the méthode champenoise tends to be high in acidity and is softened into balance by the addition of a sweet liqueur at the very end of the aging process.

Inexpensive Sparkling Wine is typically produced by the bulk process in which large containers of wine are sweetened and then receive their second fermentation under pressure in order to preserve the bubbles in the wine. Long aging is not practiced for such wines, and their character is more geared to straightforward fruit and sweetness.

SYRAH

Recall, please, the old expression: "What's in a name? A Syrah by any other name would smell as sweet." It has application in a wine world where grape names sometimes get so confused that they have no connection to reality.

Take Syrah, for instance. In Australia, it is called Shiraz, while in California, we called it Petite Sirah for the longest time. Only, it turns out the Petite Sirah is not Syrah after all but the son of Syrah and a lesser-known grape called Peloursin. Yet we struggled for years with this grape we called Petite Sirah, thinking that it was the real thing but simply did not smell as sweet—or as interesting or as grand.

The Aussies have their own problems with nomenclature. They can trace the grape back to its arrival almost two centuries ago, even before the English unloaded their prisons near what is now Sydney. But, in those days, they called grape "Hermitage" after the hillside in France's Rhône region where Syrah grows to near perfection. Eventually, under pressure from the French, the name Hermitage was dropped, and the grape took on the name Shiraz.

There must have been some person or group Down Under with a romantic streak in their choice of the grape's new name. It was the wisdom of the time that Syrah had first been cultivated in Persia near the town of Shiraz several thousands of years ago. A Crusader was reported to have brought it back to France, planted it on what is now the Hermitage hillside, and made himself and the grape famous.

Well, leave it to the Californians, who had their own problems with the grape, to set the Aussies straight. Into the local search for the truth about Petite Sirah and Syrah stepped the University of California at Davis, which also happens to be the home of a very fine program for the training of professional winemakers. The research there concluded, and then proved conclusively through DNA testing, that Syrah originated in France as the result of some extracurricular breeding between a couple of very obscure grapes.

It turns out that Shiraz never went near Shiraz just as Petite Sirah is not Syrah. And, while the name Shiraz continues in use today (apparently because the Iranians who now occupy the place have not threatened to boycott Australian goods and don't drink their wine, in any event), we now at least know that the grape that we in California call Syrah, and have only had here in any quantity for the last twenty years, is the real thing. And its rapid expansion in our vineyards from nothing to almost twenty thousand acres, little more than a twinkling of an eye in vinous time, is due to the fact that Shakespeare was right after all: Syrah does smell sweet, and it does not matter what we call it so long as we have the right grape. You might even conclude that all's well that ends well.

The Syrah story, of course, is not ended. California's understanding of the grape is a work in progress. After racing into prominence and being credited by some observers as the real deus ex machina in Merlot's seem-ing fall from grace, Syrah is now experiencing its own sales doldrums. Grape acreage shot up way ahead of marketplace acceptance, and there is a now-insignificant debate pitting the bold, highly ripened style of Syrah against a more refined style reminiscent of the best from Syrah's home in the northern Rhône district of France.

It is to Syrah's advantage that it is ideally suited to the warm microcli-mates of coastal California. Indeed, it is almost too easy for wineries to make solid, bold, highly ripened Syrahs with plenty of character, but, at the same time, it has been a lot harder to find the pretty, semirefined side of the variety. Boldness and drama are not bad things in wine, but it is bal-ance and polish, depth, and prettiness that turn drama into beauty. In the cooler parts of the coastal growing regions, Syrah has occasionally shown that it also has the ability here to succeed in a less than pushy style.

It is in this area of a more sophisticated and mannerly approach, how-ever, that Syrah has lagged to date. Syrah is here to stay; of that there can be no doubt. The question now revolves around the length of time it is going to take for Syrah to emerge into a more complete wine. It took Pinot Noir a century and a half to reach world-class status in our vineyards. Time will tell whether Syrah is a faster learner.

The recent emergence of Syrah as an important red variety in California can be seen clearly in the grape acreage chart presented earlier in table 1. In just twenty years, Syrah has moved from a blip on the vinous radar screen to discovered grape to major player. Its current standing acreage of 19,200 is spread around the state, mostly in warm to hot areas. San Luis Obispo County boasts 2,700 acres of Syrah, most in the moderately warm parts of the Paso Robles AVA. San Joaquin County rates second in acreage at 2,000, with the preponderance of those vines lying in the quite warm Lodi AVA. The more moderate growing areas in Sonoma (1,900 acres), Monterey (1,700), Santa Barbara (1,400), and Napa (1,000) counties are still mostly in the warmer parts of those places as well.

TEMPRANILLO

The rapidly improving quality and greatly increased popularity of Spain's Rioja and Ribero del Deuro districts, on the plains north of Madrid, where Tempranillo reigns supreme, has encouraged California growers and wineries to try their hands with the grape. It turns out that we have had Tempranillo here for decades under the name Valdepeñas and have grown it in the hot Central Valley where its tendency to low acidity has limited its use to jug wines. To date, the experiments with Tempranillo in cooler areas have yet to produce wines of great excitement, but, as in all things vinous, time is on the grape's side: if Spanish reds made from Tempranillo continue to be popular, so, too, will wineries be tempted to grow it. The current total of nine hundred acres remains concentrated in the fairly warm to hot California growing regions.

VIOGNIER

It might be a bit of a tall tale, but it is said in the best neighborhoods that Viognier was number one on the wine grape endangered species list only three decades earlier. It was about that time that the Joseph Phelps and Calera wineries began experimenting with the grape in California, and we just about fell for the story that total plantings of Viognier had fallen worldwide to a paltry seventy-nine acres. In fact, the total was more like three hundred acres based on odd bits of plantings spread across parts of southern France.

Still, as those first California efforts with the grape came to beautiful fruition, we believed that California had single-handedly saved Viognier from leaving this world altogether. There is some truth to the seventy-nine-acre story, for that is what was left of Viognier in the northern Rhône region of France. However, since the territory for Viognier in its home-town of Condrieu is small to begin with, there was never all that much of the grape in any event. Even today, it is estimated that Viognier plantings in Condrieu, including the attached but separate appellation of Chateau Grillet, amount to no more than five hundred acres.

It is an allowed grape in other parts of France, but thirty years ago, it was more trouble than it was worth because it often failed to produce wines capable of paying off the time and effort to cultivate it. And this is where California comes in. Our quick success with Viognier led almost instantaneously to a revival in France and to plantings elsewhere in the world. And many of those plantings were in areas that are much more hospitable to Viognier than its home territory.

Viognier has not exploded in acreage in the manner of Chardonnay or even of Merlot, but it is now up to three thousand acres here and is no longer threatened with extinction. Along the way, Viognier was introduced in some of our warmer-growing regions, and that change in the handling of the grape has led to higher production and the ability of wineries to turn Viognier into a grape that not only produces fancy and expensive wines but also is capable of yielding easy-drinking bottlings in the $10 range. Those new wines may not be the same stuff as the limited production efforts from more demanding hillside sites that remind us of its home in the Rhône region, but they are some of the most price-worthy white wines made in California

There is a case, however, for expensive Viognier. In order to make the grape into a wine that is solidly structured, complex, and age-worthy, winemakers require less productive soils and lower yields along with a fair bit of barrel aging. Wines like that are going to be more pricey than their higher-volume cousins. But, when they succeed, they will be deeper, more nuanced bottlings in which scents of flowers and white peaches are elusive wisps amid a deeper but tighter fruit core needing time to develop rather than being part of a personality that jumps out of the glass on day one.

Viognier remains something of a rare grape to this day in the cool, coastal counties where about one-third of its three thousand stands spread more or less uniformly among Mendocino, Napa, Sonoma, Monterey,

Santa Barbara, and San Luis Obispo counties, each with approximately one hundred to two hundred acres. San Joaquin County alone boasts nine hundred acres of Viognier and is the source for much of the inexpensive, often quite successful lower-priced Viognier.

ZINFANDEL

Very smart people have written whole books about Zinfandel and its origins, but not one of those extensive texts has yet convinced the world that it has the one, true answer about how Zinfandel made its way to California. As recently as three decades ago, it was accepted fact that Count Agoston Haraszthy had brought the grape here from his native Hungary. It is a reasonable story since Haraszthy is credited with bringing many grapes here back in the 1850s, and it was during that period that a grape called Zinfandel began to appear in California vineyards. The problem with that theory was that there was no record of Zinfandel in Haraszthy's log, and no evidence that any grape from the parts of Europe where he searched out grapevine cuttings had ever grown a grape called Zinfandel or had ever produced wines similar to Zinfandel.

About the same time, the leading wine historian Charles Sullivan, whose book on the subject is now considered to be one of the definitive texts, got wind of references to Zinfandel being grown in Boston in the 1830s, and he directed your authors to search through the records of the Massachusetts Horticultural Society for corroborating evidence. It was on one of our trips back home to visit family that we found records of Zinfandel earning top honors in the Society's annual competitions. And it was none other than a clipper ship captain named James Macondray, who by the mid-1850s had settled in San Francisco and was the grower of the prize-winning Zinfandel.

Not much later, prominent growers are known to have also brought Zinfandel cuttings from Boston. If all of this is at least supposition, it is solid supposition. And we do know that Zinfandel has identical DNA to a little-known grape from Croatia and that this "Crljenak Kasteljanski" looks and acts like Zinfandel. Moreover, there is a grape in Italy called Primitivo that, while it grows somewhat differently, shares identical DNA with Zinfandel. And we further know that there is no grape anywhere else in the world called Zinfandel. So the mystery persists to some extent.

There is no secret, however, about the fact that Zinfandel very quickly became a workhorse grape in California vineyards in the latter half of the nineteenth century. Indeed, there are today still some patches of Zinfandel that have been standing for well over one hundred years. Lacking the noble background of Cabernet Sauvignon and Pinot Noir, and not yielding wines of their finesse, Zinfandel became instead the backbone of sturdy red jug wine and was rarely called on to stand on its own.

Despite the occasional foray into the public's view, Zinfandel was not bottled on its own by more than a handful of wineries. And it was not until the late 1960s that Zinfandel began to take on trappings of greatness in the hands of Ridge Vineyards, still among the very best producers, and the late Joseph Swan, whose legendary Zinfandels were among the first "cult" wines of the modern wine era.

In recent times, Zinfandel has become a full-bodied, highly ripened wine with concentrated blackberryish flavors that occasionally slip into dried berry tones and can, in some hands, reach raisiny dryness. Almost all Zins these days are aged in oak for a year or more and are brought to market at one to three years of age. There have been attempts over the years to prove that Zinfandel can age like Cabernet Sauvignon, and, indeed, one will still find references in wine literature to the notion that Zinfandel will morph over time into some layered imitation of Cabernet Sauvignon. That, however, is not our finding, and after years of tasting older Zins, it is clear that most of them are at their peak of drinkability at age three to six. The occasional Zinfandel does surprise over time, as many from Ridge, Grgich Hills, and Sausal have done, and in almost every case, those have been wines with balance, restrained ripeness, and bright acidity.

True Zinfandel fanatics refuse to recognize the existence of, let alone a liking for, White Zinfandel, usually a soda-poppish pink or nearly colorless version, typically sweet, and meant for totally casual drinking. Nevertheless, it remains a popular, inexpensive quaff, and many's the winery that quietly puts out tens of thousands of cases in this style.

Today, Zinfandel is the second-most widely planted red wine grape in California, but it is worth noting that the bulk of the expanded plantings have occurred in what would be described as "warm-weather vineyards" away from the coast. Increased popularity without equivalent expansion of the best vineyards has helped push high-end Zinfandel prices up substantially, and while it is not common to find wineries whose Zin is pricier than its Cabernet Sauvignon, it is not unheard of, either. Total planted Zinfandel acres sits at 49,900, with San Joaquin County leading the way at 20,000. Sonoma County has 5,200 acres of Zinfandel, San Luis Obispo and Madera each have over 3,000 acres; and Amador, Fresno, and Mendocino all reach 2,000 acres of planted acreage.

PART TWO

California Wine Regions
and Wineries

Mendocino and Lake Counties

These seemingly faraway places up in redwood country have long been home to a small but important wine industry. Mendocino more than Lake perhaps, but the truth is that folks have known for a century and more that good wine can grow in both of these destinations. Now, with its neighbors to the south in Napa and Sonoma counties having become very heavily planted, exceptionally expensive, and beginning to run out of land for further expansion, Mendocino and Lake counties have taken on new prominence as sources of high-quality wine.

MENDOCINO COUNTY

Sufficiently removed from the urban centers of Northern California to retain its serene, woodsy, folksy setting, this temperate place is home to ten separately designated viticultural areas ranging from the cool-climate Anderson Valley to the warmer Redwood Valley. The county's 17,100 planted acres may seem small by comparison to its nearby neighbors in Sonoma and Napa, but the quality of the wine produced "up north" in Mendocino is first-rate.

Mendocino County shares borders with Sonoma County to the south and Lake County to the east. It is not unusual to see direct comparisons between Sonoma and Mendocino, usually with the greater abundance of flattering conclusions being heaped on the more famous southern sibling. Although that comparison can be useful, especially when it comes to growing conditions, it is also misleading. Unlike Sonoma, with its wide open spaces and concentration of wineries, restaurants, handsome hotels, and fancy boutiques, Mendocino is a more tightly confined, rustic throwback to another time. Its wineries are smaller, and, on the whole, their fame is considerably less.

Its grape growing, of course, is modern, but its vineyard conditions, while similar to parts of Sonoma, are less hospitable, and it is in that fact alone that Mendocino earns its spurs. Mendocino's most important growing area, the Anderson Valley, lies in relative proximity to the rugged coastline and the touring allures near Mendocino Village and Fort Bragg. Not unlike the Green Valley region of Sonoma, it provides a home to varieties like Chardonnay and Pinot Noir that demand cool climates. Its warmer appellations, of which the Redwood Valley lying east and slightly to the north of Ukiah are providing a welcoming home for Zinfandel, are, like the rest of Mendocino, more forest than agriculture. The largest portions of the county's 17,100 acres of grapes belong to Chardonnay (4,600), Cabernet Sauvignon (2,500), Pinot Noir (2,400), and Zinfandel (2,000). Red grapes outnumber whites by 10,600 acres to 6,600.

Anderson Valley

This transverse valley on the highway between the inland Alexander Valley at the northern end of Sonoma County and the ruggedly beautiful Mendocino coastline is rapidly losing its rural attitude. Wineries and restaurants, and the tourists who frequent those places, are changing the Anderson Valley into a weekend destination. Of course, it is wine quality that has been the catalyst, and, for better or worse, the admirable quality of the wine grown here is almost certain to bring about continuing expansions in acreage and in the numbers of producers filling the region. In turn, the Anderson Valley, already known to many as the home of lovely, balanced Pinot Noir, expressively spicy Gewürztraminer, and crisp, lively Sparkling Wines, is likely to become both more famous and more popular as the years go by.

The Anderson Valley is a relatively cool place for grapes, and it is, accordingly, more oriented to white wine varieties and Pinot Noir than it is to the bolder reds. When those bigger wines are attempted, it is mostly on warmer, elevated hillsides; indeed, the higher up one goes, the more hospitable the

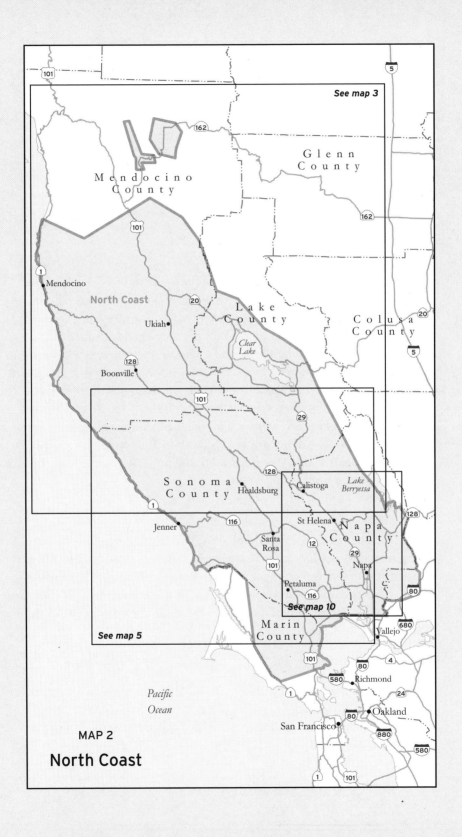

See map 3

Glenn
County

Mendocino
County

North Coast

Mendocino

Lake
County

Colusa
County

Ukiah

Clear
Lake

Boonville

Sonoma
County

Calistoga

Lake
Berryessa

Healdsburg

St Helena

Napa
County

Jenner

Santa
Rosa

Napa

Petaluma

See map 10

Marin
County

Vallejo

See map 5

Richmond

Pacific
Ocean

Oakland

San Francisco

MAP 2

North Coast

climate seems to be for grapes like Zinfandel and Cabernet Sauvignon. The Mendocino Ridge AVA lies at the southern edge of Anderson Valley and overlaps with it to a limited degree. A roster of Anderson Valley wineries, now numbering close to thirty, may not seem like much, but with vineyards like Savoy, Ferrington, and Paraboll serving wineries outside the appellation and famous Napa Valley producers like Duckhorn, Schramsberg, and Saintsbury utilizing Anderson Valley grapes, the place is no longer one of California's hidden secrets.

See Anderson Valley Winegrowers Association: www.avwines.com.

Cole Ranch

Somewhere on the lonely tract of road that passes as the route between the small metropolis of Ukiah and the Anderson Valley, up in the hills and draws of a semibarren landscape, lies a picturesque little valley that captured the imagination of John Cole almost four decades ago. He planted grapes, sold them to producers like Fetzer and Chateau St. Jean, and eventually earned American Viticultural Area (AVA) status for his tiny patch of cold-loving varieties under the name Cole Ranch. In the 1990s, Cole sold out to new owners, the Sterlings (no relationship to the Napa Winery or the owners of the Iron Horse Winery in Sonoma County's Green Valley). The Sterlings then purchased the former Pepperwood Winery in the Anderson Valley and launched their Esterlina brand, the home for most of the fruit grown in this one-owner appellation.

Covelo

If Cole Ranch is a tiny appellation by most standards, Covelo is a lone tree falling in the forest. Its reported acreage is miniscule, and it has a short growing season that is not immediately inviting to viticulture. Its standing as an AVA is the work of its one grower and is more a paean to his ability to describe its unique agricultural character than any description of the character of grapes grown there.

Dos Rios

Boasting one almost unheard-of winery and less than ten acres of grapes, the Dos Rios AVA would seem to be of significance only to those intrepid anglers and boaters who make the trek to the outback wilderness of northern Mendocino County.

McDowell Valley

Here is another of Mendocino's single-entity AVAs, but this one is different. Located in the southeast corner of the county, east of Hopland, it has history going back to the early twentieth century, and many of its still-standing old vines have turned out to be the real Syrah. Of course, the old vineyard also contains the entire Syrah/Petite Sirah family. The most noteworthy producer of grapes from this AVA is McDowell Valley Vineyards, which uses most of the yield from its 360 acres of grapes in the area. Small amounts of wine utilizing McDowell Valley grapes have also been made by Esterlina and Donkey and Goat.

Mendocino

In the sometimes-confusing world of wine nomenclature, none stands out more than county names like this one used as an AVA but meaning something less than the entire county. This V-shaped piece of territory lies in the southern end of the county and includes all of the AVAs in the county except the isolated Covelo area. The grape acreage and winery counts for the Mendocino AVA and for Mendocino County as a whole are virtually identical. Purists will point out that the AVA is far smaller than the county in terms of total acreage, but the significance of that difference is lost to most wine drinkers.

Mendocino Ridge

It is an undeniable truth that Mendocino County is awash in unusual appellations, but this one is unique. Rather than consisting of a contiguous swath of uplands, the Mendocino Ridge AVA contains a series of hilltops with a minimum elevation of 1,200 feet. About one hundred acres of vineyard are planted on these "islands in the sky," as the locals like to refer to them; and because they sit above the fog line and enjoy lots of sunshine, they are almost uniquely home to red varieties like Zinfandel with sprinklings of Syrah and the occasional Merlot and Riesling. As early as the 1970s, the Fetzer Winery was making outstanding Zinfandel from the likes of DuPratt, Zeni, and Ciapusci vineyards.

Potter Valley

Located on the eastern border of Mendocino County where it abuts Lake County, about fifty miles northeast of Ukiah, the Potter Valley has a long agricultural history. Indeed, it was the abundant and healthy grain crops grown by the Pomo Indians that attracted the brothers Potter to the valley and led them to settle there. The valley is moderately warm by Mendocino coast standards but lies at about one thousand feet of elevation and is capable of growing both cool-loving grapes and the warm-climate Zinfandel. Its appellation is rarely seen on wine labels, however, and is reported to be part of larger blends made by wineries in both Mendocino and south.

Redwood Valley

Lying just to the west of Potter Valley but somehow more in demand as a source of grapes and a home for wineries, the Redwood Valley rivals Anderson Valley for recognition among Mendocino appellations. It is home to more red grapes than white, and among its noted supporters are the local wineries Fife and Lolonis and Diageo's Rosenblum Cellars.

Yorkville Highlands

A newer and not well-known AVA but one destined to grow in prominence as its grape acreage and the number of wineries located there continue to increase, Yorkville Highlands runs from the northern terminus of Sonoma's Alexander Valley to the northwest along both sides of Highway 128 until it smacks into the Anderson Valley. To date, the most often seen name has been Yorkville Cellars; but recent bottlings from the Wattle Creek winery located there, Pinot Noir from the Weir Vineyard (he of Grateful Dead fame) under the Williams and Selyem label, and the establishment of the Meyer Family Cellars (headed by the son of the late Justin Meyer, who was the inspiration at Napa's famous Silver Oak Cellars) seem certain to bring fame and fortune to Yorkville Highlands.

LAKE COUNTY

In the nineteenth century, Lake County was a full two-day coach journey from San Francisco, yet it had a thriving wine industry boasting upward of two dozen wineries. Prohibition knocked the props out from under its feet, and from the 1930s to 1970, grapes were not often seen in Lake County. Reports of some three hundred acres at the end of Prohibition remained largely unchanged until the California wine industry as a whole began to expand rapidly in the 1970s. Plantings tripled immediately at the start of the decade to 1,000 and now total approximately 8,200. Along with grapes have come wineries, the most prominent of which is Guenoc, located on the property once owned by the famous English actress Lillie

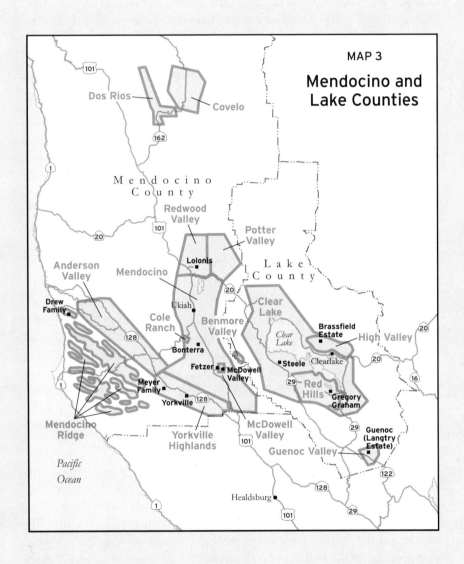

MAP 3

Mendocino and Lake Counties

Dos Rios

Covelo

162

1

Mendocino
County

Redwood
Valley

Potter
Valley

101

Lolonis

Lake
County

Anderson
Valley

Drew
Family

Mendocino

20

Clear
Lake

Ukiah

Benmore
Valley

Clear
Lake

Brassfield
Estate

High Valley

20

Cole
Ranch

128

Bonterra

Fetzer

McDowell
Valley

Steele

Clearlake

20

Meyer
Family

1

Yorkville

128

29

Red
Hills

Gregory
Graham

16

Mendocino
Ridge

Yorkville
Highlands

McDowell
Valley

29

Guenoc
(Langtry
Estate)

101

Guenoc Valley

Pacific
Ocean

122

Healdsburg

128

101

29

Langtry. Kendall-Jackson and Parducci were early users of Lake County fruit, and Jed Steele's winery, now followed by Gregory Graham's recent move to Lake County, adds the luster of success and prominence.

The county's defining feature is the twenty-mile-long Clear Lake, which occupies over half of the acreage included in the Clear Lake AVA. The Red Hills and High Valley AVAs are subappellations of the larger Clear Lake designation. The leading varieties within Lake County are Cabernet Sauvignon (3,000 acres) and Sauvignon Blanc (1,900 acres). Chardonnay, Merlot, and Zinfandel fall in the range of 400 to 600 acres apiece. Red grapes total 5,600 acres versus whites at 2,800.

See Lake County Winegrape Commission: www.lakecountywinegrape.org.

Benmore Valley

Just over the border from the southeastern corner of Mendocino County, this hilly AVA is home to one grower and few grapes. Its name, for the nineteenth-century cattle rustler Benjamin Moore, is of equal interest.

Clear Lake

The Clear Lake appellation contains more water and mountains than it does arable land, but what land it does offer to agriculture, both in the lower, flatter areas and in the hillsides, have proven hospitable to wine grapes. Here medium-warm growing conditions are more inviting to Sauvignon Blanc and Cabernet Sauvignon. Syrah is beginning to make inroads, and Petite Sirah often shows well. The Red Hills AVA at the southwestern end of Clear Lake and the High Valley AVA to the east of the lake are overlapping appellations.

Guenoc Valley

Lillie Langtry purchased this isolated property back in the 1880s and soon set about to make prize-winning wines from the few planted acres on the four-thousand-acre estate. Like the rest of Lake County, this property, by then no longer owned by Langtry, suffered at the hands of Prohibition and languished until Orville Magoon of Hawaii came along in the 1960s and refurbished the buildings and invested in new vineyards. The Guenoc Valley remains today a single-owner AVA and has about three hundred planted acres, led by Petite Sirah and followed by Cabernet Sauvignon and Merlot.

High Valley

Located in low mountains to the east of Clear Lake, this AVA is unique in its height and in the fact that it is somewhat cooler than the adjoining lower appellations. It has a reported 1,000 acres under vine, of which some 250 belong to the recently created Brassfield Winery.

Red Hills Lake County

Lying in the hills west of the Clear Lakes southern reaches, this often-visited AVA is home to such well-known names as Kendall-Jackson and Beringer, and it is also the site of a new planting belong to Andy Beckstoffer, one of the leading and most innovative vineyard owners in the Napa Valley. The area has some three thousand acres under vine at present and an additional three thousand or more plantable acres available.

See Mendocino Winegrape & Wine Commission: www.mendowine.com.

North Coast

Composed of six counties located north of San Francisco and ostensibly sharing in coastal conditions and similar grape-growing conditions, this catchall appellation is intended to be used on blended wines from all over the area. Its meaning to consumers is thus less important than the winery name and the place occupied by the wine in the winery's portfolio. There is nothing sinister about the name, but so, too, does it not convey a distinctive image of quality or style. The counties within the definition of North Coast include Marin, Sonoma, Mendocino, Lake, Napa, and Solano. Also included in that definition are almost fifty smaller-area, less than county-sized AVAs ranging from the tiny (Cole Valley, Potter Valley) to the broad and widespread (Russian River Valley, Napa Valley).

BONTERRA VINEYARDS 1993		Map 3
www.bonterra.com	707-744-7448	No Tasting
Ukiah	Mendocino County	Mendocino AVA

A pioneering grower, Bonterra was originally the early organic experiment of parent Fetzer. Indeed, its first labels were "Fetzer-Bonterra" until the 1993 vintage when Bonterra came into its own. Both are now owned by Brown-Forman, the big Kentucky spirits company that also owns Jack

Daniels, and with that company's marketing strength, Bonterra looks to produce upward of 250,000 cases annually in the next several years (50 percent Chardonnay; 20 percent Cabernet; and the remainder Merlot, Zinfandel, Syrah, and Viognier). One thousand acres are planted, of which five hundred are used for Bonterra's own estate wines (the McNab Ranch and Butler Vineyards) and the fruit from another five hundred acres is sold to Fetzer. Production growth continues to ride the coattails of the organic movement.

The wines are generally medium-full in body and meant for near- to midterm consumption. Point scores range from the low 80s to the upper 80s, thus making Bonterra a bit of a hit-and-miss situation for wine drinkers. The better-scoring wines are good values. Zinfandel often leads the way.

BRASSFIELD ESTATE WINERY 1998		Map 3
www.brassfieldestate.com	707-998-1895	Tasting by Appointment
Clearlake Oaks	Lake County	High Valley AVA

In 1973, Jerry Brassfield bought a 2,500-acre former cattle ranch in the hills east of Clear Lake. Two hundred seven of those acres were planted with grapes; and in 1998, with partner and winemaker Kevin Robinson, the winery was born. The area is underlain with volcanic and alluvial soils, and the climate changes over the 1,600- to 3,000-foot elevation range encourage the growth of a wide variety of grapes, nineteen at latest count. In 2005, a new AVA, High Valley, was designated to recognize the unique features of this location. Today, sixty thousand cases of Syrah, Zinfandel, Sauvignon Blanc, Cabernet Sauvignon, Pinot Noir, and other varieties take the names of the four vineyards: High Serenity Ranch, Monte Sereno, Round Mountain, and Volcano Ridge. The largest of these, High Serenity Ranch, with 160 acres planted, is the source of the winery's biggest seller, the Serenity white blend. The mix of white and red wines is right around 50/50. All Brassfield wines are estate grown and bottled, with no sales of grapes to or purchases from others. The planting of an additional 130 acres of grapes, the construction of aging caves, and the building of a tasting room are propelling Brassfield into further prominence. The winery's Web site is thorough and informative.

Wine quality has steadily improved over the last few years after a very inconsistent beginning, and now both medium- to full-bodied reds and whites suitable for near-term enjoyment reach into the recommended ranks with ratings in the mid- to upper 80s.

BREGGO CELLARS 2000

www.breggo.com   707-895-9589

Boonville   Mendocino County

Map 4

Tasting

Anderson Valley AVA

In 2000, Douglas Stewart and Ana Benitez-Stewart bought a 203-acre sheep ranch between Boonville and Philo in the Anderson Valley. Economics suggested that, instead of planting vineyards immediately, they would make wine from the best grapes from other Anderson Valley growers. Looking to produce Pinot Noir initially, the Stewarts bought grapes from the Savoy, Ferrington, and Donnelley Creek vineyards and from the Wiley Vineyard for Pinot Gris. Breggo now produces three thousand cases annually, primarily of their Pinot Noir and Pinot Gris, and expect to start growing their own grapes in the next two to three years.

Exceptional quality is exhibited in the winery's early releases of its balanced, fairly full-bodied, well-mannered Pinot Noir rate in the upper 80s and low 90s, while the ripe, full-bodied Savoy Chardonnay earns scores in the upper-80-point range.

DREW 2003

www.drewwines.com   707-877-1771

Elk   Mendocino County

Map 3

Tasting by Appointment

Mendocino Ridge AVA

In 2003, Jason and Molly Drew bought land and started building a winery in western Mendocino County, between the Anderson Valley and the coast. Jason had learned the trade through a range of vineyard and winery jobs, most recently as associate winemaker at Babcock in Santa Barbara County. Their objective is to make superior Pinot Noirs and Syrahs with grapes from select vineyards in the North Coast (60 percent) and Santa Barbara County (40 percent) and ultimately their own land; part of their twenty-six acres is being prepared for planting, with the first estate vintage expected in 2010. Two thousand cases are produced annually, 85 percent of which is Pinot Noir, with the remainder Syrah. Distribution is primarily online and by mailing list.

Both Pinot Noir and Syrah varieties have earned scores into the upper-80-point range to date.

ESTERLINA VINEYARDS & WINERY 2000   Map 3

www.esterlinavineyards.com   707-895-2920

Philo   Mendocino County

Tasting by Appointment

Anderson Valley AVA

John Cole bought an old sheep ranch in 1971 and planted vines on some fifty-five acres, selling the grapes to others. In the late 1990s, Cole sold the ranch to the Sterling family. The Sterlings, with patriarch Mario and his four sons at the helm, had earlier established the Esterlina brand in Sonoma County. In 2000, they bought the Pepperwood winery in Philo and consolidated production in Philo, producing 7,500 cases a year of Riesling, Pinot Noir, Merlot, and Cabernet Sauvignon. The 2006 acquisition of Everett Ridge Winery in Healdsburg will provide 60 percent more production while keeping the two labels and their winemakers distinct. The Riesling is flowery and slightly sweet, and so far it tops the winery performance charts.

FETZER VINEYARDS	1968	Map 3
www.fetzer.com	707-744-7600	Tasting
Hopland	Mendocino County	Mendocino AVA

The largest Mendocino County winery by far, Fetzer was founded in 1958 when lumberman Barney Fetzer bought a 720-acre ranch in Redwood Valley. The first vintage was a 2,500-case production of a red table wine in 1968. Early Fetzer releases of full-throttle Cabernet and Zinfandel propelled the company into prominence by the mid-1970s. Expansion followed with the ballyhooed 1978 release of Sundial Chardonnay, and the emphasis then shifted to rapid growth. Fetzer was able to grow based on value-oriented products and without wide advertising by nurturing a national wholesaling network. By the mid-1980s, production of its many wines had reached a half-million cases a year, and the winery began its experiments with organic farming and other "green" energy conservation measures, for which it would become renowned. In the early 1990s, Fetzer created the organic Bonterra label in Mendocino County and was acquired by Brown-Forman for a purported $100 million. By 2000, production exceeded 2.5 million cases. In 2001, Fetzer expanded its capacity by building a new facility in Paso Robles and launching its Five Rivers Ranch label.

Today, Fetzer produces over four million cases a year from two thousand acres in Hopland and Paso Robles, and from over one hundred other suppliers throughout the state—and indeed the world—with which Fetzer has contracts. Doing so may be a trend: Fetzer has purchased Riesling grapes from Germany and Pinot Noir from France and finishes the product in Hopland. In the opposite direction, Fetzer is selling over one million cases—fully a quarter of its production—to markets overseas. The early boldness of the Fetzer wines has now given way to a very modern, clean, medium- to full-bodied style meant for near-term consumption.

GOLDENEYE WINERY 1996

www.goldeneyewinery.com   707-895-3202

Philo   Mendocino County

Map 4

Tasting

Anderson Valley AVA

Dan and Margaret Duckhorn, of Duckhorn Vineyards in the Napa Valley, purchased an eighty-acre estate on the Navarro River in the Anderson Valley in 1996. Named Goldeneye after a diving duck of northern regions, the moniker is consistent with the Duckhorn and Paraduxx themes of the parent company. In 1997, the first harvest—375 cases—was produced and the first Pinot Noir vintage released in 2000. Ten thousand cases of Goldeneye Pinot are now produced and another three hundred to five hundred cases annually of vineyard-designated wine. Beginning with the 2001 vintage, Goldeneye grapes are also used in a second label, "Migration," which now runs to four thousand cases a year. Now up to 150 acres, Goldeneye owns four distinct estate vineyards: Confluence and The Narrows (each with fifty acres), and Abel and Gowan Creek (twenty-five acres each), which produce exclusively Pinot Noir grapes. A negligible amount of grapes are still bought from others, which will cease within the next several years as the output of the full acreage comes on line. An excellent Web site includes interesting vineyard tour and historical information.

Wine quality has been somewhat variable, but most vintages have been extremely successful, with scores of 90 points and higher for Goldeneye's ripe, full-bodied, noticeably tannic, age-worthy wines.

GREENWOOD RIDGE VINEYARDS 1972

www.greenwoodridge.com   707-895-2002

Philo   Mendocino County

Map 3

Tasting

Mendocino Ridge AVA

Situated on a western ridge top overlooking the Anderson Valley, eight acres were first planted in 1972. At 1,400 feet, the vineyard is situated entirely in the appellation and is above the fog and frost belts, encouraging a long growing season. Now expanded to sixteen acres—four each of Riesling, Cabernet Sauvignon, Merlot, and Pinot Noir grapes—Greenwood Ridge produces a total of five thousand cases a year, made almost exclusively from its own grapes except for Sauvignon Blanc, Zinfandel, and Pinot Gris from purchased grapes. Wines are available only through its wine club and at the winery. If visiting, please note the Frank Lloyd Wright–inspired tasting room designed by San Francisco architect—and longtime Wright associate—Aaron Green, father of owner-winemaker Allan Green.

The winery has enjoyed intermittent success with all varieties but more often than not scores in the mid-80-point range; true grandeur has been beyond its reach to date. Riesling is medium-sweet; Sauvignon Blanc is dry and slightly stiff; and Zinfandel is ripe, often fleshy in texture yet can be somewhat narrow in flavor for the variety.

GREGORY GRAHAM 1992		Map 3
www.ggwines.com	707-995-3500	Tasting by Appointment
Lower Lake	Lake County	Red Hills AVA

Gregory Graham was the winemaker at Rombauer Vineyards from 1988 to 2000. In 1992, he began producing, under his own label, a Carneros Pinot Noir, then a Knights Valley Viognier and a Napa Valley Viognier and Syrah. In 2000, Graham and his wife Marianne bought a thirteen-acre Zinfandel vineyard in the Red Hills of Lake County, on the southwest shore of Clear Lake where the fog-free warm days and cool nights permit long days of sunshine. Now up to twenty-five acres, all wines are made from their own grapes grown on three estate vineyards: Crimson Hill for Zinfandel and Syrah, Rolling Knolls for Sauvignon Blanc, and Bartolucci for Viognier. Production ranges from 450 to 750 cases per varietal, with a maximum total of 5,000 cases a year.

Past efforts have been high in quality—scoring into the mid-90s at times—and earning Graham exceptionally high and deserved praise for his deeply fruited, white-peach-scented Viogniers. It is not unreasonable to expect Graham's new venture to yield similar results—as have already been realized with his home-grown Viognier.

GUENOC [LANGTRY ESTATE & VINEYARDS] 1963 Map 3		
www.langtryestate.com	707-987-9127	Tasting
Middletown	Lake County	Guenoc Valley AVA

Lillie Langtry, British actress and paramour of Queen Victoria's son, Bertie, bought land in Lake County in 1888 on one of her American sojourns. She had wine made with her likeness on the label, and by 1900 the winery was a success. Tiring of the American West, she sold the property in 1906, and

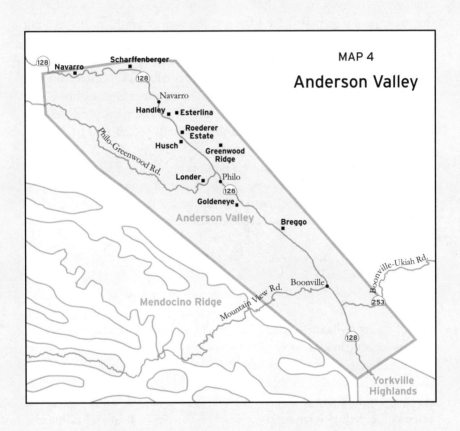

it fell into disuse. The property of twenty-two thousand acres in southern Lake and northern Napa counties was reinvigorated in 1963 as an active producer and winery, named Guenoc after the valley in which the principal vineyard was located. (The winery is now named Langtry Estate & Vineyards, but the Guenoc label remains.) The oldest and largest grower in Lake County, Guenoc was also the first single-producer AVA in the country when the Guenoc Valley designation was made in 1981. Guenoc produces 150,000 cases a year, 40 percent of its moderately priced California line and 60 percent of its Lake County and Langtry Estate lines. Under the tutelage of winemaker Paul Brasset, the winery produces Petite Sirah (30 percent), Cabernet Sauvignon (30 percent), and Sauvignon Blanc (20 percent), with Meritage, Chardonnay, Merlot, and Pinot Grigio comprising the balance. With four hundred acres under cultivation (three hundred in the Guenoc Valley appellation and the remainder on Tephra Ridge overlooking Guenoc Valley), over 70 percent of the total production is from grapes grown on the estate and the remainder purchased from other Lake County producers.

Guenoc has occasionally hit the 90-point range with special bottlings, but more often than not produces wines in the 84- to 86-point range. Top wines have good depth of fruit and balanced, usually slightly fleshy textures, while the lower-rated wines frequently tend to a bit of thinness.

HANDLEY CELLARS 1982		Map 4
www.handleycellars.com	800-733-3151	Tasting
Philo	Mendocino County	Anderson Valley AVA

One of the few woman-owned wineries in California, Handley Cellars has been successful in developing its vineyards in Mendocino and Sonoma counties into consistently strong producers of Pinot Gris, Pinot Noir, Chardonnay, Sauvignon Blanc, and vintage Sparkling Wines. Milla Handley founded the winery in 1982 after having made Chardonnay in her basement as well as learning the ropes at Chateau St. Jean and Edmeades Winery. A total of fifty-nine acres now produce grapes for fifteen thousand cases of still and Sparkling Wines. The Anderson Valley Estate Vineyard, now up to thirty acres, is home to most of the Pinot Noir and Chardonnay production. Another vineyard, the nineteen-acre Handley Dry Creek Valley Vineyard in Sonoma County, is the source of more Chardonnay and Sauvignon Blanc grapes, while the Anderson Valley T-Rex Vineyard is the source of more Pinot Noir and Pinot Gris grapes.

The winery style is one of the more refined in California, and even when very ripe, the wines are also mannerly and well balanced. It is a style, however, that has historically favored the aromatic whites, with Pinot Gris consistently nearing 90 points and both Viognier and Sauvignon Blanc rising higher in good vintages.

HUSCH VINEYARDS 1971		Map 4
www.huschvineyards.com	800-55-HUSCH	Tasting
Philo	Mendocino County	Anderson Valley AVA

In 1971, Tony and Gretchen Husch bought an orchard and started the first vineyard and winery in Anderson Valley. After several notable vintages, the vineyards were bought in 1979 by grape grower Hugo Oswald; the winery is now run by third-generation Oswalds and winemaker Brad Holstine. Today, 25 percent of the total forty-five thousand cases are from grapes grown on their twenty-two-acre Husch Estate vineyard in Anderson Valley and 75 percent from grapes of other Mendocino growers. Chardonnay tops the list at 16,000 cases, Sauvignon Blanc at 10,000 cases, and Pinot at 4,500 cases. Though in wide western-states distribution, there are several limited release wines (in the range of five hundred cases) available only at the winery.

Results have tended to group in the mid-80s range and have created little buzz, but the occasional offering ventures near 90 points, led by a recent Syrah from the La Ribera Vineyard.

LOLONIS WINERY 1982		Map 3
www.lolonis.com	707-485-7544	Tasting by Appointment
Redwood Valley	Mendocino County	Redwood Valley AVA

Family patriarch Tryfon Lolonis emigrated from Greece in 1914 and began planting vineyards in the Redwood Valley in the 1920s. It wasn't until 1982 that the family established a winery, now run by Lolonis descendants Petros, Maureen, and Phillip, and winemaker Lori Knapp. Organically grown grapes are helped along by the use of ladybugs, introduced to keep pests at bay in their northeastern Mendocino County vineyards. Today, 180 acres generate about 70 percent of the grapes used in producing 45,000 cases a year of Chardonnay, Zinfandel, Sauvignon Blanc, Cabernet Sauvignon, and Merlot. Interesting historical notes appear on the Web site.

The Redwood Valley Zinfandels, in both the regular and special bottlings, have been consistently tasty, well focused, ripe yet usually not the least bit overripe, highly rated wines, with scores ranging up to the low 90s. Other wines have been less consistent, but, on the whole, Lolonis makes enjoyable wines at reasonable prices.

LONDER VINEYARDS	1999	Map 4
www.londervineyards.com	707-895-3900	No Tasting
Philo	Mendocino County	Anderson Valley AVA

Larry and Shirlee Londer—New Mexico ophthalmologist and optical shop manager, respectively—had a vision of starting a California winery. Finding the Anderson Valley to their liking, they established the winery in 1999, with first vintages in 2001. Their first fully estate-grown Pinot Noirs were bottled in 2004. The vineyard on the south-facing hills overlooking the Navarro River has fifteen acres planted to Pinot and another acre to Gewürztraminer; 40 percent of total production is from the estate. Five thousand cases are produced, including three thousand of the winery's top-selling Anderson Valley Pinot Noir; the remainder is divided among Chardonnay, Gewürztraminer, and Syrah.

The winery's Paraboll Vineyard Pinot Noir scores in the 90-plus-point range more often than not, and the Chardonnay from the highly regarded Kent Ritchie Vineyard, located in the Sonoma Coast AVA, also comes highly recommended, with scores into the mid-90-point range. The Paraboll Pinot Noir and Londer's other Pinots are ripe yet balanced wines with a tilt toward refinement. The Chardonnay comes with the bright, slightly floral fruit that is the hallmark of its vineyard source.

MCDOWELL VALLEY VINEYARDS	1970	Map 3
www.mcdowellsyrah.com	707-744-1053	Tasting
Hopland	Mendocino County	McDowell Valley AVA

Founded in 1970 by the Crawford family, the winery and its vineyards lie between the Mayacamas Mountains and the Russian River in the McDowell Valley of southeast Mendocino County. The family received one of the first appellation designations in the state in 1982. Here are lands that had originally been planted to Syrah and Grenache grapes as much as a century ago. Those remain the principal grapes grown on the current 330 acres of vineyards, though the winery does also grow Zinfandel, Chardonnay, and Petite Sirah, and sells nearly 80 percent of its grapes to other producers. Today, most of the winery's production is Rhône varietals, principally

Syrah (the flagship McDowell varietal), Grenache, and Viognier, with the remainder Petite Sirah, Sauvignon Blanc, Chardonnay, Zinfandel, French Colombard, and Port. Eight thousand cases are produced a year, of which Syrah represents fully 60 percent.

Quality levels have varied widely over the years, with highs reaching into the upper-80-point range and the rare but occasional 90-point effort. Most wines are medium-full to full in body and are styled for nearer-term drinking.

MEYER FAMILY CELLARS 1999		Map 3
www.meyerfamilycellars.com	707-895-2341	Tasting
Yorkville	Mendocino County	Yorkville Highlands AVA

The late Justin Meyer was a teaching brother at Christian Brothers in the Napa Valley. In the 1970s, he left the order to pursue winemaking and, with Ray Duncan, established the renowned Silver Oak Cellars in Napa in 1975. In 2000, Justin and his wife, Bonny, sold their share of Silver Oak and moved north to Mendocino County, where they produced their first bottling of Meyer Family Cellars Port in 2002, just before Justin's death. The next generation, including winemakers Matt and Karen Meyer, along with matriarch Bonny, now makes their renowned Port and two Syrahs (vintage and nonvintage versions of the latter) from grapes mostly purchased from other Mendocino growers. Starting with the 2006 vintage, the Syrahs will come exclusively from Yorkville Highlands. Total production is up to five thousand cases, with Port representing 60 percent and Syrah the remainder.

There is some promise here, but it is too early to know if it will be realized. Expect Meyer wines to be full in body and to reflect the balance and richness achieved in the wines of the teacher.

NAVARRO VINEYARDS 1974		Map 4
www.navarrowine.com	800-537-WINE	Tasting
Philo	Mendocino County	Anderson Valley AVA

This winery, in the heart of the Anderson Valley on the Navarro River, was one of the first cool-climate Mendocino wineries and today produces forty-five thousand cases of wine as well as nonalcoholic grape juice and olive oil. Founded over three decades ago by Ted Bennett and Deborah Cahn, with the help of winemaker Jim Klein, their wines include Pinot Noir and Gewürztraminer (representing 30 percent of production),

Chardonnay, Sauvignon Blanc, and White Riesling. Production is from their ninety acres of vineyard and an additional 30 percent bought from other Mendocino growers.

Wines are largely unavailable except at the winery and through its wine club, but Navarro is a must stop for anyone visiting the Anderson Valley. Its Gewürztraminer is often the highest rated in California (frequently up to 92 points) and is known for capturing the spicy essence of the grape. Pinot Noir is medium/full-bodied and bright in style.

ROEDERER ESTATE 1981		Map 4
www.roedererestate.com	707-895-2288	Tasting
Philo	Mendocino County	Anderson Valley AVA

Jean-Claude Rouzaud, the fifth-generation head of the House of Louis Roederer, journeyed to California to establish an American relative of the legendary two-hundred-year-old French Champagne. In 1981, with 580 acres planted to Pinot Noir and Chardonnay grapes, Roederer Estate began making California Sparkling Wines. Its nonvintage Brut and Rosé, and the vintage-dated L'Ermitage Brut and Rosé Tetes de Cuvée, are all produced exclusively on the estate, now managed by sixth-generation Frederic Rouzaud. Sixty-five thousand cases are produced annually, of which nearly 90 percent is the Brut NV. The French parent of Roederer Estate also now owns Scharffenberger Cellars, another Mendocino Sparkling Wine producer, discussed elsewhere. The Web site is elegant.

L'Ermitage Brut, one of the most complex Sparkling Wines made in California, has earned up to 95 points and ranks among the very best in California, while the regular bottling Brut and Rosé have both ranked in the upper-80-point range, with occasional forays into the low 90s. All Roederer bubblies reflect the high-acid, brisk style of the House.

SCHARFFENBERGER CELLARS 1981		Map 4
www.scharffenbergercellars.com	707-895-2957	Tasting
Philo	Mendocino County	Anderson Valley AVA

UC–Berkeley graduate John Scharffenberger ventured into the Anderson Valley in the early 1980s and, because of the particularly conducive, relatively cool climate, began making Sparkling Wine using classic Champagne methods. In 1995, despite a positive reception to his wines, Scharffenberger sold his vineyards and winery to the French house of Louis Roederer, which had earlier established its own Roederer Estate beachhead nearby in the Anderson Valley. Roederer changed the name to Pacific Echo, but in 2004 the name reverted to Scharffenberger Cellars. (After selling the winery, John Scharffenberger went on to partner with longtime friend Robert Steinberg in an artisanal chocolate venture in Berkeley called Scharffen Berger, a pioneer of the current quality chocolate craze.) Scharffenberger Cellars now produces about twenty-five thousand cases of the modestly priced Brut NV from its 120 acres in Anderson Valley and from a very small infusion of grapes from other Mendocino County growers.

Despite the winery's great potential, quality has been spotty, with the occasional 90-point wine offset by the majority of bottlings earning in the mid- to upper 80s.

STEELE WINES 1991		Map 3
www.steelewines.com	707-279-9475	Tasting
Kelseyville	Lake County	Clear Lake AVA

Notable winemaker Jed Steele, fresh from years at Edmeades and as the original winemaker for Kendall-Jackson, needed to apply his skills to his own label. He set up shop in 1981 in a leased winery in Lake County, then in 1996 bought the former Konocti Winery near Kelseyville. Steele uses only the grapes of other producers (including buying 25 to 30 percent of Steele's needs from Jed's personal vineyards), from Lake and Mendocino counties, to Carneros in Sonoma County, to as far south as Santa Barbara County. Steele offers Chardonnay, Pinot Noir, Zinfandel, and Pinot Blanc as the top sellers from its annual production of seventy-five thousand cases, of which over two-thirds are Chardonnay and Pinot Noirs. A lower-priced label, Shooting Star, also offers a modest range of wines. And watch for the Writer's Block label being developed by Jed's son.

Zinfandel and Pinot Noir, especially Pinot from Bien Nacido Vineyard, have been the quality leaders. Steele wines are typically full-bodied and expressive with plenty of ripeness on their ledger sheets.

YORKVILLE CELLARS 1994		Map 3
www.yorkville-cellars.com	707-894-9177	Tasting
Yorkville	Mendocino County	Yorkville Highlands AVA

On thirty acres at the southernmost end of Mendocino County, in the newly designated Yorkville Highlands appellation, the Wallo family produced their first vintage in 1994. Two vineyards, Randle Hill and Rennie, total thirty acres and produce the seven main Bordeaux grapes (Sauvignon Blanc, Semillon, Cabernet Franc, Merlot, Petit Verdot, Malbec, and Cabernet Sauvignon) and bottle each variety every vintage; this may not be done elsewhere in California. Using organic growing methods, Yorkville produces a maximum of one thousand cases for each of seven principal wine types. The Web site includes an interesting history of the appellation.

Results have been mixed to date, with the occasional Cabernet reaching into the upper 80s.

Sonoma County

JUSTIFIABLY FAMOUS FOR CHARDONNAY
AND PINOT NOIR

"Number two and trying harder" might be the slogan of the grape-growing, winemaking community in Sonoma County. For years, indeed for almost all of the time that California has been in the wine business, Sonoma County has found itself eclipsed by someone else. Yes, one can point to the early days of Count Agoston Haraszthy's 1850 plantings and suggest that Sonoma had more and better grapes and a bigger place in the California wine hierarchy a century and a half ago. It was not long, however, before Napa County took the lead in wine quality, and by the time we get to the modern era in California wine industry, it is Napa that has the most important wineries, the most expensive grapes, and the most widely recognized name.

Today, Sonoma County still ranks as number two, but it is catching up. And, it is catching up in a way that does not need to compete with Napa directly. Sonoma has a different set of growing conditions, most of which invite attention to grapes like Pinot Noir and Chardonnay in its many coastal-influenced locations, and some of which are sheltered from the coast and become havens for bolder reds like Zinfandel and Syrah. In those locations, Sonoma is capable of achieving levels of excellence on its own and with grapes in which Napa does not specialize. It can be argued that the Russian River

Valley growing area is now equal to or preferred to the Napa Valley for the grapes that it grows best; and for fans of those grapes, rather than of Cabernet Sauvignon or Merlot, it is now Sonoma that reigns as the preferred territory.

It is also true that Sonoma trails but is catching up with Napa as a touring destination. Its acreage is higher; its variety of climates and locales is both broader and more spread out than Napa's; and while crowds in places like Sonoma town and in Healdsburg can be daunting, those places have a more casual, comfortable feel for many people than the formality and upscale seriousness of Napa's wine centers. With wineries ranging from south of Sonoma to west and north of Sebastopol to Healdsburg and Cloverdale in the north end of the county, Sonoma offers visitors greater distances between wineries and fewer people at some of its best-known and attractive spots.

The key to understanding Sonoma County lies in its relationship to water. At its westernmost boundary, it touches the Pacific Ocean. There are vineyards in that area, and except for those sheltered behind hills and in secluded pockets, the western extremes are cold, foggy, and inhospitable to grapes. Yet, somehow, when folks find even little bits of warmth, they plant Pinot Noir first and Chardonnay next, and somehow they succeed. Most of the coast, from San Francisco north to Mendocino, finds steep hillsides running down to the water's edge. However, there is a valley carved over the centuries by the Russian River that allows cooling ocean influences to stream eastward. It is in this area, from the coast to Santa Rosa, that some of the best Pinot Noir in the world is grown. And it is this Pinot Noir, together with a small section of river-related land to the north, that has brought Sonoma County its greatest vinous fame and fortune. One also finds very cool growing conditions in the area closest to San Francisco Bay in the Sonoma County portion of the two-county AVA known as Carneros.

This newfound renown belies the county's earlier role as a maker of hearty red wines from the warmer lands north of Santa Rosa in the Alexander and Knights valleys and from the warmer hillsides of the Sonoma Valley, which runs parallel to the Napa Valley but is smaller and less intensely farmed. Whereas Napa has become Cabernet territory, Sonoma retains much of its standing as a provider of Zinfandel, Petite Sirah, and other full-bodied reds. Little more than four decades ago, just before the start of the modern wine boom, Sonoma County was noted for substantial quantities of jug reds grown in fields whose vineyards were an old-fashioned mix of varieties. Even today, the Zinfandels of Sonoma County are much more likely to be made from very old vines with significant proportions of lesser-known red grapes. And a look back at the acreage of the mid-1960s finds Sonoma's 10,700 acres

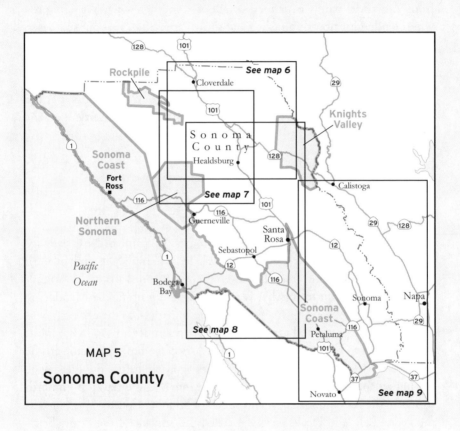

Rockpile

128

101

Cloverdale

See map 6

29

Sonoma Coast

1

Knights Valley

101

Sonoma County

Fort Ross

128

Healdsburg

Calistoga

116

See map 7

Northern Sonoma

101

29

128

116

Guerneville

Pacific Ocean

116

Santa Rosa

12

1

Sebastopol

Sonoma Coast

Bodega Bay

12

116

Sonoma

Napa

116

See map 8

Petaluma

29

1

101

MAP 5

Sonoma County

37

37

Novato

See map 9

of grapes containing 4,000 acres of Zinfandel, 1,700 acres of Carignane, 1,500 acres of Petite Sirah, and 500 acres of Alicante Bouschet. By contrast, Cabernet Sauvignon and Pinot Noir covered less than 100 acres each, and Chardonnay and Merlot were so limited as to be not counted.

The story is different today, of course. Modern winemaking has taken over and together with the expansion of plantings in the cooler areas has resulted in a massive change in direction and in the fortunes of the county. The most recent acreage survey shows 57,100 acres of grapes yet finds Zinfandel barely expanded to about 5,200 acres; while the jug red wine blenders are now diminished and show Petite Sirah at about 500 acres, Carignane down to 200 acres, and Alicante Bouschet all but gone. Today, Chardonnay with 15,100 acres, Cabernet Sauvignon with 10,900 acres, Pinot Noir with 11,000 acres, and Merlot with 6,300 acres are the dominant varieties. The county's 2,400 acres of Sauvignon Blanc puts it at the top of that variety within California, along with Napa County. And the old "Bring your jug and fill it up out of the tap" jug wine producers are nowhere to be seen.

See Sonoma County Wineries Association: www.sonomawine.com.

Alexander Valley

Cyrus Alexander arrived in the valley later to bear his name in the early 1840s and was given a parcel of land on the eastside of the valley in exchange for managing the larger land grant that covered a massive open area and surrounding hillsides that run from what is now Healdsburg up to the Mendocino County border. Among his many mercantile activities was the establishment of a vineyard, reported to have grown to 230 acres under his supervision. But it turned out to be prunes, not grapes, that became the major crop in the Alexander Valley, and as little as fifty years ago, just before the great wine boom that changed the California landscape into a vinous haven from north to south, the Alexander Valley, and much of Sonoma County, was noted as the Prune Belt, and Healdsburg was called the "Buckle of the Prune Belt." With few exceptions, the grapes of the area found their way into jug wines rather than into cork-finished bottlings. Yet, the heritage of old vines, mostly in field blends oriented toward Zinfandel, has allowed that grape to be a producer of outstanding wines both by local wineries and by makers as far away as Ridge with its famous Geyserville bottling.

The Russian River, whose westward opening to the sea allows cold marine air to flow into parts of the county to the south of the Alexander Valley, winds its way up into this valley after making a sharp turn near above Santa Rosa. And while this waterway is influential, the climate in the Alexander Valley is considerably warmer than the coastal-oriented portions of the county. One finds varieties like Cabernet Sauvignon, Merlot, Zinfandel, and Sauvignon Blanc taking over from the Chardonnay and Pinot Noir that rule in the cooler regions of the county. The whites tend to be clustered in the cooler southern end of the valley, especially in proximity to the river, while the reds are planted more extensively in the hills and in the warmer, northern end of the valley. The greater portion of the vines in the valley are planted on the deep soils in the flatlands, but there are welcoming sites off the valley floor, and it is from these more challenging locations that many of the valley's best-performing wines are grown.

Located in the northeastern corner of Sonoma County, the Alexander Valley covers some seventy-five thousand acres of land in the northeastern corner of Sonoma County and accounts for about 7 percent of the county total land mass. Its fifteen thousand acres of grapes, however, represent about 25 percent of the planted acreage in the county. Its forty wineries are also a substantial portion of the county's total, but there are fewer small, family wineries here than farther south and also fewer of world-class repute. Yet with producers like Alexander Valley Vineyards, Clos du Bois, the Francis Ford Coppola Winery (in the lovely hillside facility that was previously known as Souverain of Alexander Valley), Jordan, Sausal, Seghesio, and Simi, the Alexander Valley offers lots of well-known names and plenty of very good wine.

See Alexander Valley Winegrowers: www.alexandervalley.org.

Bennett Valley

Grape growing in the Bennett Valley, despite its century and a half of history, remains in a wonderful state of bucolic limbo. One has to search for the vines and search even harder for the wineries in this small, isolated valley southeast of Santa Rosa and west of the much larger and more organized, tourist-oriented Sonoma Valley. No main roads here—it is all meandering pathways that were carved out ages ago and remain in a state of suspended animation. A quick perusal of the growers here lists less than twenty and all with minimal plantings. The one exception to that general rule does not show up in the growers' association, but the main winery in the area is Matanzas Creek, now belonging to Kendall-Jackson, and the largest land holding is K-J's Taylor Peak property that grows grapes for several of that combine's best labels.

Carneros (Los Carneros)

This two-county AVA (see also Napa County AVAs) sits immediately north of San Francisco Bay and is cooled by it. With the exception of a few isolated hillsides and a few hardy vines with reds like Cabernet Sauvignon and Syrah, this is a place for cold-loving varieties like Chardonnay and Pinot Noir. This appellation overlaps both the Sonoma Valley AVA and the Sonoma Coast AVA, but most wineries in the area choose to put the Carneros designation on their labels. Of the almost four dozen wineries in Carneros, most reside on the Napa side, but significant labels like Buena Vista, Cline, Gloria Ferrer, and the Donum/Robert Stemmler combine are based on the Sonoma side. The larger portion of the AVA's ten thousand acres of grapes also resides in Napa.

From a touring point of view, the Sonoma side of Carneros offers a variety of interesting sites, from a NASCAR raceway to old-fashioned fruit and beef jerky stands to attractive new wineries. Its proximity to Sonoma town just a few miles to the north also makes the Sonoma side of Carneros a most interesting day trip.

See Carneros Wine Alliance: www.carneros.com;
Hospitality de Los Carneros: www.carneroswineries.org.

Chalk Hill

One can make a strong argument for Chalk Hill as its own AVA. Lying in the uplands east of Windsor and bordered by the bulk of the Russian River Valley AVA to the west, the Knights Valley to the east, and the Alexander Valley to the north, it has higher altitudes than the neighboring flatlands, has a different soil structure, and tends to grow more powerful whites and sturdier reds than immediately adjoining turf in those areas. But Chalk Hill wines seem, for the most part, to be known by other names, and the extension of the Russian River name into this distinct district dilutes the value of both names. The Chalk Hill winery and the Rodney Strong winery are the most visible users of the Chalk Hill designation on their labels.

Dry Creek Valley

Situated directly west of Healdsburg, this sixteen-mile-long valley is in reality a cigar-shaped box canyon opening to the east closed off by the high, rugged hills at the west. Two miles wide at best, it consists of valley floor, sloping hillside, and challenging uplands, especially at its western end beyond Lake Sonoma where it ends in territory it shares with the rustic Rockpile AVA. It is a warm but not hot area, and its late-night cooling helps keep acidities up while not cooling the area down so early that ripening is hindered.

Zinfandel is its best-known product, but Cabernet Sauvignon has become the number one grape here as it has in almost every location that will grow it adequately. Merlot and Chardonnay follow next, and the combination of those four varieties accounts for over two-thirds of the nine thousand or so acres currently under vine. Five dozen wineries and counting call the Dry Creek Valley home, and almost all of them make Zinfandel. There is plenty of Cabernet Sauvignon as well, but it shows up under fewer labels, in part because many Zinfandels are now vineyard designated in view of the great success that Zin has shown in this valley for the last three decades and more.

It would be unfair to say that Dry Creek is a sleepy place, yet even in the middle of summer, one can drive up and down its one main road, appropriately called Dry Creek Road, and not be in traffic jams. Wineries line the road on both sides and offer excellent visiting opportunities, but there is not much else here, and so the visiting hordes eventually head for Healdsburg with its attractive plaza, restaurants, hotels, and watering holes. And quietly hidden down a long driveway is the Sonoma County home of Gallo, where brands ranging from those labeled as Gallo to Rancho Zabaco, Frei Brothers, and a roster of others take shape in a new, modern facility so large that it has several dozen crushers sitting in wait for arriving grapes.

See Wine Growers of Dry Creek Valley: www.wdcv.com.

Green Valley of Russian River Valley

No one would blame the grapes of this multinamed AVA if they were a bit confused about what they really were. When the AVA—about eight miles from top to bottom and five from side to side, located west of the towns of Forestville, Graton, and Sebastopol, and essentially coterminous with the cool, southwestern corner of the Russian River Valley AVA—was first established, its formal name was Green Valley–Sonoma County, to distinguish it from the Green Valley of Solano County. The AVA soon became overlapped with the Sonoma Coast AVA, the Northern Sonoma AVA, and then the Russian River Valley AVA. And all too often the grapes from this Green Valley are labeled with one of those overlapping names, most likely Russian River Valley, because this is an AVA that simply has not taken hold in the marketplace. It is a shame, really, because its wines all share a bent to higher natural acidities and leaner, racier personality than the rest of the Russian River Valley or any of the other overlapping AVAs. True enough, a few grapes in the Sonoma Coast AVA are, indeed, out by the Pacific Ocean and grow in even cooler, foggier conditions, but the beauty of this AVA's conception is that its growing conditions actually are relatively similar in character from one end of the AVA to the other.

Its marine-influenced lands are most hospitable to cold-loving varieties, of which Chardonnay and Pinot Noir are the overwhelming favorites. And, while other varieties like Gewürztraminer and Riesling can grow here, and even Zinfandel can flourish in certain warm pockets and produce bright, berryish wines with zesty acidities, this is a place where those first two varieties produce wines that some might deign to compare directly to what they offer in their native France. Windy and cool, this was once apple and berry country, and it was not until the wine boom had fully taken hold and wineries realized that they needed cool locations like Green Valley for their Chardonnays, and especially for Pinot Noir, that the area gained prominence.

Knights Valley

Just over the hills from Calistoga and with a climate and soils not unlike its Napa Valley neighbor to the south, the Knights Valley at times seems more like Napa than it does the rest of Sonoma. Its location in the very southeast corner of Sonoma County, away from marine influences and thus warmer than most of the nearby AVAs in Sonoma, has made the Knights Valley a prominent home for red grapes, especially the Bordelais varieties dominated by Cabernet Sauvignon. Indeed, the largest vineyard holding here belongs to Beringer and produces a Cabernet Sauvignon that has as much or more Napa character as it does the stronger berry-like focus found in Cabernets elsewhere in Sonoma. Hillside vineyards in the Knights Valley, on the north side of Mount St. Helena, and belonging to Peter Michael and Kendall-Jackson (Trace Ridge), produce deep, concentrated red wines that compete with the best in California; the highly regarded Napa Valley winery Delectus is developing a vineyard site and aging caves there. The lush and rich Sauvignon Blancs of the Knights Valley are reflective of their hospitable location.

Once a place with a small but thriving township, today this box canyon of a valley is rural and totally unurbanized. Even its post office is in another county. Its two thousand acres of grapes are, however, domesticated and upscale.

Northern Sonoma

It has been said that this AVA does nothing more than provide a legalized frame for the Gallo family's extensive three-thousand-acre holdings that spread throughout most of Sonoma County. The AVA covers all of the county save for its southern extremes in the Sonoma Valley and Carneros, and its existence is noted on the label of only two wines, both of them Gallo's very upscale and artistically successful "Estate" bottlings of Cabernet Sauvignon and Chardonnay. Indeed, the raison d'être of the AVA seems to lie in the requirement that wines labeled Estate Bottled must come from one AVA only regardless of the gerrymandered boundaries of that AVA. Despite the obviously commercial nature of its formation, it is instructive to look back at the Napa Valley AVA and realize that its boundaries are also greatly concerned with and determined by commercial considerations.

Petaluma Gap

There is an area of relatively flat land in the midst of the coastal range starting at the Pacific Ocean and running roughly southeast past Petaluma town toward the San Francisco Bay in the western end of the Carneros District. Through this "gap," cool marine breezes and chilling fogs roll in to some extent virtually every day. Grapes are planted along the "gap," and it overlaps several AVAs, including Green Valley, Sonoma Coast, and Carneros. The marine influence it brings in greatly affects the southern portion of the Russian River Valley as well as areas near and south of Santa Rosa all the way to the western base of Sonoma Mountain. Indeed, heaviest fogs can reach all the way into the Sacramento River Valley.

The Petaluma Gap is also at the center of a brewing controversy regarding the extension of the Russian River Valley AVA southward all the way past Petaluma. The prime movers in favor of this expansion of the already-bloated Russian River AVA are the Gallo interests, whose substantial Pinot Noir holdings in the gap are now not able to take advantage of the cachet that attaches to the Russian River name. Those on the other side of the debate are the folks who enjoy the use of the Russian River name and argue that the area south of Petaluma should become its own AVA.

Regardless of how this debate comes out, it is clear that the growing conditions in the larger swath of land that is now called Petaluma Gap by the folks working there has some of the coldest growing conditions in Sonoma, and it would not be surprising to see some sort of Petaluma Gap AVA carved out along lines measured by growing conditions. At least, that is the hope.

Rockpile

The drive out Dry Creek Road from Healdsburg is one of the more enjoyable and relaxing in wine country. Just when you think you have run out of real estate as the roadway runs smack into the looming Lake Sonoma dam and the lovely parklands at its base, you realize that, in fact, there is more to come. Past the dam and up the hill to the south of the lake, the Dry Creek Valley AVA continues and overlaps the beginning of the Rockpile AVA. It is rustic, rugged territory with vineyards carved out of swales and the occasionally accommodating slope as the roadway wends its way west for another ten miles.

This is hearty red wine country, with Zinfandel predominating and Petite Sirah, Syrah, and the infrequent Cabernet Sauvignon joining in. The Rockpile AVA is relatively close to the Pacific Ocean but sits at a height (most vineyards are at an elevation of one thousand feet and higher) that keeps it from being foggy and also enjoys the moderating effects of Lake Sonoma. It can be hot during the day but still averages some ten to fifteen degrees lower than the adjoining Dry Creek Valley despite having more hours of sunshine. Very successful wines have already been made from this relatively new AVA, and the names of its supporters—including such stalwarts as Carol Shelton, JC Cellars, Rosenblum, and Seghesio—seem unlikely ever to be overrun by grapes, but for lovers of lusty, full-bodied reds, it is an AVA to remember.

Russian River Valley

If there is a vinous place in California that can challenge the Napa Valley for primary attention, the Russian River Valley must surely be it. Not only do wine lovers worship its products, but its focus on Pinot Noir and Chardonnay clearly marks it as its own special place. But unlike Napa, the Russian River Valley has not enjoyed a long and heroic standing in the California wine pantheon. Until the winegrowing world began to seek out colder-climate locations for Pinot Noir and Chardonnay (and remember, please, that Chardonnay was not even on the vinous radar screen just half a century ago), almost all of Sonoma County, including the Russian River Valley, was dedicated more to heavy reds than to lighter, brighter wines.

Indeed, whereas the name Napa Valley has been seen on wine labels for more than a century, it was not really until the wine boom of the 1970s that varietally labeled wines from this area began to take hold. Perhaps no better illustration of the Russian River Valley's rapid change of fortune exists than this quotation from one of our earlier works (circa 1979): "There are about a dozen wineries in the area, including the well-known Korbel and Sonoma Vineyards (now Rodney Strong in the current era). Most, however, are small and new."

Today, there are well over one hundred wineries within the AVA, and in all fairness, a great many are small and new. And most, not all, make Pinot Noir, which despite the greater number of Chardonnay acres planted, has become the upscale flagship wine for winery after winery after winery. And it is all because of wine quality. The cool climate, the dominant Goldridge soils in the western end of the Russian River Valley AVA, and the alluvial deposits that dominate in the northern end of the AVA as it follows the northward bend of river near Santa Rosa form a supportive partnership for those grapes and for Sauvignon Blanc in the wetter, deeper soils. In the eastern hills, which are warmer to begin with and specialize more in reds than do the cooler areas, the soils have more volcanic content. The portion of the AVA that overlaps with and contains all of the Chalk Hill AVA has a higher chalk content.

In the days before we had defined AVAs, the name Russian River Valley appeared on wines that were grown within shouting distance of the river itself. And because the coolest locations of what was to become the AVA had not been extensively planted, one finds as many Zinfandels of the 1970s labeled with the Russian River Valley name as there were Pinot Noirs and Chardonnays. When the AVA was established, it more or less adhered to past practice, but with the addition of lands on the plain west of Santa Rosa, mostly because they shared the same foggy growing conditions and soils and were growing the same varieties. In 2005, the area's boundaries were amended to include lands farther to the south, and the name of the Green Valley AVA was amended to specify its location within the Russian River Valley AVA. Whether the boundaries will extend farther south again below Sebastopol to take in the very cool growing locations near Petaluma is the subject of hot debate even as this commentary is being penned.

The Russian River Valley AVA is fairly large at this point, and its fifteen thousand acres of wine grapes not only represent some 25 percent of all the acreage standing in Sonoma County, consisting of some 6,000 acres of Chardonnay (about 40 percent of the county total) and 4,500 acres of Pinot Noir (about 45 percent of the county total), but contain more grapes than most counties in California.

See Russian River Valley Winegrowers: www.rrvw.org;
Russian River Wine Road: www.wineroad.com.

Sonoma Coast

Stretching from the Mendocino County border southward along the Sonoma County coast and then well inland to San Francisco Bay, this catchall AVA is simply too big to have any specific meaning except possibly that its grapes grow in mostly cool regions. It crosses several other AVAs, including Russian River Valley, Sonoma Valley, Green Valley of Russian River Valley, Chalk Hill, Northern Sonoma, and Carneros, and it takes in the Petaluma Gap area as well. In its best and purest use, the term is applied to wines grown west of the Russian River AVA and very near the Pacific Ocean. Several subappellations of Sonoma Coast are likely to appear in time, including Fort Ross, Seaside, and Freestone. In particular, the Freestone area, surrounding and north of the quaint village of Freestone, is alive with new vineyard activity on behalf of such well-known producers as Kistler, Torres Estate, and Joseph Phelps's new winery called Freestone.

Sonoma Mountain

The territory southeast of Santa Rosa as it stretches through both Bennett Valley and Sonoma Valley is largely defined by Sonoma Mountain, which straddles the north and east of Bennett Valley and forms the western rim of Sonoma Valley. This volcanic peak may not have erupted for the last two million years, but it has left its mark all over its slopes and indeed in the composition of the soils that surround it, especially those in the northern end of the Sonoma Valley AVA.

If one asks Patrick Campbell of Laurel Glen, this is Cabernet Sauvignon country, and he makes wine to prove it. Yet, on the same mountain is also found the Chardonnay vineyard of Richard Dinner, whose grapes make some of the highest-rated bottlings of its variety in California. Still, there are only a couple of dozen growers on the mountain and just three wineries, the biggest of which is Benziger, located in the sloping southern end of the mountain near the town of Glen Ellen. The Sonoma Mountain AVA is located entirely within the boundaries of the Sonoma Valley AVA.

Sonoma Valley

Tucked in between Sonoma Mountain and its foothills to the south on its western flank with the taller, somewhat more rugged Mayacamas Range on its eastern side, the Sonoma Valley more or less parallels the Napa Valley in its north-south orientation but is less rich in soils, more undulating in terrain, and less intensively farmed. It is, of course, almost all wine country of one sort or another from its Sonoma town terminus in the south to Santa

Rosa to the northwest. On its southern end, it abuts the Sonoma County portion of Carneros, and that part of the Sonoma Valley is more oriented to cool varieties than the up-valley portions where reds seem to do better. Still, with its twists and turns and varying elevations, the Sonoma Valley is less focused on its plantings than many other locations in the county.

The Sonoma Valley has a rich history that goes back beyond the arrival of Count Agoston Haraszthy, whose imported plantings made the valley into the early leader for wine quality and reputation. It was not long, however, that Napa grabbed top honors, and the Sonoma Valley has had to settle for second place. It may be there still, but its roster of important producers ranges from Benziger and Buena Vista to Chateau St. Jean, Kenwood, Kunde, and St. Francis. Recent estimates of planting in the Sonoma Valley AVA reach to about eight thousand acres.

See Sonoma Valley Vintners and Growers Alliance: www.sonomavalleywine.com.

A. RAFANELLI WINERY 1974		Map 7
www.arafanelliwinery.com	707-433-1385	Tasting by Appointment
Healdsburg	Sonoma County	Dry Creek Valley AVA

Now in their fourth generation, the Rafanellis had been growers and vineyard managers for many years before making their first wines in 1974. Since then, Zinfandel has been the focus, both of the fifty-acre vineyard and of the wine production, as over three-quarters of the six thousand to eight thousand cases made are well-received estate Zinfandels, with the remainder Cabernet Sauvignon. The Rafanellis were early proponents of establishing the Dry Creek Valley appellation. Wine is sold only at the winery and to mailing lists, and the winery location at the eastern end of the Dry Creek Valley near Healdsburg town makes it an easy stop for visitors to the area. The Web site is extremely sparse.

Rafanelli Zinfandels have often rated in the 90-point range although the move to winery-only sales has limited the number of recent reviews. The house style is fruit-forward with good structure and reasonable alcohol levels given the tendency of some makers to favor ripeness over fruitiness.

ACORN WINERY 1994		Map 8
www.acornwinery.com	707-433-6440	Tasting by Appointment
Healdsburg	Sonoma County	Russian River Valley AVA

Former lawyer Bill Nachbaur and his wife Betsy, a former banker, bought the Alegria Vineyard in 1990, land that had first been planted to vines in the 1850s. As with the grapes, Bill's Sonoma County roots extend back to the 1800s. The Nachbaurs expanded the vineyard to twenty-seven acres of Zinfandel, Sangiovese, Syrah, Cabernet Franc, and Dolcetto grapes and established a winery in 1994. Acorn is prone to field blends: grapes are interplanted, harvested, and fermented together, giving the dominant grape some company in the finished product. The first wine released was a Sangiovese, in '96. Since then, fewer than three thousand cases have been produced annually, with one-third Zinfandel and another third Sangiovese. Small lots of Syrah and Rosato (Rosé) fill out the roster.

The reds, identified with the Alegria Vineyard designation, tend toward high ripeness and can lose fruitiness in the process; but when they have succeeded, they score in the upper 80-point range.

ADLER FELS WINERY 1979		Map 8
www.adlerfels.com	707-539-3123	No Tasting
Santa Rosa	Sonoma County	Sonoma Valley AVA

Graphic artist and wine label maker David Coleman founded the winery in 1979 on the steep western slopes of the Mayacamas Mountains. Over time, the vineyard grew to sixty acres, and the winemaking was divided into the estate-grown and bottled wines and the much larger negotiant operation. The former is a small winery making only two varieties, a Gewürztraminer and a Sauvignon Blanc, each made in thousand-case lots. The latter, with a large new winemaking facility in Santa Rosa, churns out second labels Big Ass, Leaping Lizard, and Coyote Creek, all at modest price points. This bulk operation produces over 350,000 cases a year.

Once known for its expressive Gewürztraminers, the winery has drifted off the charts of late with its relatively inexpensive estate-grown varieties but continues to pump out lots of wine through its "buy it and bottle it" operation. Point scores for the estate wines are not encouraging.

ADRIAN FOG 1998	Map 8	
www.adrianfog.com	707-431-1174	Tasting by Appointment
Sebastopol	Sonoma County	Green Valley of R.R. Valley AVA

Jane Farrell and Stewart Dorman have built a micro-winery exclusively for single-vineyard Pinot Noir. Production runs from 50 to 350 cases per wine;

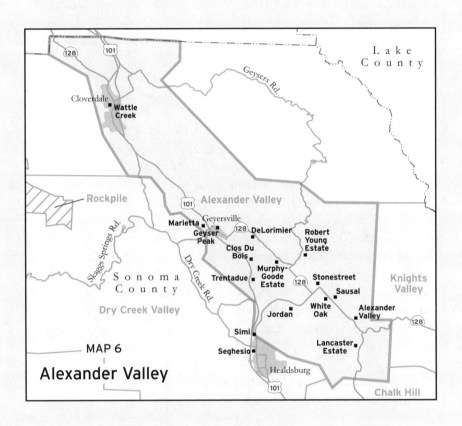

Lake County

Geysers Rd.

Cloverdale
Wattle Creek

128 101

Rockpile

101 Alexander Valley

Skaggs Springs Rd.

Marietta Geyersville
Geyser Peak 128 DeLorimier

Robert Young Estate

Clos Du Bois

Dry Creek Rd.

Sonoma County

Trentadue Murphy-Goode Estate 128 Stonestreet

Sausal

Dry Creek Valley

White Oak

Knights Valley

Jordan Alexander Valley 128

Simi

Seghesio

Lancaster Estate

Healdsburg

Chalk Hill

MAP 6

Alexander Valley

101

in the most recent vintage fewer than 700 cases were made in total. Vineyards sourced include the Savoy Vineyard in Mendocino's Anderson Valley and Two Sisters Vineyard in the Russian River Valley. With quality grapes and hands-on winemaking, Adrian Fog hits high scores in the 90-point and higher range more often than not, but the occasional klinker also appears. Wine style is ripe and high-acid, reflective of the cool sites from which the grapes are drawn.

ALDERBROOK VINEYARD & WINERY 1982		Map 7
www.alderbrook.com	800-405-5987	Tasting
Healdsburg	Sonoma County	Dry Creek Valley AVA

Partners John Crace, Phil Staley, and Mark Rafanelli (cousin to the winemaking Rafanellis) purchased a ranch and prune orchard in the southernmost part of Dry Creek Valley and turned it into a winery and vineyard. Initially, Alderbrook made primarily white varietals but, in the 1990s, converted gradually to reds, specializing in Zinfandel with half a dozen or more separate bottlings, including one blended with Syrah. Pinot Noir and Carignane also appear, but whites have disappeared from the line. The estate has expanded to sixty-five acres of vines, and the winery is now owned by the Terlato Wine Group, with Doug Fletcher the chief winemaker for the group and Bryan Parker the local winemaker. Thirty thousand cases are made annually.

The winery's location at the mouth of the Dry Creek Valley makes it one of the most accessible visitor locations in the area, and while its wines are sometimes hard to find, its location in the heart of Zin country makes them interesting. Zinfandel in a ripe, occasionally high-alcohol style is the most prominent offering.

ALEXANDER VALLEY VINEYARDS 1975		Map 6
www.avvwine.com	800-888-7209	Tasting
Healdsburg	Sonoma County	Alexander Valley AVA

In the early 1960s, Harry and Maggie Wetzel bought land near Healdsburg from heirs of Cyrus Alexander, after whom the region was named. Their son, Hank, produced the first wine in '75 and runs the winery to this day. The 130-acre estate produces some 14 grape varietals, and in most years the winery makes 17 varieties of wine, 75 percent of which is red. Their Zinfandels, with names such as Redemption Zin and the widely known

Sin Zin, are made in large quantities comprising over half of the hundred-thousand total case production. But there are many others completing the list, including Cabernet Sauvignon, Pinot Noir, Syrah, and Chardonnay, plus several proprietary blends including the Cyrus Bordeaux blend.

Wine quality has been somewhat inconsistent, but Cyrus has often scored well for its full and supple style backed by a solid spine of tannin, and the Sin Zin often rates among the reasonable values in Zinfandel.

ALYSIAN WINES 2007		Map 8
www.alysianwines.com	707-431-4410	No Tasting
Forestville	Sonoma County	Russian River Valley AVA

Noted Pinot Noir winemaker Gary Farrell has created a new label focused on small-batch Pinot Noir from the very best vineyards in the Russian River Valley. Farrell's experiences at Davis Bynum, Rochioli, and others in his formative years prepared him for this new venture, which should produce 3,500 cases, largely of Pinot Noir, annually. After selling his self-named winery in the mid-2000s, he has the luxury of blending top-notch Pinots in his new production facility on Westside Road in Healdsburg. Notable vineyards providing grapes to Alysian include Allen, Cresta Ridge, Floodgate, Hallberg, Starr Ridge, and Rochioli.

Not surprisingly, the Alysian style is very much modeled on the wines that he created at his eponymous winery and that continue to govern those latter wines as well—ripe but restrained, deep yet never over-the-top, tasty but tight, and long aging without being unapproachable when young. Critical ratings in the 90-point range are also not a surprise.

ARROWOOD VINEYARDS & WINERY 1988		Map 9
www.arrowoodvineyards.com	800-938-5170	Tasting
Glen Ellen	Sonoma County	Sonoma Valley AVA

Richard Arrowood and wife-partner Alis Demers Arrowood bought land and built a winery in the late 1980s in the Valley of the Moon. Richard Arrowood had become justifiably famous for his impressively successful stint as the first winemaker at Chateau St. Jean. Even before he left St. Jean, Arrowood and his wife established their own winery and built a strong collection of Cabernet Sauvignons (representing about 45 percent of the twenty-thousand-case total production) and Chardonnays (40 percent) from both the twenty-five-acre estate vineyard and selected other Sonoma vineyards, such as Saralee's, Alary, and Monte Rosso. Today, Dick Arrowood remains in charge despite several ownership changes, most recently a sale to Kendall-Jackson and the creation of yet another winery that remains family owned.

The handsome winery and visitors' center welcome guests year-round, and a check of the Web site is always in order to see if special events are taking place. Most recent wine ratings have been consistently near 90 points, with the occasional wine getting higher scores. Arrowood wines are lusty affairs, with depth and ripeness always evident.

B. R. COHN WINERY 1984		Map 9
www.brcohn.com	707-938-4064	Tasting
Glen Ellen	Sonoma County	Sonoma Valley AVA

Bruce R. Cohn is a rock band manager by trade, still in charge of the Doobie Brothers after some thirty-five years. In 1974, during his endless road trip, Cohn bought a ninety-acre estate and spent years restoring it and planting what are now sixty acres of vines. He sold grapes to other winemakers until his own first vintage, a Cabernet Sauvignon, in 1985. The Olive Hill Estate Vineyard still grows primarily Cabernet grapes that go into several Estate wines made today. Of the current production of twenty-five thousand cases, over 60 percent are red varietals, notably Cabernet, Pinot Noir, and Merlot. Two Chardonnays are the main white varietals, with over a quarter of total wine made. B. R. Cohn also makes and sells several olive oils from its trees. Bruce Cohn contributes his musical knowledge by sponsoring an annual benefit music festival on his property.

At times, Cohn wines have reached great heights while just as often settling for mid- to upper 80-point ratings.

BENZIGER FAMILY WINERY 1988		Map 9
www.benziger.com	888-490-2739	Tasting
Glen Ellen	Sonoma County	Sonoma Mountain AVA

Bruno Benziger, a New York wine and spirits importer, listened to his calling and moved to Sonoma in the early 1980s. Benziger established his Glen Ellen Winery, which would become a successful giant, producing more than three million cases a year. In '94, Benziger sold Glen Ellen to Heublein and started the Benziger Family Winery, making a line of more upscale varietals. With an eighty-five-acre biodynamically farmed estate vineyard providing the fruit for some of the wines made, Benziger grew into a good-sized producer through its four tiers of wines: the Family line, with production ranging from 3,000 to 52,000 cases; Reserve wines, averaging 500 cases; some 15 or so Single Vineyard wines, with 500 to 800 cases made of each vintage; and Estate wines, ranging from 100 to 2,500 cases. Chardonnay rules the roost, with a third of the 175,000-case total production. Cabernet Sauvignon is next, with 30 percent of production, and Merlot contributes another 15 percent. Chilean winemaker Rodrigo Soto and the next generation of the Benziger family run the winery today. Mike Benziger is an outspoken proponent of farming techniques designed to make the land as fertile as possible through natural techniques. And while not all wines are biodynamic, the winery joins other future-oriented producers in looking for ways to protect the land and serve the grapes at the same time.

Some of the single-vineyard bottlings, especially in Sauvignon Blanc, long a winery success, have reached into the 90-point range, and the regular bottling Sauvignon Blanc is, more often than not, a great value. Benziger wines are fairly ripe yet almost never excessive in that regard and are usually impeccably balanced, with some Sauvignon Blancs being quite high in brisk acidity.

BJORNSTAD CELLARS 2005		Map 8
www.bjornstadcellars.com	888-256-7696	No Tasting
Santa Rosa	Sonoma County	Russian River Valley AVA

Greg Bjornstad studied at UC–Davis, followed by an internship at Château Lafite Rothschild and stints at Joseph Phelps, Newton, Flowers, and Tandem (whose name reflects the partnership he formed with winemaker Greg Lafollette) before establishing his own winery. Focused on Pinot Noir and Chardonnay varieties, Bjornstad bottles about 1,500 cases at present. Grapes are sourced from several Russian River growers, including Ritchie, Hellenthal, Porter-Bass, Van der Kamp, and Barbed Oak. His wines are uniformly tight and balanced and made in a manner that encourages cellaring to let them come to their full, complex, structured potential.

Ratings at and above 90 points have been the norm to date. Bjornstad also makes wine at the new Pfendler winery with much the same style and with similarly special results.

BLACKSTONE WINERY 1990		Map 9
www.blackstonewinery.com	888-659-7900	Tasting
Kenwood	Sonoma County	Sonoma Valley AVA

Courtney Benham and his brother Derek built this substantial winery operation on a Merlot foundation. They are known for moderately priced California- or Monterey County–labeled varieties made in Kenwood and, more recently, in a newly restored facility in Gonzales, in Monterey County. Blackstone owns no vineyards but buys large lots of grapes from throughout the state. Production is well over five hundred thousand cases, of which Merlot, Zinfandel, and Monterey Chardonnay make up substantially over half. Pinot Noir, Cabernet Sauvignon, Syrah, and several Meritage blends fill out the list of varieties. The Benhams sold the winery to international drinks conglomerate Constellation Brands in 2001. Prices are moderate, and the wines often succeed for value.

BRADFORD MOUNTAIN WINERY 1988		Map 7
www.bradfordmountain.com	707-431-4433	Tasting by Appointment
Healdsburg	Sonoma County	Dry Creek Valley AVA

San Francisco financier Bill Hambrecht owns this small winery and the Grist Vineyard (sixty acres of Zinfandel and fifteen of Syrah) a thousand feet above the Dry Creek Valley and to the west/southwest of the valley floor near the western end of the AVA. Bradford Mountain grapes were sold for over a decade to the likes of Gary Farrell before winemaking began. Now three thousand cases of Zinfandel and Syrah are made, with two Zinfandels, Grist Vineyard, and Dry Creek Valley designated, representing three-quarters of the total. Wines tend to be rustic, ripe, and fairly rich with tannins that can, at times, dry out the fruit. Although the occasional wine will reach to the 90-point area, most wines score in the mid- to high 80s.

BUCKLIN OLD HILL RANCH WINERY 2000		Map 9
www.buckzin.com	707-933-1726	No Tasting
Glen Ellen	Sonoma County	Sonoma Valley AVA

In 1981, the Bucklin family obtained the Old Hill Ranch, established by William McPherson Hill in 1852. The twenty-four-acre vineyard, planted in a field-blend style primarily to Zinfandel grapes, has grown grapes for the Ravenswood Winery for many years and continues to supply fruit for what is Ravenswood's most prestigious single-vineyard bottling. In 2000, the Bucklins started their own winery, with Will Bucklin, having gained experience in France and Australia and at the notable King Estate in Oregon, in charge and making about 2,500 cases of Zinfandel (over half the total), Cabernet Sauvignon, Syrah, and Gewürztraminer. The other Bucklin ranch, Oak Hill Farm, grows and sells produce and flowers.

Despite the fame of the estate, the winery has had mixed results with its wines. Ripeness has run rampant at times, and fruit has not always been a prime player in the bold, rustic wines produced. As the result, the six Zinfandels produced to date have ranged in score from 85 to 91. Still, the vineyard has outshone its peers more often than not, and that is reason enough to expect the wines to gain in consistency over time.

BUENA VISTA WINERY 1857		Map 9
www.buenavistacarneros.com	707-252-7117	Tasting
Sonoma	Sonoma County	Carneros AVA

In 1857, Hungarian Count Agoston Haraszthy founded the Buena Vista Winery after stints as a state legislator from San Diego and sheriff of San Diego County. Just over a century later, the winery had changed hands several times but, in 1969, a campaign to redevelop the thousand-acre Ramal Vineyard in Carneros began, led by journalist Frank Bartholomew and the legendary winemaker Andre Tchelistcheff. Now owned by the Ascentia group, along with such other noted producers as Gary Farrell and Geyser Peak, Buena Vista has shifted focus under winemaker Jeff Stewart (experienced at Kunde, De Loach, and La Crema wineries) from low-cost, bulk wines to premium wines in the Carneros and Estate Vineyard Series tiers. About sixty thousand cases are produced each year, with Chardonnay leading the pack at nearly 40 percent of the total. Pinot Noir is next at about 30 percent, while Merlot, Cabernet Sauvignon, and Syrah bottlings each represent 10 percent of production. Buena Vista uses estate-grown fruit principally from its five-hundred-acre plantings on the Ramal Vineyard in Carneros. The legendary stone winery, closer to Sonoma town, was established in the 1860s and still serves as the tasting room; it is recognized as a California Historic Landmark. It is still one of the most interesting places to visit in all of wine country, as it has been for years.

Buena Vista quality rankings have escalated along with the change in focus, and the winery's upscale Pinot Noirs deserve notice for their continuing string of 90-point and higher scores. Even the more modestly priced regular bottling of Pinot Noir has typically outscored its price point peers of late. Chardonnay has done well also. Regular bottlings typically are medium/full-bodied, balanced, and reasonably fruity. Special bottlings, typically vineyard designates, have been fuller, deeper, and equally well balanced.

CARLISLE WINERY & VINEYARDS 1998		Map 8
www.carlislewinery.com	707-566-7700	No Tasting
Santa Rosa	Sonoma County	Russian River Valley AVA

Mike Officer, frustrated software developer, moved to Sonoma and made hobby wines for several years. In 1998, Officer started the winery and produced 650 cases. His focus has been old-vine Zinfandel and Syrah; today, with the help of co-winemaker Jay Maddox, the winery produces three thousand to five thousand cases a year, split fairly evenly between the two varieties. The vineyards sourced include several in Sonoma County such as the Ray Teldeschi Ranch and Gold Mine Ranch Vineyards in Dry Creek Valley and Rosella's Vineyard, farther afield in the Santa Lucia Highlands of Monterey County.

The Carlisle style is variously described as full-bodied, densely stuffed, concentrated, and hedonistic or alternatively as over the top. For fans of the style, it is about as good as it gets, and many reviewers rate the wine in the 90s on a consistent basis. Others, ourselves included, have had decidedly mixed reactions, feeling that the wines are superb when the fruit matches the rest of the wine but harder to take when size and ripeness dominate all else.

CAROL SHELTON WINES 2000		Map 8
www.carolshelton.com	707-575-3441	Tasting by Appointment
Santa Rosa	Sonoma County	Russian River Valley AVA

After UC–Davis, Carol Shelton paid her winemaking dues at Mondavi, Buena Vista, and, for many years, Windsor vineyards before setting up her own shop, devoted to small-batch Zinfandel. Five vineyard-designated Zinfandels and an upscale specialty Zin are typically made, along with a very successful dry Rosé that relies on Carignane for its fruit. Shelton finds fruit sources from vineyards as far afield as Mendocino County, Cucamonga, the Russian River Valley, and Rockpile, with wine names such as Monga, Karma, and Wild Thing, among others. Four thousand cases are produced in total.

Like most popular Zinfandel makers, Shelton emphasizes ripeness in her wines, but the reason that they score consistently in the lower to mid-90s is the delicious, well-focused fruit that is each wine's first focus. Monga is typically ripest; Rockpile, the most succulent; and her Maple Zin, from one of the Dry Creek Valley's finest Zinfandel vineyards, the out-and-out fruitiest. The winery, located in an industrial building in Santa Rosa, is not of much interest, but spending an hour with the energetic Shelton tasting through her wines is an opportunity not to be missed.

CASTALIA WINES 1993		Map 8
www.castaliawines.com	707-857-3376	No Tasting
Geyserville	Sonoma County	Russian River Valley AVA

Terry Bering started making garage wines and moved on to his own label Pinot Noir beginning in 1993. He remains cellar master at Rochioli, from where he sources all his fruit and where he makes the wine. A single vintage-dated Pinot Noir is produced each year in 350-case lots. These well-crafted, keenly focused wines are expensive but not outrageously so when compared to other wines made from Rochioli grapes. Scores into the mid- to upper 90s are the rule rather than the exception. Although these wines are rare now and likely to remain so, it is clear that they are worth knowing about.

CHALK HILL ESTATE VINEYARDS & WINERY 1980		Map 8
www.chalkhill.com	707-838-4306	Tasting by Appointment
Healdsburg	Sonoma County	Chalk Hill AVA

In 1974, attorney Fred Furth bought a 650-acre ranch and planted 260 acres to vines in the hilly Chalk Hill area east of Windsor. Today's 350 vineyard acres produce grapes for all the estate-bottled wines, with particular focus on Chardonnay. Under the watch of winemaker Steven Leveque, formerly of Robert Mondavi, production of Chardonnay, Cabernet Sauvignon, Sauvignon Blanc, Pinot Gris, and Merlot totals in excess of sixty thousand cases.

All Chalk Hill wines are made in ripe but not excessively concentrated styles and reflect substantial oak barrel influences. Chardonnay has been the quality leader in most vintages, followed by Sauvignon Blanc and Pinot Gris. Merlot has been the leader among the reds, with Cabernet Sauvignon trailing a bit behind. Top vintages have scored in the 90- to 95-point range, more often for whites than for reds. Pinot Gris, made in an aggressively outgoing, oaky style, is among the deepest, most expressive versions of the grape anywhere in the world, but it also veers away from the aromatic, fruit-driven direction that is Pinot Gris's dominant styling.

CHARLES CREEK VINEYARD 2002		Map 9
www.charlescreek.com	707-996-6622	Tasting
Sonoma	Sonoma County	Sonoma Valley AVA

Midwesterners and former financial professionals Bill and Gerry Brinton (Bill is a descendant of John Deere) came west to further their business careers. After several other ventures, including growing grapes on Sonoma Mountain, the Brintons chose to make their own wines. With veteran winemaker Kerry Damskey in charge, several vineyard-designated Chardonnays, Merlots, and Cabernet Sauvignons are produced in small lots, with total production over eight thousand cases. Grape sources included the well-known Hyde, Sangiacomo, and Stagecoach vineyards.

To date, the many Chardonnays have been pleasantly constructed, of medium depth and rich in oak. Ratings have ranged from the mid- to upper 80s, with the occasional Merlot reaching into the low 90s.

CHASSEUR 1994		Map 8
www.chasseurwines.com	707-829-1941	No Tasting
Sebastopol	Sonoma County	Russian River Valley AVA

Winemaker and proprietor Bill Hunter (English for "*chasseur*") had a Davis degree and a dozen years' experience at Bonny Doon in Santa Cruz and Rombauer in St. Helena before launching his own label in 1994. Dedicated to small-batch Chardonnay and Pinot Noir from grapes grown by some fourteen vineyards, most in the western part of the county, in ocean-influenced, cool-climate vineyards as well as the occasional Carneros bottling, Chasseur makes about a dozen vineyard-designated bottlings each year more or less evenly split between its two varieties, with a total production of five thousand cases.

In recent years, Chasseur has ranked at the very top of the list in both varieties, and if Hunter's unfiltered, slightly hazy-appearing Chardonnays seem a little murky in appearance, they compensate with deep, rich, complex flavors in which ripe apple, sometimes citrus-tinged fruit is set against layered notes of roasted grains and creamy oak. Scores for Chardonnay are now regularly in the 90-point range, with several bottlings exceeding 95 points and taking down top honors year in and year out. Chasseur Pinot Noirs have not lagged far behind and also consistently earn scores above 90 points.

CHATEAU ST. JEAN 1973		Map 9
www.chateaustjean.com	707-833-4134	Tasting
Kenwood	Sonoma County	Sonoma Valley AVA

Among the first of the modern wineries to set up shop in the Sonoma Valley and change the face of its winemaking efforts, Chateau St. Jean specialized early on in Chardonnay and Riesling under founding winemaker, Richard Arrowood. Changes of ownership from the original California-based founders to two sets of overseas owners led to changes in focus toward red wines and the eventual departure of Arrowood, who went on to found his eponymous winery. The picturesque "chateau," named for the wife of the original owner and not a canonized Frenchman, has been expanded over the years and is one of California's most interesting wineries. Winemaking is now under the direction of Margo Van Staaveren, who oversees production that has reached two hundred thousand cases made up of a broad line of varieties. Ownership of Chateau St. Jean is now in the hands of the Beringer Blass wine division of Foster's Group.

Wine quality, as is often the case at wineries of this size, can be variable, but vineyard-designated Chardonnay continues to set the pace. La Petite Étoile Fumé Blanc is also a quality leader. The winery makes a broad array of red wines in a full-bodied rich style. At the other end of the price range, Chateau St. Jean is one of the leaders in moderately priced Chardonnay and Sauvignon Blanc.

CLINE CELLARS 1982		Map 9
www.clinecellars.com	707-940-4000	Tasting
Sonoma	Sonoma County	Carneros AVA

Fred Cline, descendant of the Jacuzzi whirlpool and spa family, grew nuts and wine grapes before settling on winemaking. In 1982, Cline purchased the former Firpo Winery in Oakley (Contra Costa County) and its 140 acres of vineyards. In '91, Cline moved the winery to a 350-acre Carneros estate, where it remains today. From the total of nearly five hundred vineyard acres in the two regions, Cline makes large batches of modestly priced Zinfandel and smaller quantities of numerous Rhône varieties, including Syrah, Viognier, Marsanne, and Roussanne. Second labels Oakley and Jacuzzi Family Vineyards are produced at the Carneros headquarters.

Cline is best known for its Zinfandels made from aged vines in Contra Costa County and following the very ripe, concentrated, somewhat desiccated but deeply drawn, rustic flavors the grapes from those hot, sandy vineyards typically produce. Ratings for the Zins have been somewhat inconsistent, with scores ranging form the mid-80s up to the 90-point area on occasion. The Bridgehead and the Big Break Zinfandels have been the ratings leaders. Lately, a Carneros AVA Syrah has joined in those two wines in receiving admirable scores in the high 80s to low 90s.

CLOS DU BOIS WINES 1974		Map 6
www.closdubois.com	707-857-3100	Tasting
Geyserville	Sonoma County	Alexander Valley AVA

In the early 1970s, Frank Woods purchased one hundred acres in the Dry Creek Valley and another five hundred in Alexander Valley. The year 1974 was the first vintage of Clos du Bois (literally, "enclosure in the woods"), and over the next three decades the vineyards grew to over nine hundred acres and the winery grew into a megabrand, now making several dozen varieties of wines totaling over two million cases in Classic, Reserve, and Proprietary lines. Clos du Bois is owned by the international drinks conglomerate Constellation Brands.

Among the Clos du Bois claims to fame are its position as one of the leading sellers of Merlot; its continuing allegiance to Riesling, a grape that has fallen out of favor in the marketplace but enjoys a small, loyal following; and the success of its full-bodied, tightly structured Marlstone proprietary red that contains a mix of Bordelais varieties led by Cabernet Sauvignon and Merlot.

COLLIER FALLS VINEYARDS 1997		Map 7
www.collierfalls.com	707-433-7373	Tasting
Healdsburg	Sonoma County	Dry Creek Valley AVA

Barry Collier and the late Susan Collier purchased a hundred-acre estate from the Ferrari-Carano interests in the hills toward the northwest corner of Dry Creek Valley, overlooking Lake Sonoma. The twenty-five-acre-vineyard provided all the fruit for the winery's production of three thousand cases, of which Zinfandel is about half; Primitivo, Zinfandel's twin, adds in another three hundred cases. Cabernet Sauvignon checks in at about one thousand cases, and the rest is devoted to Petite Sirah.

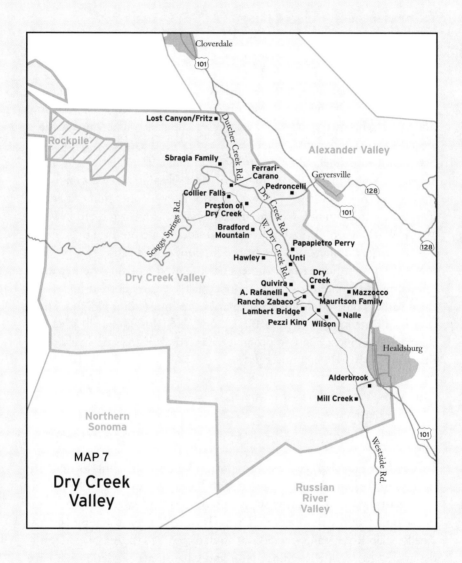

MAP 7

Dry Creek Valley

Wine quality has been inconsistent in the early vintages, with scores reaching into the 90-point range in first outings, then falling off after that. Recent results suggest that the winery may be finding its rhythm again. Collier wines follow the typical Dry Creek model of ripe and rich in best vintages.

COPAIN WINE CELLARS 2000		Map 8
www.copainwines.com	707-836-8822	Tasting by Appointment
Healdsburg	Sonoma County	Russian River Valley AVA

Founder and winemaker Wells Guthrie learned the business at Chapoutier in the northern Rhône and Turley on the California Central Coast before undertaking his own winery and custom crush facility. The Copain wines are all vineyard-designated, small lot varieties, with the focus on Pinot Noir, Syrah, and Zinfandel. The vineyard sources range from six to eight in the Anderson Valley that make up the Pinot Noir selection and a dozen Syrahs from as far afield as Garys' Vineyard in Monterey County, James Berry in Paso Robles (a blend of Grenache and Mourvèdre), and a vineyard in Walla Walla, Washington. A total of five thousand cases are produced.

With large numbers of wine in production, results can vary a bit, but, more often than not, critical success has followed Copain whether in its limited production efforts or its more available efforts bottled under seasonal names rendered in French such as L'Automne (Pinot Noir), L'Hiver (Syrah), Printemps (Sauvignon Blanc), or L'Été (Rosé). Copain is among those wineries most likely to produce balanced, fruit-focused, lively wines that favor midsized weight over power.

DAVIS BYNUM WINERY 1975		Map 8
www.davisbynum.com	707-433-5852	Tasting
Healdsburg	Sonoma County	Russian River Valley AVA

Former San Francisco newspaper reporter Bynum was living in Berkeley in the 1950s when he experimented with home winemaking. The experiment morphed into a nearby warehouse winery and later to eighty acres in Sonoma County that became Davis Bynum Winery in the mid-1970s. The Russian River Valley ranch contributed grapes to the mainly vineyard-designated roster of RRV Pinot Noir and Chardonnay varieties that have long fetched top dollar. The ten-thousand-case winery was sold in 2007 to Tom Klein of Rodney Strong Vineyards, but the label will remain separate. Meanwhile, the next generation of Bynums is starting up a second label,

River Bend, which will continue to use the family-owned vineyards and Bynum winery facility. Time will tell how much is accomplished under new ownership, but it is clear that the Bynum label will show improved results—if only because it will get more and better attention than it had received in recent years. Stay tuned.

DAVIS FAMILY VINEYARDS 1997		Map 8
www.davisfamilyvineyards.com	866-338-9463	Tasting
Healdsburg	Sonoma County	Russian River Valley AVA

Guy Davis was first exposed to the world of wine as a college student in Idaho where he worked at a French restaurant. After several stops, Davis found a small vineyard in the Russian River Valley and set up shop in the late 1990s, making small lots of Pinot Noir, Syrah, Zinfandel, and Chardonnay, largely from his own fruit. A third of the four-thousand-case output is Pinot Noir. Davis travels to New Zealand each year to make Gusto, a second-label Sauvignon Blanc.

Chardonnay has been the quality leader to date, with recent wines reaching 90 points, while Pinot Noir has been good enough to earn recommendations in the mid- to upper 80s.

DELOACH VINEYARDS 1975		Map 8
www.deloachvineyards.com	707-526-9111	Tasting
Santa Rosa	Sonoma County	Russian River Valley AVA

Retired San Francisco firefighter Cecil DeLoach tended a small Russian River Valley vineyard until weak grape demand led him to winemaking, becoming a leading Pinot Noir and Chardonnay producer in the region. The original 200 acres of vineyards grew to 450 and production to over 120,000 cases. DeLoach has nearly twenty wines on offer, with Pinot Noir still leading the way in a three-tiered group of wines: modestly priced RRV, the "OFS" (Our Finest Selection), and a dozen or more vineyard-designated wines from vineyards in Sonoma and Lake counties. In 2003, DeLoach sold the winery to the French drinks group Boisset Family Estates, with mixed results under the new ownership but potential aplenty.

DELORIMIER WINERY 1985		Map 6
www.delorimierwinery.com	800-546-7718	Tasting
Geyserville	Sonoma County	Alexander Valley AVA

San Francisco surgeon Dr. Alfred DeLorimier planted a vineyard near Geyserville that evolved into eighty-five acres over three nearby sites. Over the years, production grew to some 25,000 cases of Chardonnay, Merlot, Sauvignon Blanc and two Meritage bottlings, and ownership changed and then changed again. DeLorimier is now in the hands of the Wilsons (of Wilson and Mazzocco) and the winery is turning its focus to Cabernet Sauvignon. Owner Diane Wilson partners with Antoine Favero in crafting the wines.

DEERFIELD RANCH WINERY 1982		Map 9
www.deerfieldranch.com	707-833-5215	Tasting by Appointment
Glen Ellen	Sonoma County	Sonoma Valley AVA

Berkeley garage winemaker Robert Rex bought the ranch in 1982 but made his wines elsewhere until a winery facility was completed in 1996. A long list of primarily reds are made with fruit from some fifteen or more contracted area vineyards, including Ladi's, Cohn, Los Chamizal, and Trio. In addition to straightforward varieties, Rex makes several Meritage blends, most Cabernet Sauvignon based. Lots of 250 to 2,000 cases contribute to the total production of 12,000, which will grow to a maximum of 45,000 cases.

Scores in the middle to upper 80s have predominated to date.

DEHLINGER WINERY 1976		Map 8
www.dehlingerwinery.com	707-823-2378	No Tasting
Sebastopol	Sonoma County	Russian River Valley AVA

Trained at UC–Davis, enologist Tom Dehlinger initially planted fourteen hilly acres that, over time, grew to the present forty-five acres planted principally to Pinot Noir and Chardonnay. The estate-grown and -bottled varieties follow suit, with the Pinot Noir and Chardonnay representing over two-thirds of the seven-thousand-case total produced, with smaller quantities of Syrah and Cabernet Sauvignon also bottled. Over three-quarters of production is sold through a subscriber list. Despite two decades of incredible success, the winery has remained a small, hands-on producer.

The Dehlinger style emphasizes ripeness and richness with Pinot Noir, especially the Reserve, the Octagon, and the Goldridge bottlings—all having enormous success with scores in the low to middle 90s. Goldridge is typically the most open of the wines in style; the Octagon bottling, taken from a patch at the top of the sloping site, tends to be most tightly structured and the longest lived.

DEUX AMIS WINERY	1987	Map 7
www.deuxamiswines.com	707-431-7945	No Tasting
Healdsburg	Sonoma County	Russian River Valley AVA

The "two friends" who created this winery are longtime winemakers Phillis Zouzounis and Jim Penpraze. Their first vintage in 1987 was a hundred cases of Zinfandel made from purchased grapes. The focus has remained firmly on Zinfandel, with four now made: a Sonoma County bottling, a Dry Creek Valley wine, and two vineyard-designated examples, most recently from the Shadick and Halling vineyards. A Petite Sirah is also produced. Total output is just over 1,500 cases, with the vineyard-designated batches as small as 150 cases.

Critical evaluation of Deux Amis wines has revealed a maddeningly inconsistent track record, but fans of the winery remain steadfast, in part because its wines continue to seek a balanced style instead of the boldness that has become the norm for the grapes it produces.

DONUM ESTATE	2001	Map 9
www.thedonumestate.com	707-939-2290	No Tasting
Sonoma	Sonoma County	Carneros AVA

Formerly part of the adjacent Buena Vista estate, the 120-acre Donum Estate Vineyard dates to the 1970s. In 2001 the first Donum vintage was bottled by owner-grower Anne Moller-Racke of the German wine and spirits group Racke International. Under Moller-Racke and winemaker Kenneth Juhasz, Donum has produced notable Pinot Noir from its vineyards both in Carneros and in the Russian River Valley. Production tops out at two thousand cases of Pinot Noir. See also the entry for Robert Stemmler, which is under the same management and winemaking team and uses the same vineyard sources, all of which make Donum the upscale label of the same organization.

It is worth noting that in most vintages, Donum Pinot Noir has been exceptionally well received, with scores at and above 90 points and some wines rating as among the very best of the vintage. The Carneros bottling is the tighter of the two, while the Russian River Valley is more open and more directly fruity in style. Both are very representative of their respective provenances.

DRY CREEK VINEYARD 1972		Map 7
www.drycreekvineyard.com	800-864-9463	Tasting
Healdsburg	Sonoma County	Dry Creek Valley AVA

David Stare moved west in the early 1970s and built a winery modeled on châteaux of the Loire Valley. It was to be the first new, small premium winery built in Dry Creek Valley since Prohibition, and Stare began with Chenin Blanc and Fumé Blanc, then added Zinfandel, with the latter pair becoming his "flagship" wines (just as the label art recognized the family's proclivity for sailing ships). Stare was also an early proponent of establishing the Dry Creek Valley AVA and among the first to use the now near-ubiquitous Old Vines and Meritage. The winery is currently in the hands of the next generation, Don and Kim Stare Wallace, with winemaker Bill Knuttel helping focus on fewer wines than at the turn of the century. Production has been consciously reduced to just over a hundred thousand cases, still relying heavily on the Fumé Blanc and Zinfandels. Fairly new are the vineyard-designated Zinfandels from Dry Creek Valley's Somers Ranch and Beeson, as well as a Cabernet Sauvignon from the Endeavour Vineyard. Much of the Dry Creek line is from grapes grown on the two-hundred-acre estate.

The winery has concentrated more of its efforts on making solid, well-focused wines, and its efforts with its basic Fumé Blanc and its Heritage Zinfandel have become accepted as some of the best values around in moderately priced wines. The vineyard designates of these varieties, also fairly reasonably priced, can occasionally achieve ratings in the 90-point range. And like everything else about this young but maturing winery, its Web site its attractive, accessible, and filled with value.

DUTTON-GOLDFIELD WINERY 1998		Map 8
www.duttongoldfield.com	707-823-3887	Tasting
Sebastopol	Sonoma County	Russian River Valley AVA

Renowned grower Steve Dutton, of Dutton Ranch, and winemaker Dan Goldfield had collaborated since the early 1990s and formed a partnership in 1998. Goldfield came from Philadelphia, where he was a research chemist, until lured west. Here he studied at Davis and began his winemaking career with stops at Mondavi, Schramsberg, La Crema, and Kendall-Jackson's Hartford Court. Dutton's father, Warren, had first planted grapes in the region in 1964; now the Dutton Ranch has 1,150 planted acres in some 60 discreet vineyards that are owned, leased, or managed by Dutton; another 150 acres are planted to apples. The Dutton-Goldfield partnership now produces some ten thousand cases annually, with Chardonnay 45 percent of the total and Pinot Noir another 40 percent. Very small quantities of Zinfandel, Syrah, and Pinot Blanc are also bottled.

From the outset, Dutton-Goldfield wines have searched for balance and focus at the expense of depth and concentration. As the result, it is not unusual for the winery to offer wine that is higher in acidity and lower in alcohol than the competition. The risks of underachievement are great with that chosen strategy, yet the rewards when the wines work out are substantial, and Dutton-Goldfield has earned a fair degree of deserved praise for its wines. Morelli Lane Zinfandel has been a real favorite with lots of scores in the lower to mid-90s, making it one of the highest-rated Zinfandels in California in recent vintages.

FERRARI-CARANO VINEYARDS & WINERY 1981		Map 7
www.ferrari-carano.com	800-831-0381	Tasting
Healdsburg	Sonoma County	Dry Creek Valley AVA

Don Carano, owner of the El Dorado Hotel in Reno, bought land in the Alexander and Dry Creek valleys in the late 1970s. The 60 acres grew into the current 1,400 acres on 19 separate vineyards in the Alexander Valley, Russian River Valley, Dry Creek Valley, and Carneros. Ferrari-Carano, under the guidance of winemakers Sarah Quider (white wines) and Aaron Piotter (reds), make over 150,000 cases of a wide range of wines in numerous styles and tiers, with a focus on Merlot, Chardonnay, Zinfandel, Sauvignon Blanc, and several proprietary blends. A very well-situated, Italianate winery and tasting room, called Villa Fiore, complete with a spectacular view of the west end of the Dry Creek Valley, welcomes visitors and is among our favorites.

Ferrari-Carano succeeds at virtually all levels, from its midpriced bottlings of Fumé (Sauvignon) Blanc, and Chardonnay to its upscale "Reserves" of Chardonnay and its blended reds. The regular bottling Fumé is perhaps its most consistent wine, with scores in the upper 80s to low 90s—quite high for its price niche. Whites run from ripe and brisk for Sauvignon Blanc to full bodied and balanced for Chardonnay, while reds tend to fullness and a bit of fleshiness in the usually well-muscled architecture.

FISHER VINEYARDS 1973		Map 9
www.fishervineyards.com	707-539-7511	Tasting by Appointment
Santa Rosa	Sonoma County	Not in an AVA

Fred and Juelle Fisher—he is the grandson of the General Motors body manufacturer ("Body by Fisher")—bought twenty-two acres on the Sonoma side of the Mayacamas Mountains after leaving the automotive and financial businesses. Fisher has consistently made small batches of Cabernet Sauvignon, Chardonnay, and Merlot, with an even smaller amount of Syrah and a Cabernet-based blend, Cameron. The next generation, including winemaker Whitney, Robert, and Cameron, is now the winery's future. Most wines are made from grapes grown on the two estate vineyards, the home estate in Sonoma County, and another in northeastern Napa County; there are eighty planted acres in total. Production totals from six thousand to eight thousand cases, of which the several Cabernet selections equal 50 percent.

Frequently superb, always made with care and an eye for balance, Fisher wines generally score in the high 80s to low 90s, with Chardonnay being the leading performer over the years.

FOPPIANO VINEYARDS 1896		Map 8
www.foppiano.com	707-433-7272	Tasting
Healdsburg	Sonoma County	Russian River Valley AVA

The historic, family-run winery is now in its fifth generation, started by Genoa immigrant Giovanni Foppiano in 1896 after panning for gold didn't pan out. The Foppianos weathered the Prohibition storm and its jug wine image when, in the late 1960s, they hopped onto the varietal wine bandwagon. The Foppiano estate vineyards include 140 planted acres in the Russian River Valley and contribute fruit to much of the better wines, sourcing the rest from numerous California vineyards. The focus is on reds exclusively, and Foppiano produces some fifty thousand cases of them, with a Sangiovese blend accounting for 45 percent of production and Petite Sirah another 25 percent. Second label Riverside by Foppiano makes another twenty-five thousand cases of low-priced whites.

Foppiano wines are fairly inexpensive for North Coast varieties, and while their scores have ranged from the mid- to the upper 80s at best, they are often fairly priced for what they deliver. Recent Pinot Noir and Petite Sirah have shown best.

FORT ROSS VINEYARD & WINERY 1994 — Map 5

www.fortrossvineyard.com	415-701-9200	No Tasting
Fort Ross	Sonoma County	Sonoma Coast AVA

Located on steep ridges less than a mile from the Pacific Ocean near the town of Fort Ross, and possessing possibly the closest vineyard to the Pacific in all of California, the Fort Ross winery was established by South Africans Linda and Lester Schwartz. Their 44-acre vineyard overlooks the ocean at elevations ranging from 1,200 to 1,700 feet, useful for the principally Pinot Noir and Chardonnay production, totaling some 2,500 cases, all made with estate-grown grapes. A Rosé and a "Pinotage" blend are also made in very small quantities.

Success has been an early visitor to this producer, and scores for both Pinot Noir and Chardonnay are 90 points and higher more often than not. The wines are reflective of the coastal, uplands heritage in their combination of high acidity and high ripeness.

FREEMAN VINEYARD & WINERY 2001 — Map 8

www.freemanwinery.com	707-823-6937	No Tasting
Sebastopol	Sonoma County	Green Valley of R.R. Valley AVA

Den and Akiko Freeman found a disused winery in Sebastopol in 2001 and launched a small winery specializing in Pinot Noir and Chardonnay in small batches. With winemaker Ed Kurtzman in charge, late of Chalone and Testarossa, Freeman makes something less than six thousand cases—the Pinot Noir comprises 90 percent of production—from grapes grown on nearby vineyards, including Bailey, Guidici, and Keefer Ranch.

Early results have been encouraging, with wines frequently rated 90 points and higher. The Kurtzman hand shows here in the wines' good balance amid high but not overdone ripeness.

FREESTONE VINEYARDS 1999 — Map 8

www.freestone.com	707-874-1010	Tasting
Freestone	Sonoma County	Sonoma Coast AVA

Freestone is the Joseph Phelps Vineyards' new venture near the ocean, making exclusively Pinot Noir and Chardonnay varieties. Run by Bill Phelps, Joe's son, the family acquired one hundred acres near the town of Freestone, dedicating eighty-eight of those acres to Pinot Noir and the remainder to Chardonnay, bringing in the first vintage in 2006. The vineyards are divided into four parcels, two of which fit just inside the western boundary of the Russian River Valley AVA and two of which are farther west yet. Since then, under the watchful eye of winemaker Theresa Heredia, Freestone has produced very limited quantities of three tiers of Pinot Noir and Chardonnay, principally from its estate-grown grapes along with the occasional vineyard-designated bottling. Please note, however, that this Freestone bears no relation to wines with the same name that were produced in the early 2000s by the Von Strasser winery in the Napa Valley.

The wines of the first vintage were pleasant and garnered 90-point ratings for the ripe yet firm personalities. The 2007 Chardonnays rated in the mid- to upper 90s and came in a refined, restrained, firm yet deep and layered style that moved the standards for California-produced Chardonnay. Clearly, this is a label that demands attention. With prices running high for the Freestone-labeled wine, one can look to wines labeled as Ovation and Fog Dog at more moderate but certainly not inexpensive prices.

FRITZ WINERY 1979		Map 7
www.fritzwinery.com	800-418-9463	Tasting
Cloverdale	Sonoma County	Dry Creek Valley AVA

San Franciscans Jay and Barbara Fritz bought the site at the northern end of Dry Creek Valley in 1970 and built a subterranean winery and cellars in 1979. Now under the watch of winemaker Christina Pällman (whose winery backgrounds include such stalwarts as Domaine Dujac in Burgundy and Felton Road at the southern tip of New Zealand), Fritz makes twelve thousand cases of reds: Cabernet Sauvignon, Zinfandel, Pinot Noir, and Syrah; and whites: Sauvignon Blanc and Chardonnay. Most of the fruit is grown in the Fritz estate vineyard; the accomplished Merry Edwards serves as consulting winemaker, and second-generation member Clayton Fritz is day-to-day hands-on manager. Lost Canyon wines (see entry) and winery are a recent purchase and are now moved to Fritz, Sonoma County.

After working with noted winemakers Tom Dehlinger, Davis Bynum, and Joe Rochioli, Farrell launched his own label in 1982 with fifty cases of Pinot Noir. Over the years, Farrell became the leading exponent of balanced, restrained layered Pinot Noirs, and while his wines have never been fruit-forward when they were young, they were almost always more age-worthy than their peers. Indeed, more than one tasting has seen older Farrell wines mistaken for French. In 2000, he built a new, large facility on a hilltop overlooking the Russian River Valley and expanded production substantially. In '07, the winery and name was acquired by Beam Wine Estates and in turn sold in '08 to the local investment group Ascentia Wine Estates.

With Farrell having excused himself for less corporate pastures, the winery now proceeds under the practiced hand of winemaker Susan Reed (experienced at Matanzas Creek) and produces some twenty-five thousand cases, 45 percent of which is Pinot Noir and 30 percent Chardonnay, followed by smaller quantities of Cabernet Sauvignon, Sauvignon Blanc, Zinfandel, and Merlot. The selection is extensive, featuring single-vineyard bottlings from the best vineyards in Sonoma County as well as from the forty-five-acre Farrell estate.

Pinot Noir has long been the leader for Farrell, under both regimes, with bottlings from the best Westside Road vineyards like Howard Allen and Rochioli setting the pace and often earning scores ranging into the stratospheric end of the 90-point range. The stylistic direction set by Gary Farrell continues with all wines being relatively firm in structure, nicely fruited without excess, and capable of long aging. It is a style that produces very good to great wines in top vintages but can flounder in weak vintages.

The winery, known over the years principally for its bulk wines, was founded in 1880. Revived in 1972 when acquired by Milwaukee's Schlitz brewery from the Bagnani family, Geyser Peak grew within three years to two hundred thousand cases and then to over a million on the back of its Summit brand of low-cost product. In '83 the winery was bought by the local Trione family, which sold the Summit brand and focused on varietal wines, dropping production to some four hundred thousand cases. For a time, Trione was in partnership with Australian winemaker Penfolds, but Trione reacquired the Penfold share in '92. The ownership saga continued when, in '98, it was acquired by Beam Wine Estates, then Constellation Brands, and, in '08, by a local investment group, Ascentia Wine Estates.

Today's production stands at 250,000 cases of the many Geyser Peak wines, 90 percent of which consists of the modestly priced varietals—a California Sauvignon Blanc accounts for nearly half the total production—with smaller batches of reserve and vineyard-specific bottlings sold at significantly higher prices. Geyser Peak owns 1,200 acres of vineyards in the Alexander Valley, Russian River Valley, and Lake County. A few upscale efforts are attempted under the Block Collection subset of the Geyser Peak label, but success remains a less than consistent commodity for this winery whose products can be great values in top vintages. Regular bottlings are modest, everyday efforts that can be good values when successful. The reserves are riper and richer and can occasionally break the 90-point barrier.

GLORIA FERRER WINERY 1984		Map 9
www.gloriaferrer.com	707-996-7256	Tasting
Sonoma	Sonoma County	Carneros AVA

The Spanish Ferrer family, makers of Catalonian Cava and the Freixenet Sparkling Wine, started this *méthode champenoise* winery in Carneros in 1984. A new winery and extensive aging cellars were built in 1988 with an eighty-thousand-case capacity. In 1991, Ferrer started making still wines as well as sparklers. Since then, the winery's production has grown to over two hundred thousand cases annually, of which 70 percent are Sparkling Wines and 30 percent still, largely Pinot Noir, all under the auspices of longtime winemaker Bob Iantosca. Ferrer grows its own fruit on a 200-acre estate vineyard and holds long-term leases on another 130 acres. The winery's hillside location west of Sonoma town affords wonderful views over its own vineyards and its Carneros District neighbors, and the many activities sponsored by the winery make it a special highlight of our visits to the area.

Wine quality is high for the prices asked, with its midpriced Sparkling Wines showing classic Sparkling Wine character competing equally with and often outranking its price point competition, and the Pinot Noir can also excel for the money. Two upscale bubblies, the middle-aged Royal Cuvée and the long-aged Carneros Cuvée, are also high achievers, with critical ratings that can reach into the 90-point range. A brand-new bubbly is Va de Vi, a fruit-forward, flowery, Muscat-inspired offering that makes for easy warm-weather sipping.

GUNDLACH-BUNDSCHU WINERY 1973		Map 9
www.gunbun.com	707-938-5277	Tasting
Sonoma	Sonoma County	Sonoma Valley AVA

Gundlach-Bundschu traces its ancestry back to 1858 when Jacob Gundlach acquired four hundred acres that he named Rhinefarm. Ten years later fellow German immigrant Charles Bundschu joined the winery and the family by marrying Gundlach's eldest daughter. Prior to Prohibition, the winery was noted for its table and fortified wines and after Repeal for its vineyards. In 1973, the family decided to return to winemaking; today the winery is run by the sixth generations. Gundlach-Bundschu is best known for its Merlot, which represents over 40 percent of the fifty-thousand-case total production and relies on its full-bodied, rich character for success. The 200-acre Rhinefarm Vineyard and leased 150-acre vineyard produce most of the fruit for the range of largely red varieties offered. Recent changes in winemaking responsibility have seen the arrival of Keith Emerson at the helm. His experiences at Cakebread and Vineyard 29 in the Napa Valley and his time at Palliser in New Zealand suggest that things are going to be on the upswing at Gundlach Bundschu.

Long praised for the richness and fullness of its Rhinefarm Merlot and Zinfandel, both of which have rated up into the 90-point range in years past, Gundlach-Bundschu wines have lately scored in the mid-80s.

HALLECK VINEYARD 1999		Map 8
www.halleckvineyard.com	707-738-8383	Tasting by Appointment
Sebastopol	Sonoma County	Sonoma Coast AVA

Ross Halleck began his wine career as a marketer whose clients included several major producers. After moving to Sonoma County in the early 1990s, he and wife, Jennifer, planted their small, single-acre Pinot Noir vineyard and brought out their first vintage in 1999. Production averages three thousand cases and currently includes five single-vineyard Pinot Noirs and a Sauvignon Blanc, all made in small lots sourced from the estate vineyard and two or three others nearby.

Both the Pinot Noirs and the Sauvignon Blanc have been exceptionally well received, often scoring high into the 90-point range. Halleck may not be as widely known as its famous neighbors up there in Sonoma's Pinot country, but this is a winery worth following. Its wines are mannerly, well filled, and brightly balanced.

HANNA WINERY 1985		Map 8
www.hannawinery.com	800-854-3987	Tasting
Healdsburg	Sonoma County	Russian River Valley AVA

Dr. Elias Hanna, a heart surgeon who emigrated from Syria at an early age, first acquired twelve acres in the Russian River Valley in the 1970s and produced homemade Chardonnay and Cabernet Sauvignon. Since then, the planted vineyards have grown to 250 acres in four locations in the Russian River, Sonoma, and Alexander valleys. Now run by daughter Christine Hanna and longtime winemaker Jeff Hinchliffe, Hanna's production averages forty thousand cases of all estate-grown and -produced wines, with a single Sauvignon Blanc accounting for 60 percent and several Cabernets for 25 percent. Pinot Noir, Syrah, Zinfandel, and Cabernet Franc varieties round out the roster. Hanna has tasting rooms in both Healdsburg and Santa Rosa.

Not surprisingly, the ripe, expressive Sauvignon Blanc has been our favorite Hanna wine over the years.

HANZELL VINEYARDS 1957		Map 9
www.hanzell.com	707-996-3860	Tasting by Appointment
Sonoma	Sonoma County	Sonoma Valley AVA

In 1948, industrialist and Ambassador James Zellerbach bought a two-hundred-acre site on a remote hillside in the Mayacamas Mountains. In '53, Zellerbach planted six acres of Pinot Noir and Chardonnay, thought to be the oldest Pinot Noir planting in America. A first vintage was made in '57 under the Hanzell label (a contraction of Hana and Zellerbach). Over time, Zellerbach built what would become one of the first showcase wineries, modeled on Clos de Vougeot in Burgundy. Among the Hanzell accomplishments was the introduction of French oak for aging. Now owned by Alexander de Brye and family, Hanzell produces six thousand cases annually (75 percent Chardonnay and 25 percent Pinot Noir) from grapes grown on the forty-two-acre estate vineyard. Bob Sessions, now holding the title of winemaker emeritus, oversaw production at Hanzell for decades, and the Sessions family is still very much involved in the running of Hanzell.

The winery has enjoyed iconic status for its early successes and continued emphasis on deep character, but it also had lean years in which the wines were simply not up to snuff. Recent results are better, but time will tell if this proud producer reacquires its premier status.

HARTFORD FAMILY WINERY 1993		Map 8
www.hartfordwines.com	707-887-8010	Tasting
Forestville	Sonoma County	Green Valley of R.R. Valley AVA

Don and Jennifer Hartford (daughter of Jess Jackson of Kendall-Jackson) acquired a new facility built for Laurier and named it Hartford Court. The winery produces some 7,500 cases in total, including 50 percent Pinot Noir under the Hartford Court vineyard-designated label, another 20 percent Hartford Court Chardonnay, and the remainder a Zinfandel line under the Hartford label. All wines are full-bodied. The estate vineyard of fewer than ten acres and a dozen or so vineyards of others in Sonoma County are the sources of fruit. Pricing has been high, and wine quality usually follows suit.

HAWLEY WINERY & VINEYARDS 1996		Map 7
www.hawleywine.com	707-431-2705	Tasting
Healdsburg	Sonoma County	Dry Creek Valley AVA

As Clos du Bois's first winemaker, John Hawley helped that winery expand exponentially in the 1990s before working for Jess Jackson and eventually founding his own winery in 1996. With ten acres of Merlot, Cabernet Sauvignon, Zinfandel, and Voignier grapes on the Hawley Vineyard on Bradford Mountain, overlooking the Dry Creek Valley, Hawley now produces five thousand cases of some ten wines each year, from Viognier to Chardonnay, Pinot Noir, and Cabernet, using his own grapes and those of several other noted Sonoma growers. Sons Paul, director of the 2008 wine spoof *Corked*, and Austin now run the show.

Wine quality has been varied over the years, with Chardonnay and Zinfandel leading the way and seemingly every variety produced making the grade in some years and falling short in others. Still, this is a winery with potential, as its many successes indicate.

HOOK & LADDER VINEYARDS 2004		Map 8
www.hookandladderwinery.com	707-546-5712	Tasting
Santa Rosa	Sonoma County	Russian River Valley AVA

In 1970, San Francisco firefighter Cecil De Loach and wife Christine acquired twenty-four acres of old-vine Zinfandel grapes in the Russian River Valley and started making De Loach wines in '75, growing to a substantial winery that De Loach sold to French winemaker Boisset in '03. In 2004, De Loach and the next two generations started the Hook & Ladder winery. With 375 acres of vineyards still cultivated by the De Loach family, Hook & Ladder now produces some thirty thousand cases of a dozen moderately priced wines under the guidance of winemaker Jason De Loach, Cecil's grandson.

Wines have been adequate for the prices asked, but, at those moderate prices, one does not expect a lot of scores above 90 points.

HOP KILN WINERY 1975		Map 8
www.hopkilnwinery.com	707-433-6491	Tasting
Healdsburg	Sonoma County	Russian River Valley AVA

The drop-dead gorgeous early twentieth-century stone hop kiln, originally built to cook hops for beermakers, dominates the hillside premises overlooking the Russian River. Acquired by physician Marty Griffin in the 1970s and converted to a winery, Hop Kiln has a forty-five-acre vineyard that contributes fruit to the production of ten thousand cases of ten varieties, including several proprietary blends (Big Red and Thousand Flowers) under the watch of winemaker Erich Bradley. A second label, HK Generations, is reserved for a top-of-the-line Pinot Noir and Chardonnay. The kiln is on state and national registers of historic places and is a must-see along Westside Road just at the start of that area's outstanding Pinot patch.

It is too early to offer definitive commentary on the HK line, but given the outstanding growing area occupied by the winery, these wines have a chance to join the list of attractions from their provenance. Other Hop Kiln wines have been ripe and outgoing when good, but overall quality has been something of a hit-and-miss situation. Nevertheless, we always stop in when in the area because it is a very fine touring visit.

IRON HORSE VINEYARDS 1978		Map 8
www.ironhorsevineyards.com	707-887-1507	Tasting
Sebastopol	Sonoma County	Green Valley of R.R. Valley AVA

In the early 1970s, Audrey and international attorney Barry Sterling (no relation to Napa's Sterling Vineyards) acquired a three-hundred-acre ranch from Rodney Strong that included a railroad junction called Iron Horse. In the early days Fumé Blanc took center stage, but gradually *méthode champenoise* Sparkling Wines came to the fore and approached half of the total winery production. Now run by the next generation, Joy Sterling and brother Laurence, with winemaker David Munksgard, Iron Horse produces over forty-five thousand cases, nearly half of which are composed of six sparkling Cuvées and the remainder a wide range of still wines featuring Chardonnay and Pinot Noir. Most wines, both still and Sparkling, are made with fruit grown on 160 estate acres in the Green Valley.

Iron Horse Sparkling Wines enjoy great popularity based on their rich, slightly open styling and lofty intentions. Scores range as high as 90 points and generally lead those for its table wines.

J VINEYARDS 1987		Map 8
www.jwine.com	888-594-6326	Tasting
Healdsburg	Sonoma County	Russian River Valley AVA

Judy Jordan, daughter of Tom Jordan of his own winery, decided to go on her own and established her brand, J, in 1987 for the production of Sparkling Wine. Other varieties, principally Pinot Noir and Chardonnay, soon followed and were joined by lesser amounts of other varieties, most notably one of California's most elegant and desirable Pinot Gris. In 1996, the winery purchased the former Piper Sonoma winemaking facility in Healdsburg, in the heart of the Russian River Valley, and has turned it into one of the wine country's most interesting visitor stops, where the house chef works to create wine and food pairings that make you want to come back for more.

Wine quality, always high from the start, remains so today, and with emphasis on a light, airy style of Sparkling Wine, J has regularly pulled in scores of 90 points and higher. Its magnum-sized offering is aged a year longer than the wine in regular-sized bottles and emerges with a rich, creamy, refined character that has made it a great favorite. Vineyard-designated Pinot Noirs have also earned their fair share of plaudits.

JORDAN VINEYARD & WINERY 1976   Map 6

   www.jordanwinery.com   800-654-1213   Tasting by Appointment

   Healdsburg   Sonoma County   Alexander Valley AVA

Tom Jordan came to the county fresh from a successful career in oil and gas exploration in Colorado and acquired 275 acres of prune orchards and another 1,300 acres of woodlands. The orchard would become the estate vineyard planted to Cabernet Sauvignon, Merlot, and Cabernet Franc and used for the production of a single annual Cabernet Sauvignon and Chardonnay, totaling 75,000 cases. From its earliest days, Jordan set out to lift the standards for Alexander Valley wines and succeeded. Lately, however, its wines have been less well received, and even a change of vineyard from the deep soils of midvalley to the sparser soils in the hills behind the winery has not brought about a significant uptick in ratings. Despite the great popularity enjoyed by Jordan wines, most critical evaluations come up no higher than the mid- to upper-80-point range for wines of medium ripeness but little range or richness relative to the competition.

KENDALL-JACKSON 1982   Map 8

   www.kj.com   800-769-3649   Tasting

   Fulton   Sonoma County   Russian River Valley AVA

In 1974, San Francisco attorneys Jess Jackson and then-wife Jane Kendall acquired an 80-acre pear and walnut orchard in Lakeport, which was converted to vineyards. Building on the success of Vintner's Reserve Chardonnay. K-J expanded production into virtually every nook and cranny of the California under the auspices of winemaker Randy. Most Kendall-Jackson wine is from grapes grown on the 14,000 acres of owned vineyards and almost every popular variety is offered. Jackson expanded vertically as well, with several tiers of select, vineyard-specific and other niche varietals. Production is well over four million cases from some thirty-five wineries around the world operating under the Jackson Wine Estates umbrella.

Quality ranges from adequately appropriate for the simple, correct wines under the Vintner's Reserve monicker to much higher for special bottlings with concomitant increases in quality for very correct, expressive wines drawn from very good vineyards.

KISTLER VINEYARDS 1978		Map 8
www.kistlervineyards.com	707-823-5603	No Tasting
Sebastopol	Sonoma County	Russian River Valley AVA

Steve and John Kistler acquired land in the 1970s on a Mayacamas Mountains ridge two thousand feet above the Sonoma Valley. Their first vintage, in 1979, produced a Pinot Noir and a Chardonnay, the only varieties made to this day. Under winemaker Mark Bixler, Kistler makes twenty-five thousand cases each year with much of the wine made from the grapes grown on their sixty acres of vineyards; the remainder comes from such Sonoma vineyards as Dutton Ranch, Durell, and Hudson.

Kistler wines are highly regarded, sought after, and expensive but generally worth it, with scores of 90 points and higher the rule rather than the exception. The Chardonnays, especially, are rich, complex affairs, usually with very good balancing acidity.

KORBEL CHAMPAGNE CELLARS 1882		Map 8
www.korbel.com	707-824-7000	Tasting
Guerneville	Sonoma County	Russian River Valley AVA

The reigning champion when it comes to the quantity of *méthode champenoise* Sparkling Wine, Korbel continues its role as the leading purveyor of bottle-fermented bubbly in the United States. Its products are among the lowest priced of the type but are consistent in their serviceability. The winery operates out of its attractive location along River Road in Guerneville, and both the ride out there and reception when you arrive are worth the visit as a break from the upmarket wineries that are the centerpieces of vinous life in the Russian River Valley. The winery today controls two thousand acres of vineyard, some of which are visible in the rolling hills surrounding the winery, and it also draws grapes from all over California for its various products. In addition, Korbel Brandy is the sales leader in its category.

Over the years, we have been more favorably impressed by Korbel's Brut Rosé, Blanc de Noir, and sparkling Chardonnay; each rates, more often than not, among our highest recommendations for value. The style is more commercial than special, but with most of the production selling for $12 or so, we have no argument with the way the wines are made.

KOSTA BROWNE WINERY 1997   Map 8

    www.kostabrowne.com   707-823-7430   No Tasting

    Sebastopol   Sonoma County   Russian River Valley AVA

Michael Browne and Dan Kosta were working at the highly regarded John Ash restaurant when they decided to make a little wine on their own. With old and rustic equipment, they started in business and by 2001 had partnered with Chris Costello and acquired both the business management acumen and the local contacts to begin to grow. Now, the winery is heading toward ten thousand cases of production, almost all consisting of some dozen separate Pinot Noirs and one Syrah. The appellation bottlings, labeled Russian River and Sonoma Coast, are the volume leaders at approximately three thousand cases apiece, while the many vineyard designates make up the rest. Grapes are sourced from leading growers both in Sonoma County and the Santa Lucia Highlands. Kosta Browne has very quickly become one of the most sought-after names among Pinot Noir producers. As of 2009, investors Vincraft have taken controlling interest.

Recent vintages from Kosta Browne have ranged from 90 points to the upper 90s. The appellation bottlings, while not inexpensive, also earn big-time plaudits and have become special-occasion wines on their own. These are wines of great depth, concentrated fruit, keen varietal focus, and the promise of plenty of age worthiness for the variety. Great Web site.

KUNDE ESTATE WINERY & VINEYARDS 1904   Map 9

    www.kunde.com   707-833-5501   Tasting

    Kenwood   Sonoma County   Sonoma Valley AVA

Founder Louis Kunde emigrated from Germany and, in 1904, acquired the thousand-acre Wildwood Vineyards, originally planted by grower John Drummond in 1879 with Cabernet Sauvignon cuttings from Châteaux Margaux and Lafite Rothschild. The Kunde family made wine until World War II but continued to grow grapes, which they sold to Sebastiani and other nearby producers. In 1990, in a newly built winery, Kunde restarted its winemaking business, now under the supervision of the fourth and fifth generation of Kundes and winemaker Tim Bell. Six discreet estate

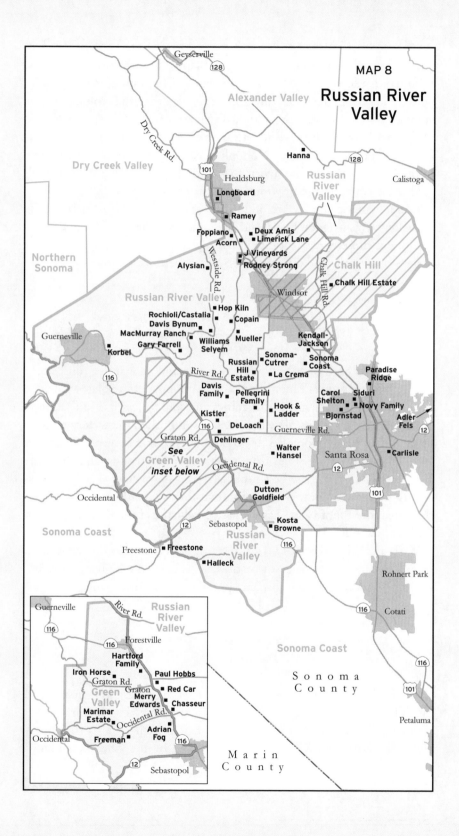

MAP 8

Russian River Valley

Geyserville

128

Alexander Valley

Dry Creek Valley

Dry Creek Rd.

101

Healdsburg

Longboard

Ramey

Foppiano

Acorn

Deux Amis

Limerick Lane

J Vineyards

Rodney Strong

Alysian

Westside Rd.

Russian River Valley

Hop Kiln

Rochioli/Castalia

Davis Bynum

MacMurray Ranch

Gary Farrell

Korbel

Guerneville

116

Williams Selyem

Copain

Mueller

River Rd.

Russian Hill Estate

Davis Family

Kistler

DeLoach

Graton Rd.

116

Dehlinger

See Green Valley inset below

Occidental Rd.

Occidental

Sonoma Coast

Freestone

Freestone

Halleck

Sebastopol

12

116

Russian River Valley

Hanna

128

Calistoga

Russian River Valley

Chalk Hill Rd.

Chalk Hill

Chalk Hill Estate

Windsor

Kendall-Jackson

Sonoma-Cutrer

Sonoma Coast

La Crema

Pellegrini Family

Hook & Ladder

Guerneville Rd.

Walter Hansel

Santa Rosa

12

Paradise Ridge

Carol Shelton

Siduri

Novy Family

Bjornstad

Adler Fels

12

Carlisle

101

Dutton-Goldfield

Kosta Browne

Rohnert Park

116

Cotati

Sonoma Coast

Sonoma County

116

101

Petaluma

Green Valley inset

Guerneville

River Rd.

Russian River Valley

116

116

Forestville

Hartford Family

Iron Horse

Graton Rd.

Green Valley

Marimar Estate

Occidental

Freeman

12

Sebastopol

Paul Hobbs

Red Car

Graton

Merry Edwards

Chasseur

Occidental Rd.

Adrian Fog

116

Marin County

vineyards total over seven hundred acres planted to some twenty varietals. Production exceeds 125,000 cases, of which Chardonnay represents 40 percent, and Cabernet and Sauvignon Blanc are the other volume leaders among a long list of varieties and quality levels offered. The lovely Kunde winery, with its exquisite sylvan setting, is often used by Hollywood's leading lights for their weddings. Not only is Kunde a fine stop in the middle of the Sonoma Valley, but a visit to the winery's attractive Web site will land you a coupon for complimentary tastings at the winery.

Kunde wines generally are midpriced, and we have been partial to its Chardonnay, Sauvignon Blanc, and Zinfandel over the years. If not entirely consistent, those wines will rate in the highly respectable upper-80-point range in most years and offer plenty to like at their asking price.

LA CREMA WINERY 1979		Map 8
www.lacrema.com	800-314-1762	Tasting
Windsor	Sonoma County	Russian River Valley AVA

La Crema was born in a Petaluma warehouse and grew into a full-fledged winery making serious Pinot Noir and Chardonnay. In the late 1980s, the ownership ran into financial difficulties and sold to Jess Jackson's Artisan & Estates cluster of upscale wineries. Jackson pushed the winery to grow to an annual production of 150,000 cases of the same two varieties at two levels: the Appellation series from several Sonoma regions and the Nine Barrel selection from the best nine barrels in the winery. La Crema has a forty-five-acre estate vineyard with two-thirds Chardonnay grapes and the remainder Pinot Noir. Tastings are conducted at the Kendall-Jackson facility in Windsor.

With a checkered history, La Crema does not have a consistent track record. Recent results suggest that the label is being given greater play and attention and suggests that this once proud name is rising again.

LAMBERT BRIDGE WINERY 1975		Map 7
www.lambertbridge.com	800-975-0555	Tasting
Healdsburg	Sonoma County	Dry Creek Valley AVA

In 1969, Gerard Lambert (no relation to C. L. Lambert who first built a ranch here in the 1920s) bought 120 acres and planted a vineyard. In '75 a winery was built with a modest, 5,000-case capacity. In '93 the winery and seventy-five-acre vineyards were acquired by the Chambers family, who run the company today. The production of ten thousand cases is overseen by winemaker Jill Davis, experienced at Beringer, Buena Vista, and William Hill. Merlot and Chardonnay represent about 20 percent of production each, while Sauvignon Blanc and Zinfandel are also well represented. A red Meritage called Crane Creek Cuvée is a fan favorite. Lambert Bridge wines have varied widely in quality over the years, with the full-bodied Merlot and the rich Crane Creek Cuvée leading the way.

LANCASTER ESTATE WINERY 1995		Map 6
www.lancaster-estate.com	707-433-8178	Tasting by Appointment
Healdsburg	Sonoma County	Alexander Valley AVA

Proprietor Ted Simkins was a distributor when he acquired the former Maacama Creek Winery in 1995. In the hills that mark the confluence of the Alexander Valley, Chalk Hill, and Knights Valley AVAs, Lancaster Estate built a winery and caves in '01 to make wine from the fruit of its fifty-acre vineyard. Production stands at about 6,500 cases—all estate-grown, -produced, and -bottled—of Cabernet Sauvignon, Cabernet-based blends, and Sauvignon Blanc under the hand of winemaker Jesse Katz.

Early wines were more rustic than accomplished, but recent vintages, all sturdy in construction, have scored in the 90-point range because of added depth and suggest that Lancaster is hitting its stride as its vines mature and the winemaking team gets a handle on what they are dealing with. The addition of the redoubtable David Ramey as consulting winemaker reinforces the notion of future success.

LANDMARK VINEYARDS 1974		Map 9
www.landmarkwine.com	707-833-0053	Tasting
Kenwood	Sonoma County	Sonoma Valley AVA

Founded by the Mabry family of Sonoma winegrowers, Landmark was acquired by Damaris Deere Ford, great-great-granddaughter of John Deere, in 1989. A move from the urban sprawl of Windsor to Kenwood was followed by construction of a new winery and planting of an eleven-acre vineyard. Now run by Mike Deere Colhoun, his wife Mary, and winemaker Eric Stern, Landmark produces twenty-five thousand cases of Chardonnay and Pinot Noir, with a small quantity of Syrah for good measure. Several other Rhône-style varieties should be part of the 2010 vintage.

Chardonnays labeled as Lorenzo and Damaris are the quality leaders, often scoring in the low 90-point range; while the Overlook Chardonnay, a blend from coastal vineyards in both Northern and Southern California, often reaches recommended levels in the upper 80s. Landmark Chardonnays aim for a fruity, juicy center with good acid balance and oaky richness for added range of character.

LAUREL GLEN WINERY 1977		Map 9
www.laurelglen.com	707-526-3914	Tasting
Glen Ellen	Sonoma County	Sonoma Mountain AVA

Patrick Campbell—owner, winemaker, vineyard manager, violist—bought the three-acre Laurel Glen Vineyard and made his first bottle of Cabernet Sauvignon in 1981. The vineyard, now expanded to thirty-five acres on the east-facing slopes of Sonoma Mountain one thousand feet above Glen Ellen, was one of the first in this region, which Campbell pushed for AVA status early on. Campbell now makes small batches of Sonoma Mountain Cabernet using his own fruit, Zinfandel from Lodi grapes, called ZaZin, and Malbec in the Mendoza area of Argentina. Five thousand cases are produced.

Laurel Glen Cabernets were among the first to show the potential of Sonoma Mountain, and Campbell was among the first American vintners to explore the potential of South America, first in Chile and then in Argentina. His tasting room is off-site up north in Geyserville. His front-line Cabernet is balanced with firm fruit and oaky richness. ZaZin reflects its Lodi heritage with evident ripeness and the lush feel of such wines, and its balance and avoidance of excess, all at a very attractive price, make it one of the better-valued Zinfandels around.

LEDSON WINERY & VINEYARDS 1999		Map 9
www.ledson.com	707-537-3810	Tasting
Kenwood	Sonoma County	Sonoma Valley AVA

Owner-winemaker Steve Ledson has created an eye-popping faux Normandy-style winery at which legions of wines are produced. A dozen Zinfandels, eight Merlots, a half-dozen Cabernet Sauvignons, are just the tip of the varietal iceberg here, with some seventy-five total wines made totaling forty-five thousand cases. A thirty-six-acre estate vineyard with Merlot and Zinfandel grapes complements those bought from growers throughout Northern California. Numerous couples have started their married lives here.

Prices are relatively high at Ledson, reflecting the winery's high ambitions and extracted approach to winemaking. The Chardonnays, especially the Reserve, have been more likely to live up to that ambition than other wines. Still, this winery, at the northern end of the Sonoma Valley, makes an interesting stop.

LIMERICK LANE CELLARS 1986		Map 8
www.limericklanewines.com	707-433-9211	No Tasting
Healdsburg	Sonoma County	Russian River Valley AVA

A winery that describes the taste of its first Pinot Noir as "Think lingerie rather than leather" can't be all bad. Former San Francisco firefighter Michael Collins, along with Realtor brother Tom and friend Ted Markoczy, bought thirty acres on Limerick Lane in Healdsburg at the eastern end of the Russian River Valley. For a decade they sold grapes to other winemakers but finally made their own wine, beginning in 1986 with their first Zinfandel. Now Zinfandel accounts for 90 percent of the five-thousand-case production, all made from grapes grown on their thirty-acre estate. Small batches of Pinot Noir, Syrah, and dessert wines round out the roster.

Early results with the berryish, balanced, nicely fruity Zinfandel saw scores ranging up to and above 90 points and put Limerick Lane on the map. Recent results are less encouraging, but the potential remains high. Stay tuned.

LONGBOARD VINEYARDS 1998		Map 8
www.longboardvineyards.com	707-433-3473	Tasting
Healdsburg	Sonoma County	Russian River Valley AVA

Israeli surfer dude Oded Shakked came to the United States to study winemaking at Davis, and the access to the beach kept him from going home. Having spent time at J, where he made some excellent table wines, he has now partnered with Robert Williams and Bruce Lundquist to run Longboard. With the eleven-acre DaKine Vineyard planted to a red field mix, and additional grapes purchased from the likes of Rochioli, Redgrave, and O'Neel vineyards, Longboard produces about ten thousand cases of Syrah (33 percent of volume), Sauvignon Blanc and Merlot (20 percent each), and smaller quantities of Pinot Noir and Cabernet Sauvignon.

The tasting room features, of course, bitchin' vintage surfboards and surfing films.

This is a winery on the rise. Early results with solidly constructed, ripe-fruited Syrah have reached into the 90-point range, and with vineyards of its own along the highly acclaimed Westside Road area and access to other famous properties, Longboard promises to show up regularly on the radar screens of wine lovers.

LOST CANYON WINERY 2001		Map 7
www.lostcanyonwinery.com	707-894-3389	Tasting
Cloverdale	Sonoma County	Dry Creek Valley AVA

Started in 1978 as a home winemaking adventure, partners Jack States, Randy Keyworth, and Bob Riskin established Lost Canyon as a commercial winery in 2001. The Oakland winery offers small lots of vineyard-designated Pinot Noir and Syrah from the Russian River Valley, Carneros, and the Sonoma Coast. Production is in the neighborhood of 2,500 cases, each bottling in the 300- to 500-case range and evenly distributed between Pinot Noir and Syrah, with an occasional Viognier thrown in for good measure. Vineyards sourcing the grapes include Alegria, Dutton Ranch, Las Brisas, and Stage Gulch.

Quality levels have been well above average, with qualitative ratings for the ripe yet decently balanced Pinot Noirs reaching into the 90-point range on occasion. A recent sale to the Fritz Winery principals has seen winemaking shift to the Fritz Winery in Cloverdale from the winery's original home along the waterfront in Oakland.

MACMURRAY RANCH 1941		Map 8
www.macmurrayranch.com	888-668-7729	No Tasting
Healdsburg	Sonoma County	Russian River Valley AVA

Actor-comedian Fred MacMurray bought the 1,500-acre ranch and vineyards, located in a drop-dead gorgeous box canyon off Westside Road, in the early 1940s from the Porter family, whose ancestor Colonel George Porter returned as a Mexican War hero to settle the ranch in 1846. With MacMurray's passing, ownership was taken up by the Gallos, who created a label named after MacMurray. Longtime winemaker Susan Doyle, an Australian with experience in the Yarra Valley and Tasmania, produces limited quantities of Pinot Noir and Pinot Gris from grapes grown on the ranch as well as on the Sonoma and Central coasts.

The vineyard designates have often reached into the 90-point range, but the lower-priced, larger-volume bottlings identified with a broad appellation have only stayed in the middle 80s for the most part. Pinot Gris is fruity in an off-dry, deeply cast manner, and the home-ranch Pinot Noir has also scored well for its keen focus, good manners, and medium depth.

MACROSTIE WINERY & VINEYARDS 1987		Map 9
www.macrostiewinery.com	707-996-4480	Tasting by Appointment
Sonoma	Sonoma County	Carneros AVA

Winemaker Steve MacRostie, who had spent nearly a decade at Hacienda when that label belonged to a highly successful Sonoma Valley winery, founded his own winery in 1987. MacRostie's focus was always on Chardonnay made from grapes grown by the noted Sangiacomo Vineyard. Ten years later, MacRostie planted fifty-eight acres to Chardonnay, Pinot Noir, and Syrah varietals on the Wildcat Mountain Vineyard near the borders of Carneros and the Sonoma Coast appellations. Today's forty-thousand-case production, guided by winemaker Kevin Holt, is derived from the estate vineyard and other Sonoma vineyards including Bennett, Beckstoffer, Sangiacomo, and Durell. Chardonnay still represents 70 percent of production, with Pinot Noir next at 20 percent.

Chardonnay, both the Wildcat Mountain bottling and the Carneros bottling, have been broad successes for their good depth and balance tied to well-focused varietal character and have been recommended in most years with scores ranging mostly in the upper 80s. Wildcat Mountain Syrah, made in a ripe, firm style, has also been a favorite of ours and has been rated at 90 points and over in recent vintages. With prices that are typically lower than those of its nearby competition, MacRostie wines typically offer good value for the money.

MARIETTA CELLARS 1979		Map 6
www.mariettacellars.com	707-433-2747	No Tasting
Geyserville	Sonoma County	Alexander Valley AVA

Chris Bilbro, whose family once owned Bandiera, has long made moderately priced red wines in a small winery just outside Geyserville. As founder-winemaker, Bilbro has a hand in all aspects of the winery, now producing thirty-five thousand cases a year, with Zinfandel the predominant variety. Grapes are sourced from the Alexander Valley and Mendocino for the

Zinfandels, Petite Sirah, Cabernet Sauvignon, and an occasional Port. A proprietary red blend called Old Vine Red is sold only to mailing list members. Angeli Cuvée is a Zinfandel-based blend.

Both ripe, fruity Zinfandel and more complex Angeli Cuvée occasionally rate in the 90-point range, while the Old Vine Red, now hard to find, earned an early reputation as a great value in a rustic red wine reminiscent of wines made decades ago before California wines became more polished.

MARIMAR ESTATE 1986		Map 8
www.marimarestate.com	707-823-4365	Tasting
Sebastopol	Sonoma County	Green Valley of R.R. Valley AVA

Marimar Torres, direct descendant of the renowned Torres wine producer in Spain's Priorat region south of Barcelona, has established a family outpost here in the New World. Marimar Torres settled in San Francisco in the 1970s and started her winery in the 1980s, choosing to locate in the cool Green Valley region near the western edge of the Russian River AVA. The Sonoma estate includes thirty acres of Chardonnay and Pinot Noir grapes in Green Valley known as the Don Miguel Vineyard after her father and another thirty acres of vines recently planted even closer to the Pacific near the burgeoning Freestone area of the Sonoma Coast AVA and known as Doña Marguerita after her mother. All wines are made from estate-grown fruit, and Torres now makes about sixteen thousand cases annually, evenly divided between Chardonnay and Pinot Noir varieties. Marimar Torres is also known for the several books she has written on Spanish cuisine and wine.

With the winery's reliance on cool-climate fruit, a house style stressing bright acidity to go along with fairly ripe grape character has evolved. The wines are often still developing when released and often mature in incredibly rewarding libation as they reach their sixth to eighth birthdays. At times, the wines can seem green and acidic, but the ones that succeed are among the best-balanced, longest-lived versions of the varieties made in California. Because of the house style, ratings can be somewhat inconsistent, but Marimar Estate garners enough ratings in the upper 80s and low to mid-90s to be rightfully considered as a top performer.

MATANZAS CREEK WINERY 1977		Map 9
www.matanzascreek.com	800-590-6464	Tasting
Santa Rosa	Sonoma County	Bennett Valley AVA

Sandra and Bill MacIver founded this small winery and vineyard in the little-known Bennett Valley appellation, in the northwest corner of Sonoma Valley, in the late 1970s. A modest beginning of three thousand cases and forty acres of vineyard grew over time to forty thousand cases and eighty acres of estate plantings today. In 2000, Kendall-Jackson acquired the winery for Jess Jackson's Artisan & Estates group. François Cordesse of France is winemaker, with Merlot the production and popularity leader, though Matanzas Creek also makes Sauvignon Blanc, Chardonnay, Pinot Noir, and Syrah. As a sidelight, an acre has been devoted to commercial production of lavender.

At one point in its history, Matanzas Creek stood out as a quality leader, and while there are the frequent successes still coming from the winery, the wines are less consistent than they were. An upscale Merlot from the nearby Jackson vineyard development in the hills across from the winery called Jackson Park Vineyard is once again raising the sights of this exceptionally handsome winery. It is a place we often visit for its beauty, its wines, its gardens, and because the Bennett Valley, while immediately contiguous to and easily accessible from the very popular Sonoma Valley, is a quieter place.

MAURITSON FAMILY WINERY 1998		Map 7
www.mauritsonwines.com	707-431-0804	Tasting
Healdsburg	Sonoma County	Dry Creek Valley AVA

Mauritson ancestors first planted grapes in Dry Creek Valley in the 1880s, but they shipped the product home to Sweden. Over the years, the family became a major grower, with a total of more than four thousand acres of ranchland and vineyards; three-quarters of that land is now under Lake Sonoma. The sixth generation of the family, represented by winery owner-winemaker Clay Mauritson—a former Oregon linebacker with winemaking experience at Kenwood, Taft Street, and Dry Creek Vineyards—made his first vintage in 1998. Wines are produced from grapes grown on several estate vineyards totaling more than three hundred acres in three locations: the Dry Creek and Alexander valleys and Rockpile. Mauritson is fast heading toward the ten-thousand-case capacity of its new winery facility, with Zinfandel leading the varietal pack with nearly 50 percent of total production. Sauvignon Blanc represents 30 percent and Cabernet Sauvignon another 10 percent.

Mauritson Zinfandels under the family name and also labeled as Rockpile are highly ripened, rich, focused on ripe blackberries and often high achievers, with critical ratings reaching into the lower and mid-90-point range. The winery, located along the middle of the Dry Creek Valley, makes a pleasant stop. The Rockpile Zinfandel has only an *M* hidden at the lower corner of the label to identify its familial lines.

MAZZOCCO VINEYARDS 1984		Map 7
www.mazzocco.com	800-501-8466	Tasting
Healdsburg	Sonoma County	Dry Creek Valley AVA

Prominent eye surgeon Dr. Thomas Mazzocco acquired an eighteen-acre Chardonnay vineyard in the Alexander Valley named River Lane. Subsequently, an additional thirteen acres of Cabernet Sauvignon were planted. The winery changed hands several times in the 1990s until Ken and Diane Wilson, of their 220-acre eponymous vineyards nearby, bought the winery and 20-acre estate vineyard. Today some fifteen thousand cases are produced in Sonoma County, Vineyard-Designated, and Reserve lines, with Zinfandel the leader at 40 percent of volume. Another 30 percent is Chardonnay and 15 percent each of Cabernet and Merlot. Winemaker–general manager Antoine Favero has pedigrees from UC–Davis, Sebastiani, and Gundlach-Bundschu.

Over the years, Mazzocco wines have changed styles, and, now under the Wilsons' leadership, you can count on wines that are extremely high in ripeness, concentrated in character, and of a style that aficionados of large-scaled wines will love but others will find over-the-top.

MERRY EDWARDS WINES 1973		Map 8
www.merryedwards.com	888-388-9050	Tasting by Appointment
Sebastopol	Sonoma County	Russian River Valley AVA

With a degree in hand from UC–Davis, Edwards learned winemaking from the ground up, making wines for others—such as Mount Eden, Matanzas Creek, Liparita, Lambert Bridge, and Fritz—for over a quarter century. The first Merry Edwards–labeled wines were made in 1997. Edwards planted her first vineyard acreage in 1998, the twenty-four-acre Meredith Estate Vineyard in the Sonoma Coast region, and later an additional nine acres on the Russian River Valley Coopersmith Vineyard. Merry Edwards has become, dare we say, a cult wine, producing several Pinot Noir varieties and a Sauvignon Blanc from her estate vineyards and others in the county such as Pellegrini's Olivet Lane and Klopp Ranch

Vineyards. Production approaches fifteen thousand cases, mostly of Pinot Noir.

From her early days at Mount Eden right up to the present day, Edwards has shown a magic touch with Pinot Noir. Most of her many Pinots rate above 90 points, and the best have jumped up to and past 95 points in virtually every vintage. Moreover, her deep, tightly fruited, well-focused Sauvignon Blanc, although not inexpensive for the variety, is also one of the most highly regarded renditions of that variety; it, too, has regularly earned ratings up in the mid-90s.

MILL CREEK VINEYARDS & WINERY 1974		Map 7
www.millcreekwinery.com	877-349-2121	Tasting
Healdsburg	Sonoma County	Dry Creek Valley AVA

The Kreck family settled in Sonoma County and first planted vines in 1965 and blended its first vintage in '74, followed by building a winery in '76. The '77 vintage Cabernet Sauvignon was light in color, so it was named Cabernet Blush. The subsequent rage for "blush" wines was a windfall for the Krecks, who had craftily (or luckily) trademarked the term *Blush* and have received royalties for its use on labels ever since. Now operated by the third generation, Mill Creek makes a full line of wines, led by Sauvignon Blanc (at 25 percent of the ten-thousand-case annual production), Merlot (another 25 percent), and Chardonnay and Cabernet Sauvignon (each 20 percent). All wines are estate grown and bottled, using Sauvignon Blanc, Chardonnay, Merlot, and Cabernet grapes from a fifty-five-acre vineyard in the Dry Creek Valley and an eight-acre Cabernet vineyard in the Alexander Valley.

Mill Creek wines are reasonably priced; and while they do not often pick up the highest critical rankings, they are nevertheless very often worth the asking price. Lately, both Sauvignon Blanc and Syrah have outperformed their price point competition and are well worth pursuing.

MUELLER WINERY 1992		Map 8
www.muellerwine.com	707-837-7399	Tasting by Appointment
Windsor	Sonoma County	Russian River Valley AVA

Veteran winemaker Robert Mueller made wine for many others before building his own small winery and launching the Mueller label in the early 1990s. Grapes are sourced from vineyards in the Russian River Valley, with

Jim Ledbetter's Vino Farms a frequent contributor. Four thousand cases are produced with Pinot Noir, Chardonnay, and Pinot Gris leading the pack, each with about 25 percent of the total. Smaller lots of Zinfandel and Syrah are also offered.

The winery's nicely focused Pinot Noirs have been the quality leaders with ratings into the mid-90s in top efforts, and Chardonnay has not trailed far behind.

MURPHY-GOODE ESTATE WINERY 1985		Map 6
www.murphygoodewinery.com	800-400-7644	Tasting
Geyserville	Sonoma County	Alexander Valley AVA

Vineyard developer Tim Murphy, vineyard manager Dale Goode, and winemaker David Ready collaborated on the creation of the winery, using three hundred acres of combined Alexander Valley vineyard holdings as the basis of this fully estate-grown and -bottled winery. Originally noted for its Fumé Blanc and Chardonnay, over time the emphasis shifted to red varieties, with Cabernet Sauvignon—including several Cabernet-based Clarets—and Merlot leading the way. Production is heading toward 150,000 cases annually, including the inexpensive second label Tin Roof. Jess Jackson of Kendall-Jackson purchased the winery, but not all the vineyards, in 2006.

Over the years, Sauvignon Blanc in its various guises and Zinfandel have been the quality leaders. Recent Zinfandels have been somewhat elevated in ripeness but have succeeded because they have also carried attractive berryish fruit.

NALLE WINERY 1984		Map 7
www.nallewinery.com	707-433-1040	Tasting
Healdsburg	Sonoma County	Dry Creek Valley AVA

Doug Nalle, with wife Lee and son Andrew, run this small producer, making 2,000 to 2,500 cases, principally of Zinfandel with small bottlings of Pinot Noir and Chardonnay for good measure. Some grapes are grown on the estate vineyard, with the bulk coming from other growers, in particular Hopkins Ranch in the Russian River Valley. Winemaker Doug Nalle had wide experience, from Jordan to Souverain to Quivira, before putting it to work on his own label. Illustrator Bob Johnson's cartoons are featured on each year's label, and the Web site doesn't take itself seriously. The winery houses a pétanque court and horseshoe pit for visitors.

Zinfandel may be the volume leader, but the Hopkins Ranch Pinot Noir has scored better of late. The Zins tend to be medium to full-bodied with relatively high acidity for the variety.

NOVY FAMILY WINES 1998		Map 8
www.novyfamilywines.com	707-578-3882	Tasting by Appointment
Santa Rosa	Sonoma County	Russian River Valley

Novy is the newer expression of Siduri's owners-winemakers Adam and Dianna (Novy) Lee and their families, and the Novy wines are made in the same facility as the Siduri bottlings. While Siduri focused exclusively on Pinot Noir, Novy makes principally Syrahs with a few excursions into Zinfandel, Chardonnay, and the occasional dessert wine. The Lees were wine retailers in Texas who took the plunge to "build" their warehouse winery, making an extensive list of single-vineyard bottlings sourced from twenty-five or more excellent vineyards ranging from Oregon's Willamette Valley to Santa Lucia Highlands in Monterey County with names such as Garys', Rosella's, and Pisoni vineyards. Novy Family Wines makes five thousand cases, of which Syrah represents 85 percent.

Siduri Pinot Noirs are among California's best, and while Novy has yet to reach that exalted level, the label does rate well more often than not. The Syrahs are, not surprisingly, more full and expressive than the winery's Siduri Pinot Noirs, but they have lacked the special grace that is so much a part of the Siduri line.

PAPAPIETRO PERRY WINERY 1998		Map 7
www.papapietro-perry.com	877-467-4668	Tasting
Healdsburg	Sonoma County	Russian River Valley AVA

Another Sonoma Pinot Noir specialist, Papapietro Perry was founded by San Francisco newspapermen Ben Papapietro and Bruce Perry, friends who shared an interest in garage winemaking. (Fellow employee Bert Williams contemporaneously created Williams Selyem wines.) In 1998, Papapietro and Perry established their winery, and the early vintages were well received. Winemaker Ben oversees the production of more than five thousand cases of Pinot Noir (two-thirds of production) and Zinfandel (one-third) with fruit from several noted growers in the Russian River and Dry Creek valleys, including Elsbree, Pauline's, and Charles vineyards.

Its wines never lack for ripeness, but with great vineyards and solid wine-making, Papapietro Perry Pinot Noirs regularly rank above 90 points and are widely recognized as important members of the Russian River Pinot brigade.

PARADISE RIDGE WINERY 1991		Map 8
www.prwinery.com	707-528-9463	Tasting
Santa Rosa	Sonoma County	Russian River Valley AVA

In the late 1970s, Holland-born Walter Byck and the late Marijke Byck-Hoenselaars discovered what was to become their 156-acre estate in the hills just north of Santa Rosa near the site of the historic Fountain Grove Winery. Seventeen acres were planted to Chardonnay and Sauvignon Blanc, and in '91 they built their winery. Today the winery is owned and run by the next generation, Rene Byck and Sonia Byck-Barwick, with Dan Barwick serving as winemaker. Four thousand to five thousand cases are bottled each year; Syrah and Cabernet Sauvignon lead the way with about 25 percent of production each.

Hidden up the hill and behind housing subdivisions, this handsome winery and its extraordinary sculpture garden are well worth the few minutes' diversion needed to be found. Once there, you will find lots to like both on the grounds and in the tasting room. At some point or other, almost every wine in the Paradise Ridge portfolio has scored 90 points and higher. Its Rockpile-grown Cabernet Sauvignon is big and rich, while its Sauvignon Blanc is bright and rich.

PAUL HOBBS WINERY 1991		Map 8
www.paulhobbs.com	707-824-9879	Tasting by Appointment
Sebastopol	Sonoma County	Russian River Valley AVA

The well-traveled Paul Hobbs learned winemaking at UC–Davis, Robert Mondavi, and Simi before plying his trade as a consulting winemaker in Chile and Argentina, in the last of which he founded Vina Cobos in the Mendoza region of Argentina. Hobbs started his own winery in 1991 focused on single-vineyard Chardonnay, Cabernet Sauvignon, and Pinot Noir, now making a dozen or more individual bottlings, totaling ten thousand cases a year. The winery's great success relies both on some of California's finest vineyards and on Hobbs's ability to extract and deliver on the potential of the grapes he gets. Hobbs wines never lack for depth or richness, but their success is based on the balance of elements that allows every aspect of the wine to show well.

Hobbs has used the fruit from notables like Hyde and Beckstoffer To Kalon for Cabernet Sauvignon, Hyde and Valdez for Pinot Noir, and Richard Dinner and Kent Ritchie for Chardonnay—each of which has topped the charts at some point in the mid- to upper 90s. The *San Francisco Chronicle* recently dubbed Hobbs "a supernova in the cult wine galaxy." Although we might shy away from such terminology, we did name Hobbs as the Connoisseurs' Guide Winery of the Year in 2008 because virtually every wine offered matched or outpointed its peers in that year, including our two highest-rated wines of the year.

PEDRONCELLI WINERY 1927		Map 7
www.pedroncelli.com	800-836-3894	Tasting
Geyserville	Sonoma County	Dry Creek Valley AVA

The third generation of the Pedroncelli family continues to make wine where John Pedroncelli Sr. started in 1927. The family managed the transition, in the '60s and '70s, from bulk wines to varietals. With 105 acres of vineyards on several Dry Creek Valley locations and grapes purchased from some dozen other area growers, Pedroncelli makes seventy thousand cases of a wide range of wines, from Zinfandel to Cabernet Sauvignon to Chardonnay, all sold at modest prices.

There are as many misses as hits here, but the hits always rank as good values, and the ripe Zinfandel has often been the winery's best offering.

PELLEGRINI FAMILY VINEYARDS 1933		Map 8
www.pellegrinisonoma.com	800-891-0244	Tasting by Appointment
Santa Rosa	Sonoma County	Russian River Valley AVA

The third and fourth generations of Pellegrinis are now running the winery and vineyards under the direction of Robert Pellegrini and winemaker Kevin Hamel (formerly of Preston). The ancestors had emigrated from Tuscany early in the twentieth century and established one of the first vineyards in the county. After Prohibition, the family turned to winemaking to complement their vineyards. There are now three vineyards, Olivet Lane, Cloverdale Ranch, and Eight Cousins, in the Russian River and Alexander valleys totaling 130 acres of vines. The thirty-five-thousand-case production includes about a dozen different wines, all estate grown and bottled at a new winemaking facility.

Wines from the home vineyard on Olivet Lane, including those made by others like Merry Edwards, tend to be bright in acidity and precise in fruit. Most wines have earned scores in the upper 80s to the low 90s, and they are often among the better values from the area.

PETER MICHAEL WINERY 1982		Map 11
www.petermichaelwinery.com 707-942-4459		No Tasting
Calistoga	Sonoma County	Knights Valley AVA

London technology businessman Sir Peter Michael bought vacation property overlooking the Knights Valley and began developing small vineyards that would grow to a total of nearly fifty planted acres on the western slopes of Mount St. Helena at elevations from one thousand to two thousand feet. In the late 1980s, Michael built what would remain the only winery in the Knights Valley appellation; the winery was built in two parts, one for white wines and the other for reds. The first winemaker was the legendary Helen Turley; today's is Nicolas Morlet from the Champagne region with experience in France and at Joseph Phelps in California. Twelve thousand cases of single-vineyard wines are made, with Chardonnay leading the list. Two Cabernet Sauvignon-based proprietary reds are made with the names Les Pavots (the poppies) and L'Espirit des Pavots. A single Pinot Noir is made from grapes grown by Pisoni Vineyards in Santa Lucia Highlands in Monterey County.

Hard to find and expensive, Peter Michael wines regularly earn ratings in the upper 80s to mid-90s and are considered among the elite of the California offerings. They are universally deep, rich, complete, and complex.

PEZZI KING VINEYARDS 1993		Map 7
www.pezziking.com	800-411-4758	Tasting by Appointment
Healdsburg	Sonoma County	Dry Creek Valley AVA

San Franciscan James Rowe bought this 135-acre estate and winery in 1993 and gradually rebuilt the west-facing hillside vineyards to 110 acres while upgrading the winery into a state-of-the-art facility. Today, about a dozen wines, all estate grown and bottled, comprise the thirty-thousand-case production; they include Cabernet Sauvignon, Zinfandel, and Chardonnay as the leading varieties. Winemaker Patrick Saboe, replacing longtime overseer Paul Brasset in 2007, brings extensive experience at the likes of Hanna and Keller wineries.

The winery's early penchant for wholly inconsistent results has steadied of late, and recently reviewed wines have clustered in the respectable mid- to upper-80-point range.

PRESTON OF DRY CREEK 1973		Map 7
www.prestonvineyards.com · 707-433-3372		Tasting
Healdsburg	Sonoma County	Dry Creek Valley AVA

Dairy farmer Lou Preston and his family developed 115 acres of vineyards in the early 1970s with the intention of selling most of his crops to other vintners. But Preston started making his own wines in '73—Sauvignon Blanc, Zinfandel and Cabernet Sauvignon—and built a winery in '82 for production of his burgeoning roster of wines, reaching a peak of thirty thousand cases made in '89. In the 1990s, Preston cut back on production to the current eight thousand cases in favor of maintaining other crops, such as vegetables and olives, all farmed organically. Today's wines include the original varieties and a range of Rhône varieties such as Mourvèdre, Roussanne, Marsanne, and Viognier.

If quality is not always consistent at this iconoclastic producer, it has been high enough to make Preston an important player in the production of Rhône varieties. Recent reviews of Viognier, Marsanne, Zinfandel, and Sauvignon Blanc have all touched 90 points and keep Preston top of mind for Dry Creek Valley visits. Few wineries are as welcoming to drop-in visitors—or as warmly funky. Sip a glass on the patio, pet the never-ending supply of cats, and enjoy Lou's specialty breads.

QUIVIRA VINEYARDS 1981		Map 7
www.quivirawine.com	800-292-8339	Tasting
Healdsburg	Sonoma County	Dry Creek Valley AVA

Henry and Holly Wendt acquired land on the west side of the Dry Creek Valley in the early 1980s and developed a vineyard that would grow to ninety acres today, permitting the winery to make all of its wines with estate-grown fruit. Production is currently in the thirty-thousand-case range, with Zinfandel leading the way at about 45 percent of production, followed closely by Sauvignon Blanc. Second label Steelhead is used for larger-batch, lower-priced Zinfandel and Sauvignon Blanc. The Wendts sold the winery to Pete Knight in 2006. The winery has taken a strong environmentally friendly stand with its solar panels, biodynamic farming, and support for the revitalization of Wine Creek and the return of wild steelhead runs.

Wine quality has always been high over both ownerships, with both Zinfandel and Sauvignon Blanc scoring well, often into the 90-point area, and offering lots to like at the prices asked.

RAMEY WINE CELLARS 1996		Map 8
www.rameywine.com	707-433-0870	Tasting by Appointment
Healdsburg	Sonoma County	Sonoma County AVA

David Ramey found his way to winemaking through the classic route: UC–Davis to Château Pétrus in France to Chalk Hill to Matanzas Creek to Dominus Estate to Rudd Estate. As winemaker for these notable wineries, Ramey helped build their reputations but finally put his own on the line in 1996 when he and his wife, Carla, founded their own label. Ramey, as owner and winemaker, produces some twelve thousand cases of Cabernet Sauvignon, Chardonnay and Syrah from some of the best vineyards in Sonoma and Napa counties (prestigious names such as Ritchie, Hyde, Hudson, Rodgers Creek, and Jericho Canyon). Ramey produces primarily appellation-specific bottlings in moderate quantities and chart-topping single-vineyard wines in limited quantities.

Ramey Chardonnays have been so good over the years, knocking down blockbuster scores from the low to the upper 90s in virtually every outing, that they have somewhat shaded the successes of its reds, both Cabernet and Syrah. Needless to say, Ramey's wines are not to be missed. And David Ramey's consulting gigs at places like Rodney Strong have yielded similar results in the initial outing among the winery's priciest Chardonnays and Cabernet Sauvignons. Expect Ramey Chardonnays, whether the appellation bottlings or the fancier vineyard designates, to be ripe, wonderfully fruity and complex, with plenty of vital acidity.

RANCHO ZABACO WINERY 1994		Map 7
www.ranchozabaco.com	866-972-6246	No Tasting
Healdsburg	Sonoma County	Dry Creek Valley AVA

E & J Gallo created this label in the early 1990s, based on one of the earliest Mexican land grants called Tzabaco Rancho. Originally called Zabaco Vintners, the current version produces a range of Zinfandels focused first on moderately priced offerings but also featuring pricey, limited edition

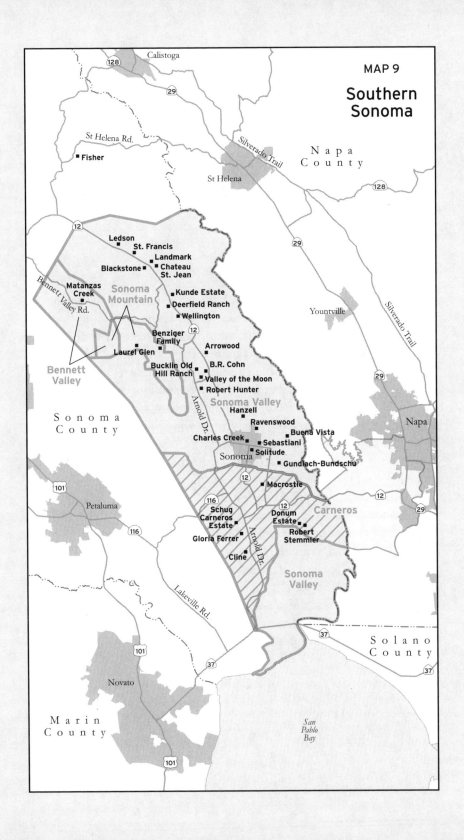

MAP 9

Southern Sonoma

Calistoga

128

29

St Helena Rd.

Silverado Trail

N a p a
C o u n t y

■ Fisher

St Helena

128

12

Ledson
■   St. Francis
■
Landmark
Blackstone   ■ Chateau
■   ■ St. Jean

Matanzas
Creek
■   Sonoma
Mountain

Bennett Valley Rd.

■ Kunde Estate

■ Deerfield Ranch

■ Wellington

Yountville

29

Silverado Trail

29

Benziger
Family
■
Laurel Glen
■

12

■ Arrowood

Bennett
Valley

Bucklin Old
Hill Ranch
■   ■ B.R. Cohn
■
■ Valley of the Moon
■ Robert Hunter

S o n o m a
C o u n t y

Sonoma Valley
■ Hanzell

■ Ravenswood
■
Charles Creek ■ ■ Buena Vista
■ ■ Sebastiani
■ Solitude
Sonoma   ■ Gundlach-Bundschu

Napa

Arnold Dr.

101

Petaluma

116

12

■ Macrostie

116
Schug
Carneros
Estate ■
■ Gloria Ferrer

12

■ Donum
Estate

Carneros

12

29

■ Cline

Arnold Dr.

■ Robert
Stemmler

Sonoma
Valley

101

Lakeville Rd.

37

S o l a n o
C o u n t y

101

37

37

37

Novato

M a r i n
C o u n t y

San
Pablo
Bay

101

bottlings from the famed Monte Rosso Vineyard, acquired by Gallo as part of its purchase of the Louis Martini Winery. Total production is in excess of one hundred thousand cases, which includes the low-priced second label Dancing Bull.

Most of the lower-priced offerings have proven to be reasonable values, while the expensive bottlings have often stressed very high ripeness and have had high appeal to the limited audience for that style.

RAVENSWOOD WINERY 1976		Map 9
www.ravenswood-wine.com	888-669-4679	Tasting
Sonoma	Sonoma County	Sonoma Valley AVA

Co-owner and winemaker Joel Peterson was raised by East Bay chemists and earnest wine aficionados. His father was a founder of the influential wine-tasting group, the Vintners Club, in San Francisco, and his mother, Francis, later became a major contributor to one of the early wine newsletters. Peterson inherited the bug and apprenticed with Zinfandel guru Joseph Swan in the early 1970s and then made his first wine in 1976, a whopping 350 cases. By 1981, Peterson and partner Reed Foster built their own winery, with Zinfandel the continuing focus, and built it into a qualitative leader. Over the years, at a time when red wines were growing in popularity, the winery made vast numbers of bottlings at every level, from the top-drawer vineyard designates—featuring Sangiacomo, Teldeschi, Old Hill, and Big River vineyards—to the midlevel County Series to the modestly priced bulk Vintners Blend. In 2001, international conglomerate Constellation Brands purchased Ravenswood. Today over a million cases are produced, with well over three-quarters the many Zinfandel labels. The Web site is worth perusal.

Joel Peterson maintains his hands-on role in making the limited production vineyard-designate Zinfandels, and their early success has continued right up to the present, with lots of ratings rising into the low to mid-90s and keeping Ravenswood at the top of the Zinfandel leader board. The vineyard-designated Zinfandels never lack for ripeness and, true to the Peterson preference, are high in enlivening acidity. The Old Hill bottling is the boldest, toughest of the lot.

RED CAR WINE 2000		Map 8
www.red-car-wine.com	707-829-8500	Tasting
Graton	Sonoma County	Sonoma Coast AVA

Film industry Angelinos Carroll Kemp, a producer and garage winemaker, and the late Mark Estrin, a screenwriter, established the winery in 2000, making a mere fifty cases in the first release. The winery was named Red Car in homage to the defunct trolley system that served the Los Angeles basin for decades. Today, Sonoma County is the HQ, as the migration north began in 2004 with grapes almost exclusively from the Sonoma Coast appellation, though currently the wines are made in rented space in Santa Maria. Several tiers of wines are produced, principally of Pinot Noir and Syrah varieties. Several small estate vineyards, all in the Sonoma Coast area, are beginning to bear fruit. Total production runs to 6,500 cases, of which two-thirds are Pinot and Syrah bottlings.

Syrahs bearing such intriguing names as Tomorrowland and Fight, as well as the new Cuvée 22, made in a more refined style, have earned top-of-the-table ratings all the way past the 95-point level at times.

ROBERT HUNTER WINERY 1980		Map 9
www.roberthunterwinery.com 707-966-3056		Tasting by Appointment
Sonoma	Sonoma County	Sonoma Valley AVA

Bob and Ann Hunter began with their forty-two-acre Hunter Farms Vineyard growing Chardonnay, Pinot Noir, Cabernet Sauvignon, and Merlot grapes. Early production focused on Brut de Noirs Sparkling Wine, and that wine remains a constant. It is one of the longer-aged bubblies offered in California and is now joined in the line by tables wines made from the winery's other estate-grown grapes. Bob Hunter's son, Robert III, whose winemaking career has seen him making outstanding wines at places like Markham and Sterling in the Napa Valley, now has his hand on the winemaking regimen at the family winery. The winery is located at the back of the family's lovely property off Arnold Drive in the Sonoma Valley.

ROBERT STEMMLER WINERY 1976		Map 9
www.robertstemmlerwinery.com 800-939-2293		Tasting
Sonoma	Sonoma County	Carneros AVA

Born in Germany and trained as a winemaker, Robert Stemmler came to California and worked in the business for Inglenook, Krug, and Simi before starting his own label while a consultant. By 1982, Stemmler was making ten thousand cases based on his reputation for Pinot Noir. In '89, Racke USA, owners of Buena Vista, acquired the Stemmler winery, though Robert continued his own production. In '01, Racke sold Buena Vista to Allied Domecq but kept the Donum Estate Vineyard, the largest of three Stemmler vineyards at seventy acres in the Carneros District. Production, under owner Anne Moller-Racke and winemaker Kenneth Juhasz, stands at twelve thousand cases today, largely composed of several Pinot Noir estate bottlings, with a Chardonnay and Vin Gris made in smaller bottlings. The Donum name appears on the "reserve-level" Pinot Noir, and Donum and Stemmler wines are made in the same winery by the same winemaker.

The Stemmler Pinot Noirs, including a bottling from the Russian River Valley, and Donum edition are typically rated in the low to mid-90s and make Stemmler and Donum names to remember.

ROBERT YOUNG ESTATE WINERY 1963		Map 6
www.ryew.com	707-431-4811	Tasting
Geyserville	Sonoma County	Alexander Valley AVA

Peter Young came from upstate New York for the Gold Rush in 1858 and stayed for the farming. The fifth generation now runs the Robert Young Winery on their 500-acre estate, 320 acres of which are planted to Chardonnay, Merlot, and Cabernet Sauvignon. Other crops are also grown, but the majority of the fruit goes toward estate Chardonnay, Merlot, and Cabernet, including a Cabernet-based blend, Scion. Winemaker Kevin Warren, from Krug and Belvedere, makes about 7,500 cases annually, ranging from a Chardonnay representing half of the output to small, vineyard-block-specific Cabernets made in 150-case lots.

Wine quality has been good, if occasionally inconsistent, with scores ranging from the mid-80s to lower 90s. Both Chardonnay and Scion have shared in the successes and are capable of delivering real drinking pleasure in good vintages. The wines have tended to be ripe and balanced, with more finesse than bombast to their personalities.

ROCHIOLI VINEYARDS & WINERY 1979		Map 8
www.rochioliwinery.com	707-433-2305	Tasting
Healdsburg	Sonoma County	Russian River Valley AVA

The Rochioli family has farmed in the Russian River Valley since the 1930s, becoming one of the noted early grape growers. They started making their own wines with a thousand-case first vintage in '82 and grew slowly to the current ten-thousand-case annual production of Pinot Noir (at over 50 percent), Chardonnay, and Sauvignon Blanc. Under winemaker Tom Rochioli—representing the third generation—Rochioli has made its name on its estate wines as well as on selling grapes from the 125-acre Rochioli Vineyards to the likes of Gary Farrell and Williams-Selyem. Rochioli's longer production items are marketed by the international drinks conglomerate Terlato Wines Group, but his limited-production and highly sought-after wines are available only by mailing list.

Based on his location in the very center of Pinot's sweet spot along Westside Road, Rochioli Pinot Noirs, always high in ripe and finely focused fruit, whether under his own label or bottled by others, are among the highest rated in California and are significantly responsible for the widely recognized and admired reputation of Russian River Valley Pinots.

RODNEY STRONG VINEYARDS 1959		Map 8
www.rodneystrong.com	800-678-4763	Tasting
Healdsburg	Sonoma County	Russian River Valley AVA

Founded some fifty years ago by the late Rod Strong, a professional dancer trained in ballet, who, having performed on Broadway, developed a love of wine while dancing in Paris. As his professional career was winding down, he moved into the wine business by starting a brand called Tiburon Vintners, an operation out of an old house in that Marin County town just north of San Francisco. He soon expanded his mailing list strategy to the production of table wines under the Sonoma Vineyards brand before renaming it Rodney Strong in 1984, more or less coincident with the winery's sale to a large national distributor, Renfield Importers. Renfield was sold to Schenley, which sold to Guinness, which then sold to Klein Foods. With production measured in the hundreds of thousands of cases, the winery has mostly been a maker of lower-priced, everyday wines from its own and nearby vineyards. In recent years, owner Tom Klein has created a winery within a winery where limited-production wines take advantage of the quality that can be found in Sonoma County grapes. Consulting winemaker David Ramey helps guide this new approach, and the result is the best wines from this now-venerable company in some years.

The winery, located immediately next door to J Vineyards, is a handsome place that sees lots of visitors; and even though it is now several decades old, the winery building remains an architectural jewel both inside and out. Longer production whites tend to be balanced, medium-bodied bottlings that earn scores in the mid-80s. The recent upscale Chardonnay and Cabernet Sauvignons have been rated in the low to mid-90s.

RUSSIAN HILL ESTATE 1997		Map 8
www.russianhillestate.com	707-575-9428	Tasting
Windsor	Sonoma County	Russian River Valley AVA

Medical researchers Edward Gomez and Ellen Mack acquired two modest vineyards and a winery in the late 1990s and began making Pinot Noir and Syrah varieties, principally from their own grapes. Under winemaker Patrick Melley, a former restaurateur, Russian Hill produces about seven thousand cases annually, of which two-thirds is Pinot Noir and the remainder distributed among Syrah, Chardonnay, and the occasional Port and Rosé.

Wine quality from the outset has generally been positive, with more scores in the upper 80s and low 90s than anything else. Most recent Pinot Noirs in a balanced, moderately oaky, tightly fruity style, from several designated vineyards, and the occasional Syrah have led the parade at this fledgling winery.

SAUSAL WINERY 1973		Map 6
www.sausalwinery.com	800-500-2285	Tasting
Healdsburg	Sonoma County	Alexander Valley AVA

In 1956, the Demostene family, originally from Genoa, acquired the 125-acre Sausal Ranch, on which red varietals had been planted as early as the 1890s. For several decades, Sausal sold grapes to others—much of them purchased by Grgich Hills—before Dave Demostene began making wine in 1973. The third generation is now making some fifteen thousand cases, primarily of Zinfandel and Cabernet Sauvignon, with smaller lots of Petite Sirah and Sangiovese, all from their estate-grown fruit.

The house style from the outset has stressed balance and lively acidity, and while the number of superb wines has often been matched by the quantity of less successful efforts, Sausal's best Zinfandels have topped the charts in many vintages and make the winery one that continues to enjoy a high standing with critics and consumers alike.

SBRAGIA FAMILY VINEYARDS 2004		Map 7
www.sbragia.com	866-222-4342	Tasting
Geyserville	Sonoma County	Dry Creek Valley AVA

Ed Sbragia made his name as the longtime winemaker for Beringer from 1984 until 2008, when he became the "emeritus" winemaker. In 2004, with son Adam, Sbragia launched his own label, making five thousand cases of Cabernet Sauvignon and Zinfandel from the family's thirty-plus acres of vineyards located at the northwestern end of the Dry Creek Valley and from grapes grown in favorite Napa locations.

Now entirely on his own, Sbragia has endowed his wines with far more depth and heft than was understandably the case at a big commercial winery like Beringer. And while some will say his wines are over the top, no one doubts that they have substance and personality. The best rate in the low to mid-90s and are genuine head turners.

SCHUG CARNEROS ESTATE WINERY 1980 Map 9

| www.schugwinery.com | 800-966-9365 | Tasting |
| Sonoma | Sonoma County | Carneros AVA |

Educated at Geisenheim, Germany's prestigious wine institute, Walter Schug and his wife Gertrude came to California in the early 1960s. Walter worked for Gallo, then was the founding winemaker at Joseph Phelps from '73 to '83 while making his own wines on the side. In '90, Schug bought fifty acres in Carneros and planted forty-two acres to Chardonnay and Pinot Noir grapes. His estate vineyards are supplemented by grapes purchased from notable growers, including Sangiacomo, Ricci, and Vineburg vineyards. Today's production is near capacity at twenty-five thousand cases, half of which are Pinot Noir varieties, while Chardonnay is another third of the output. Other wines include Cabernet Sauvignon, Merlot, and a small batch of Rouge de Noirs Sparkling Pinot Noir.

Schug wines are typically medium-full in body and carry noticeable acidity, even in the upscale line called Heritage Reserve. The special bottlings have been the more successful, with scores of recent wines reaching up to 90 points. Other wines have tended to rate in the mid-80s.

SEBASTIANI VINEYARDS & WINERY 1904 Map 9

| www.sebastiani.com | 800-888-5532 | Tasting |
| Sonoma | Sonoma County | Sonoma Valley AVA |

Founded by Italian immigrant Samuele Sebastiani in 1904, the winery began with access to original vineyards planted by Franciscan fathers as far back as the mid-1820s. The Sebastiani family is now in its fourth generation of winemaking, having started with Samuele's purchase of the small winery on the outskirts of the town of Sonoma. For decades, Sebastiani was content with selling his wines to other local winemakers. In the mid-1940s, the reins were handed to August Sebastiani, who expanded the bottled wine business dramatically. By the 1960s, the bulk wine business gave way to bottled generic varieties; indeed, by then Sebastiani was now buying bulk wine from others to satisfy his customers' demand. By the end of the 1970s, Sebastiani was producing over four million cases. In 1980, Sam Sebastiani succeeded his father and dramatically changed course, bringing down production substantially in favor of higher-quality varietal wines. The cost of revamping production took its toll on family unity, and, by the end of the decade Sam was voted out and his sister Mary Ann Cuneo took over. Today, some 280,000 cases—out of a million-case capacity—are produced with an emphasis on quality in the three tiers: a Proprietor's Selection line, an Appellation Selection group, and a large-volume Sonoma County tier. With this shift in focus has come continued family conflict and, in December 2008, Sebastiani was acquired by the Foley Wine Group of Santa Barbara (labels Foley Estates, Firestone, and several others). The Sebastiani family still owns vineyards in the heart of Sonoma County.

While there are new chapters to be written in this century-old story, Sebastiani wines for the moment occupy an interesting niche. The basic and slightly upscaled reds, especially Zinfandel and Merlot, are rich and supple and earn ratings in the upper 80s, with occasional excursions to higher levels; they rate as some of the best values around. But whether the Foley success with Chardonnay and Pinot Noir down in Santa Barbara County translates to Sebastiani remains to be seen. It might extend the label's very successful run of late.

SEGHESIO VINEYARDS & WINERY 1895   Map 6

www.seghesio.com	707-433-3579	Tasting
Healdsburg	Sonoma County	Alexander Valley AVA

Founder Edoardo Seghesio emigrated from the Piedmont region of Italy in the late nineteenth century, planted his first vines in the Alexander Valley in 1895, and built a winery in 1902. Before and after Prohibition, Seghesio supplied bulk wine to Italian Swiss Colony and others. Seghesio was one of the last of the Sonoma winemakers to shift from bulk wines to varietals, but in the mid-1990s, the current generation of the family reduced production dramatically—from some 130,000 to 30,000 cases—and focused on making wines from their own impressive vineyards, with some 415 acres scattered around the valley in seven locations and from purchased grapes. The focus remains on Zinfandel, which represents well over half of the production, with a number of Italian varieties (Sangiovese, Barbera, Pinot Grigio, and Arneis) made in smaller batches.

The Seghesio style has been a bit of a work in progress. The winery's initial varietal bottlings were fruity, balanced, and rich. Then, when Zinfandel ripeness started climbing, Seghesio was among the makers whose Zins began to push the limits, and some of its offerings began to lose the delectable, concentrated fruit that brought such early success to the winery. More recently, we have seen a slight moderation in concentration and a concomitant increase in ratings. Seghesio has the potential to rate in the top handful of Zinfandel producers, and it often does earn scores in the 90-plus point range.

SIDURI WINES 1994		Map 8
www.siduri.com	707-578-3882	Tasting by Appointment
Santa Rosa	Sonoma County	Russian River Valley AVA

Texas wine retailers Adam and Dianna Lee set out for California to make wine and, in 1994, set up shop in a Santa Rosa warehouse. Within three years they were making four vineyard-designated Pinot Noirs that gained notoriety for their quality. The rest is history: Siduri makes some fifteen thousand cases of twenty-five separate Pinot Noir bottlings from twenty-seven vineyards from Santa Barbara to the Willamette Valley in Oregon. The vineyards represented include such household names as Garys', Pisoni, and Rosella's. Sister winery Novy Family Wines makes a similar range of Syrah bottlings and shares the winemaking facilities. (Incidentally, Siduri is the Babylonian goddess of wine.)

With a roster of Pinot Noirs now pushing past two dozen, and using grape sources from one end of the West Coast to the other, Siduri regularly reaches the peak of perfection in Pinot but can occasionally plum the depth of thinness and angularity that is the flip side of the varietal spectrum. Still, many of its vineyard designates earn over 90 points; most recently its Sonatera bottling has led the way. And with the occasional grand success with its $20 appellation offerings, Siduri is a winery that must be considered whenever Pinot Noir is on the menu.

SIMI WINERY 1876		Map 6
www.simiwinery.com	800-746-4880	Tasting
Healdsburg	Sonoma County	Alexander Valley AVA

Tuscan brothers Giuseppe and Pietro Simi immigrated to San Francisco during the Gold Rush and subsequently founded their eponymous winery in 1876 when they moved from the city to Sonoma County. Both brothers died in 1904, leaving Giuseppe's daughter, Isabelle, to take over the winery at age eighteen, running it through Prohibition, a weak demand for wine, and two world wars until selling the property at age eighty-four in 1970. Ownership changes included a sale to Moët-Hennessy and, in 1999, to current owners Constellation Brands' Icon Estates group (labels Franciscan, Mount Veeder, Robert Mondavi). Winemaker Steve Reeder—of Kendall-Jackson and Chateau St. Jean—has supervised the nine hundred acres of vineyards in the Alexander and Russian River valleys, and production of some half a million cases a year since 2003. Reeder's focus is on the large-volume Sonoma County Chardonnay and Alexander Valley Cabernet Sauvignon, which represent 75 percent of total production, but he also has had success with Merlot, Sauvignon Blanc, Zinfandel, and a proprietary white blend.

Simi is one of the most reliable wineries for its large production wines. And while you can pay a lot more for some of the popular restaurant brands, Simi typically matches them for quality and outshines them for value.

SOLITUDE WINES 1986		Map 9
www.solitudewines.com	707-573-8240	No Tasting
Sonoma	Sonoma County	Carneros AVA

Richard Litsch, Solitude Wines' owner-winemaker/chief bottle washer, gained his experience after UC–Davis at Rombauer, in Australia and New Zealand, and as assistant winemaker at Chalone. While at Chalone, Litsch made his Solitude wine on the side and, in 1988, focused on Solitude. Litsch makes less than two thousand cases in total, with his Chardonnay from the Sangiacomo Vineyard representing all of that recently but Pinot Noir having also been in the line.

More success has been the order of the day at Solitude, with scores for Chardonnay often rising into the 90-point range.

SONOMA COAST VINEYARDS 2001		Map 8
www.sonomacoastvineyards.com	707-874-1993	No Tasting
Windsor	Sonoma County	Sonoma Coast AVA

In the western reaches of the county, four to six miles from the ocean, lies the "extreme" Sonoma Coast, from which the grapes for this winery are grown. Vineyards including Freestone, Peterson, and Balistreri provide the fruit for winemaker Anthony Austin (formerly the founding winemaker at Firestone in Santa Barbara County), who produces 6,500 cases, half of which is Pinot Noir and the remainder Chardonnay and Sauvignon Blanc bottlings. John and Barbara Drady are the owners and are active in all kinds of wine country activities, including "training sessions" for aficionados and competitions they organize and run for commercial gain. And giving their wines due credit, they have often reached the 90-point plateau.

SONOMA-CUTRER VINEYARDS 1973		Map 8
www.sonomacutrer.com	707-528-1181	Tasting by Appointment
Windsor	Sonoma County	Russian River Valley AVA

Founder Brice Jones and winemaker Bill Bonetti established Sonoma-Cutrer solely as a vineyard but, in 1981, started making wines as well with a focus on Chardonnay. Growth led to a state-of-the-art winery and, in '99, sale of the winery and one thousand acres of vineyards to drinks giant Brown-Forman. Under winemaker Terry Adams, Sonoma-Cutrer now produces over one hundred thousand cases, 95 percent of which are Chardonnays, ranging from a broadly distributed Russian River Ranch Chardonnay to a limited-bottling Founders Reserve.

It is a big brand but one that has lost its flair at the quality end of the spectrum and now produces no better than average results at the price levels asked. With more brisk acidity than fruit depth in its wines, this winery has dropped from the list of makers to be remembered.

ST. FRANCIS WINERY 1979		Map 9
www.stfranciswine.com	707-833-4666	Tasting
Kenwood	Sonoma County	Sonoma Valley AVA

San Francisco businessman Joe Martin acquired the hundred-acre Behler Ranch in Kenwood in 1973. After several years of selling grapes to other vintners, Martin built his own winery in '79. Over time—and with the partnership with Kobrand Wine & Spirits in '88—the modest winery grew to today's 250,000-case giant, bottling some two dozen varieties, much of it made from grapes grown on the 525 acres of estate vineyards. Tom Mackey is the longtime winemaker.

St. Francis is one of those love-them/hate-them labels. When its wines are on song, they can be incredibly deep, rich, full of flavor and complexity, and well worth their middle-of-the-road prices. But all too often, things go awry here. Merlot has been the winery's strongest varietal of late. Have a look at the winery's Web site for the many tasting opportunities and options that make a visit to St. Francis worthwhile.

STONESTREET WINERY 1989		Map 6
www.stonestreetwines.com	800-355-8008	Tasting
Healdsburg	Sonoma County	Alexander Valley AVA

San Francisco haberdasher Edward Gauer bought the former Zellerbach Vineyards, primarily as a horse ranch. By 1986, Gauer had planted four hundred acres to vineyards and began making wine; in 1989, the property was acquired by Jess Jackson's Artisans & Estates group. Five years later, Jackson bought the adjacent Alexander Mountain Estate and merged the two properties into a nine-hundred-acre vineyard, contributing fruit to the thirty-thousand-case production of Chardonnay, Cabernet Sauvignon, and several Cabernet-based blends, notably the Legacy bottling. As with most of Jackson's upscale labels, the wines of Stonestreet are typically quite ripe, but they vary in fruit depth and have mostly earned ratings in the mid- to upper 80s.

TRENTADUE WINERY 1969		Map 6
www.trentadue.com	888-332-3032	Tasting
Geyserville	Sonoma County	Alexander Valley AVA

Family patriarch Leo Trentadue farmed fruit orchards in the South Bay until encroaching urbanization forced him from what would become Silicon Valley to the Alexander Valley. Initially, Trentadue grew grapes on his 160-acre vineyard and sold them to other vintners until the late 1960s, when he started his own label. Most of the range of wines—Zinfandel is the leader in the production department with about half of the thirty thousand cases made—is from estate-grown fruit and modestly priced. Bulgarian winemaker Miro Tcholakov has introduced several limited-production "La Storia" blends and even a bubbly. The winery encourages weddings and special events.

The house style can be a bit rustic at times, and quality is not always entirely consistent. However, Trentadue sits on prime property for the making of lusty reds, and its best efforts from Merlot to Zinfandel sport lots of rich, ripe fruit. Its wines are more likely to earn scores in the mid- to upper-80 range.

UNTI VINEYARDS 1997		Map 7
www.untivineyards.com	707-433-5590	Tasting by Appointment
Healdsburg	Sonoma County	Dry Creek Valley AVA

The Unti family—George, Linda, and Mack—first planted what would become their sixty-acre estate vineyards in 1990 and established the winery in 1997 focused on small lots of estate-grown and -bottled red varieties. Under winemakers Sebastien Pochan and Mick Unti, they produce seven thousand cases, with Zinfandel leading the way at a third of the total. Organic farming methods are employed. The Untis, father and son, have a long and significant history in the wine business going back to their days in the Safeway grocery store chain when, under their leadership, wine became a major point of focus for the company.

The handsome winery in the midst of the Dry Creek Valley is a good stopping-off point. To date, most Unti wines have rated in the very respectable range of the mid- to upper 80s.

VALLEY OF THE MOON WINERY 1941		Map 9
www.valleyofthemoonwinery.com	707-939-4500	Tasting
Glen Ellen	Sonoma County	Sonoma Valley AVA

Valley of the Moon has history as far back as 1863 when it was first operated as a winery. Two decades later, it was sold and renamed Madrone Vineyards, which remained in operation until 1941 when Enrico Parducci and Peter Domenici took over. They, in turn, sold to Heck Estates, owner of several wineries, most notably Korbel and now including Kenwood and Lake Sonoma. Heck brought the winery full circle, naming it Valley of the Moon once again. Today, under the auspices of winemaker Harry Parducci Jr., the winery produces over forty-five thousand cases of numerous varieties, including the volume leader Chardonnay, a Pinot Noir, Cabernet Sauvignon, and a popular Pinot Blanc. A small estate vineyard contributes its old-vine Zinfandel grapes.

With most wine prices at the lower end for Sonoma County, this winery often provides good value even though its qualitative ratings are typically in the mid-80s, with only the occasional bottling reaching above that level.

At the southern tip of the Russian River Valley lies this seventy-five-acre vineyard—planted to Chardonnay and Pinot Noir—and winery. The first vines were planted by Walter in 1978 and the first wines made for the '96 vintage. Current proprietor Stephen Hansel's real job is ownership of several Sonoma auto dealerships, but serious attention is paid to the ten-thousand-case production of estate-grown and -bottled Chardonnay and Pinot Noir varieties.

With its advantaged Russian River Valley location and hands-on production, Hansel has succeeded in garnering plenty of 90-plus point ratings and earning its way into the pantheon of highly regarded producers of Chardonnay and Pinot Noir. Hansel wines are ripe but balanced, tasty but refined.

WATTLE CREEK WINERY 1994   Map 6

www.wattlecreek.com   707-894-5166   Tasting

Cloverdale   Sonoma County   Alexander Valley AVA

Australians Chris and Kris Williams bought the former Pat Paulsen property in northern Alexander Valley and revived its 30-acre vineyard and developed a 120-acre vineyard on a 600-acre property in the Yorkville Highlands region of southern Mendocino County. With winemaker Michael Scholz—also from Australia, where he grew up on a family vineyard in the Barossa Valley Wattle Creek makes well over ten thousand cases of estate-grown and -bottled wines, including Chardonnay, Sauvignon Blanc, Pinot Noir, and even a Sparkling Wine. "Wattle" is the name of the Australian equivalent of the acacia tree.

The winery is open by appointment only, but there is a tasting room in San Francisco's Ghirardelli Square.

WELLINGTON VINEYARDS 1989   Map 9

www.wellingtonvineyards.com   800-816-WINE   Tasting

Glen Ellen   Sonoma County   Sonoma Valley AVA

Father and son John and Peter Wellington found a ten-acre vineyard in Glen Ellen and built a winery on it in 1989. The vineyards have expanded somewhat to thirty-five acres, providing about half the grapes needed for their ten-thousand-case production of a wide range of wines. The list is led by Cabernet Sauvignon, Syrah, and Zinfandel plus several unique varieties such as Marsanne, Roussanne, and Grenache. Peter remains the winemaker.

Qualitative ratings have been led recently by Syrah, Viognier, and Sauvignon Blanc—all reaching the lofty 90-point plateau. Other wines have scored lower and have occasionally been bothered by a leathery, earthy edge.

WHITE OAK VINEYARDS & WINERY 1980		Map 6
www.whiteoakwinery.com	707-433-8429	Tasting
Healdsburg	Sonoma County	Alexander Valley AVA

Angeleno Bill Myers had been a contractor and Alaskan fisherman before settling in the Sonoma Valley and building a small winery and vineyard just off the Healdsburg town square. In the 1990s, Myers partnered with the developers Burrell Properties; acquired 750 vineyard acres in the Alexander, Russian River, and Napa valleys; and built a handsome, inviting winemaking facility tucked in between the Sausal and Stonestreet wineries in the southeastern corner of the Alexander Valley. White Oak now uses only 10 percent of the grapes grown on the estates and sells the remainder to other area vintners. White Oak produces twenty-five thousand cases, led by Cabernet Sauvignon, Sauvignon Blanc, and Chardonnay.

Prices have been kept at reasonable levels over the years, and while not every vintage has been the stuff of dreams, White Oak has hit 90 points with balanced, accessible Sauvignon Blanc and Chardonnay. Its wines can be among the most price-worthy relative to quality on those occasions. Moreover, it is a very pleasant stop along the wine trails.

WILLIAMS SELYEM WINERY 1981		Map 8
www.williamsselyem.com	707-433-6425	No Tasting
Healdsburg	Sonoma County	Russian River Valley AVA

Founders Burt Williams and Ed Selyem were garage winemakers prior to establishing their eponymous winery in the early 1980s, specializing at the time in Zinfandel. Over the next two decades, the Williams Selyem reputation grew substantially when they chose to focus on Pinot Noir from some of the best growers in the county, including Rochioli, Heintz, and Allen vineyards. In '98, Williams Selyem was acquired by New York state winery owners John and Kathe Dyson, whose only major change was to develop two nearby vineyards of their own, Drake and Litton Estates, totaling eighty-five acres. The list of grape purveyors has grown to a dozen or more and represents 85 percent of the fruit needed for winemaker Bob Cabral's current production of eleven thousand cases; Pinot Noir remains the leading variety, with Chardonnay and Zinfandel made in more limited editions.

Pinot Noir has set the pace at Williams Selyem for two decades now, with the top-rated bottlings reaching the very highest levels and making the winery one of the most admired and desirable producers of this sometimes-difficult variety. Lately, the Chardonnays have also come into the 90-plus point range and now challenge the leaders in that variety as well. The Pinots, especially the top vineyard designates, are some of the most refined, keenly focused versions of the variety made in California. The Chardonnays are ripe, somewhat direct, and fairly deep, but they are also far less consistent performers than the Pinot Noirs.

WILSON WINERY 1993		Map 7
www.wilsonwinery.com	800-433-4353	Tasting
Healdsburg	Sonoma County	Dry Creek Valley AVA

Diane and Ken Wilson bought vineyard land in the Dry Creek Valley beginning in 1988 and an old tin barn/winery on West Dry Creek Road that formerly housed the Fredson Winery. The vineyard grew to 220 acres of Zinfandel, Cabernet Sauvignon, Syrah, and Merlot grapes, used for their own wines and sold to others. Their first foray into winemaking, under the direction of Diane Wilson, was in 1994, making a Cabernet Sauvignon. Since then, very limited bottlings of Cabernet, Zinfandel, and Syrah have totaled about three thousand cases annually. Over time, Wilson has acquired the Mazzocco Winery and Matrix in the Dry Creek Valley, de Lorimier (formerly Mosaic) in the Alexander Valley, and Jepson in Mendocino County.

Wilson Zinfandels, the mainstay of the line, are almost always very high in ripeness, with dried grape notes in aromas and flavors, and alcohols often exceeding the 16 percent level. Needless to say, they are not universally liked, but the style has its devotees, and the best of the wines do impress.

Napa County

Most winegrowing counties in California manage to have their own countywide personality, even where the territories included in the county as a whole are so disparate as to have little to do with one another from a grape-growing perspective. Napa County is a little bit different in that regard. Because virtually every grape grown in the county has historically been able to use the "Napa Valley" tag on its label, the notion of Napa County has all but been overwhelmed by the power of the Napa Valley name. And so it is that the valley lying between two sets of north-south hills is called the Napa Valley, and so, too, for wine-labeling purposes, are places high in those hills and in adjoining lands.

It is a fact that most of the grapes in Napa County are thus in the Napa Valley AVA, but it is also a fact that most of the grapes within the AVA are also either on the valley floor or in the hills that face the valley. There are, of course, places like the Wild Horse Valley, Chiles Valley, Pope Valley, and Carneros that are not part of what might be called the "Napa Valley proper" but do have substantial grape-growing populations. Some—Carneros, especially—is so unique and special in its own right that its AVA has become widely recognized and can stand on its own. Others, like Stags Leap District (spelled without an apostrophe *s* for political reasons),

Oakville, and Rutherford, have become the geese that lay the golden eggs of California wine.

Indeed, it is almost commonplace to think first of the Napa Valley when defining California wine and then to think of Rutherford and Stags Leap as the places that define the Napa Valley, and finally to think of Cabernet Sauvignon as the wine that defines those places. Such is the hierarchy of California wine that the small, delimited places in the Napa Valley have come to define the quality end of the spectrum for millions of wine aficionados all over the world.

Napa County grape growing has blossomed along with the growth of the industry, but nowhere does one see the concentration of the most expensive grape varieties as in Napa, and that is, of course, related to the fact that no other region in California has such expensive turf. From a base of about ten thousand acres before the wine boom of the 1970s, acreage in Napa County has now grown to 45,400, and the greatest part of that is devoted to Cabernet Sauvignon (19,100 acres) and its red wine mates from Bordeaux, including Merlot (6,800), Cabernet Franc (1,200), Petit Verdot (600), and Malbec (300). Pinot Noir comes next among reds (2,800), with Zinfandel (1,500), Syrah (1,000), and Petite Sirah (700) all quite limited by comparison. Chardonnay (7,100) and Sauvignon Blanc (2,500) are the leading whites, with others not getting above a few hundred acres apiece. See also the section later on the Napa Valley AVA for historical grape-growing data.

Atlas Peak

Occupying the high ground (from 760 feet to the summit) of this promontory rising out of the hills to the northeast of Napa City, Atlas Peak has a shorter, hotter growing season than the valley proper. Temperatures can be lower than those on the valley floor, but since much of the AVA lies above the fog line, Atlas Peak fruit gets more hours of sunshine and tends to ripen sooner and at higher sugar levels. Cabernet Sauvignon has become the leading variety in the area, but Zinfandel acreage is also significant.

Calistoga

It has taken years—too many years—but the forces arguing over formation of the Calistoga AVA have finally been told, as of the turn of 2010, by the government that their seemingly unending debate is over. Calistoga, the town lying at the very northern end of the Napa Valley, has certainly been deserving of the recognition. More red grapes than white grow here, and

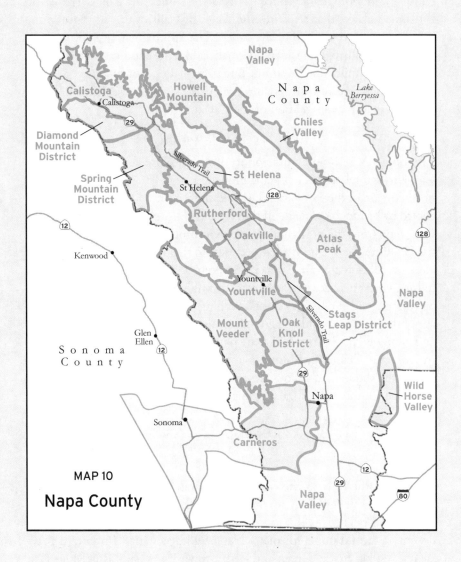

Napa Valley

Napa
County

Lake
Berryessa

Calistoga

Calistoga

Howell
Mountain

Chiles
Valley

Diamond
Mountain
District

Silverado Trail

St Helena

St Helena

Spring
Mountain
District

Rutherford

Kenwood

Oakville

Atlas
Peak

Yountville

Yountville

Stags
Leap District

Napa
Valley

Glen
Ellen

Mount
Veeder

Oak
Knoll
District

Silverado Trail

S o n o m a
C o u n t y

Napa

Wild
Horse
Valley

Sonoma

Carneros

MAP 10

Napa County

Napa
Valley

whether one is talking about hillside wineries like Storybook Mountain or flatlanders like Chateau Montelena, the growing conditions are warm and dry and produce concentrated wines, often with very admirable longevity. Cabernet Sauvignon is the generally preferred variety, and it is a much sturdier and more highly concentrated style, sometimes a bit over-the-top for some palates, that separates the wines of Calistoga from those in the middle and southern end of the valley. The approximately 2,500 acres of vines make Calistoga considerably smaller than the commune-based AVAs that line the valley to the south; but it is quality, not quantity, and the concentrated nature of the wines grown there that have demanded and finally earned the designation of the Calistoga AVA.

Carneros (Los Carneros)

The only AVA to go across county lines and also to have two names, Carneros is a relatively cool grape-growing region lying immediately at the northern end of the San Pablo Bay extension of the San Francisco Bay. It is cooled by breezes blowing in off the bay, but it also gets late afternoon winds that come from the north and flow down through the Sonoma Valley and the Petaluma Gap. The vineyards closest to the bay tend to be heavily oriented to cold-loving varieties like Chardonnay and Pinot Noir, while some hillside vineyards back from the bay are willing hosts to Merlot, Cabernet Sauvignon, and Syrah. Grapes for Sparkling Wine take a significant percentage of the Carneros yield and go to famous wineries like Domaine Carneros and Gloria Ferrer, both of which are physically located in Carneros, and also to Domaine Chandon, Mumm Napa, and Schramsberg. Of the approximately ten thousand acres of grapes in Carneros, the greater majority lie on the Napa County side of the dividing line.

See Carneros Wine Alliance: www.carneros.com;
Hospitality de Los Carneros: www.carneroswineries.org.

Chiles Valley

Located in the hills to the east of the Napa Valley floor, but included in the Napa Valley AVA for historical rather than wine style reasons, this upland pocket (at elevations from 800 feet and up) has increasingly become a second home for many Napa Valley wineries. Important players like Volker Eisele, Green and Red, Brown Estate, and RustRidge lead the way in the Chiles Valley. In part because its grapes can be classified as Napa Valley, and in part because of the late growing season, Cabernet Sauvignon is popular here and does very well even if producing somewhat less complex wines generally. Zinfandel is another frequently planted grape in the Chiles Valley, with the latter three of the wineries named all specializing in that grape rather than in Cabernet. Vineyard acreage is estimated in the neighborhood of 1,100.

Diamond Mountain District

Situated in the Mayacamas range along the west side of the Napa Valley between St. Helena and Calistoga, the Diamond Mountain District is today red wine country. Ironically, its most famous winery for years was Sparkling Wine producer Schramsberg, but even Schramsberg has now converted its Diamond Mountain vineyard to Cabernet Sauvignon and moved its Sparkling Wine vineyards to appropriately cooler locations. The district is somewhat bifurcated along north-south lines, with wineries like Diamond Creek, Von Strasser, Schramsberg, and Reverie in the southern and somewhat cooler and better-irrigated parts, while others to the north have far less water to work with and noticeably drier and hotter climatic conditions. The AVA runs from 400 feet of elevation up to 2,200 and contains something under 1,000 acres of vines, mostly planted to red grapes, which, in the Napa Valley these days, means mostly Cabernet Sauvignon and other Bordelais varieties.

Howell Mountain

High in the hills east of St. Helena, this AVA was one of the first to be established yet is one of the least heavily planted among the Napa Valley's list of recognized places. Officially running from six hundred feet in elevation up to the peaks at over two thousand feet, the Howell Mountain AVA finds most of its several hundred acres of mostly red grapes growing at elevations around a thousand feet. It is rugged territory and long, sunny, west-facing exposures together with a drier than normal climatic setting combine to produce tough, deep, concentrated Cabernet Sauvignons and Zinfandels more often than not. But there are pockets and winemakers who somehow tame the beast, and one sees wines like Dunn Cabernet and Beringer Bancroft Ranch Merlot achieving at least a semblance of refinement that too often eludes the typically bold wines of the area.

Mount Veeder

The Mayacamas Range separates the Napa Valley from the Sonoma Valley, and the hills that face east contain a string of AVAs that start east of Napa city and run north past St. Helena (the Spring Mountain District) and then up to Calistoga (the Diamond Mountain District). The Mount Veeder AVA, like its hillside neighbors to the north, starts at six hundred feet of elevation and runs up to the peaks; and like its neighbors, it is a mix of steep canyons and plantable slopes. Its soils run from sparse and rocky to the occasional alluvial fan, and its wines are among the more refined, for the most part, of Napa's hillside AVAs—although Spring Mountain certainly gives it a run for its money in that regard. Because Mount Veeder is the farthest south, and because its southern end abuts the uplands of Carneros, it is the coolest of the hillside AVAs, and one finds more white grapes in these hills than farther north. Plantings on Mount Veeder are nevertheless more oriented to Bordelais reds and Zinfandel than to whites and total less than a thousand acres.

Napa Valley

It is the most famous piece of geography in the wine world of the United States, and it is known around the world by wine collectors as the place that defines wine in California. What is less well-known, however, is that its use on wine labels goes far beyond the borders of the valley proper and takes in virtually ever square inch of Napa County except for a few rugged, isolated pockets of the county's northeast corner—places that have not ever been and are unlikely, in the future, to ever be home to wine grapes. Its various wine regions run from the cool, maritime-influenced Carneros District to the hot corners of Calistoga and the Wild Horse Valley. Its grapes grow in deep, rich soils in the middle of the valley floor and on thin, spartan soils in its rugged hillsides. Its wines are the most expensive that are produced in California, and its economic impact, from wine sales to tourism, dwarfs that of any other wine place in the state.

It was not always thus, of course. Two hundred years ago, before the arrival of settlers from the east, the Napa Valley was the fertile, lush home to the Wappo Indians, who fished its abundant streams for salmon and who feasted on migrant fowl and local elk and bear. Its land supported wild crops, and indeed, it had an abundance of grapes even then. In 1836, George Yount received the first land grant to what was then Spanish-held territory. He established himself in the lower part of the valley, but it was not long before other settlers arrived, and soon the fertile soils became one of the burgeoning homes for wine grapes brought by European immigrants and by transplants from the eastern United States. By 1846, California had become part of the United States, and it did not take long for folks like Jacob Schram and Charles Krug to start producing small quantities of wine. Still, despite the success over the next century of producers like Beaulieu, Inglenook, Krug, Beringer, Christian Brothers, and others, the Napa Valley was still a sleepy place at the end of World War II. Its twelve thousand acres of grapes at the time actually fell off over the next twenty years until it had dropped to about ten thousand acres by 1964. Petite Sirah with almost two thousand acres led the way, and Zinfandel was second at just under a thousand acres. There were five hundred acres of Cabernet Sauvignon, two hundred acres of Pinot Noir, and no recorded acreage of Chardonnay.

In the years that followed, first slowly and then in a rush as the wine boom of the 1970s took hold in the Napa Valley in a big way, the valley was transformed into a playground for food- and wine-loving adults. Its best products can fetch hundreds of dollars per bottle when young, and thousands as they mature. Grape plantings have risen to forty-five thousand acres. Now Cabernet Sauvignon, at nearly eighteen thousand acres, is king, with Chardonnay and Merlot both boasting some seven thousand acres; these three grapes account for 75 percent of the Napa Valley harvest.

Today, the concentration of famous names that dot the valley have acquired their own AVAs. On the valley floor, running straight up the valley from Napa to Calistoga are what we chose to call the "commune AVAs." From the Oak Knoll District to Yountville, Oakville, Rutherford, St. Helena, and Calistoga, these growing regions, named for the towns (save Oak Knoll, which has no urban center and lies in the nine-mile stretch from Napa to Yountville), occupy most of the territory that we see when we drive through the valley proper and are blessed with the greatest portion of the acreage credited to the Napa Valley AVA. At the fringes are the cool Carneros region near the bay, the hillside regions on either side of the valley, and the adjoining upland valleys to the east.

See Napa Valley Vintners: www.napavintners.com; Napa Valley Wine Library Association: www.napawinelibrary.com; Silverado Trail Wineries Association: www.silveradotrail.com.

Oak Knoll District of Napa Valley

Occupying the southern end of the valley above the town of Napa and below Yountville, the Oak Knoll District (note the reference to the Napa Valley in the official title of the AVA) is a bit of a mixed bag in terms of growing conditions. Its midvalley flatlands are particularly hospitable to cooler varieties like Chardonnay but are not so cool that Pinot Noir is a major player there. And yet the area also seems to find enough warmth so that it ripens Merlot and Cabernet Sauvignon toward the end of harvest.

There are also hillside vineyards on both sides of the valley, and the higher one gets, the warmer the site and the more likely it is to be tilted to the production of red grapes rather than white.

Vine acreage numbers about 3,500, with Merlot and Chardonnay both over 500 but less than 1,000 and Cabernet Sauvignon just under 500. Trefethen and Monticello are the most prominent wineries in the district among the roughly thirty in all. Other important producers include Darioush, Hagafen, and Luna. The district has a limited but useful Web site, www.oakknolldistrictofnapavalley.com.

Oakville

Along with the Rutherford AVA, Oakville lies at the heart of the Napa Valley, and its wines are among the most expensive and widely recognized of any growing area in the United States. The alluvial fans along the western edge of the valley have been planted to grapes for well over a century, and Hamilton Crabb's 1868 holdings on the western alluvial fan known as the West Rutherford Bench that he called, for lack of a more inclusive term, To Kalon, remain today as one of the recognized superstars among all California vineyard sites. Wineries like Robert Mondavi, Paul Hobbs, and Provenance are making stellar wines from this superb location, and nearby wineries like Harlan and Screaming Eagle are able to sell their Cabernet Sauvignons at prices that are exceeded only by the most storied First Growths of Bordeaux. Not surprisingly, the dominant grapes in Oakville are Cabernet Sauvignon and its complementary varieties, headed by Merlot.

See Oakville Winegrowers: www.oakvillewinegrowers.org.

Rutherford

It is here in Rutherford that the most famous wineries of the past century were founded, Beaulieu and Inglenook (now Francis Ford Coppola's Rubicon Estate). And it is here in Rutherford that Beaulieu's legendary post-Prohibition winemaker, Andre Tchelistcheff, coined the famous phrase "Rutherford dust" to explain the extraordinary rich and complex character that Cabernet Sauvignon acquires in this hallowed turf. Indeed, when the Rutherford folks proudly proclaim that "this is Cabernet country," they mean it. Of the almost five thousand planted acres in Rutherford, fully 70 percent of them contain Cabernet Sauvignon, and Merlot, Cabernet's partner in crime, makes up an additional 15 percent. Nothing else even comes close.

The climate within the AVA resembles its neighbors', and being up-valley from Oakville, it is just a bit warmer, although not by enough to worry about. The alluvial fans that make up the West Rutherford Bench are paralleled on the east by smaller outcroppings of alluvial soils, and because the east gets late afternoon sun, it is the warmer part of the AVA and tends to make wines that are a bit fleshier overall. Still, there is virtually no part of this "commune AVA" that does not make very good, and very expensive, wine. Some fifty wineries, large and small, call Rutherford home, and another fifty make wines that are either entirely or partly grown there.

See Rutherford Dust Society: www.rutherforddust.com.

Spring Mountain District

Lying west of the St. Helena AVA in the sloping hills of the Mayacamas Range, Spring Mountain has a long history of grape growing and has had its share of renown over the years. As one heads out of St. Helena up Spring Mountain Road, it becomes clear that this is not "easy" territory. Vineyards get carved out of accommodating pockets and swails but then run out of turf as the land becomes steep and just plain unwelcoming. About two dozen wineries work this challenging land, the most well-known of which are Pride Mountain, sitting at the very top of the AVA at elevations ranging up to two thousand feet, Newton, Cain, Paloma, and Spring Mountain Vineyard, which occupies one of the older sites and has caves carved into the hills in the nineteenth century.

Stags Leap District

The red rock promontories that form the eastern border of this growing area, located at the eastern edge of the Yountville AVA a half dozen miles north of Napa town, are said to be the home of the famous leaping quadruped. It is also these rocky outcroppings that capture and reflect the late afternoon sun and provide warm growing conditions later in the day than other locations in the southern end of the valley. Nighttime temperatures, however, drop off rapidly as this valley within a valley gets cooled by breezes off the bay. The result is both a long growing season and very good balancing acidity in the grapes. With about 1,500 acres under vine, most of it in Cabernet Sauvignon and Merlot, the Stags Leap District has become well-known for its supple and sumptuous red wines, the best of which rate near the top of the Napa Valley collectible list.

In the wine boom of the 1970s, the district became almost instantly famous when the Stag's Leap Wine Cellars 1973 Cabernet Sauvignon won a tasting in Paris in which French winemakers chose that wine out of a blind tasting as better than any of their own. When an adjoining property to SLWC was developed and named itself Stags' Leap Winery, the first of several legal battles over the name began. Years later, when the district was awarded AVA status, its name further exacerbated hurt feelings when the name selected had no apostrophe at all—resulting in three spellings for *Stags* and a lifetime of stories over the courtroom haggling.

When the wineries are not suing each other, they form a strong and identifiable group, almost each of which, from Shafer to Silverado to Pine Ridge and the two named Stags, has achieved a fair degree of fame and success.

See Stags Leap District Winegrowers Association: www.stagsleapdistrict.com.

St. Helena

Lying just north of the valley center, but the recognized central village on the Napa Valley floor, St. Helena is somewhat less well-known for its wines than its brethren in Rutherford and Oakville or even its northern neighbor up-valley in Calistoga. Expect that circumstance to change, however, with the adoption of the St. Helena AVA. Now, wineries never associated with place are able to proclaim their common provenance, and based on the long history of brilliant wines from the area, the name St. Helena will become more than a place of lovely boutiques, restaurants to die for, and the historic wineries of Beringer, Charles Krug, and Christian Brothers (now the Greystone visitors center).

Like the other "commune"-styled AVAs in the Napa Valley, the St. Helena AVA is located on the valley floor and encompasses the low-lying foothills and alluvial fans running out of the hills on either side of the valley. But, unlike its neighbors, it is longer rather than broader because the valley pinches to something like a mile wide at what one would call the "waistline" of a distinctly hourglass shape. The areas below the waistline, which occurs just north of St. Helena town, are quite similar in soil, temperature, and layout to the vineyards of Rutherford and Oakville. These areas include a continuing of the West Rutherford Bench that runs right up into the west side of St. Helena proper and is home to significant wineries like Corison, just south of town, and Spottswoode, directly west of town.

Wild Horse Valley

Lying at the eastern border of Napa County far to the east of the Napa Valley proper but still able to use that important name on its grapes for historical reasons rather than for commonality of weather, soils, or exposure, this sparsely populated AVA sports little over one hundred acres of grapes and no tourist attractions. It is notable more because of its alignment to the Napa Valley in a legal sense than for any other reason, vinous or otherwise.

Yountville

No history of the Napa Valley is complete without reference to George Yount. It was Yount who became the first white settler in the Napa Valley in the early 1830s, and by 1836 he received a land grant called Rancho Caymus that eventually became much of what we know as the Napa Valley's heart from Yountville to Rutherford. Having planted the first European vines in the Napa Valley, Yount later became a land developer laying out the framework for Yountville town in the 1850s and ironically naming it Sebastopol, although there existed (and still exists) a city by the same name in Sonoma County. After his death, his Sebastopol was renamed Yountville.

Because Yountville lies more south than north in the valley, it has cooler growing conditions than its up-valley neighbors and tends to produce firmer, tighter wines, whether red or white. Among the important wineries in Yountville are Dominus, which grows its tannin-bound red wines in the alluvial soils on the western edge of the valley, and Domaine Chandon, whose lovely building is one of our favorite touring stops. Yountville, in addition to its vinous importance, is home to a number of very fine hotels and even finer restaurants as well as other shopping possibilities.

ACACIA VINEYARD 1979		Map 16
www.acaciavineyard.com	877-226-1700	Tasting by Appointment
Napa	Napa County	Carneros AVA

Acacia was a pioneer in the Carneros region as one of the first winemakers focusing on vineyard-designated wines, Pinot Noir in particular. Founded by Mike Richmond and his backers, Acacia initially bought grapes from nearby vineyards. Today, 150 acres of corporate-owned vineyards, including the Lone Tree and Winery Lake vineyards, provide the majority of grapes for the 160,000-case annual production (55 percent Chardonnay and

45 percent Pinot Noir). Acacia is now owned by the conglomerate Diageo Chateau & Estate Wines, and its wines range from relatively inexpensive entry-level bottlings to limited-production vineyard-designated offerings.

Over its three decades of existence, the winery has gone from quality leader to laggard and is now somewhere in the middle. While few wines win top awards, the best earn admirable scores in the low 90s, especially Chardonnay. The Acacia style, when successful, mirrors the Carneros tendencies to produce firm, tightly fruity wines of good depth.

ALTAMURA VINEYARDS & WINERY 1985		Map 15
www.altamura.com	707-253-2000	Tasting by Appointment
Napa	Napa County	Napa Valley AVA

Napa Valley native Frank Altamura worked the vineyards, fresh out of high school and learned the business at Sterling, Trefethen, and Caymus before making his own wines. In 1980, Altamura purchased seventy acres on the Silverado Trail that he sold in favor of a four-hundred-acre ranch in the Wooden Valley bowl, in the remote southeastern Napa Valley. The initial thirty-five-acre vineyard was planted to Cabernet Sauvignon and Sangiovese, with a first bottling of some three thousand cases in '92. Today, the vineyard runs to sixty-five acres, including sixty acres of Cabernet. Production now totals six thousand cases, of which two-thirds are Cabernet, another 20 percent Sangiovese, and the remainder small batches of Sauvignon Blanc and the overlooked Nebbiolo.

Altamura wines combine ripeness and depth but can occasionally come up short of overall fruit concentration. Still, more often than not, they are well received and rate in the recommended ranks, with scores in the upper 80s to low 90s.

ANCIEN WINES 1997		Map 15
www.ancienwines.com	707-255-3908	No Tasting
Napa	Napa County	Carneros AVA

Ken and Teresa Bernards established a small winery of their own after experience with, and consulting for, other Napa Valley winemakers. Their efforts produced a small winery focused on Pinot Noir—representing two-thirds of the 2,500-case production—and Chardonnay. Vineyard sources include Toyon in Carneros, Red Dog in Sonoma Mountain, and Fiddlestix in the Santa Rita Hills of Santa Barbara County. Quality has been somewhat inconsistent: although there have been many successes that reached stratospheric scores, there have also been as many ordinary efforts. Most recent Chardonnays and Pinot Noirs have been back on track, and Ancien remains a winery to be watched. Ancien Pinot Noirs are typically full-bodied and balanced with noticeable oak.

ANDERSON'S CONN VALLEY VINEYARDS 1983		Map 12
www.connvalleyvineyards.com	800-946-3497	Tasting by Appointment
St. Helena	Napa County	Napa Valley AVA

Gus Anderson and his son Todd , after divergent careers in orthodontia and geophysics, built a winery east of St. Helena where Conn Creek flows out of Howell Mountain. Over twenty-six acres of vines on a forty-acre estate produce the majority of grapes used in making their primarily red range of wines, from the Estate Cabernet to a Pinot Noir to an Éloge blend. A Chardonnay rounds out the offerings, which near their sixteen-thousand-case capacity. The Andersons have done best over the years with their ripe, rich, somewhat fleshy-textured Cabernet Sauvignon, often hitting scores in the 90-point range and justifying the high prices for the wine.

ANDRETTI WINERY 1996		Map 14
www.andrettiwinery.com	888-460-8463	Tasting
Napa	Napa County	Oak Knoll District AVA

Race-car legend Mario Andretti teamed up with former Kmart executive Joe Antonini to build the winery of Mario's dreams. With fifty-three planted acres in the Oak Knoll district, Andretti produces a total of more than twenty thousand cases in three lines: the moderately priced Selections line of multiple wine types from several vineyard sources; the Napa Valley line of estate-grown varieties, particularly Chardonnay, Merlot, and Sauvignon Blanc; and three limited estate-grown releases under the Montona label—Chardonnay, Merlot, and Cabernet Sauvignon—available only at the winery. Quality has rarely risen above average for Napa Valley wines, making Andretti much more of a winner on the track than off.

ANOMALY VINEYARDS 1997		Map 12
www.anomalyvineyards.com	707-967-8448	No Tasting
St. Helena	Napa County	St. Helena AVA

Lawyers Steve and Linda Goldfarb moved to the Napa Valley from Berkeley in 1997 and released their first vintage that year; their winery was completed in 2002. Fruit from their eight acres of vineyards is made into high-end Cabernet Sauvignon sold only through a mailing list and at a small number of top-drawer restaurants. Their latest releases remain at the thousand-case level and holding. The wine is made in a ripe yet balanced style with firm tannins for age worthiness. Quality levels have varied widely and tend to mirror the highs and lows of Napa Valley Cabernet vintages. Its St. Helena location delivers ripe fruit of medium intensity, and the fairly refined house style can leave the wines short on depth in weak years.

ARAUJO ESTATE WINES 1990		Map 10
www.araujoestate.com	707-942-6061	No Tasting
Calistoga	Napa County	Calistoga AVA

San Francisco businessman Bart Araujo bought the justifiably famous Eisele Vineyard in 1990. The vineyard, first planted in the 1800s to Zinfandel and Riesling, more recently provided fruit for two decades to Joseph Phelps for that winery's top-rated Eisele Vineyard Cabernet Sauvignon. When Araujo purchased the land, he replanted some twenty of the estate's thirty-eight acres to Cabernet Sauvignon grapes and new plantings of Syrah, Sauvignon Blanc, and Viognier. Current wine production includes two thousand cases of the estate-grown Cabernet Sauvignon Eisele Vineyard and a second estate label, Altagracia, and another two thousand of Syrah, Sauvignon Blanc, and, occasionally, Viognier.

To date, Araujo Cabernet has consistently scored above 90 points and is considered one of the Napa Valley's rare and special bottlings. Its style is always full and bold, and there are those who think it may trade away a bit of refinement for increases in intensity. However, such concerns seem not to have affected the enormous demand for the wine.

ARTESA VINEYARDS & WINERY 1991		Map 16
www.artesawinery.com	707-224-1668	Tasting
Napa	Napa County	Carneros AVA

Founded in 1991 as Codorniu Napa, the winery produced Sparkling Wines exclusively, along the lines of the Spanish parent Codorniu Group. In 1997, the name became Artesa, and the focus changed to still wines. Today Artesa makes Cabernet Sauvignon, Pinot Noir, Merlot, and Sauvignon Blanc from grapes grown on its four hundred planted acres in the Carneros, Alexander Valley, and Sonoma Coast regions, as well as from grapes bought from several other regions. Artesa has grown into a substantial producer, with over 65,000 cases produced in its accessible Classic line, another 17,000 cases of Reserve wines, and 7,500 more in smaller batches. Futuristic architecture, berms, waterfalls, and sculpture gardens greet the visitor and make Artesa one of the most interesting places to visit in the Carneros region.

Wine quality has varied from very good to ordinary, in part because the winery uses such a wide variety of sources and offers a range of price points. Still, Artesa wines can offer good value for the money when they overachieve, and visits to the winery always seem to uncover new and interesting ideas. Depending on the grape source and the price point of the wine, Artesa bottlings run from mild to sturdy and from average scores around 85+ to the 90s on occasion. New "Elements" wines, under $20, are often good values.

ATLAS PEAK VINEYARDS 1989		Map 15
www.atlaspeak.com	707-252-7971	No Tasting
Napa	Napa County	Atlas Peak AVA

Originally founded by British megabrewer Whitbread along with Tuscan winemaker Antinori and Bollinger of Champagne, Atlas Peak is now held by conglomerate Beam Wine Estates, which was recently acquired by Constellation Brands, which then sold it onward to Ascentia Wine Estates along with Buena Vista and Gary Farrell wineries. Originally a Sangiovese producer, Atlas Peak saw the writing on the wall and reinvented the business to produce nearly exclusively mountain-grown Cabernet Sauvignon. Five Napa Valley mountains are the source of grapes for these wines, including Atlas Peak's own five-hundred-acre vineyard and others on Mount Veeder, Spring Mountain, Howell Mountains, and Diamond Mountain. Current production of its premium Cabernet and a Claret blend of Cabernet, Merlot, and Petit Verdot is just north of five thousand cases. Excess vineyard production is sold to some dozen Napa wineries, including Conn Creek, Darioush, Silver Oak, and Stag's Leap. Recent Cabernets were well-received, but this is a brand in search of a consistent identity.

AUGUST BRIGGS WINES 1995		Map 11
www.augustbriggswines.com	707-942-4912	Tasting
Calistoga	Napa County	Calistoga AVA

After winemaking apprenticeships in Oregon and Sonoma County, August "Joe" Briggs built his modest winery in Calistoga in 2004. Though Briggs does have a 1.5-acre estate vineyard planted to Petite Sirah, the large majority of grapes are sourced from over a dozen vineyards in Napa and Sonoma counties, including Frediani, Green Island, Page-Nord Monte Rosso, and Leveneroni. Briggs makes about 1,500 cases each of Pinot Noir, Cabernet Sauvignon, and Chardonnay varieties, and smaller lots of Zinfandel, Charbono, Petite Sirah, and Syrah. Current total production runs about 5,500 cases of the winery's 10,000-case capacity.

Early results under this label were good to spectacular, with Zinfandel being a leader statewide, then the winery's quality took a tumble, and it is only recently returning to consistent form without yet consistently finding the near perfection that marked so many of its earlier efforts. The house style runs to ripe and somewhat rustic, especially in the heavier reds, with the most recent Zinfandel seemingly back on track.

BALDACCI FAMILY VINEYARDS 1997		Map 15
www.baldaccivineyards.com	707-944-9261	Tasting
Napa	Napa County	Stags Leap District AVA

Thomas Baldacci and his family purchased the winery and vineyard, located on a southern slope in the Stags Leap District, in 1997. Under the guidance of winemaker Rolando Herrera, with experience at Stag's Leap and several other Napa wineries, Baldacci has specialized in estate-grown Cabernet Sauvignon with Pinot Noir, Syrah, and Gewürztraminer produced for good measure. The seventeen-acre estate vineyard is planted to Cabernet Sauvignon and Cabernet Franc grapes. Production runs to over three thousand cases, more than half of which is Cabernet.

Prices for front-line Cabs are fairly steep but not out of line for limited-production wines from the Napa Valley. Quality has been good, with scores in the upper 80s for the most part and the occasional 90-point winner. The reds, its most important wines, are full in body with well-focused fruit and evident tannins and are a bit brusque for wines from the Stags Leap District.

BALLENTINE VINEYARDS 1992		Map 12
www.ballentinevineyards.com	707-963-7919	Tasting by Appointment
St. Helena	Napa County	St. Helena AVA

Libero Pocai first planted grapes at this location in 1906 after being chased from San Francisco by the earthquake. John Ballentine bought the closed winery during Prohibition and began making wine in the 1930s. Van Ballentine of the next generation married Betty Pocai and sold grapes from the 110 acres of vineyards to neighboring wineries. In 1992, Van revived the winery and released the first contemporary vintage. Ballentine now specializes in estate Zinfandel, Merlot, and Syrah varieties, with a Cabernet Sauvignon in the works. Production runs at about nine thousand cases of a ten-thousand-case capacity.

With prices ranging from moderate to somewhat pricey, Ballentine often hits the rating charts in the upper 80s and can offer good value with many wines, especially Zinfandel. Ripe Zinfandels are the winery's most often seen efforts.

BARNETT VINEYARDS 1983		Map 11
www.barnettvineyards.com	707-963-7075	Tasting by Appointment
St. Helena	Napa County	Spring Mountain District AVA

A family-owned winery and vineyard near the top of Spring Mountain has grown from fourteen acres and one hundred cases in 1983 to close to forty acres and six thousand cases. Specialties are the estate-grown Rattlesnake Hill Cabernet Sauvignon and Spring Mountain Cabernet, both primarily sourced from estate-grown grapes and representing half of the total production. Limited bottlings of other varieties use grapes purchased from more distant vineyards, including Pinot Noir from Tina Marie in the Russian River Valley, Chardonnay from the Savoy in the Anderson Valley, and Sangiacomo in Carneros. Hal and Fiona Barnett built the winery and run it with winemaker David Tate.

The quality leader to date has been the pricey but highly regarded Rattlesnake Hill Cabernet, with scores in the mid-90 range not uncommon. Savoy Vineyard Chardonnay and Russian River Pinot Noir can also gain scores at that level, and while Barnett is not always spoken of in the hushed tones reserved for the Napa Valley's royalty, its success is going to push it in that direction very quickly. When successful, whether with solidly structured Cabernets or Pinot Noir and Chardonnay in ripe and brighter styles, Barnett wines never lack for oaky richness and admirable depth.

BEAULIEU VINEYARD 1900		Map 13
www.bvwines.com	800-264-6918	Tasting
Rutherford	Napa County	Rutherford AVA

By almost any standard, Beaulieu is the winery that has defined the fine wine trade in California for the greater part of the twentieth century. Its role as quality leader in Cabernet Sauvignon, which was unchallenged after Prohibition, actually began not long after its founding in 1900. By 1936, the winery had moved to the very front of the quality lists with the release of its Georges de Latour Private Reserve, named for the winery founder. That wine, whether in 1936 or 1951 or 1970, was arguably the leading player in the most expensive and ultimately the most defining game in the varietal wine portion of the industry. When the wine boom hit in the 1970s, and with Beaulieu being bought out by increasingly larger and larger corporate interests, things changed, but even with an increase in competition and despite the selling off of some of its best vineyard sites, Beaulieu Private Reserve Cabernet remains one of the defining wines for California.

Beaulieu got its start at the beginning of the twentieth century when Georges de Latour bought and planted grapes in the West Rutherford area of the Napa Valley. The winery, along with Inglenook (now Francis Ford Coppola's Rubicon Estate), became an industry leader even then, and despite Prohibition—which saw so much good vineyard land either abandoned or pulled out altogether—de Latour kept his grapes well tended and was able to resume production in 1934 with the enactment of Repeal. His decision, in 1938, to hire a young Russian winemaker named André Tchelistcheff, who had stopped off in France's Champagne region to learn his trade, as the head of production at Beaulieu, turned out to be yet another masterstroke by de Latour. After de Latour's death in 1940, Tchelistcheff brought the winery to the very pinnacle of quality, with defining efforts in both Cabernet Sauvignon and Pinot Noir. By the time he retired from Beaulieu some three decades later, Tchelistcheff was America's most celebrated winemaking genius and Beaulieu was its most collectible wine.

After the 1970 vintage, a great one for Beaulieu, the winery went through a series of ownership changes that has resulted today in Beaulieu being one in a string of wineries owned by Diageo, the international investment chain. For a period of time in the 1970s and 1980s, as production rose, the quality of Beaulieu wines came into question; but by 1990, the winemaking team headed by Joel Akin was allowed to make changes in the winemaking regimen that eventually restored Beaulieu to the upper end of the quality ranges for its top wines. No longer a small family-run winery, Beaulieu's production across all of its wines runs into the hundreds of thousands of cases. It now makes Reserve wines of all stripes and regular and high-production bottlings at the low to middle end of the price spectrum.

Quality varies widely across the winery line, but Georges de Latour Private Reserve Cabernet Sauvignon, still a classic Napa Valley wine with curranty and cola notes supported by sweet oak and balancing tannins, can now be counted on to rate in the 90-plus range in most vintages, and the other Reserve bottlings are not far behind. In good vintage, a reasonably priced Cabernet Sauvignon labeled with the Rutherford appellation excels for value among a rising tide of very expensive Napa Valley Cabernets. Tapestry Reserve is typically full-bodied and less refined than the winery's flagship bottling; it will rate as high as 90 points in good vintages. Reserve Chardonnay from Carneros is ripe, oaky, and slightly citrusy. The Beaulieu tasting room, right on the highway in Rutherford, has long been one of our favorites.

BELL WINE CELLARS 1991		Map 14
www.bellwine.com	707-944-1673	Tasting by Appointment
Yountville	Napa County	Yountville AVA

Bell was founded in 1991 by South Africa-born winemaker Anthony Bell and grower John Baritelle. Ten years later, the winery was purchased by San Diego Chargers owner Alex Spanos and wine wholesaler Ron Berberian, but both Bell and Baritelle have stayed on. The initial release of five hundred cases has expanded to over fourteen thousand of the winery's sixteen-thousand-case capacity. Chardonnay and Merlot grapes are grown on the small estate vineyard, while the remainder of the fruit is grown nearby and, in the case of the Syrah, in the Sierra foothills. Some fifteen or so varieties are produced, principally including Cabernet Sauvignon, Syrah, Merlot, Chardonnay, and Sauvignon Blanc.

With the winery's advantageous location and the money behind it, success should have followed, but regardless of ownership, Bell has been a continuing underperformer with scores more often in the low to mid-80s.

BERINGER VINEYARDS 1876		Map 12
www.beringer.com	707-967-4412	Tasting
St. Helena	Napa County	St. Helena AVA

The brothers Beringer founded this historic winery just at the north end of St. Helena proper almost a century and a half ago and built the handsome Rhine House, still one of the most beautiful winery buildings in the Napa Valley. By the 1970s, with the winery having lost some of its lustrous standing, the family sold out to the Nestlé chocolate interests of Switzerland, which in turn sold to investors who then, in 1999, sold to the Foster's brewing empire of Australia. Foster's, it turns out is also a major player in the Australian wine scene with its world-renowned Wolf Blass label. With Beringer and Blass as its crown jewels, and with labels like Etude, St. Clement, and others as part of its operations, the entire enterprise took on the name Beringer Blass.

Today, Beringer has expanded into a million-case line of wines that range from exquisite special bottlings from some of the Napa Valley's best vineyards to long-selling lines of table wines at popular price levels. Beringer's concentrated yet mannerly special bottlings of Cabernet Sauvignon, Chardonnay, and Merlot often earn ratings at the very top of the scale, while the rest of the line comes in with respectable scores for the prices asked. A visit to the Rhine House is still one of our favorite choices in the Napa Valley.

BROWN ESTATE WINERY 1981		Map 14
www.brownestate.com	707-963-2435	Tasting by Appointment
St. Helena	Napa County	Chiles Valley AVA

Establishing their family vineyard in the Napa Valley's Chiles Valley District, the Browns planted grapes beginning in 1985, built their winery in 2001 and caves in '05. The forty-acre estate is two-thirds planted to Zinfandel, with the remainder in Cabernet Sauvignon and Chardonnay grapes. Today's production runs to two thousand cases of estate-grown, -produced, and -bottled Zinfandel and another thousand of Cabernet and Chardonnay.

The lush, full-bodied Zinfandel has gained the most fame to date for its very high levels of ripeness and fruity intensity; it has consistently earned chart-topping points in the 90- to 93-point range.

BUEHLER VINEYARDS 1978		Map 12
www.buehlervineyards.com	707-963-2155	Tasting by Appointment
St. Helena	Napa County	Napa Valley AVA

MAP 11

Northwestern Napa

Knights
Valley

Napa
Valley

Napa
County

Howell
Mountain

Peter
Michael ■

■ T-Vine

Chateau
Montelena ■

Robert
Pecota ■

Calistoga

Storybook
Mountain ■

128

■ Zahtila

Kenefick
Ranch ■

Calistoga
■ Cellars

29

Araujo
■ Estate

Summers
Estate ■

Calistoga

■ August
Briggs

Clos
Pegase ■

Sterling
■

Cuvaison
■

Von Strasser ■

■ Diamond Creek

Paoletti
■

Diamond
Mountain
District

■ Reverie on
Diamond
Mountain

Schramsberg
■

Frank
■ Family
Madrigal

Silverado Trail

29

St Helena

Pride
Mountain
■

Barnett
■

Terra
Valentine
■

St. Helena Rd.

Smith-Madrone
■

Spring Mountain Rd.

■ Stony Hill

Paloma
■

Robert Keenan
■

Spring Mountain
■

Newton
■

■ Cain

St. Clement
■

Spring
Mountain
District

Sonoma
County

Napa
Valley

12

Kenwood

A small, family-owned winery and vineyard, Buehler was established in 1971 by retired Bechtel engineer John Buehler Sr. with the planting of the first vines. Located in the remote hills east of St. Helena and above Lake Hennessey, the vineyards were developed by John Jr., who oversees the operation to this day. Noted for its Cabernet Sauvignon, Zinfandel, and Chardonnay, the estate varieties use grapes from the twenty-six-acre vineyards around the winery. Total production approaches twenty-five thousand cases, with over half Cabernet bottlings.

Once a leader in the midpriced Zinfandel sweepstakes and offering reasonable value for its Russian River Valley Chardonnay, Buehler has not kept up with the pace of late and is decidedly "off the boil" relative to its past glories.

BURGESS CELLARS 1972		Map 12
www.burgesscellars.com	800-752-9463	Tasting by Appointment
St. Helena	Napa County	Napa Valley AVA

Former military and commercial pilot Tom Burgess bought twenty acres of the former Souverain Cellars vineyards—which had known winemaking since the 1880s—on the western slope of Howell Mountain. Expanding the vineyards over time to a total of 105 planted acres, the winery now makes Cabernet Sauvignon on the western slope Ranch Vineyard, Syrah on the eastern slope Ink Grade Road Vineyard, and Merlot in Yountville on the Triere Vineyard. All wines are estate grown and bottled; thirty thousand cases are made currently.

The Burgess style emphasizes tight fruit when young and age worthiness, but the wines have often lacked the stuffing to justify the time needed to have them open up. As a result, ratings have typically landed in the mid- to upper-80 range with the very occasional 90-pointer cropping up for the winery's Bordeaux blend called Enveiere. Still, the wines are not expensive by Napa Valley standards, and they rightfully enjoy a following among those who like a more firmly structured wine.

CAFARO CELLARS 1986		Map 12
www.cafaro.myshopify.com	707-963-7171	Tasting by Appointment
St. Helena	Napa County	St. Helena AVA

Renowned winemaker Joe Cafaro, who had made wine for the likes of Chappellet, Keenan, Acacia, and Sinskey, as well as consulting to others, began his own label in 1986. In '96 the fifteen-acre Cafaro Family Vineyard on the eastern hills just south of the Stags Leap District was planted to Cabernet, Merlot, Cabernet Franc, and Petite Verdot, with a first harvest in '99. Three thousand cases, evenly distributed among Cabernet Sauvignon, Merlot, and Syrah, are produced with a goal of another thousand in the future. All wines are made from estate-grown fruit.

The winery style looks for structure and balance but does not always find the depth of character to lift the wine into the upper rating levels, and more often than not, Cafaro wines have rated in the mid- to upper 80s with occasional excursions above 90 points.

CAIN VINEYARD & WINERY 1983		Map 11
www.cainfive.com	707-963-1616	Tasting by Appointment
St. Helena	Napa County	Spring Mountain District AVA

In 1980, Joyce and Jerry Cain purchased land on the top of Spring Mountain, nearly two thousand feet above the valley floor, where they could plant all five Bordeaux grape varieties. Though part owners Jim and Nancy Meadlock took full control of the winery in'91, winemaker Christopher Howell was a constant. Today, 84 acres on a 540-acre ranch are planted, and the grapes are the source of most of the three principal wines produced: Cain Five, the top-end estate-grown blend of Cabernet Sauvignon, Merlot, Malbec, Cabernet Franc, and Petit Verdot grapes; and two other more modestly priced blends, Cain Concept and Cain Cuvée. The latter represents 50 percent of the twenty-five thousand cases of total production; the remainder is split between Cain Five and Cain Concept.

Cain wines have been something of a mixed blessing for wine lovers over the years. At times, they have risen to the top of the ratings table; at others, they have seemed overly coarse and low on fruit. Still, Cain Five, one of the first wines in California to feature all five of the Bordeaux red grapes, enjoys a bit of a cult following.

CAKEBREAD CELLARS 1973		Map 13
www.cakebread.com	800-588-0298	Tasting by Appointment
Rutherford	Napa County	Rutherford AVA

Well over thirty years ago, while simultaneously operating his family's auto repair business in Oakland and pursuing a career in photography (he studied with Ansel Adams), Jack Cakebread came to the valley to photograph it for a book and wound up buying a vineyard and establishing a winery along Highway 12. Some thirty years later, with son Bruce and six other Cakebreads in tow, along with winemaker Julianne Laks, winery production ranges well over fifty thousand cases of a wide selection of wines including Sauvignon Blanc, Chardonnay, Pinot Noir, Merlot, Syrah, Zinfandel, and Cabernet Sauvignon. Thirteen vineyard sites, totaling 340 planted acres throughout the valley, produce fruit for Cakebread's broad and generally well-received line of varietal offerings.

At some point or other, almost every variety made has enjoyed a fair measure of success within the winery's rich yet balanced style. Sauvignon Blanc and Chardonnay are the varieties most likely to succeed, with Cabernet Sauvignon not far behind.

CALISTOGA CELLARS	1998	Map 11
www.calistogacellars.com	707-942-7422	Tasting
Calistoga	Napa County	Calistoga AVA

Back in the mid-1990s, wine country veteran Roger Louer got together with some friends and purchased a vineyard. A few years later, with the help of widely traveled winemaker, Barry Gnekow, the Calistoga Cellars label was born. Today, the winery has expanded its line to include Chardonnay, Sauvignon Blanc, Zinfandel, Merlot, Cabernet Sauvignon, a vineyard-designated Cabernet from Louer's vineyard, and a Cabernet Sauvignon Port. When the Calistoga AVA was officially designated in January 2010, the winery's name was specifically challenged. After three years, the name Calistoga will no longer be allowed to appear on wines that do not meet the requirements (85 percent of grapes grown there) of the Calistoga AVA.

Zinfandel has so far been the quality leader, with scores that have risen into the 90s more often than not. Chardonnay and the Louer Cabernet Sauvignon are close behind, but results can be inconsistent.

CARDINALE ESTATE	1990	Map 14
www.cardinale.com	800-588-0279	Tasting by Appointment
Oakville	Napa County	Oakville AVA

Part of Kendall-Jackson's Artisan & Estates group of wineries, Cardinale Estate, under the auspices of A&E's winemaker Chris Carpenter, makes a single Cabernet Sauvignon-based blend each vintage. Typically, the blend is about 90 percent Cabernet Sauvignon and 10 percent Merlot. Capacity of the winery, shared with Lokoya, is fifty thousand cases. The owned vineyards total just over 130 acres, with 68 acres at the Keyes Vineyard and 63 acres at Veeder Peak, plus a small representation at the To Kalon Vineyard.

The wine is a big, inky-colored, intense, and somewhat exaggerated version of Cabernet Sauvignon, and it has won both wide acclaim and the occasional brickbat for its willingness to push the envelope. Yet, for aficionados of the style, the frequent ratings in the low to mid-90s seem appropriate.

CARNEROS CREEK WINERY 1971		Map 16
www.briarcliffwines.com	707-253-9464	Tasting
Napa	Napa County	Carneros AVA

Original owners Francis and Kathleen Mahoney established the first winery in Carneros since Prohibition and met with immediate success for their estate-grown Pinot Noir as well as for Zinfandel sourced from Amador County. Mahoney worked closely with UC–Davis on studies of clonal selections of Pinot and was among the first to separate the various clones into potential by depth, color, and character. In 2004, the Mahoneys sold the winery to the Briarcliff Wine Group in 2004 (they also own Wildhurst), and the new owners retained winemaker Ken Foster. Now mostly a Pinot Noir specialist, Carneros Creek produces as much as eleven thousand cases each vintage of a Reserve and a more limited "Grail" Pinot Noir in addition to the occasional Chardonnay. The 160-acre Mahoney Vineyard remains the major source of grapes under the new ownership.

CAYMUS VINEYARDS 1972		Map 13
www.caymus.com	707-963-4204	Tasting by Appointment
Rutherford	Napa County	Rutherford AVA

Founded by noted, longtime Napa Valley growers Charlie and Lorna Wagner, and now managed by their son Chuck, Caymus focuses on Cabernet Sauvignon made from grapes grown on their own sixty-acre estate vineyard as well as grapes purchased from Jan Krupp's renowned Stagecoach Vineyard in the Atlas Peak AVA. A Napa Valley Cabernet Sauvignon and a high-end Special Selection Cabernet make up the lion's share of the fifty-thousand-case production. A second label, Conundrum, is a white blend of Sauvignon Bland, Chardonnay, and Muscat grapes. The family also controls the Belle Glos and Mer Soleil labels for Pinot Noir and Chardonnay made by the next generation of Wagners. For some years, Caymus made the Liberty School line of modestly priced wines, but the Wagners sold their controlling interest in 1997.

From the very outset, Caymus Cabernet Sauvignon went to the top of the rating charts and has stayed there ever since. In its early days, when all the wine produced came from the twenty-five acres surrounding the midvalley vineyard, both the regular bottling and the heavily oaked Special Selection delivered some of the purest expressions of the curranty, rich Rutherford character one could find. Expansion has changed the character of both wines to some extent, but nothing has dented the continuing run of Cabernet success at Caymus. Ratings in the 90- to 95-point range are achieved more often than not, and Caymus rightfully deserves to be mentioned among the royalty of Napa Valley Cabernet producers.

CHAPPELLET WINERY 1967		Map 14
www.chappellet.com	800-4WINERY	Tasting by Appointment
St. Helena	Napa County	Napa Valley AVA

Donn and Molly Chappellet were modern pioneers when they planted grapes on high-elevation eastern hillsides in the Napa Valley. After selling a successful food service business in Southern California, the Chappellets bought land and a winery on Pritchard Hill, past Lake Hennessey and well above the valley floor. Founded in 1967, the winery now makes twenty-five thousand cases a year of notable Cabernet Sauvignons (the Signature Cabernet and the limited-production Pritchard Hill Estate Vineyard Cabernet), Merlot, and Chardonay, principally from the fruit grown on the 110-acre Pritchard Hill Vineyard.

There have been a few missteps along the way, but Chappellet has had the benefit of a good location and a string of highly talented winemakers, including current overseer, Philip Titus. Even as early as 1969, its Cabernet showed that it needed to be included in the top ranks. It is not unusual for each of its wines to earn scores in the high 80s and low 90s and for the top-of-the-line Pritchard Hill Estate Vineyard Cabernet to rise even higher to the very pinnacle of the ratings, including having been named the Connoisseurs' Guide Wine of the Year. The Chappellet style of ripe, well-fruited, somewhat tightly structured wines is dictated in part by preference and in part by the hillside site.

Cesare Mondavi, father of Peter Mondavi, who ran Krug in succession from Cesare, and Robert Mondavi who rebelled and started his own eponymous winery in 1966, was a grape grower and winery owner in Lodi who also had wine interests in the Napa Valley. In 1943, he bought the Charles Krug winery from the family of German immigrant Krug and moved his operations there. At his passing in 1959, his wife Rosa became the nominal head of operations, but winemaking fell to Peter while Robert was in charge of sales and marketing. Despite the Krug history of innovation under Peter, Robert felt that many of the winery's concepts were out of date; and after clashing with his brother, he left the family business and created a rift in which the Krug Winery and the Mondavi winery were at odds with each other for years. The resolution of the legal battle between the two saw Robert awarded money and vineyards and left the Charles Krug Winery without funding to move with the times.

Even today, with the winery having updated itself, it still feels somewhat out of date, and its wines, while greatly improved from the dull offerings of two decades ago, rarely win high honors in any category. The occasional Cabernet Sauvignon will reach to 90 points, but most wines are of medium depth at best and search for concentration and modern styling.

Chase has a long history in the Napa Valley dating to the late 1800s when a St. Helena ranch was purchased by Sarah Esther Chase Bourn. Her son built Greystone Cellars in 1888 at the north end of St. Helena. In 1894, phylloxera hit many valley vineyards, including Bourn's, and they sold to the Christian Brothers; it's now the home of the Culinary Institute of America. In 1998, Bourn's great-great-grandson, Andrew Simpson, harvested grapes from the twelve-acre estate vineyard and bottled the first vintage at Chase Family Cellars. Today, two thousand cases are produced, principally Zinfandel, plus limited bottlings of Cabernet Sauvignon and Petite Sirah.

The Chase Zinfandel, always ripe—and full of berryish fruit when successful—is a bit of a hit-or-miss proposition, but it can carry the Napa Valley stamp in best vintages, and the winery deserves kudos for sticking with a variety that can do so well in Napa when all around it are converting to Cabernet Sauvignon.

CHATEAU MONTELENA 1972		Map 11
www.montelena.com	707-942-5105	Tasting
Calistoga	Napa County	Calistoga AVA

Chateau Montelena will always be known for its defeat of France's best at the Paris Tasting of 1976, at which the Montelena Chardonnay beat all contending whites. But the winery didn't just arrive on the scene with a blue ribbon. The winery dates to 1882 when Alfred Tubbs bought 254 acres north of Calistoga. Winemaking ended with Prohibition but roared back in 1972 when lawyer James Barrett brought forth his first vintage. The wines taken to Paris had been made by winemaker Mike Grgich, soon to depart to form his own label, Grgich Hills. Now under the guidance of Barrett's son Bo, the winery focuses on estate-grown and -bottled Cabernet Sauvignons and Chardonnays. Montelena grows grapes on its eight vineyard blocks, totaling ninety-five acres, principally planted to Cabernet. Forty thousand cases are produced, with Cabernet over half the output and Chardonnay, Zinfandel, and even a small quantity of Riesling rounding out the production. The medieval stone winery remains to this day and is one of the most picturesque in the Napa Valley.

Over three decades, Chateau Montelena has stayed near the top of the ranking scale, and while scores in the 90s are not unusual for this prestigious producer, its wines have occasionally suffered from being tighter than they are fruity. Still, there are very few wineries anywhere with better track records and fewer still that have rightfully become legends in their own time.

CHATEAU POTELLE 1988		Map 14
www.chateaupotelle.com	707-255-9440	Tasting
Napa	Napa County	Mount Veeder AVA

A young French winemaking couple, Jean-Noël and Marketta Formeaux, came to California charged with investigating the U.S. side of the business. Instead of reporting back, they stayed and started their own projects here. Purchasing 200 acres high on Mt. Veeder, under the winemaking auspices of Marketta, their production reached 20,000+ cases of Chardonnay, Cabernet Sauvignon, Zinfandel and Sauvignon Blanc at its peak. They also founded a second label, Gravity Hills, located in west Paso Robles, with a further 50 planted acres and production of 11,000 cases, mostly of Zinfandel. But success did not have a happy ending. Things got rocky. The winery was sold to the Kendall-Jackson interests and sales slowed.

Building on the success of its upscale, full-bodied wines, labeled with the monicker VGS, the winery has delivered a wide-ranging set of rankings from the mid-and upper 80s to the occasional 90-pointer.

CHIMNEY ROCK WINERY 1980		Map 15
www.chimneyrock.com	800-257-2641	Tasting
Napa	Napa County	Stags Leap District AVA

New Yorker Hack Wilson, an executive with Pepsi-Cola and for several years active in the South African brewing industry, became interested in wine. Wilson bought the 185-acre Chimney Rock golf course on the Silverado Trail, near Clos du Val in the small Stags Leap District AVA, and planted nine holes (seventy-five acres) to Cabernet Sauvignon, Merlot, Chardonnay, and Sauvignon Blanc. Ultimately, a total of nearly 120 acres would be planted from the flatlands of the trail up into the eastern hills. In 1987, Doug Fletcher, with experience at the original, legendary Martin Ray winery and later at Steltzner Vineyards, became winemaker. The Terlato family bought the Wilson family interests in 2000, and Chimney Rock joined the Terlato Group, which includes Rutherford Hill, Alderbrook in Sonoma, and Sanford in Santa Barbara County. More than thirty thousand cases of Cabernet Sauvignon, Elevage Bordeaux (a blend of Merlot, Cabernet, and Cabernet Franc), Elevage Blanc, and Fumé Blanc are produced today.

The Chimney Rock style from the very outset was a reflection of winemaker Fletcher's preference for balanced wines that work well with food and have good aging potential. The winery has shied away from the fleshy, youthfully precocious direction taken by many of its neighbors in the Napa Valley and instead relied on firm acids and tannin-laced structures in the reds. It is a style that can be difficult to execute in California, and results have not always been inspired, but Elevage has scored well in almost every vintage, often reaching into the low-90-point range, and so has the Cabernet Sauvignon. The Fumé Blanc, typically rated in the mid-80s, has been less successful overall. Fletcher now directs winemaking for the entire Terlato group, with Elizabeth Vianna the hands-on winemaker at Chimney Rock, but the house style has not changed and is not likely to.

CLARK-CLAUDON VINEYARDS 1989		Map 12
www.clarkclaudon.com	707-965-9393	No Tasting
St. Helena	Napa County	Howell Mountain Valley AVA

Fellow Peace Corps graduates Tom Clark and Laurie Claudon founded Clark-Claudon after Tom's apprenticeships at Souverain, El Retiro, and Spring Mountain led to a vineyard management company of his own. They planted twenty acres on Howell Mountain in 1990 and made a first Cabernet Sauvignon vintage of fewer than two hundred cases in 1993. Today, about one thousand cases of estate Cabernet Sauvignon and Sauvignon Blanc are produced.

After indifferent results with the first releases of Cabernet Sauvignon, the winery has seemed to hit its stride with a string of highly recommendable bottlings whose focused character and good aging potential has earned ratings in the upper 80s and low 90s.

CLIFF LEDE VINEYARDS 2002		Map 15
www.cliffledevineyards.com	800-428-2259	Tasting
Yountville	Napa County	Stags Leap District AVA

Canadian businessman Cliff Lede bought the S. Anderson winery and sixty acres in the northern end of the Stags Leap District in 2002. With Michelle Edwards as winemaker (formerly of Coglin), they set about to plant the acreage to Bordeaux varietal grapes, leading to a first release in '04. Lede specializes in estate-grown Cabernet Sauvignon, Sauvignon Blanc, and Petite Sirah. Their Poetry label consists of a high-end, limited-edition Cabernet. The winery has continued to use the S. Anderson label for its limited-production Sparkling Wines. Total production approaches eighteen thousand cases, with the Cliff Lede label accounting for 80 percent. A small hotel, the Poetry Inn, is located just across the Silverado Trail on additional acreage controlled by the winery.

Almost from the outset, the winery has been successful with most varietals. Poetry and a recent Sauvignon Blanc have garnered scores in the 90s, while most of the rest have been rated in the upper 80s, with the occasional mid-80s proving to be the exception to the general rule.

CLOS DU VAL WINERY 1972		Map 15
www.closduval.com	707-259-2200	Tasting
Napa	Napa County	Stags Leap District AVA

American businessman John Goelet and French winemaker Bernard Portet, the latter having spent years in Bordeaux working with his father at Château Lafite, discovered the Stags Leap District when they acquired 150 acres and founded Clos du Val (a "small estate of a small valley") in 1972. A year later, they purchased an additional 180 acres in the Carneros region. Their first Cabernet Sauvignon vintage, in '72, was one of only six Cabernets selected for the Paris Tasting of 1976, at which American Cabernets took the measure of their Bordeaux competitors. Today Clos du Val makes over 65,000 cases annually, ranging from some 35,000 cases of its Classic Cabernet to 250 cases of its Reserve Cabernet and Chardonnays. John Clews has taken up the winemaking reins, while Portet tends to Clos du Val holdings in Australia and France.

The winery is maddeningly inconsistent in quality. Some bottlings rival the best in the valley, and many rate simply no better than average for their not immoderate price levels. Clos du Val enjoys its high reputation based on its few great successes and its avoidance of total clunkers. From the outset, Clos du Val has made wines that show a European influence in their restrained ripeness and higher acidities.

CLOS PEGASE 1984		Map 11
www.clospegase.com	707-942-4981	Tasting
Calistoga	Napa County	Calistoga AVA

Owner and art collector Jan Shrem bought land south of Calistoga in the early 1980s and hired renowned architect Michael Graves to design his state-of-the-art, modernistically handsome winery. Vineyard acreage has grown to over 450 in three locations: 50 at the estate Home Ranch, another 40 at the Palisades Vineyard north of Calistoga, and another 360 acres in Carneros, in Mitsuko's Vineyard named after Shrem's wife. From these three vineyards comes the fruit for some fifty thousand cases of Cabernet, Chardonnay, Pinot Noir, Sauvignon Blanc, and Merlot. A museum-quality sculpture collection graces the premises, and the interior is dotted with modern art as well. For those who would combine the arts with their ventures in the Napa Valley, Clos Pegase is a mandatory stop.

After somewhat mixed results in the beginning, Clos Pegase now succeeds with virtually each of its offerings. In particular, those wines labeled Hommage, all of which are deep and rich yet do not abandon the house style, regularly score in the 90-plus range; the other bottlings rate from a recommended 87-point level up to the low 90s. Even when ripe, Clos Pegase wines have always been geared to a level of elegance that separates them from the bolder style often prevailing at wineries within its price niche.

COLGIN CELLARS 1992		Map 12
www.colgincellars.com	707-963-0999	No Tasting
St. Helena	Napa County	Napa Valley AVA

Former art and antiquities expert and auctioneer Ann Coglin of Beverly Hills founded this ultrapremium winery and vineyard on Pritchard Hill, east of and above St. Helena, overlooking Lake Hennessey. The small winery, completed in 2002, produces about 2,500 cases a year of Cabernet Sauvignon, Syrah, and a red blend in five bottlings, two from the 20-acre estate vineyard and three from others in the region. The largest bottling is about 1,200 cases of the IX Estate Red, from estate grapes. Individual bottles, available only to mailing list subscribers and top-drawer restaurants, retail for $290 and up. Winemaker Allison Tauzlet joins noted vineyard manager David Abreu in making these elite wines.

With ratings in the mid- to upper 90s and prices as stratospheric as the wines' ratings, Colgin has become one of the most highly sought-after wines in California due to its immensely powerful yet polished efforts.

CONN CREEK WINERY 1973		Map 13
www.conncreek.com	707-963-9100	Tasting
St. Helena	Napa County	Rutherford AVA

Former electronics exec Bill Collins founded Conn Creek in 1973 and sold it thirteen years later to US Tobacco, parent of Ste. Michelle Wine Estates, the current owner. Conn Creek now farms a three-acre estate vineyard in Rutherford and holds contracts for the output of several more, including Collins Vineyard north of St. Helena, Palisades Ranch northeast of Calistoga, and the Stagecoach Vineyard on Atlas Peak. Production is level at 25,000 cases, three-quarters of which is the Napa Valley Cabernet, and another 3,500 cases of the proprietary Meritage red blend called Anthology. In the last year or so, Mike McGrath has assumed the winemaking mantle at Conn Creek, replacing Jeff McBride who has moved to an executive position at Stag's Leap Wine Cellars. No change in winemaking style would seem to be in the works.

The winery's Cabernet Sauvignon comes recommended in more years than not, typically with scores in the upper 80s, while Anthology has reached into the low 90s every so often and offers good value in those vintages.

CORISON WINERY 1987		Map 12
www.corison.com	707-963-0826	Tasting by Appointment
St. Helena	Napa County	St. Helena AVA

Cathy Corison started her own label in 1987 after ten years as winemaker at Chappellet Vineyards. In '96 she bought ten acres of land—the old Kronos estate—and planted eight to Cabernet Sauvignon. She makes four hundred to five hundred cases of the Kronos Vineyard Cabernet Sauvignon, another three thousand of the Corison Napa Valley Cabernet from grapes grown on several other vineyards on the western bench of Rutherford and St. Helena, and a very limited quantity of Gewürztraminer from a vineyard in the Anderson Valley.

The Corison style is considerably more refined and elegant than most of its competitors. When the wines succeed, they are exquisite examples of the genre, but in lesser vintages, they can be somewhat too limited in character. High scores, which reflect the winery's ability to make some of the best-mannered wines in the Napa Valley, reach into the mid- and upper 90s—making Corison an important winery in our cellars and a worthwhile stop along Highway 12, the main road through the Napa Valley.

COSENTINO WINERY 1980		Map 14
www.cosentinowinery.com	707-944-1220	Tasting
Yountville	Napa County	Oakville AVA

Owner-winemaker Mitch Cosentino was a Central Valley wine wholesaler who started making wines in a corner of one of his warehouses. The small start in 1980 has grown into a group of wineries stretching from Yountville to Lodi and includes labels Cosentino, M Coz, and CE2V, among others. Just over a hundred acres are planted on three vineyards in Oakville, Pope

Valley, and Lodi. Production of Cosentino wines runs to twelve thousand cases of Cabernet Sauvignon, Zinfandel, Chardonnay, and several Meritage blends; indeed, Cosentino was among the pioneers in developing Meritage blends in California. Another five thousand cases are bottled at the Crystal Valley Cellars in Lockeford, in the Lodi AVA.

Quality has been about average for the prices charged. Ripeness sometimes gets the better of the wines, while at other times, the wines have lacked a sufficiently fruity center.

CULLER WINES 1997		Map 14
www.cullerwines.com	707-257-0567	No Tasting
St. Helena	Napa County	St. Helena AVA

Karen Culler makes Syrah, with the occasional excursion into Cabernet Sauvignon. A former chemist in the Northwest, Culler left for Columbia Cellars in Washington, a degree from UC–Davis, and more than a decade learning the business from Robert Mondavi, leading her to become the winemaker for Vichon. In 1997, Culler started making her own wine as well as becoming consulting winemaker to others in the Napa Valley. Total current production is shy of one thousand cases of three separate vineyard-designated Syrahs, from the Griffin's Lair Vineyard near Petaluma, Sawi Vineyard in Sonoma, and a Syrah blended from grapes grown on the Alexander Ranch and Cortese Vineyards in the Napa Valley.

Culler's wines are always well received but also hard to find. Her Syrahs have often achieved high ratings because they are deep, balanced, ripe but not over-the-top in the search for the strength of that variety.

CUVAISON WINERY 1969		Map 11
www.cuvaison.com	707-942-6266	Tasting
Calistoga	Napa County	Calistoga AVA

Multiple ownership in the early days led to a lack of focus and production of myriad wine styles. Finally, in 1986, the industrialist Alexander Schmidheiny's family of Switzerland took over and concentrated on the critically acclaimed Chardonnay, which now represents over two-thirds of the production of sixty-five-thousand cases, with the remainder divided among Cabernet Sauvignon, Merlot, Pinot Noir, and Syrah. Under the guidance of winemaker Steven Rogstad, grapes are grown for the Cuvaison bottlings on the 400-acre Carneros estate—planted to Chardonnay, Pinot

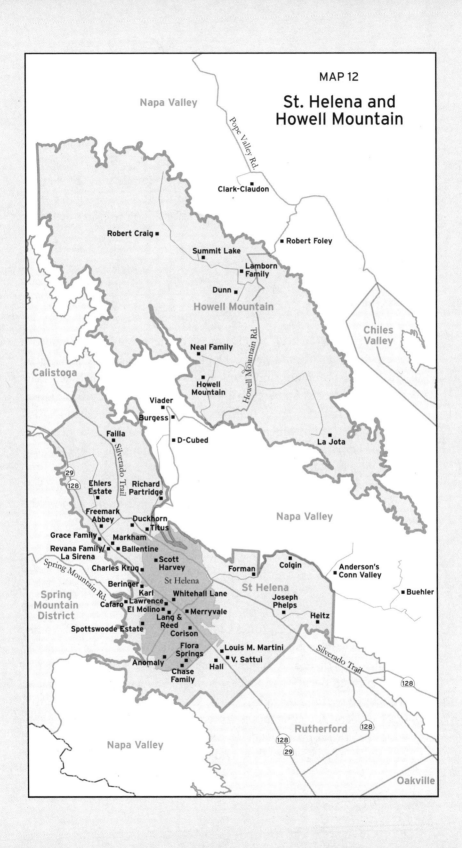

MAP 12

St. Helena and Howell Mountain

Napa Valley

Pope Valley Rd.

Clark-Claudon ■

Robert Craig ■

Robert Foley ■

Summit Lake ■

Lamborn
Family ■

Dunn ■

Howell Mountain

Chiles
Valley

Calistoga

Neal Family ■

Howell Mountain Rd.

Howell
Mountain ■

Viader ■

Burgess ■

Failla ■

D-Cubed ■

La Jota ■

Silverado Trail

29
128

Ehlers
Estate ■

Richard
Partridge ■

Napa Valley

Freemark
Abbey ■

Duckhorn ■
Titus ■

Grace Family ■

Markham ■

Revana Family/
La Sirena ■

Ballentine ■

Spring Mountain Rd.

Charles Krug ■

Scott
Harvey ■

Forman ■

Colgin ■

Anderson's
Conn Valley ■

St Helena

St Helena

Buehler ■

Spring
Mountain
District

Beringer ■

Karl ■

Whitehall Lane ■

Joseph
Phelps ■

Cafaro ■

Lawrence ■
El Molino ■

Merryvale ■

Heitz ■

Lang &
Reed ■

Spottswoode Estate ■

Corison ■

Flora
Springs ■

Louis M. Martini ■

Silverado Trail

Anomaly ■

Hall ■

V. Sattui ■

Chase
Family ■

128

Napa Valley

Rutherford

128

128

128
29

Oakville

Noir, and Merlot—and on the 170-acre Brandlin Ranch on Mount Veeder, of which 32 are planted to Cabernet.

Besides residing in one of the more handsome modern wineries in the Napa Valley, located on the east side along the Silverado Trail, Cuvaison has also become one of the more consistent producers, with most wines wholly recommendable and some scoring up to 90 points. Its flagship Chardonnay is made in a tight, brisk style that reminds some of French wines and enjoys a fair degree of popularity because it is always a good mate to lighter seafood and most shellfish preparations. The reds are medium/full- to full-bodied with good balance.

D-CUBED CELLARS 1994		Map 12
www.dcubedcellars.com	707-963-5212	Tasting
Angwin	Napa County	Napa Valley AVA

With a name such as Duane David Dappen, it's inevitable that "D-Cubed" would leap forth as a brand name. Dappen, with experience at Grgich Hills, Storybook Mountain, and Frank Family Vineyards, concluded that Zinfandel would be his focus, even though less than 2 percent of grapes grown in the Napa Valley are of that varietal. Dappen now produces 2,500 cases, well over a third of which is his flagship Napa Valley Zinfandel. The remaining production is of vineyard-designated Zinfandels from Howell Mountain, St. Helena, and Chiles Valley vineyards.

From the outset, quality has been high; each of the deeply drafted D-Cubed efforts earn ratings in the highly recommended range of 90-plus points as often as not.

DALLA VALLE VINEYARDS 1986		Map 14
www.dallavallevineyards.com	707-944-2676	No Tasting
Oakville	Napa County	Oakville AVA

Gustav Dalla Valle, from a centuries-old Italian winemaking family, came to winemaking late in life, at seventy. Most of Gustav's life had been spent as a deep-sea diver and equipment manufacturer. Then, with spouse Naoko, he planted twenty-five acres of Cabernet Sauvignon grapes on an eastern slope above the Silverado Trail in Oakville. After Gustav's death, in 1995, Naoko continued operating the vineyard and winery and brought their wines to critical prominence among the small-production wines of the Napa Valley. Today, three thousand cases of the Dalla Valle Cabernet are made each year, and a Cabernet–Cabernet Franc blend named Maya after their daughter is produced in annual lots of fewer than five hundred cases. Distribution is very limited, through a now-closed mailing list and a few other channels.

The wines enjoy a fine reputation and are typically rated near 90 points and higher. High demand now means that the oak-enriched, firmly but not brusquely structured, age-worthy Dalla Valle wines make only rare appearances in wine stores.

DARIOUSH WINERY 1997		Map 10
www.darioush.com	707-257-2345	Tasting
Napa	Napa County	Napa Valley AVA

The Darioush Winery perches in its grand Persian splendor just off the Silverado Trail. Darioush Khaledi was raised in Iran's Shiraz region, where his father was a winemaking hobbyist. Khaledi the younger immigrated to Southern California in the late 1970s and was originally a civil engineer; then, with his family, he built a regional grocery business. His passion for wine led him to plant ninety-five acres of Bordeaux-style grapes in Oak Knoll, Carneros, and elsewhere in the valley and, in '04, build his Persian-temple winery. Today, a total of over fifteen thousand cases are made of Cabernet Sauvignon (two-thirds of total production), Merlot, and Chardonnay. Visit the interesting Web site, full of good photos and plentiful information about the wines and winery. And, if you are touring in the Napa Valley, visit the winery.

Darioush wines are typically full-bodied, plush, intensely flavored examples of the hedonistic approach that is more likely to come from California than from most other wine-producing regions. Qualitative ratings in the low to mid-90s are the norm, but be aware that these are wines for people who like the big, dramatic, mouth-filling style.

DAVID ARTHUR VINEYARDS 1978		Map 14
www.davidarthur.com	707-963-5190	Tasting by Appointment
St. Helena	Napa County	Napa Valley AVA

David Long's father Don bought land in the 1950s on Pritchard Hill, above the Silverado Trail near Lake Hennessey as an investment. David worked at Chappellet, Phelps, and Schramsberg to learn winemaking while planting forty acres to Chardonnay and eventually to Bordeaux varietal grapes. Today's production of over 3,500 cases consists of an estate Cabernet named Elevation 1147 after the height of the vineyard; a Meritaggio composed of Cabernet Sauvignon, Merlot, and Sangiovese (and representing a third of total winery production); Merlot; Sauvignon Blanc; and Chardonnay.

Wine quality has varied widely over the years: scores in the 90s have appeared side by side with ratings in the mid-80s, far lower than the ambitious prices might suggest. Still, the latest releases from David Arthur were among its best to date, with the top-rated wines having both depth and classic structures in which supple centers are well supported by a firming but unobtrusive spine of tannin.

DELECTUS WINERY 1995		Map 15
www.delectuswinery.com	707-255-1252	Tasting by Appointment
Napa	Napa County	Napa Valley AVA

Gerhard Reisacher comes from an eight-generation Austrian winemaking family. After graduating from Austria's premier viticultural college, Gerhard set out for the States and worked at Far Niente, Pine Ridge, and Clos du Val before starting to make his own wine, with wife Linda, in 1995. Today's roster includes several Cabernet Sauvignons, Merlot, Syrah, and four or five red-based blends, with the best earning premium prices. The family dogs are featured on the labels of several Merlot-based blends with names such as Dog-Gone Good, Dog in Style, and Dirty Old Dog. A new, forty-acre vineyard in Knights Valley immediately north of and bordering Mount St. Helena has been planted to the five red Bordeaux varietals. Located at 1,200 to 2,200 feet, it is to be the home of a new estate winery with a 7,500-case capacity.

Everything that Delectus makes is supple, full-bodied, somewhat more tannic than most of its competition, and sturdy. As tasty as they are when young, these wines, whose ratings are typically in the upper 80s and low 90s, are even more enjoyable as they age.

DIAMOND CREEK VINEYARDS 1968		Map 11
www.diamondcreekvineyards.com	707-942-6926	No Tasting
Calistoga	Napa County	Diamond Mountain District AVA

Diamond Creek was one of the state's first Cabernet Sauvignon-only estate vineyards and has been exceptionally successful in maintaining that focus for many years. The redoubtable Al Brounstein left his Southern California pharmaceutical business to buy seventy-nine acres on Diamond Mountain, west of Calistoga. Four separate vineyards, totaling twenty-two acres, were planted to Cabernet grapes and provided the fruit for the separate vineyard-designated Cabernets that have become cult wines, among the best and highest-priced in the valley. Now Phil Steinschriber, the winemaker since 1991, has taken over since Brounstein's death in 2006; he is gradually replanting the vineyards and continues to make fewer than two thousand cases of this very limited-distribution wine.

Diamond Creek wines have been treated as some of the Napa's crown jewels from the beginning, but the tannin-heavy wines of its early days were also too stern for some and often met with resistance from those looking for a more balanced approach. Over the years, the winery tempered its style somewhat, and while the wines remain incredibly age-worthy, they are much more approachable than they used to be and no longer demand two decades and more of cellaring before they come into their own. As a result, Diamond Creek wines, from three adjoining parcels with somewhat differing soils and exposures and labeled as Gravelly Meadow, Red Rock Terrace, and Volcanic Hill, have all received high critical acclaim, with ratings in the mid- to upper 90s regularly seen. A tiny parcel planted near the winery's private lake and carrying the name Lake Vineyard is sold only to the mailing list.

DOMAINE CARNEROS 1987		Map 16
www.domaine.com	800-716-BRUT	Tasting
Napa	Napa County	Carneros AVA

A partnership of France's Champagne Taittinger and Kobrand distributors, Domaine Carneros uses the *méthode champenoise* to make a Brut, Brut Rosé under the moniker Cuvée de Pompadour, and a Reserve Blanc de Blancs labeled as Le Rêve in the style of the French parent. An impressive winery, built in the grand style of the Taittinger Château de la Marquetterie near Reims, can produce sixty thousand cases of Sparkling Wines. A second facility was more recently built out back for Pinot Noir and can make up to eighteen thousand cases of still wines.

Winemaker–managing director Eileen Crane, with Sparkling Wine credentials from Domaine Chandon and Gloria Ferrer, oversees production from principally estate-grown grapes on 190 acres of vineyards. Le Rêve often rates with the very best bubbly produced in California.

The Brut, Rosé, and Blanc de Blancs regularly earn ratings in the upper 80s to low 90s, while Le Rêve can be rated as high as the mid-90s, which places it at the very pinnacle of California Sparkling Wine ratings. It is Crane's stylistic predilections that dictate the very successful, invitingly crisp, yeasty, bright approach that each of the Domaine Carneros wines delivers.

DOMAINE CHANDON 1973		Map 14
www.chandon.com	707-944-8844	Tasting
Yountville	Napa County	Yountville AVA

The first in a series of investments in California by some of the leading houses from Champagne, Chandon is the child of the Moët & Chandon establishment (which also has wineries in Argentina, Australia, and India). Its wines are made in the classic method of producing the bubbles directly in the bottle and are intended as a blending of French styling and the somewhat riper California fruit. With a modern winery located across the highway from Yountville, and sporting a destination restaurant and very active tasting room, this distinctive winery was instrumental in changing the face of Sparkling Wine in California.

Its early success places its products, a traditional Brut and a Blanc de Noirs, at the top of the quality ladder, and the addition of a Reserve bottling and a new and upscale line entitled Étoile has kept Chandon moving with the changes and improvements that have taken place in the almost four decades since its arrival. Chandon owns some one thousand acres of vineyards in the cool, southern end of the Napa Valley, mostly in Carneros but also on Mount Veeder. Total production is in the hundreds of thousands of cases, and Chandon Sparkling Wine has become a respected and reliable staple. With most California Sparkling Wine houses, including Chandon, offering long-aged wines, the Brut and Blanc de Noirs now compete with other entry-level bubblies and garner ratings in the upper 80s, which keeps them very competitive with their price-level peers.

DOMINUS ESTATE 1982		Map 14
www.dominusestate.com	707-944-8954	No Tasting
Yountville	Napa County	Yountville AVA

This historic vineyard located directly north of Domaine Chandon, the history of which extends as far back as George Yount, who planted the first vineyards in 1836, passed through several owners to John Daniels, who also owned Inglenook in Rutherford (now Rubicon Estate) and operated the vineyard in its heyday of the 1930s to 1960s. On his death, it passed to his two daughters, Robin Lail and Marcia Smith. In 1982, Christian Moueix, winemaker for the famous Château Pétrus of Pomerol, entered a joint venture with the Daniels daughters establishing Dominus Estate. Some years later, in 1995, Moueix took full control. Since '83, the Dominus proprietary Cabernet Sauvignon-based red blend has been made each vintage; seven thousand cases were made most recently. A second red blend, typically lighter on the Cabernet and with slightly more Cabernet Franc and Petit Verdot in the mix, is called Napanook; five thousand cases were made in the most recent vintage. The 108-acre Napanook Vineyard is the sole source of grapes for both blends. The handsome, low-slung, environmentally innovative stealth winery was completed in 1997 by Swiss architects Herzog & de Meuron, designers of London's Tate Modern, San Francisco's de Young Museum, and Beijing's "Bird Cage" Olympic Stadium.

Dominus, whose early labels featured a stern-looking Christian Moueix, has always been a bit of a stern wine with tannins and earthy characteristics having prominent roles as part of a tight, well-focused, correct fruit personality. Recent vintages have softened the image somewhat, but Dominus remains a solid, age-demanding wine whose ratings at 90 points and up help justify its optimistic pricing.

DUCKHORN VINEYARDS 1976		Map 12
www.duckhorn.com	707-963-7108	Tasting
St. Helena	Napa County	St. Helena AVA

Banker Dan Duckhorn was lured to Napa on business and decided to start a vineyard and winery. With ten other families as investors, Duckhorn released its first small output of Merlot and Cabernet Sauvignon in 1978, and a Sauvignon Blanc followed in 1982. Known particularly for its Merlot, Duckhorn now typically produces five Merlot varieties, four Cabernets, and a Sauvignon Blanc each vintage year, with total production totaling sixty-five thousand cases. Seven owned vineyards in the Napa Valley and on Howell Mountain total 180 acres, principally of Merlot, Cabernet, Sauvignon Blanc, and Zinfandel grapes. Bill Nancarrow, a New Zealander from the winegrowing Hawkes Bay region, is winemaker for Duckhorn and its siblings, the Paraduxx and Anderson Valley's Goldeneye labels.

Duckhorn red wines are rich and deep with plenty of youthful tannin for age. They have been leaders in Merlot for three decades and hit the mark with Cabernet Sauvignon as well. Ratings in the 90- to 95-point range are the norm and attest to the continuing success that has followed this winery since its inception. Sauvignon Blanc has likewise excelled across the years, often rating as the top in many vintages—although recent efforts, while quite recommendable, have dropped into the upper 80s.

DUNN VINEYARDS 1982		Map 12
www.dunnvineyards.com	707-965-3642	No Tasting
Angwin	Napa County	Howell Mountain AVA

Randy and Lori Dunn (Randy was winemaker at Caymus) revived an old Cabernet Sauvignon vineyard on their property in the Howell Mountains east of St. Helena and built a winery on the site in the 1980s. Today the production has gradually increased to about five thousand cases of only two well-received Cabernets: a Howell Mountain bottling with 100 percent Howell Mountain grapes grown on their thirty acres of vines; and a Napa Valley Cabernet with 85 percent Howell Mountain grapes and the remainder purchased from other Napa vineyards. The Dunn family sells a high proportion of their wines to mailing list subscribers. Randy Dunn is a staunch opponent of the trend toward higher-alcohol wines that he sees as being built more for winning tastings than for enjoying.

In the 1980s especially, Dunn Cabernets enjoyed cult status as some of Napa's most highly collectible bottlings. The advent of newer wineries with a richer style and a slight fall-off in Dunn quality may have turned the heat down a bit, but Dunn's keenly focused, age-worthy Cabernets remain popular, hard to get, and expensive. The Napa Valley designate is the slightly softer of the two. Both can earn ratings above 90 points for their firm, balanced styles.

EHLERS ESTATE 1993		Map 12
www.ehlersestate.com	707-963-5972	Tasting
St. Helena	Napa County	St. Helena AVA

The Ehlers Estate—originally Ehlers Grove—was first planted as early as 1886, along with the construction of the winery, still extant. In the late 1980s, Jean Leducq, a French laundry magnate, was casting about for a winery in the Napa Valley after building a vineyard and winery operation in Virginia, near Thomas Jefferson's original acreage. Leducq and family bought the Ehlers Estate's forty-two acres, on which Bordeaux varieties now grow. Today, several years after Jean's death, the Leducq foundation owns the property, run by winemaker Rudy Zuidema, experienced in Napa Valley and Australia. Production stands at ten thousand cases of estate wines, focused on two Cabernet Sauvignons that comprise 70 percent of the output.

The potential here is quite high, and over the years, the winery has enjoyed a great deal of success; but there have been too many moments of inconsistency, and both price and quality have suffered. Now, with stable leadership, recent Merlots and Cabernet Sauvignons, especially the reserve-quality bottling labeled 1886, have prospered and scored into the 90-point range.

EL MOLINO 1981		Map 12
www.elmolinowinery.com	707-963-3632	Tasting by Appointment
St. Helena	Napa County	St. Helena AVA

El Molino, the bale mill, and an original stone winery were built in the 1870s as one of the earliest Napa Valley wineries and were restored in 1981 by the late Reg Oliver. Now run by his daughter Lily Oliver and her husband Jon Berlin, El Molino makes limited quantities of Pinot Noir and Chardonnay. Production is about two thousand cases a year, evenly divided, all made from grapes grown on their Star Vineyard in Rutherford despite the winery's address in St. Helena.

In more vintages than not, the winery has earned scores in the 90s for both varieties, and even though the immediate area is far better known for Cabernet Sauvignon, El Molino has proven that its chosen varieties can succeed there as well. Both wines are ripe and rich, reasonably well balanced, and have shown that they can age as well as their peers even though coming from a noticeably warmer site than most upscale versions of Chardonnay and Pinot Noir.

ELIZABETH SPENCER 1998		Map 13
www.elizabethspencerwines.com	707-963-6067	Tasting
Rutherford	Napa County	Rutherford AVA

A confluence of lucky events brought wine marketer Elizabeth Pressler together with distributor, importer, and spouse Spencer Graham to craft their small winery in Rutherford. With winemaker Matthew Rorick, Elizabeth Spencer makes a modest range of wines from grapes grown on others' vineyards in the Napa Valley (Cabernet Sauvignon), the Sonoma Coast (Chardonnay, Pinot Noir and Syrah), and Mendocino (Sauvignon Blanc). About 2,500 cases of the Elizabeth Spencer Cabernet, Pinot Noir, Syrah, and Sauvignon Blanc joins another 300 cases of the very limited E X S-labeled Chardonnay and Pinot Noir.

Quality has been fairly consistently good, scoring in the upper 80s to low 90s, and it is not unusual for the balanced, medium-depth Elizabeth Spencer wines to offer more value for the money than their Napa Valley peers.

ELYSE WINERY 1987		Map 14
www.elysewinery.com	707-944-2900	Tasting
Napa	Napa County	Napa Valley AVA

Ray and Nancy Coursen came west without the expressed intention of becoming winemakers, but, after a series of apprenticeships at all levels of the industry, including Ray's very successful stint as winemaker at the Whitehall Lane Winery, they made a 1987 Zinfandel from the Morisoli Vineyard that started them on their way. Buying a small winery in 1997, the Coursens have made an increasing variety of wines, ranging from vineyard-designated Cabernet Sauvignon to Zinfandel to Syrah, all from some fifteen vineyards scattered throughout the Napa Valley. A white blend called L'Ingénue and red blend called Le Corbeau round out the Elyse offerings. A pricey, very limited Jacob Franklin-labeled Cabernet Sauvignon and Petite Sirah are new to the scene. Total production is in the vicinity of fifteen thousand cases, of which half is Zinfandel.

The Elyse style tends to richness and a fair degree of brawn. When the wines have the fruit to bring everything into balance, they succeed, often reaching 90 points and beyond, especially the Zinfandels, but a few have been more rugged than they are attractive.

ETUDE WINES 1982		Map 14
www.etudewines.com	707-257-5300	Tasting by Appointment
Napa	Napa County	Napa Valley AVA

Founder Tony Soter, formerly a winemaker for hire, established Etude with winemaker Jon Priest in 1982. The focus has always been on Pinot Noir and

Cabernet Sauvignon, though they represent about 60 percent of the twenty-thousand-case production, with Merlot, Rosé, and Pinot Gris bringing up the rear. The Pinot is made from Carneros Estate-grown grapes; others are purchased from several well-regarded Napa Valley vineyards, including Schoenstein, Vine Hill Ranch, and Frediani. A second label, Fortitude, is a small-batch line using so-called endangered varietals such as Semillon, Charbono, Carignane, and Validquié. Etude is now owned by the international Foster's Group.

The most successful wines to date have been Pinot Noir, both the regular bottling and the upscale Heirloom Pinot Noir, and the nicely concentrated, fruity Pinot Gris. Scores for those wines reach into the 90s, and very few Pinot Gris in California are its equal.

FAILLA 1998		Map 12
www.faillawines.com	707-963-0530	Tasting
St. Helena	Napa County	Napa Valley AVA

Originally named Failla Jordan, after winemaker Ehren Jordan and wife Anne-Marie Failla, the word *Jordan* was excised in 2002 due to legal difficulties with Jordan Vineyard & Winery (no relation). Ehren Jordan gained experience at Joseph Phelps and in the Rhône Valley. Back in California, Jordan worked at Neyers Vineyard, where he remains as winemaker in partnership with the Neyers family. Failla bought grapes for their earliest wines, Syrah and Viognier, and still purchase most of their grapes from the likes of Keefer Ranch and Hirsch. Ten acres of Syrah, Chardonnay, and Pinot Noir grapes are now being grown on the ten-acre estate vineyard on the Sonoma Coast, just inland from Gualala. Production averages 2,500 cases each vintage, featuring more Pinot Noir than anything else, with Syrah and Chardonnay also significant portions of the production. A limited bottling of Viognier rounds out the line.

In top vintages, Failla's expressive, rich, well-balanced wines can earn scores up into the 90-point range.

FAR NIENTE VINEYARDS 1979		Map 14
www.farniente.com	707-944-2861	Tasting by Appointment
Oakville	Napa County	Oakville AVA

Built in the 1880s and abandoned at Prohibition, Far Niente was lovingly restored by Gil and Beth Nickel and neighboring grower Dick Stelling in 1978. After the untimely passing of Gil Nickel, Beth Nickel remains in control, with day-to-day management provided by Dirk Hampson who has winemaking experience in Germany, in Burgundy, and at Château Mouton-Rothschild in Bordeaux. Annual production is upward of forty thousand cases of premium-priced Chardonnay (over half) and Cabernet Sauvignon from Napa Valley grapes and the two-hundred-acre estate vineyards. Second label Nickel & Nickel makes limited bottlings of a range of single vineyard-designated wines, and Dolce is the dessert wine branch of Far Niente.

Far Niente wines are pricey, ripe, and high in oak and full in body. They have the trappings of grandeur and age worthiness in good vintages but have lacked sufficient fruit at times.

FARELLA VINEYARD 1985		Map 15
www.farella.com	707-254-9489	Tasting by Appointment
Napa	Napa County	Napa Valley AVA

Tom Farella started his business as a grower for other winemakers, then began making his own wines after apprenticeships at Neyers and Flora Springs in the Napa Valley, Meursault, and Oregon. Farella owns and manages a twenty-six-acre estate vineyard in the Coombsville neighborhood at the base of the Vaca Mountains in the southeast corner of the valley. He still sells fruit to the likes of Honig, Pahlmeyer, and a dozen others, as well as renting space at the winery for a handful of custom crush vintners. Farella makes about 1,200 cases in total of Cabernet Sauvignon, Syrah, Merlot, and Sauvignon Blanc as well as a Bordeaux blend of 70 percent Cabernet and 30 percent Merlot called Farella Alta.

Farella and Farella Park wines have performed at levels expected of small Napa wineries.

FLORA SPRINGS WINERY & VINEYARDS 1978		Map 12
www.florasprings.com	707-963-5711	Tasting
St. Helena	Napa County	St. Helena AVA

Two generations of the Komes family have built this large winery and extensive vineyards. Jerry, a retired president of international construction giant Bechtel, and his wife, Flora, bought their first vineyard in 1977. Their son, John, and daughter, Julie Garvey, were the initial winemakers, now the job of Ken Deis; Julie's husband, Pat, manages the vineyards. They own over six hundred acres in twelve vineyards in six appellations throughout the Napa Valley, with nearly half in the Pope Valley, east of St. Helena and south of Howell Mountain. About 70 percent of the grapes are sold to other vintners, and today's production is well over fifty thousand cases of Cabernet Sauvignon, Merlot, Chardonnay, and Sangiovese. Flora Springs makes several single-vineyard Cabernets with very limited distribution and two proprietary blends in larger circulation: Trilogy, including Cabernet, Merlot, Cabernet Franc, and Malbec; and a blend of Sauvignon Blanc grapes called Soliloquy.

Maddening inconsistency has dogged Flora Springs wines almost from the start, and while there have been a fair number of ratings in the high 80s and low 90s, virtually every wine in the arsenal has had its ups and downs. Top-rated Trilogy, once a coequal blend of the three major Bordeaux varieties, is now dominated by Cabernet Sauvignon. It is made in a ripe, brightly balanced manner; and when the fruit is up to the task, it is a quite enjoyable wine.

FOLIE À DEUX WINERY 1981		Map 14
www.folieadeux.com	800-535-6400	Tasting
Oakville	Napa County	Oakville AVA

Larry and Eva Dizmang set forth in 1981 to satisfy their "shared fantasies" by building a winery. Sold in '95 to longtime Napa Valley winemaker, Dick Peterson and partners, they in turn sold in '04 to Trinchero Family Estates, owners of Sutter Home. With a twenty-two-acre vineyard just north of Calistoga, Folie à Deux makes over thirty thousand cases of modestly priced Cabernet Sauvignon, Merlot, Chardonnay, and Sauvignon Blanc from Napa Valley grapes and a Zinfandel from Amador County. A second label, Ménage à Trois (or the blending of three) provides even more accessible white, red, and Rosé blends.

Changing ownership patterns has led to inconsistent quality over the years and changes in style.

FORMAN VINEYARD 1983		Map 12
www.formanvineyard.net	707-963-0234	Tasting by Appointment
St. Helena	Napa County	Napa Valley AVA

Ric Forman was the first winemaker at Sterling in 1968, at age twenty-four. In 1977, when Coca-Cola bought Sterling, Forman became a partner in a new venture with Sterling's founder, Peter Newton. In 1982, Forman set out on his own, starting a winery on Howell Mountain with six acres planted to Cabernet Sauvignon grapes. Over time, the vineyard grew to a total of eighty-nine acres, spread among three discreet vineyards in St. Helena and on the Rutherford Bench. Today, Forman focuses on just two wines, a Cabernet, representing two-thirds of the 3,500-case total production, and a barrel-fermented Chardonnay that makes up the other third.

Forman has a wide and dedicated following, and occasional inconsistencies over the years have not done much to limit the ardor for his carefully crafted wines whose alcohols are always in check and whose acidity is always there for good balance.

FRANCISCAN OAKVILLE ESTATE 1973		Map 13
www.franciscan.com	707-963-7112	Tasting
Rutherford	Napa County	Rutherford AVA

For a winery that has existed little more than three decades, Franciscan has certainly had its share of changes. It was founded in 1973, and its original ownership moved on even before its first wines debuted. More changes ensued, and in 1985, Franciscan came under the practiced hand of Chilean vintner Augustin Huneeus, and its present personality was formed. New wines were added, quality increased, other wineries were added to the family; and with its favored location directly on the highway and its attractive winery building and inviting tasting room, Franciscan found stability of sorts. It was purchased by the Constellation Group, which also own Ravenswood and Robert Mondavi, among others, and Franciscan remains an important, midpriced Napa Valley brand.

Wine quality is about average for the winery size and price point, which means that its midpriced offerings are wholly reliable and enjoyable, and its upscale bottlings, Magnificat, a red Bordeaux-style blend, and Cuvée Sauvage Chardonnay, fermented with wild yeasts, will occasionally reach into the 90-point range. Both of the special bottlings tend to fullness without heaviness and can be complex in best vintages. Other offerings are middle-of-the-road, medium/full-bodied wines.

FRANK FAMILY VINEYARDS 1992		Map 11
www.frankfamilyvineyards.com	800-574-9463	Tasting
Calistoga	Napa County	Calistoga AVA

It's the classic story: Hollywood mogul (Rich Frank, boss of Disney's and Paramount's TV divisions and now agent to the stars) weekends in Napa Valley and decides to get into winemaking. Mogul buys old Hans Kornell sparkling winery, built in 1880s south of Calistoga, and plants vineyard, now grown to two hundred acres in three locations. Mogul develops winery with experienced, established Napa Valley denizen, Koerner Rombauer of Rombauer Vineyards, and eventually buys out wine expert. Mogul now makes over seventy thousand cases of Cabernet Sauvignon, Zinfandel, Chardonnay, and Sparkling Wine that sells at a premium. Second labels Winston Hill and Napa Cellars help the bottom line.

Wine mogul lives happily ever after making wines that are rich and deep, the best of which routinely earn ratings in the high 80s to mid-90s. Winston Hill, an upscale bottling, can reach to the mid-90s in ratings for its full, supple, concentrated flavors.

FRAZIER WINERY 1995		Map 15
www.frazierwinery.com	707-255-3444	Tasting by Appointment
Napa	Napa County	Napa Valley AVA

In 1982, proprietor and longtime airline pilot Bill Frazier bought fifteen acres in southeast Napa Valley for his family home. In 1990, he planted ten acres of Cabernet Sauvignon and Merlot grapes on hillsides just below his Coombsville area residence in the proposed Tulocay AVA. In 1998, another eleven acres were planted; and in 2001, the winery was completed. A final ten acres were planted in 2008. Frazier has focused on Cabernet and Merlot bottlings, and the five-thousand-case production, all made from estate-grown fruit, is fairly evenly divided between the two. A second label, Lupine Hills, makes somewhat more modestly priced Cabernet and Merlot.

While Frazier has yet to find a consistent path to high ratings, its Cabernets are nicely structured and fairly full-bodied, with good varietal character in most vintages.

FREEMARK ABBEY WINERY 1967		Map 12
www.freemarkabbey.com	800-963-9698	Tasting
St. Helena	Napa County	St. Helena AVA

Josephine Marlin Tychson was the first female California winery owner in 1886; the site of Tychson Cellars is now Freemark Abbey. The winery and vineyards changed hands several times until the Freemark Abbey name—a blend of the names of the three Southern California investors—was introduced in 1939. The business was revived in 1967 by a group of seven partners who drove its growth, but through the 1990s and early 2000s, Freemark Abbey lost focus, going through several ownership groups. In 2006, Kendall-Jackson's top-end Jackson Family Wines bought Freemark Abbey. Ted Edwards, winemaker since 1986, remains the constant, supervising the production of three vineyards totaling two hundred acres and of forty thousand cases of wine, including about 40 percent Cabernet Sauvignon, 20 percent Chardonnay, and 16 percent Merlot, plus several smaller-quantity bottlings of Syrah, Zinfandel, Late Harvest Riesling, and a Cabernet-Merlot blend named Josephine after the founder of many years ago.

Limited-production, single-vineyard Cabernets from the Bosché and Sycamore vineyards have set the quality pace of late and even the long-production, regular-bottling Cabernet has been recommendable of late. The Freemark Abbey preference for balanced, mannerly wines has continued from its beginnings over four decades ago. The 1970 Cabernet Bosché was and remains one of the legendary bottlings from the era when California Cabernets came to full prominence.

FROG'S LEAP 1981		Map 13
www.frogsleap.com	707-963-4704	Tasting
Rutherford	Napa County	Rutherford AVA

The historic Red Barn winery building started in 1884 as Adamson Winery and was renovated in 1994 by Frog's Leap and the Williams family. At the turn of the twentieth century, the property had been used to raise frogs and, in particular, their legs for gourmets. Knowing this, John Williams decided on the name Frog's Leap, in part as a word play on the successful Stag's Leap Wine Cellars. Under Williams's constant direction, production hovers around sixty thousand cases a year, over 30 percent of which is Sauvignon Blanc. The remainder is fairly evenly divided among Cabernet Sauvignon, Merlot, Zinfandel, and Chardonnay, with the odd Napa Gamay, Petite Sirah, and Riesling thrown in for good measure. Frog's Leap uses the grapes from its 230 acres of vines as well as other Napa producers. The animated Web site includes a daily Zen quotation and interesting wine commentary.

Under Williams's direction, the winery adamantly adheres to its stylistic preference for wines balanced toward the high-acid end of the spectrum. The style works for the occasional Sauvignon Blanc, and the winery has its followers, as its sales figures so clearly indicate. But it is a style not widely favored, and Frog's Leap wines, regardless of the winery's greatly admired sense of humor, need to be approached with an understanding that they march to a different drummer.

GIRARD WINERY 1980		Map 14
www.girardwinery.com	707-968-9297	Tasting by Appointment
Yountville	Napa County	Yountville AVA

Pat Roney, a former sommelier, importer, marketing man at Christian Brothers, and president of specialty food retailer Dean & Deluca, took over as principal owner of Girard in 2000. With winemaker Marco DiGiulio, Girard farms forty acres of vineyards, eighteen of which are in the Pritchard Hill area of Oakville, near Colgin and Chappellet vineyards. Girard production currently approaches forty thousand cases, of which Sauvignon Blanc is the volume leader at 40 percent, followed by a Russian River Valley-sourced Chardonnay at 25 percent, the Artistry proprietary red blend, and a Petite Sirah, each representing 15 percent of volume. Girard recently acquired nearby Harrison Vineyards, which stopped making wine in the Napa Valley in favor of its Pinot Noir project in New Zealand.

The winery has had its ups and downs over the years, making some of Napa's best Cabernet Sauvignons in the 1980s but showing far less consistency in the 1990s. The new ownership has reinvigorated the brand, and, led by the Cabernet-based Artistry bottling with scores into the 90-point range, Girard is once again earning solid reviews.

GRACE FAMILY VINEYARDS 1978		Map 12
www.gracefamilyvineyards.com	707-963-0808	No Tasting
St. Helena	Napa County	St. Helena AVA

Dick Grace, former San Francisco stockbroker, moved with his wife, Ann, to the Napa Valley in 1974 and planted Cabernet Sauvignon grapes on an acre parcel adjacent to their home. At first, the grapes were processed by Caymus and made as a vineyard-designated bottling under the Caymus name, becoming an early cult wine; the Cabernet has been made by Grace since '83. To this day, Grace Family is a wine made in extremely limited quantities—measured in the hundreds of cases—sold only to an effectively closed mailing list and at charity auctions benefiting causes that fit Grace's Buddhist philosophies. Individual bottles have fetched record amounts at auction, reflecting the high standing enjoyed by the Grace Cabernet Sauvignon.

GREEN AND RED VINEYARD 1977		Map 10
www.greenandred.com	707-965-2346	No Tasting
Chiles Valley	Napa County	Chiles Valley AVA

Jay Heminway gave up teaching and moved to the Chiles Valley in 1970, buying a 160-acre farm that had fallen into disrepair. By 1972 he had planted a sixteen-acre vineyard on land ranging in elevation from nine hundred to two thousand feet. The soils are red iron veined with green serpentine; ergo the vineyard's name. Heminway was a pioneer in the Chiles Valley and pushed for an AVA designation, finally received in 1999. The vineyards have expanded to thirty-one planted acres spread over three individual vineyards, Chiles Mill, Catacula, and Tip Top. Principally a Zinfandel producer, Green and Red makes a total of about 6,500 cases, with Zinfandel representing fully 90 percent of output.

More likely to reach ratings in the upper 80s than higher for its medium/full- to full-bodied wines, Green and Red keeps its prices within reason and is well received for the value offered.

GRGICH HILLS CELLAR 1977		Map 13
www.grgich.com	800-532-3057	Tasting
Rutherford	Napa County	Rutherford AVA

Grgich Hills Cellar was formed in 1977 as a partnership between Croatian winemaker Miljenko "Mike" Grgich and Austin Hills of the Hills Bros. Coffee family. When Hills Bros. was sold in 1976, Austin decided to expand his small Napa Valley vineyard holdings and to plunge into the winery business. Mike Grgich had made wine for all the big names in the industry, including Souverain, Christian Brothers, Beaulieu, and Robert Mondavi. But it was as winemaker for Chateau Montelena that he truly made his name; during his tenure, the Montelena '73 Chardonnay took the prize at the famous 1976 Tasting of Paris. Now Grgich Hills uses the grapes from five vineyards in the valley, totaling 366 acres, to make its line of estate-grown and -bottled wines. Production stands at seventy thousand cases annually, of which the landmark Chardonnay still holds sway with just under half of the production, followed by Cabernet Sauvignon and Fumé Blanc at about 20 percent each. Grgich Hills also makes a Zinfandel and

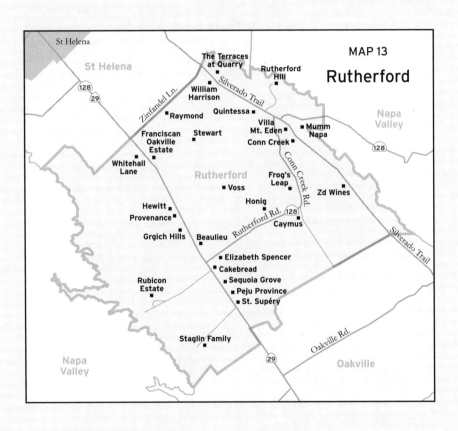

MAP 13

Rutherford

St Helena

St Helena

Napa
Valley

The Terraces
at Quarry

Rutherford
Hill

Zinfandel Ln.

Silverado Trail

William
Harrison

Raymond

Quintessa

Villa
Mt. Eden

Conn Creek

Mumm
Napa

128

Franciscan
Oakville
Estate

Stewart

Whitehall
Lane

Rutherford

Conn Creek Rd.

Voss

Frog's
Leap

Zd Wines

Honig

Hewitt

Provenance

Rutherford Rd.

128

Caymus

Grgich Hills

Beaulieu

Silverado Trail

Elizabeth Spencer

Cakebread

Rubicon
Estate

Sequoia Grove

Peju Province

St. Supéry

Staglin Family

Napa
Valley

29

Oakville Rd.

Oakville

Merlot and recently introduced a dessert wine called Violetta for Grgich's daughter. Overall production control has now shifted to Grgich's nephew, Ivo, who continues to improve the wines.

If not ringing the gong in every vintage with every variety, Grgich Hills is nonetheless more consistently good than almost all wineries its size. The house style combines fully ripe flavors with plentiful underlying acidity, and it results in wines that typically age longer and better than most of its peers. The Fumé Blanc and Chardonnay have been quality leaders, and Zinfandel usually follows suit as well—all capable of rating up into the 90s in top vintages. Essence, the winery's upscale Sauvignon Blanc from biodynamically grown grapes, has reached the very top of the Sauvignon Blanc ratings in some vintages.

HAGAFEN CELLARS 1979		Map 14
www.hagafen.com	707-252-0781	Tasting
Napa	Napa County	Napa Valley AVA

In Hebrew, *hagafen* means "the vine," and Hagafen Cellars was the first kosher winemaker in Northern California. Hagafen Cellars was founded by Zack Berkowitz and Ernie Weir, the latter serving as winemaker and now sole proprietor-winemaker. Hagafen produces eight thousand cases using the juice from its two vineyards just east of the Silverado Trail and from some half-dozen other sources in the valley as well as a White Riesling from Lake County. The winery makes a fairly wide range of wines, from Cabernet Sauvignon to Pinot Noir to a Sparkling Wine on occasion.

Hagafen wines have been something of a hit-or-miss proposition from year to year, but a new, upscale label called Prix has met with good success in its initial outings. White Riesling has had a bit of success, which is something of a surprise given the difficulties the grape has historically had in Napa; but it, too, can be inconsistent from vintage to vintage.

HALL WINES 2003		Map 12
www.hallwines.com	866-667-HALL	Tasting
St. Helena	Napa County	St. Helena AVA

Kathryn and Craig Hall own the place. Kathryn's father was a winegrower in Mendocino County, and she was an attorney before becoming U.S. ambassador to Austria during the first Clinton administration. Craig is a Dallas financier and, more recently, winery and vineyard owner. With winemaker New Zealander Richard Batchelor, Hall focuses on Bordeaux varieties. Its 350 planted acres, on over 3,000 total acres of land, provide fruit for the 50,000 cases produced. Over half is Cabernet Sauvignon, made in both a large bottling as part of its Napa Valley line, and a much smaller line of wines under the moniker Artisan Collection, which can range from 50 to 500 cases produced. The Web site features some excellent photos and videos of the Gehry project as well as good information about each wine.

This ambitious winery is still in the beginning phases of its development, and while quality has been inconsistent with few scores reaching into the 90-point range, the intent and potential are obvious. Time will tell how much of that potential is realized, but this is a winery to be watched. Construction of a new winery and visitors center designed by the forward-thinking architect, Frank Gehry, is slated for completion in 2010 or thereabouts.

HARLAN ESTATE WINERY 1990		Map 14
www.harlanestate.com	707-944-1441	No Tasting
Oakville	Napa County	Oakville AVA

Bill Harlan, real estate investor and wine lover, set out to create one of Napa's great wines. With an estate in the hills west of Oakville, and under the guiding hand of winemaker Bob Levy, Harlan has succeeded in offering a number of extraordinarily expensive, impossible-to-find, very ripe and dense wines that are rated in the mid- to upper-90-point range more often than not. There are those who claim that Harlan wines are over-the-top and lack grace, but others contend that depth, intensity, focus, richness and age worthiness are as much the hallmarks of greatness as any other measure. The bottom line, however, is that Harlan wines are so expensive that if you have to ask what they cost, you cannot afford them.

HARTWELL VINEYARDS 1990		Map 15
www.hartwellvineyards.com	800-366-6516	Tasting by Appointment
Napa	Napa County	Stags Leap District AVA

In 1985, after careers in aerospace and plumbing, Bob Hartwell bought a small vineyard on the west side of the Silverado Trail in the heart of the Stags Leap District. With the help of winemaker Celia Welch Masyczek at first and now Benoit Touquette of France and South Africa and Andy

Erickson with local experience, Hartwell has built a strong reputation for Cabernet Sauvignon in particular, but the winery also makes exceptional Merlot and Sauvignon Blanc as well. Production hovers around 3,500 cases, of which Cabernet bottlings comprise over 50 percent. Fifteen acres of vineyards contribute most of the fruit used by Hartwell.

Each of the Hartwell wines has at times reached the very top of the rating scale and is usually found in the range of 90+ points. The winery style is rich, deep, nicely fruited, and mannerly—and its following and the somewhat elevated prices for its wines are well earned and deserved.

HDV WINES 1979		Map 15
www.hdvwines.com	707-251-9978	Tasting by Appointment
Napa	Napa County	Carneros AVA

Larry Hyde, from a multigeneration California farming family, owns and manages Hyde Vineyards in Carneros, one of the most celebrated vineyard sites in all of California. His wife's cousin is none other than the world-famous Aubert de Villaine, the co-owner of the unparalleled Burgundian winery Domaine de la Romanée-Conti. Combining the initials into HdV, the partnership has brought forth a hugely successful winemaking operation, using the Hyde grapes, de Villaine quality standards, and the guiding hand of winemaker Stéphane Vivier. Grapes not used in HdV winemaking are sold to a couple of dozen of the biggest names in the valley, including Paul Hobbs, Kistler, Patz & Hall, Robert Mondavi, and Schramsberg. HdV makes four wines: Belle Cousine, a Merlot–Cabernet Sauvignon blend; Syrah; and two Chardonnays. Each bottling runs from 1,000 to 1,800 cases, with a total production of about 6,000 cases.

From the outset, quality has been very high, with both Chardonnay and Syrah pulling down top honors. HdV makes very tasty, perfectly balanced wines with impeccable varietal credentials.

HEITZ WINE CELLARS 1961		Map 12
www.heitzcellar.com	707-963-3542	Tasting
St. Helena	Napa County	St. Helena AVA

Joe Heitz came to the Napa Valley some fifty years ago, working first at Beaulieu under the tutelage of the legendary Andre Tschellicheff before founding his own winery long before it became the fashionable thing to do. Making Pinot Noir at first, a variety that was dropped from the Heitz arsenal not long afterward, along with Cabernet Sauvignon and Chardonnay, Heitz soon joined the lists of the top producers of both varieties. By the late 1960s and early 1970s, he was producing wines that quickly made him one of Napa's most celebrated winemakers. His cantankerous personality may have earned him few friends, but his wines were among the very best, led by his Martha's Vineyard Cabernet Sauvignon. The halcyon days of the 1970s were not to be repeated in the 1980s as a combination of age and stubbornness led to deteriorating wine quality.

And while Heitz enjoys near legendary status among those who remember his two decades of exceptional results, the winery's loss of focus and its failure to recapture past glories under the management of his children has led to inconsistency in its flagship Cabernets, both Martha's Vineyard and Bella Oaks, and total loss of form for the Chardonnay. The mintiness of the Martha's Vineyard wines sets them apart from almost everything else in the Napa Valley.

HENDRY WINES 1995		Map 14
www.hendrywines.com	707-226-8320	Tasting by Appointment
Napa	Napa County	Napa Valley AVA

George Hendry was a nuclear physicist and inventor with medical technology giant Siemens in Berkeley; indeed, he remains involved as president of a manufacturer of particle accelerators for medical research. Hendry also dabbled in growing grapes on the very parcel where he grew up in southern Napa County immediately west of the town of Napa. He sold grapes to other producers until he decided to make his own wine, and now very little Hendry Vineyard wine is made by others. His intimate hillside winery, with its underground aging cellar, focuses on Zinfandel and Chardonnay made from the 117 acres of estate-grown grapes. Production ranges from ten thousand to twelve thousand cases a year, a third of which is Zinfandel, another third Chardonnay, and the remainder Cabernet Sauvignon and a proprietary red blend. Several of Hendry's wines identify the vineyard block number on the label to make very precise the terroir brought to a specific vintage.

Greatest success to date has been with Zinfandel in the hands of both inimitably delightful George Hendry and, until recently, Rosenblum Cellars. The Hendry Zins, and a wine labeled Primitivo for that particular variant of Zinfandel, are made in a rich, ripe, high-alcohol style that succeeds best in vintages where adequate fruit joins the all-out ripeness.

HEWITT VINEYARD 2000

www.hewittvineyard.com   707-968-3633

Rutherford   Napa County

Map 13

No Tasting

Rutherford AVA

First planted in 1880 and located in the very heart of the West Rutherford Bench, the vineyard was purchased by William Hewitt, a retired John Deere executive, in 1962. For nearly forty years, Hewitt expanded the vineyard and sold the Cabernet Sauvignon grapes to other winemakers in the valley. Now at sixty acres of vineyards west of Highway 29, at the foot of the Mayacamas Range, Hewitt uses only grapes from its own vineyard in the making of its wines. Tom Rinaldi, the general manager and winemaker, came to Hewitt in 2000 after over two decades as winemaker at Duckhorn, and he made the first Hewitt wines in 2001. Since then, about five thousand cases of the Hewitt Vineyard-designated Cabernet Sauvignon have been made annually. In 2000, Chalone purchased the property after William's death in 1998. In 2005, the Chalone Wine Group was itself purchased by the international Diageo Chateau & Estate Wines.

Some find the wine too high in ripeness for their preferences, but its deep fruit and its ability to portray the currancy, varietally focused character of the best wines from the Rutherford Bench have consistently earned it scores in the 90s in our view—with that ripeness duly noted.

HONIG VINEYARD & WINERY 1980

www.honigwine.com   800-929-2217

Rutherford   Napa County

Map 13

Tasting by Appointment

Rutherford AVA

Louis Honig bought a sixty-eight-acre ranch in Rutherford in 1964 and began planting Cabernet Sauvignon and Sauvignon Blanc grapes. These two varieties would remain the winemaking focus long after Louis died; the first vintage was brought in by his progeny in '81. Honig is now run by Michael, Louis's grandson; Elaine, Louis's wife; and other family members. Winemaker Kristin Belair has been on scene since '97 and continues making estate-grown and -bottled Sauvignon Blanc (about thirty thousand cases annually) and Cabernet (ten thousand cases), both reasonably priced and gaining attention. The Web site reveals the eye-opening marketing postcards that have become a kind of underground trademark.

Honig Sauvignon Blanc occasionally rises to the 90-point level, while the Cabernet has struggled to reach beyond the mid-80s in most vintages.

The wines are balanced, reasonably fruity, and never threaten to go over the top.

HOWELL MOUNTAIN VINEYARDS 1988   Map 12

www.howellmountain.com   707-967-9676   Tasting by Appointment

Rutherford   Napa County   Howell Mountain AVA

Howell Mountain Vineyards was first established in 1988 as a small-lot Zinfandel and Cabernet Sauvignon producer. In 2005, Peter and Vicky Chow acquired the winery and vineyards after his long career in international transport and logistics. There are two vineyards totaling fifty-two acres, Beatty Ranch and Black Sears, which are planted to Zinfandel (75 percent) and Cabernet Sauvignon. Howell Mountain produces about five thousand cases annually, with Zinfandel again leading the way with over three-quarters of volume. A Cabernet and a Chardonnay are bottled as well, though at a rate of only five hundred to six hundred cases each.

Despite using grapes from some of the best-known sites on Howell Mountain, the winery has had a spotty track record to date. Its recent change of ownership offers hope for the future, as does the employment of longtime Napa Valley winemaker Jack Stuart.

JARVIS WINERY 1992   Map 15

www.jarviswines.com   800-255-5280   Tasting by Appointment

Napa   Napa County   Napa Valley AVA

William Jarvis, fresh from the telecommunications business, purchased a Napa Valley retreat along with twenty-five acres of vineyards near Atlas Peak. The vineyards grew to thirty-seven acres, and an impressive underground winery was built. Cabernet Sauvignon was the focus from the first vintage and now represents half of the winery's nine-thousand-case production, followed by Chardonnay and a red blend named Lake William. Jarvis and his wife, Letitia, also started a community music conservatory and dance workshop.

Jarvis wines have always teased with glimmers of the quality that their site and their ambitions should produce, but expectations notwithstanding, quality rankings have been decidedly mixed, as every high-ranking effort has been seemingly matched by rather average scores for others. If one were visiting other producers in this corner of the Napa Valley, Jarvis would be an enjoyable stop.

JOSEPH PHELPS VINEYARDS 1972   Map 12

www.jpwines.com   707-963-2745   Tasting by Appointment

St. Helena   Napa County   St. Helena AVA

Colorado construction magnate Joseph Phelps had a better idea. After helping build the winery now known as Rutherford Hill and having met vineyard owners and invested with them as part of his increasing interest in wine country, Phelps built his own handsome, wood-sided winery in a little valley immediately off the Silverado Trail just east of St. Helena. With winemaker Walter Schug in charge, Phelps added new ideas to the California wine scene with a gorgeous Bordeaux blend, Insignia, that is still the winery's flagship effort; exceptional late harvest Rieslings; and the introduction of Rhône varietals, Syrah, and Viognier. Today, Phelps enjoys an international reputation for high quality and has wide distribution based on its production in the range of one hundred thousand cases. The winery, which started with just its estate vineyard, now owns important holdings all over the Napa Valley. In a new project, it has developed a new winery and brand called Freestone based on holdings of Pinot Noir and Chardonnay in western Sonoma County. As of 2008, there was a complete change in management and winemaking at Phelps, as the first generation of family and staff gave way to younger voices. An interesting and valuable feature of the otherwise straightforward Phelps Web site is the listing of food pairing recommendations for every wine on offer.

Joseph Phelps Cabernet Sauvignons and its Bordeaux blend, Insignia, are among the Napa Valley's best and have been for the winery's three-decade existence. Both Insignia and the famous Backus Cabernet Sauvignon routinely earn scores over 90 points and more often 95 points and up. The regular-bottling Cabernet Sauvignon can rate into the 90s; Chardonnay, Merlot, Sauvignon Blanc, Syrah, and Viognier are never far behind and also can jump to the top of the ratings list on occasions. Insignia is a rich, mannerly, fairly supple wine whose continuing success has made it into one of the highest-volume upscale "clarets" in the Napa Valley. The Backus Cabernet is often more intense and more rugged than Insignia, if somewhat less mannerly. Both wines carry price tags of $200 and up.

KARL LAWRENCE CELLARS 1991   Map 12

www.karllawrence.com   707-255-2843   No Tasting

Napa   Napa County   Napa Valley AVA

Winemaker Michael Trujillo and his partner, ob-gyn Bryan Henry—the latter said to have delivered more than six thousand Napa Valley babies—together built this Cabernet Sauvignon–focused winery that produces about 1,500 cases of the Karl Lawrence Cabernet plus a second label, Aldin, which is used for a Chardonnay and red blend. Grapes are sourced from the renowned Lamb Family Vineyard on Howell Mountain and the Morisoli Vineyard in Rutherford. "Karl Lawrence" is a combination of the middle names of the partners.

Cabernet Sauvignon quality has generally been high, not surprising given the reputation of the vineyard sources, with scores often reaching 90 points and higher, especially considering the not over-the-top prices for the wine. Karl Lawrence wines tend to fullness without brashness and plenty of depth yet never seem to lose their good manners.

KENEFICK RANCH 2002		Map 11
www.kenefickranch.com	707-942-6175	No Tasting
Calistoga	Napa County	Calistoga AVA

San Francisco neurosurgeon Thomas Kenefick acquired a 125-acre vineyard in the foothills of the Palisade Mountains in Calistoga and began growing Cabernet Sauvignon, Cabernet Franc, Syrah, and Sauvignon Blanc grapes. Under the supervision of winemaker Robbie Meyer, Kenefick has produced an average of 2,500 cases of Cabernet Sauvignon, Sauvignon Blanc, and Merlot over the past several years. Kenefick also sells excess grapes to the likes of Etude, Joseph Phelps, Robert Mondavi, and Rosenblum.

Kenefick Ranch Merlot and Cabernets are not inexpensive, but at $40 to $60, and with critical ratings of 90 to 93 points, they are better values than many of the higher-priced wines being produced today in the Napa Valley. They reflect the rich soils and warmer temperatures of their Calistoga provenance by being full in body and deep in ripe, concentrated flavor, but they are also a carefully constructed lot that avoids the perils of overripeness.

KRUPP BROTHERS 1991		Map 15
www.kruppbrothers.com	707-226-2215	Tasting
Napa	Napa County	Napa Valley AVA

In 1991, brothers Jan and Bart Krupp acquired a forty-one-acre ranch hidden in a box canyon behind the Stags Leap hills, straddling Atlas Peak. Ultimately, the vineyards grew to 700 acres planted to grapes of 1,100 owned acres in total, and they are divided into three separate vineyards: the original Krupp Vineyard, Krupp Brothers Vineyard, and the widely respected Stagecoach Vineyard. Excess grape production is sold to the likes of winemakers J.C. Cellars and Miner. Under the watchful eye of Australian winemaker Nigel Kinsman, Krupp produces over eight thousand cases in total of its Veraison Cabernet Sauvignon, Black Bart Marsanne, and Krupp Merlot.

Krupp wines have a rustic quality; yet because their fruit is so deep and well defined, they are prized for both depth and focus and, as such, earn scores ranging from the upper 80s to the mid-90s. The Stagecoach Vineyard name has appeared in very highly rated wines from the other producers mentioned.

KULETO ESTATE FAMILY VINEYARDS 1992   Map 16

| www.kuletoestate.com | 707-963-9750 | Tasting by Appointment |
| St. Helena | Napa County | Napa Valley AVA |

In 1992, Pat Kuleto assembled five parcels from cattle ranchers to create a 760-acre ranch on the eastern edge of the Napa Valley overlooking Lake Hennessey and Pritchard Hill. Kuleto had built his long career on designing restaurants (think of Fog City Diner, Postrio, and Boulevard in and around San Francisco) and later building them for his own management. With winemaker David Lattin, most recently from Acacia, Kuleto produces about nine thousand cases a year, led by Cabernet Sauvignon at just under three thousand and followed by Syrah, Zinfandel, and Sangiovese. The winery's full capacity is about fifteen thousand cases. Planted acreage is nearing 100 and seems unlikely to grow beyond 125 acres of the hillside terrain, led by Cabernet Sauvignon.

Still, it has been the ripe, richly oaked Zinfandel, more than any other variety, that has shown the way for quality to date, with scores that have reached up into the 90-point range. This "modern" rustic winery enjoys a setting that is among the most spectacular in Napa, and the trek off the valley floor to find it is well worth the effort.

LA JOTA VINEYARD CO. 1898   Map 12

| www.lajotavineyardco.com | 877-222-0292 | Tasting |
| Angwin | Napa County | Howell Mountain AVA |

In 1898, San Francisco newspaperman Frederick Hess bought over three hundred acres of ranch lands on Howell Mountain and built a stone winery that remains on the property today. Bill Smith, an oil exploration executive, bought the derelict property in 1974 to pursue his garage-winemaking proclivities. Smith planted vineyards and restored the La Jota name, making his first vintage Cabernet Sauvignon in 1982. Today, Cabernet remains king, representing virtually all the 4,500-case production. Grapes are grown on three separate vineyards totaling twenty-five acres; Cabernet grapes account for two-thirds. In '01, Markham Vineyards took over the company which, in turn, was purchased in '05 by Kendall-Jackson's Artisan & Estates holdings.

Early quality under Smith was quite high, with the long-aging wines, especially the upscale Anniversary Bottling, picking up scores in the mid-90s and rivaling the best-rated wines of the time. Things went off the boil for a period of time, however, with fruit not keeping up with bold tannins. Kendall-Jackson has promised to right the ship, so La Jota's future may well emulate its former successes.

LAMBORN FAMILY VINEYARDS 1982		Map 12
www.lamborn.com	925-254-0511	Tasting by Appointment
Napa	Napa County	Howell Mountain AVA

The late Bob Lamborn, a San Francisco private eye, bought land with son Michael atop Howell Mountain in the early 1970s and made his first vintage: one hundred cases of Zinfandel in 1982. Over the years, the second and now third generations of Lamborns continued to make small batches of Zinfandel and Cabernet Sauvignon to high standards, exemplified by the hiring of winemaker Heidi Barrett in 1996. Barrett has extensive winemaking experience, having been the original winemaker for Screaming Eagle, and she makes her own wine, La Sirena. Four acres of estate Zinfandel grapes and four of Cabernet are used to make the annual vintages of one thousand cases each of Zinfandel and Cabernet wines.

The Zinfandel is the better known of the two, especially since the Cabernet is newer on the scene. In its best vintages, the big, bold style of the Zinfandel has been well regarded, but there have also been ups and downs along the way, and ratings have ranged from the dreary low 80s to the recommended 90-point range.

LA SIRENA 1994		Map 12
www.lasirenawine.com	707-942-1105	No Tasting
St. Helena	Napa County	St. Helena AVA

Heidi Barrett, famous Napa Valley winemaker and daughter of the near-legendary Richard Peterson of Beaulieu fame and wife of Bo Barrett of the Chateau Montelena Barretts, started her own label in 1994. Barrett gained experience with a wide range of international winemakers before establishing her reputation by becoming the original winemaker for Screaming Eagle in 1992. As a consulting winemaker, she currently works for Amuse Bouche, Paradigm, and Lamborn Family, among others, as well as owning her own label (which means "the mermaid" in Spanish and Italian). Barrett makes several small-batch Syrahs and Cabernet Sauvignons as well as an atypical dry Muscat. Total production approaches three thousand cases. La Sirena makes a Barrett Vineyard Syrah and uses purchased grapes for its other wines.

The winery style so far has been to emphasize power and mass, and, although that direction has proven very popular with some reviewers, an equal number prefer Heidi Barrett's efforts at other wineries. Despite having a Calistoga PO Box address, the wines are made at Revana Family Vineyard in St. Helena, one of Barrett's many significant clients.

LANG & REED WINE COMPANY 1996		Map 12
www.langandreed.com	707-963-7547	No Tasting
St. Helena	Napa County	St. Helena AVA

John and Tracey Skupny, originally from Kansas, worked for several decades in Napa Valley wineries before launching Lang & Reed—named for their children—in 1996. Concluding that Cabernet Franc is more than just a blending grape, Lang & Reed has specialized in this varietal ever since, sourcing grapes from a handful of vineyards in Lake County, the North Coast, and the Napa Valley. Current production tops out at three thousand cases, of which nearly 90 percent is their 100 percent Cabernet Franc offering.

The winery has done a very good job of overcoming the grape's hard-edged tendencies in California vineyards, and both its Premier Etage bottling and the North Coast bottling, released young and fresh, have attracted a wide following and scores in the upper 80s, with the Premier Etage reaching 90 points. An upscale bottling called Right Bank debuted recently and has become a 90-point + hit.

LEWIS CELLARS 1992		Map 14
www.lewiscellars.com	707-255-3400	No Tasting
Napa	Napa County	Napa Valley AVA

Randy Lewis, a former race car driver abroad and in the United States, with spouse Debbie and son Dennis, run this moderately sized but brilliantly successful winery specializing in Cabernet Sauvignon and Chardonnay. Grapes are bought from select vineyards in Oakville, Rutherford, Pritchard Hill, Carneros, and the Russian River Valley and, with winemaker Brian Mox, are made into fewer than nine thousand total cases annually, with Cabernet leading the way (45 percent of production), then Chardonnay (40 percent), and small quantities of Syrah and Merlot.

Results have been spectacular over the winery's existence. Recent releases have upped the ante again as Chardonnay has vaulted into the upper-90 range, and everything else has consistently earned mid-90-point rankings. Lewis wines, so full of quite ripe yet comfortably balanced fruit and filled out by rich oak, have well and truly established their places at the pinnacle of the quality leaders among California producers.

LIPARITA CELLARS 1988		Map 12
www.liparita.com	707-963-2775	No Tasting
Yountville	Napa County	Napa Valley AVA

History had been kind to Liparita; unfortunately, recent history has not. Its first vineyards on this Howell Mountain site were planted in the 1800s and named for the resemblance of the land to Sicily's Lipari Islands. In the 1980s, San Franciscan Robert Burrows revived the winery and planted eighty acres before selling the vineyards to Kendall-Jackson and the winery to lawyer Spencer Hoopes in the late 1990s. Time then seemed to stand still for Liparita, with vintages stacking up a bit and the winery losing visibility, but it has always been a winery with potential that has sometimes been reached and sometimes not. Most recently, it has cut back production to less than two thousand cases of Napa Valley Cabernet Sauvignon.

LOUIS M. MARTINI 1922		Map 12
www.louismartini.com	707-963-2736	Tasting
St. Helena	Napa County	St. Helena AVA

This venerable winery, whose offerings were the favorites of generations of wine drinkers right up to the time of the 1970s California wine boom, was very quickly surpassed in quality by the hundreds of newcomers. Despite giving up its jug wine program, the winery became known for light and clean varietal wines offered at reasonably competitive prices.

Still, when Louis M. Martini, the son of founder Louis P. Martini, passed away, his children decided to sell to Gallo; and under Gallo, with the Martini next generation still somewhat in charge, the winery has made a comeback. Old winemaking procedures have been abandoned and ambitious new projects undertaken. New upscale wines are appearing, such as the very successful Lot No. 1 Cabernet Sauvignon and a recent Monte Rosso Vineyard Cabernet.

This is not the same winery of the good old days, but it is making up for the loss of continuity with improving quality and new directions. And its tasting room is still a treat to visit. The upscale Cabernets are returning Martini to the ranks of interesting wineries to follow.

LUNA VINEYARDS 1996		Map 14
www.lunavineyards.com	707-255-5862	Tasting
Napa	Napa County	Oak Knoll District AVA

Two Beringer execs, George Vare and Mike Moone, bought the former St. Andrews Winery on the southern end of the Silverado Trail in 1995 and had the audacious vision of focusing on Pinot Grigio and Sangiovese. Their first order of business was to replant the twenty-two-acre Chardonnay vineyard to Pinot Grigio and to source their remaining grape needs from the Game Farm Vineyard in Oakville and Chafen Vineyard in Rutherford. The first winemaker was the noted John Kongsgaard, formerly of Newton, who was succeeded by Mike Drash and more recently by Jim McMahon. Over fifty thousand cases are produced, largely of Pinot Grigio and Sangiovese, plus several interesting blends, including Freakout (Pinot Grigio, Chardonnay, and Sauvignon Blanc) and the Canto red blend. For golfers, please note that the Arnold Palmer wines are second labels of Luna. Most recently, Luna has become a significant player in the Merlot and Cabernet Sauvignon sweepstakes with wines that are big and bold.

The winery's Pinot Grigio, which tastes more like a wine from Alsace with California leanings than anything the grape has ever done in Italy, is one of California's best. Even though the bold, very ripe, tannic-laden reds are not for every palate, they still rate in the 90+-point range more often than not.

MADONNA ESTATE 1922		Map 16
www.madonnaestate.com	707-255-8864	Tasting
Napa	Napa County	Carneros AVA

Since 1922, the Bertolucci family has made wine in Carneros. Andrea "Andy" Bertolucci emigrated from Italy in 1912 and within a decade bought twenty-four acres of vineyard in Carneros and a winery across from Mont St. John. Some four generations later the family is still making wine, now called Mont St. John Madonna Estate. Up to 25,000 cases are made each year, using only the grapes grown on the 160-acre family estate vineyard. Varieties include Cabernet Sauvignon, Pinot Noir, Chardonnay, and more exotic wines such as Dolcetto and Muscat.

Over the years, quality has varied up and down more than most, but the highs have been very high, and with one of the best vineyards in Carneros under the winery's control, the potential remains high.

MADRIGAL VINEYARDS 1995		Map 11
www.madrigalvineyards.com	707-942-6577	Tasting by Appointment
Calistoga	Napa County	Calistoga AVA

The Madrigal family had farmed the vineyards of Napa Valley for three generations until Jess and Chris Madrigal decided to make their own wines in 1995. The Madrigal Vineyards are on thirty acres planted to Cabernet Sauvignon and Merlot grapes, located in the Larkmead District between St. Helena and Calistoga that was formerly owned by Duckhorn and managed by the Madrigals. Today, Madrigal makes just over a thousand cases of Cabernet, Pinot Noir, Petite Sirah, Merlot, and a Port. A new production facility can handle upward of seventeen thousand cases, so the Madrigals use it as a custom crush facility as well as for their own winemaking.

The early wines, while likeable, were on the unpolished side, and only by dint of attractive underlying fruit did they find success. More recent efforts show a more mature and sophisticated approach, and the current batch of wines has been the best yet while not giving up the Madrigal penchant for solid, highly structured bottlings. Not surprisingly, the house style has made the winery's Petite Sirah into one of California's best. Prices, though not inexpensive, remain among the more attractive in the Napa Valley, especially when the wines reach into the 90-point range.

MAHONEY VINEYARDS 1992		Map 16
www.mahoneyvineyards.com	707-253-9463	Tasting
Napa	Napa County	Carneros AVA

Francis and Kathleen Mahoney, longtime co-owners of Carneros Creek Winery, created the Mahoney label to make estate-only varieties from the grapes they grow on 160 total acres in Carneros. The focus has always been on Pinot Noir, nudged along by winemaker Ken Foster, a Pinot expert from David Bruce, among others. Other wines include Chardonnay, Syrah, and small batches of interesting Italian and Spanish varieties. The Carneros acreage—including the Las Brisas, Mahoney Ranch, and Gavin vineyards—is sufficient for Mahoney's own twenty-thousand-case production as well as sales to other winemakers. In 2006, Mahoney sold the winery production facilities to the Michael Mondavi family, but the Mahoneys have retained their vineyards and continue to produce the Mahoney wines in the facility.

Mahoney has not left the scene, however, and now makes wine in industrial space in Sonoma. Pinot Noir remains the focus under the Mahoney label, with most efforts seeking balance rather than out-and-out boldness. Production under Mahoney stands at some six thousand cases, while a secondary label, Fleur de California is now stretching past twenty thousand cases, again with an emphasis on Pinot Noir. The winery tasting room is in the Oxbow Market near downtown Napa, while winemaking is conducted about fifteen miles away.

MARKHAM VINEYARDS 1977		Map 12
www.markhamvineyards.com	707-963-5292	Tasting
St. Helena	Napa County	St. Helena AVA

Bordeaux immigrant Jean Laurent established a winery in 1874 with five acres of vineyards in St. Helena. Five years later he built the stone cellar still used today. In 1977, Bruce Markham bought the disused site and revived the cellar and built a viable winery. Markham, in turn, sold the winery and over 350 acres divided into four vineyards to the Japanese winemaking and importer Mercian, Inc., which works in concert with the international Terlato Wine Group marketers.

Today, under the watchful eye of winemaker Kimberlee Nicholls, Markham produces well over one hundred thousand cases of a fairly wide range of accessibly priced, competently made varieties, from Merlot (40 percent of production) to Sauvignon Blanc (25 percent) to Cabernet Sauvignon (10 percent).

MASON CELLARS 1993		Map 15
www.masoncellars.com	707-944-9159	Tasting
Napa	Napa County	Napa Valley AVA

After some twenty years of winemaking and vineyard management for the likes of Chappellet and Lakespring, Randy Mason established his own label in 1993. Concurrently, he helped start up the Napa Wine Company, a custom crush facility in Oakville, where the Mason Cellars wines are made today. The focus here is on Sauvignon Blanc. Grapes from Yountville and the Russian River Valley are blended into Mason Cellars Sauvignon Blanc and a second label, the modestly priced Pomelo. The success of these wines has led to substantial production, topping out at about sixty thousand cases, the vast majority of which are the several Sauvignons. A Merlot and Cabernet Sauvignon are also made in limited quantities.

On occasion, the ripe, tightly constructed Mason Cellars Sauvignon Blanc has reached into the 90-point range while Pomelo Sauvignon Blanc, a wine of more modest proportions, has often been one of the leading values in that variety.

MAYACAMAS VINEYARDS 1941		Map 14
www.mayacamas.com	707-224-4030	Tasting by Appointment
Napa	Napa County	Mount Veeder AVA

In 1941, Jack and Mary Taylor bought an abandoned stone winery and distillery dating from 1889 and restored both the winery and nearby vineyards on the slopes of Mount Veeder. After working the vineyard through the 1960s, the Taylors sold to Bob and Elinor Travers, who run Mayacamas to this day. The 52 acres of vineyards, at elevations ranging from 1,800 to 2,400 feet, are planted principally to Cabernet Sauvignon and Chardonnay, plus small blocks of Sauvignon Blanc and Pinot Noir. The wines are made in small batches, with the Mayacamas Cabernet and Chardonnay topping out at two thousand cases each and Sauvignon Blanc and Pinot Noir averaging five hundred cases.

There was a time, when the Traverses first took over Mayacamas, during which both Cabernet and Chardonnay were as good as it gets in a ripe, deep way. But, as the industry grew and overall wine quality increased, Mayacamas failed to keep up, and today's wines are rather hit-or-miss affairs at best. When they succeed, it is because they find enough central fruit to fill out their medium/full-bodied architecture.

MELKA WINES 1995		Map 14
www.melkawines.com	707-963-6008	No Tasting
Oakville	Napa County	Oakville AVA

Philippe Melka, born and trained in Bordeaux, where he had originally studied geology, became interested in wine and learned throughout Bordeaux and Australia before settling in Oakville, where he remains a consulting winemaker to several top labels, including Gemstone and Vineyard 29. With his wife, enologist Cherie Melka, they started making their own wine in 1995. The Melkas make just two wines today, the CJ Cabernet Sauvignon and a proprietary red blend, Métisse. About 500 cases of the CJ Cabernet and 1,500 of the Métisse are made each year from grapes grown by David Abreau on a four-acre plot in St. Helena and elsewhere in the Napa Valley.

Many of Melka's wines, both for his own label as well as for other producers, have been big winners, and as a result, his talents are widely recognized. His wines of late have been less consistent, but they remain hot commodities for their potential to pop up at the top of the charts.

MERRYVALE VINEYARDS 1983		Map 12
www.merryvale.com	707-963-2225	Tasting
St. Helena	Napa County	St. Helena AVA

Sunny St. Helena Winery was the first winery built in the Napa Valley after the end of Prohibition in 1933. Some half a century later, Swiss entrepreneur Jack Schlatter bought the property from Bill Harlan, who set off to found Harlan Estate, renamed and revived it with the help of son René and winemakers Larry Cherubino and Sean Foster. Today's Merryvale is a blend of three tiers of wines: the Merryvale line of fairly high-priced varieties, including Cabernet Sauvignon, Chardonnay, Pinot Noir, and Merlot; an even higher-priced Prestige range, including a proprietary Chardonnay blend called Silhouette, a Cabernet blend called Profile, and several wines made with Beckstoffer Vineyard grapes; and the more modestly priced Starmont label, now produced at its own winery south of Napa town near the entrance to the Napa Valley, with Sauvignon Blanc, Cabernet, Merlot, and Chardonnay on offer. Ten thousand cases of Merryvale and

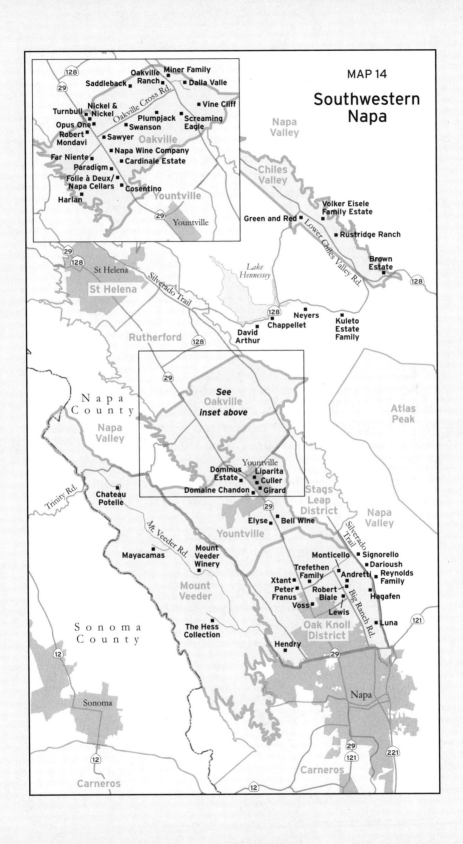

MAP 14

Southwestern Napa

128
29
Oakville
Saddleback ■ Ranch
■ Miner Family
■ Dalla Valle
Turnbull ■ Nickel &
■ Nickel
Opus One ■
Robert
Mondavi ■
■ Vine Cliff
Oakville Cross Rd.
Plumpjack ■
Swanson ■
■ Screaming
Eagle
■ Sawyer
Oakville
Far Niente ■
Paradigm ■
■ Napa Wine Company
■ Cardinale Estate
Folie à Deux/
Napa Cellars ■
■ Cosentino
Harlan ■
Yountville
29
Yountville

Napa
Valley

Chiles
Valley

Volker Eisele
Family Estate
Green and Red ■
Lower Chiles Valley Rd.
■ Rustridge Ranch

Brown
Estate ■

29
128
St Helena
Silverado Trail
St Helena

Lake
Hennessey

128

Rutherford
128
128
Neyers ■
Chappellet ■
David
Arthur ■
Kuleto
Estate
Family ■

Napa
County
Napa
Valley

*See
Oakville
inset above*

29

Atlas
Peak

Trinity Rd.
■ Chateau
Potelle

Yountville
Dominus
Estate ■
Domaine Chandon ■
Liparita ■
Culler ■
Girard ■

Stags
Leap
District

Napa
Valley

Mt. Veeder Rd.
■ Mayacamas
Mount
Veeder
Winery ■
Yountville
Elyse ■
■ Bell Wine

Mount
Veeder

Silverado
Trail

Monticello ■
Signorello ■
■ Darioush
Trefethen
Family ■
Andretti ■
Reynolds
Family ■
Xtant ■
Peter
Franus ■
Robert
Biale ■
Hagafen ■
Voss ■
Lewis ■
Big Ranch Rd.
■ Luna
121

Sonoma
County

■ The Hess
Collection

Oak Knoll
District

12
Hendry ■
29

Sonoma

Napa

12
29
121
221

Carneros
12
Carneros

ninety thousand cases of Starmont wines are made each year. Grapes are sourced from the seventy-acre estate vineyards and from other growers around the valley.

Quality levels are reasonable for the prices charged, but Merryvale rarely dents the highest score ranges and settles instead on being good, reliable, and interesting. The tasting room at the main winery just south of St. Helena on Highway 29 is a very pleasant place to stop. Starmont wines carry prices at the lower end of the Napa Valley scale.

MINER FAMILY VINEYARDS 1998		Map 14
www.minerwines.com	800-366-9463	Tasting
Oakville	Napa County	Oakville AVA

Founded by Dave and Emily Miner (Dave had headed up Oakville Ranch) in the eastern hills of Oakville, the winery produces a broad range of varieties under the guidance of winemaker Gary Brookman, formerly of Joseph Phelps. Miner purchases grapes from several well-respected vineyards, including Stagecoach in Napa, and Garys' and Rosella's vineyards in the Santa Lucia Highlands of Monterey County. A total of twenty-five thousand cases are produced at the Miners' custom crush facility, which has a hundred-thousand-case capacity and currently eight customers in addition to Miner. Three-quarters of the Miner production is red, principally Cabernet Sauvignon, Pinot Noir, and Merlot; and another quarter is white, nearly all of which is Chardonnay. Lesser amounts of several other varieties are produced, including a very successful Viognier from Madera County.

Over half the wines reviewed from Miner in the past decade have scored 90 points and more, with a recent Wild Yeast Chardonnay reaching up to 95 points. Even when ratings are less than spectacular, most wines still fall in the comfortably recommended range at the upper end of the 80-point level. Miner wines are bold and usually fairly dramatic, and they are consistently successful. The Viognier is rich, ripe, and luscious yet very well balanced, and it frequently reaches the top of charts with ratings of 90 points and beyond.

MONTICELLO VINEYARDS 1970		Map 14
www.corleyfamilynapavalley.com	707-253-2802	Tasting
Napa	Napa County	Oak Knoll District AVA

Jay Corley set out from Southern California for Napa in 1969 to find a vineyard. Now run by sons Kevin, Chris, and Stephen Corley, the winery produces a relatively modest total of fifteen thousand cases of a substantial variety of wines made from the grapes grown on the family's five distinct vineyard properties in the Oak Knoll, Yountville, Rutherford, and St. Helena areas. Under its own label, Monticello makes moderately priced estate wines including Pinot Noir, Chardonnay, Cabernet Sauvignon, Syrah, and Merlot. Under the Corley label is a proprietary red blend and a Cabernet. And at the top of the line rests the Corley Reserve label with an Estate Chardonnay from Home Ranch grapes. Jefferson Cuvée is an important wine in the line and adds to the double entendre related to both the Corley ties to the family's Virginia roots and the importance of the names Jefferson and Monticello in Napa County. The winery building is influenced by the architecture of Thomas Jefferson's Monticello.

Monticello and Corley wines, made in a fairly full-bodied, balanced, reasonably polished style, are not inexpensive but, by Napa standards, are somewhat more affordable. Ratings have varied over the years, yet scores into the highly recommended 90-point range are no strangers to this handsome, quality-oriented winery. It is well worth a visit when you are in the area.

MOUNT VEEDER WINERY 1973		Map 14
www.mtveeder.com	707-967-3830	Tasting by Appointment
Napa	Napa County	Mount Veeder AVA

In the mid-1960s, founders Michael and Arlene Bernstein planted twenty acres of vines on the slopes of Mount Veeder. Several subsequent ownership changes later, the winery and vineyards are now owned by international holding company Constellation Brands and overseen by winemaker Janet Myers. Vineyard acreage has grown to forty, spread among three sites on the slopes of Mount Veeder and planted to all five classic Bordeaux varietals. Ten to twelve thousand cases in total of two wines are produced: the lion's share is a Cabernet Sauvignon and a smaller batch of a Reserve red blend of Cabernet and Merlot.

The winery's Cabernets typically reflect their mountain origins in their high levels of ripeness and concentration. Top vintages have scored in the 90-point range, and the regular-bottling Cabernet is one of the better values in the Napa Valley when it reaches that rating level.

MUMM NAPA 1985   Map 13

www.mummnapa.com   800-686-6272   Tasting

Rutherford   Napa County   Rutherford AVA

In 1983, after a four-year search, Mumm of Champagne and Seagram founded the California Sparkling Wine house as a joint venture. Then called Domaine Mumm, the firsts sparklers appeared in '86, initially produced at nearby Sterling, and the Mumm winery was completed in '88. Now owned by French drinks conglomerate Pernod Richard, Mumm is overseen by winemaker Ludovic Dervin, a native of Champagne and experienced at Charles Heidseick and G. H. Mumm in France and California's Piper Sonoma. Made according to the traditional methods of Champagne, the current production in excess of 250,000 cases ranges from the old favorite Brut Prestige, through a Blanc de Noirs and Blanc de Blanc, to the top-of-the-line DVX (named for founding winemaker Guy Devaux). A small vineyard, also named after Devaux, in Carneros is the source of Chardonnay, Pinot Noir, and Pinot Meunier grapes as well as up to fifty different vineyards throughout the valley.

In its early years, Mumm made Sparkling Wine that was high in fruit flavors and greatly enjoyed by those who were willing to forgive those wines for favoring California succulence over French austerity. But, true Champagne, even though fruitier today than it was in the past, is still not about fruit but about balance, richness, depth, and complexity, and today's Mumm products have moved in that direction. The Prestige line of wines typically earns recommended to highly recommended scores of mid- to upper 80s, with the occasional reach to the 90-point level. The DVX wines, both Brut and Rosé, are made in a more classic, crisp, and chalky style; more often than not, they rate at the very highest among locally produced Sparkling Wines, with scores of 95 and up not uncommon.

NAPA CELLARS 1996   Map 14

www.napacellars.com   707-944-2565   Tasting

Oakville   Napa County   Oakville AVA

Founded in 1996 by Rich Frank and Koerner Rombauer, the small winery on Highway 29 next to Mustards was purchased by Trinchero Family Estates in 2006 and is now under the watchful eye of winemaker Joe Shirley. Grapes are sourced from throughout the valley and made into six varieties: Chardonnay, Sauvignon Blanc, Cabernet Sauvignon, Merlot, Zinfandel, and Syrah, with Chardonnay leading the pack in terms of volume, with about ten thousand cases out of the total of more than thirty thousand cases produced each vintage.

Prices have been historically low by Napa Valley standards, and quality has been about average for those prices. New leadership has seen both quality and prices advance. At this writing, it appears as though a new script is in the process of being written at Napa Cellars. Recent wines are considerably fuller and deeper in character.

NAPA WINE COMPANY 1877		Map 14
www.napawineco.com	800-848-9630	Tasting
Oakville	Napa County	Oakville AVA

The Nouveau Medoc Winery was the first occupant of what is now the Napa Wine Company's winery and in 1877 was only the ninth bonded winery in California. After decades of ownership changes, the Pelissa family of winegrowers bought the winery and vineyards in the 1950s. Today, the company is run by Andrew Hoxsey, grandson of the Pelissas. The Napa Wine Company is in fact an agglomeration of four distinct entities: the Napa Wine Company's own label, producing 7,500 cases of Cabernet Sauvignon, Zinfandel, Sauvignon Blanc, and Pinot Blanc; 600 acres of vineyards, including 210 acres in Oakville and 390 in Yountville, the grapes from which go into the home-label wine as well as being offered to other vintners; a custom crush facility, blending for some 60 customers, including the Napa Wine Company's label; and a large sales/tasting room (unfortunately named Cult Wine Central) for some two dozen local winemakers.

To date, Sauvignon Blanc, made in a rich, ripe, yet firmly balanced style, has been the quality leader with scores often at 90 points and beyond. Zinfandel has also occasionally cracked the 90-point barrier, but Cabernet Sauvignon has so far remained in the mid- to upper 80s.

NEAL FAMILY VINEYARDS 1997		Map 12
www.nealvineyards.com	707-965-2800	Tasting by Appointment
Angwin	Napa County	Howell Mountain AVA

Family patriarch Jack Neal established a vineyard management service in 1968. After Jack's '94 death, son Mark continued the business, which farms nearly two thousand acres today. In '97, Mark began making his own wine from grapes grown on the ten-acre Howell Mountain estate as well as vineyard-designated wines from several top valley vineyards farmed by Neal. The Neal family produces about 3,500 cases, mostly of Cabernet Sauvignon, with a small quantity of Zinfandel and Sauvignon Blanc. Organic farming methods are used exclusively for their own grapes and those served by the management company.

Prices for these hard-to-find wines have been below the Napa Valley norm for the quality delivered, but the search is typically worth the effort, especially for the balanced Cabernet Sauvignon and the ripe, fruity Zinfandel.

NEWTON VINEYARD 1977		Map 11
www.newtonvineyard.com	888-242-6195	Tasting by Appointment
St. Helena	Napa County	Spring Mountain District AVA

Newton was established in 1977 by the late Peter and Dr. Su Hua Newton when they sold their founders' interest in Sterling to Coca-Cola. The Newtons began developing the 560 acres of land that they acquired on Spring Mountain, west of St. Helena on the eastern slopes of the Mayacamas range. There are now 200 acres planted to Merlot, Cabernet Sauvignon, Cabernet Franc, and Petit Verdot at elevations ranging from 500 to 1,600 feet. Production has been steady at 28,000 cases of Cabernet, Merlot, Chardonnay, and a red Bordeaux blend, The Puzzle, all unfiltered. Newton Vineyard is now owned by Domaine Chandon.

Merlot and the upscale Chardonnay, labeled Unfiltered, have been quality leaders, with the Chardonnay more often than not reaching into the highly recommended ranks with scores in the 90s. The wines produced from the hillside-grown grapes have typically been full in body, relatively high in fruit, richly oaked, and decently balanced.

NEYERS VINEYARDS 1992		Map 14
www.neyersvineyards.com	707-963-8840	Tasting by Appointment
St. Helena	Napa County	Napa Valley AVA

Bruce Neyers, a former research chemist, was attracted to the valley and winegrowing at the end of army service in the Bay Area. Starting in the Mayacamas Vineyards cellars, Neyers became acquainted with Joe Phelps and, in 1975, signed on to run the new winery, Joseph Phelps Vineyards, where he remained until 1992, when he started his own winery. With wife

Barbara and longtime winemaker Ehran Jordan, Neyers has set up shop near Pritchard Hill on the east side of Napa Valley. Their estate vineyard, Conn Valley Ranch, has fifty acres planted to Merlot, Cabernet Sauvignon, and Cabernet Franc, and it provides a quarter of the grapes for the Neyers wines. The remaining grapes are grown by the likes of a half-dozen growers in the valley and Sonoma, including the Sangiacomo family in Sonoma, Lee Hudson in Carneros, and Tofanelli in Calistoga. Production runs to fifteen thousand cases, 60 percent of which is Chardonnay, another 20 percent Zinfandel, and the remainder small quantities of Cabernet, Syrah, and Merlot. Neyers is also well-known within wine-collecting circles for his role as import manager for Berkeley's iconoclastic Kermit Lynch Imports.

The winery style runs to rich and full-bodied across the entire spectrum of offerings. Single-vineyard bottlings of Chardonnay and Zinfandel have led the impressive parade of hits authored by Neyers, while Syrah, both in the Hudson Vineyard release and in a special blend called Cuvée d'Honneur have often joined in the 90- to 95-point ranks of exceptional Neyers wines.

NICKEL & NICKEL 1997		Map 14
www.nickelandnickel.com	707-967-9600	Tasting by Appointment
Oakville	Napa County	Oakville AVA

The Nickel family, led by the late plant nursery mogul and motorcycle aficionado Gil Nickel, founders of Far Niente, established their own label in 1997 devoted to 100 percent single-vineyard wines from Napa growers and their own vineyard. Their estate, Sullenger Vineyard, is planted solely to Cabernet Sauvignon, one of the principal varieties made in the restored 1800s homestead, now winery. The list of current varieties is long: nine separate single-vineyard-designated Cabernets, four Chardonnays, three Merlots and Syrahs, and two Pinot Noirs and Zinfandels. These two dozen varieties use the grapes of a wide range of growers, including Rock Cairn, Truchard, Hudson, and Suscol Ranch. Production is in the 45,000-case range, with individual bottlings ranging from as few as 250 cases to as many as 3,500.

Everything about this winery, from its spectacular stone winery building to its eye-pleasing grounds to its packaging, speaks to upscale intent, and that intent has more often than not been equaled by wine quality. The wines are rich and ripe and are enhanced by not immodest oak influences;

not surprisingly, given the care and expense that goes into their making, they tend to be somewhat pricey. Depending on vintage and vineyard, wine ratings have ranged from the mid-80s to the lower 90s.

OAKVILLE RANCH VINEYARDS 1989		Map 14
www.oakvilleranchvineyards.com 707-944-9665		No Tasting
Napa	Napa County	Oakville AVA

Founders Bob Miner, after leaving the helm of Oracle, Inc., and Randy Lewis, subsequently of Lewis Cellars, bought a 350-acre ranch 1,400 feet above the valley floor on the eastern slopes above the Silverado Trail. The original ranch had fifty-five acres planted to Chardonnay, Cabernet Sauvignon, Cabernet Franc, and Merlot. Now run by Miner's widow, Mary Miner, and winemaker Ashley Heisey, the vineyards have grown to eighty acres, but the production of two thousand cases remains modest. Varieties offered include several Cabernet bottlings, a Chardonnay, a Merlot-based blend, and a Cabernet Franc-based wine named Robert's Blend in homage to the founder.

Ripe and reasonably balanced, full, sometimes fleshy in style, Oakville Ranch wines occasionally reach the 90-point level.

OPUS ONE 1979		Map 14
www.opusonewinery.com	707-944-9442	Tasting
Oakville	Napa County	Oakville AVA

Located directly across the highway from the Robert Mondavi winery in Oakville, Opus One was started by the combined efforts of Robert Mondavi and the Baron de Rothschild, owner of Château Mouton Rothschild in Bordeaux. It represented at the time—and still represents today—the single-most significant collaboration ever between Bordeaux and Napa. The goal at Opus One was to focus on one Cabernet Sauvignon-based wine and to make it as an estate wine in the manner of the Bordeaux châteaux. From its outset, Opus One achieved high levels of richness and near-perfect focus. Even when its own vineyards came into maturity, necessitating a slight change in the wine, quality remained high. Today, its mostly below-ground winery remains one of the technological leaders in the Napa Valley, and the wine has changed little over time. The sale of the Robert Mondavi winery to Constellation leaves Opus One more or less intact, with a drift in management toward the de Rothschild side of the equation, whereas it was the Mondavis who were previously doing most of the management activities.

The wine is full-bodied, well balanced, richly oaked, and layered. In most vintages, its critical ratings exceed 90 points and can range as high as 95. While other Napa Valley wines have come along and passed Opus One in price and prestige, it remains today one of the most respected names among California wines.

PAHLMEYER WINERY	1987	Map 15
www.pahlmeyer.com	707-255-2321	No Tasting
Napa	Napa County	Napa Valley AVA

Jayson Pahlmeyer, a former Bay Area trial attorney, developed vineyards in Coombsville, Atlas Peak, and on the Sonoma Coast before taking up winemaking for his own label. The first Bordeaux-style vintages were made by winemaker Randy Dunn from grapes grown on former partner John Caldwell's vineyard east of Napa. Now Pahlmeyer and longtime wine-maker Erin Green produce serious Chardonnay, Pinot Noir, and Merlot and Cabernet Sauvignon blends from Jayson's seventy-two-acre Waters Vineyard above Napa and thirty-acre Wayfarer Farm on the Sonoma Coast. Production is approaching twenty thousand cases, with nearly half devoted to Chardonnay.

Jayson's wines are as barrel-chested as he is, and they are prized by collectors for their intensity, depth, and boldness. High scores into the 90s are the norm for these dramatic efforts that appeal to fans of weighty, complex wines.

PALOMA VINEYARD	1995	Map 11
www.palomavineyard.com	707-963-7504	No Tasting
St. Helena	Napa County	Spring Mountain District AVA

Former Texans Jim and Barbara Richards moved to the Napa Valley in 1984 and planted fifteen acres of their estate to Merlot and Cabernet Sauvignon grapes. For a decade they only sold grapes to other well-known winemakers but in '84 made their first vintage of Merlot, to the modest tune of six hundred cases. The fifteen acres are still bearing fruit, producing grapes for a renowned estate-grown Merlot and a very small batch of Syrah. Total production runs between two thousand and three thousand cases a year, 90 percent of which is the flagship Merlot.

The Paloma Merlot is about as good as it gets with this variety. Not only does the wine capture lots of rich, deep, succulent Merlot fruit, but, because of its hillside vineyard, the wine takes on added structural dimension that contributes to its long-aging ability. Don't miss this one. Although not inexpensive, it sells for half or less than Napa Valley Cabernet Sauvignons of comparable quality and aging potential.

PAOLETTI VINEYARDS 1994		Map 11
www.paolettivineyards.com	707-942-0689	Tasting by Appointment
Calistoga	Napa County	Calistoga AVA

Los Angeles restaurateur (of the well-regarded Ristorante Peppone) Gianni Paoletti is a Napa Valley vintner as well, and his winery reflects his Italian heritage. Assisted by winemaker Tim Crowe, Paoletti makes an interesting line of wines and blends totaling about 3,500 cases in most years, of which fully three-quarters is Cabernet Sauvignon or blends based on Cabernet. Merlot and Merlot-based blends make up another 20 percent, with several Tuscan varieties rounding out the total. Most wines are made from grapes grown on the Paoletti vineyards, thirty-six acres planted to Cabernet, Merlot, and Sangiovese.

The wines have been intensely flavored and somewhat rustic in styling, and they have often been among the most highly praised wines of their type. In the top vintages, the wine have rated up into the mid- to upper 90s.

PARADIGM 1991		Map 14
www.paradigmwinery.com	707-944-7683	Tasting by Appointment
Oakville	Napa County	Oakville AVA

Ren and Marilyn Harris come from long lines of California ancestors: Ren's family came to California in the 1760s, while Marilyn's emigrated from Italy to grow grapes in the valley in the 1890s. The Harrises established Paradigm Vineyards in 1976 and began making their own wines in 1991. With renowned winemaker Heidi Peterson Barrett using grapes from the estate vineyard laid out by her father, famous Napa Valley luminary Dick Peterson, Paradigm makes up to six thousand cases each year, with its signal Cabernet Sauvignon representing fully three-quarters. They also make small batches of Merlot, Zinfandel, and Cabernet Franc, all from the estate. The fifty-five-acre vineyard is now two-thirds planted to Cabernet, with the remainder in Merlot and Cabernet Franc. Paradigm uses 30 percent of the grapes produced and sells the remainder to other local winemakers.

Paradigm wines typically exhibit an inviting combination of richness, good fruit, reasonable balance, and a degree of complexity owing to both the highly regarded vineyard sited on the western benchlands as well as the winemaker's practiced hand.

PEJU PROVINCE 1983		Map 13
www.peju.com	800-446-7358	Tasting
Rutherford	Napa County	Rutherford AVA

While running his LA landscape architecture and nursery businesses, Tony Peju visited the Napa Valley in 1979 and not long after came away with an established vineyard of thirty acres planted to Cabernet Sauvignon and French Colombard. Now up to 450 acres spread among three vineyards (Rutherford Estate, Persephone, and Wappo), Peju makes a wide variety of wines under the guidance of winemaker Sara Fowler, late of Franciscan and Mount Veeder. Peju's Cabernet and other red varietals lead the pack in the production of thirty-five thousand cases a year. The popular visitors center, in a landmark faux French Provincial tower, lures scores of tourists who enjoy the professionally run, informative tastings provided. Indeed, the better part of Peju's sales are direct to the consumer, either at the winery or through its wine club.

Rich, full-bodied reds with midterm aging potential are the Peju hallmark, and while some will find them too inviting and not classically structured, most tasters like the fact that the wines provide lots of drinking pleasure without demanding lengthy stays in the cellar. Inconsistent critical ratings have ranged from the mid-80s to the mid-90s, but those who visit the winery and participate in its lengthy, for-fee tastings invariably find something to their liking.

PETER FRANUS WINE COMPANY 1987		Map 14
www.peterfranus.com	707-945-0542	Tasting by Appointment
Napa	Napa County	Napa Valley AVA

Peter Franus was raised in Connecticut but came west to attend the University of California, after which his newfound interest in wine led him to enroll in the viticulture and enology program at Fresno State. Several winemaking experiences later, Franus wound up as winemaker at the Mount Veeder Winery from 1981 to 1992. He made his first wine, a Zinfandel, in '87 for his own label. Today, Franus makes his wines from the grapes of several select Napa Valley growers, including Stewart, Truchard, and Brandlin vineyards. This small producer makes in the neighborhood of 3,500 cases a year, featuring a Cabernet Sauvignon, Zinfandel, and Sauvignon Blanc.

Each of those wines has garnered high scores, with the Brandlin Ranch Zinfandel frequently spoken of as one of Napa's best. The Zin is focused on ripe berries, comes with a fair bit of tannin, but is not ever a massive, overdone wine.

PINE RIDGE WINERY 1978		Map 15
www.pineridgewinery.com	800-486-0503	Tasting
Napa	Napa County	Stags Leap District AVA

In 1978, Gary Andrus headed a partnership that started with a fifty-acre vineyard on the Silverado Trail, now grown to over three hundred acres in five valley appellations. By 1980, a new small winery was in place and produced twelve thousand cases a year. Now up to eighty-five thousand cases, of which half is Pine Ridge's unique Chenin Blanc–Viognier blend, most wines are made from estate-grown grapes. Longtime winemaker Stacy Clark oversees the production of six Cabernet Sauvignons, three Chardonnays, and a smattering of other varieties and blends. The partnership has been sold to Leucinda National Corp., a diversified holding company with two wineries, Pine Ridge and Archery Summit in Oregon.

More often than not, Pine Ridge reds have been enjoyed for their mix of fruit and richness, but there is the occasional inconsistency here that keeps the label from rising to the top of the charts. Most wines are made with balance and polish; the best get scores in the 90s, and the rest range from the mid- to upper 80s.

PLUMPJACK WINERY 1995		Map 14
www.plumpjack.com	707-945-1220	Tasting
Oakville	Napa County	Oakville AVA

Founded by recent mayor of San Francisco Gavin Newsom, and backed by philanthropist-socialite-composer Gordon Getty, PlumpJack is best described as part of a cottage industry of luxe restaurants, inns, and shops in Northern California, all named in honor of Jack Falstaff. At press time there were sixteen discrete businesses under the PlumpJack umbrella. In 1995, the group bought a century-old, fifty-acre vineyard property in Oakville and made a successful Cabernet Sauvignon. Now under the guidance of winemaker Anthony Biagi—late of Duckhorn and Neal Family Vineyards—PlumpJack makes ten thousand cases of Cabernet, Merlot, Syrah, and Chardonnay to high standards. Second label Cade is just out of the chute but makes its own Cabernet and Sauvignon Blanc.

The Cabernet Sauvignon, made in the ripe, black cherry, and sweet oak style, has shown best, with the Reserve bottling reaching the top of the ratings chart with 90-point and higher scores in many vintages.

PORTFOLIO LIMITED EDITION 1998		Map 15
www.portfoliowinery.com	707-265-6555	No Tasting
Napa	Napa County	Napa Valley AVA

A very small—"cult," if you will—family winery, Portfolio was founded in 1998 by Luc and Genevieve Janssens. Genevieve is the winemaker in the family; from France and a line of vintners. She worked at Opus One and remains the director of winemaking for Robert Mondavi. Luc is a Belgium-born artist—ergo the winery's name. Each vintage year, Portfolio bottles only about 250 cases of a Cabernet Sauvignon–Cabernet Franc blend. The Cabernet grapes are exclusively from the Hendry Ranch Vineyard in southwest Napa, and the Cabernet Franc grapes are from the Weitz Vineyard in Oakville.

Year in and year out, these polished, rich, perfectly focused wines have scored at the top of the charts, with ratings nearly always in the 90s and often reaching the very pinnacle of critical acclaim.

PRIDE MOUNTAIN VINEYARDS 1991		Map 11
www.pridewines.com	707-963-4949	Tasting by Appointment
St. Helena	Napa County	Spring Mountain AVA

The late Jim Pride, a dentist and dental management entrepreneur, with wife Carolyn, acquired an estate and vineyard on Spring Mountain—partially in Napa and partially in Sonoma County—called Summit Ranch, where the first known vineyards were planted in the 1860s. Planting the original fifty acres, the first Pride Mountain wines were produced in 1991. In later years, an additional thirty acres were planted to Cabernet Sauvignon, Cabernet Franc, Petit Verdot, and Merlot, and a modern winery was constructed.

The winery and vineyards are now managed by Jim's widow and their children, Suzanne and Steve, with the guidance of winemaker Sally Johnson and consulting winemaker Bob Foley. Twenty thousand cases are made each year, including Cabernet (at about 40 percent of the total), Merlot (30 percent), Viognier, Chardonnay, and Cabernet Franc. The Web site thoroughly reflects the interesting history of the area as well as providing detailed profiles of the wines on offer.

Every wine made at this winery has shown well in the chosen style that emphasizes high ripeness and generous oaky richness but also comes with solid structures and good aging potential. The Viognier is often among the most intense in California, while the sturdy reds are among the best for cellaring. Ratings of 90 points and up are the norm for this attractive, wonderfully sited winery. It is among our favorite places to take visitors in the Napa Valley.

PROVENANCE VINEYARDS 1999		Map 13
www.provenancevineyards.com	707-968-3633	Tasting
Rutherford	Napa County	Rutherford AVA

Winemaker and general manager Tom Rinaldi skipped vet school in favor of enology at UC–Davis and set out to make a name for himself in Napa Valley wineries, including Freemark Abbey, Rutherford Hill, and, for twenty-two years, as the founding winemaker at Duckhorn. In 1999, Rinaldi made his first vintage of Provenance Cabernet Sauvignon. In 2002, now owned by international spirits conglomerate Diageo, Provenance bought the former Chateau Beaucanon winery in Rutherford. Provenance has grown rapidly and currently makes over fifty thousand cases a year, with over 40 percent of that Cabernet, another 35 percent Merlot, and smaller quantities of Sauvignon Blanc and a Port. Several Provenance bottlings use estate grapes from the forty-five-acre home vineyard. Other notable vineyard-designated wines include a Beckstoffer To Kalon Cabernet and a Paras Merlot.

The winery's location on the West Rutherford Bench and its access to good-quality fruit has allowed it, under Rinaldi's guiding hand, to succeed more often than not. While not inexpensive, the winery's midpriced Cabernets can be fairly good values relative to its competition.

QUINTESSA 1993		Map 13
www.quintessa.com	707-967-1601	Tasting by Appointment
Rutherford	Napa County	Rutherford AVA

In the 1960s, Chilean Agustin Huneeus grew a small winery in Chile, Concha y Toro, into his country's largest. Political upheaval drove him to move from Chile to head up Seagram's worldwide wine operations. In the United States, he later founded Noble Vineyards, which subsequently acquired Concannon in the Livermore Valley. He also served for a time as the head of Franciscan Vineyards. With Valeria, his wife and an accomplished viticulturist and biochemist in her own right, the couple worked together to develop the Quintessa Vineyards and winery, focusing on a single red Meritage blend, estate-grown Quintessa, based on Cabernet Sauvignon, Merlot, and Cabernet Franc; today, just under ten thousand cases are produced, but the winery's capacity is six times that number. The 280-acre Quintessa estate includes 170 acres planted to Cabernet (75 percent of the grapes), Merlot, Cabernet Franc, Petit Verdot, and Carmenere. When developed in the '90s, the Huneeuses were fortunate that the vineyards had not been developed earlier in the heyday of phylloxera. The striking, crescent-shaped winery is built unobtrusively into an eastern-facing hillside on the Rutherford estate, running between the Napa River and the Silverado Trail. The Web site is loaded with good information and photographs that will encourage a visit.

Early Quintessa wines, not made from the still-developing estate, were quite popular, but the first editions from home-grown grapes were less well received. Lately, with more mature fruit coming into the winery and greater understanding of how to handle that fruit, Quintessa has returned to the top of the ratings pack and now can be expected to continue its recent string of 90- to 95-point successes. The wine reflects the riper, black cherry style of fruit that comes from the east side of the valley and is typically made with a sturdy, age-worthy undercarriage.

RAYMOND VINEYARD & CELLAR 1971		Map 13
www.raymondvineyards.com	800-525-2659	Tasting
St. Helena	Napa County	Rutherford AVA

The winery was founded in 1971 by Roy Sr., Roy Jr., and Walter Raymond. The Raymond family dates to 1876 when Jacob and Frederick Beringer founded Beringer Bros. Five generations later, Craig and Krisi Raymond continue winemaking, and Roy Jr. and Walter still run the business, even though in 1989 the family sold a majority interest to the Japanese Kirin Brewing Co. The majority of grapes are grown on three owned vineyards: the 90-acre Rutherford estate with Cabernet Sauvignon and Merlot grapes; 10 acres of Cabernet in St. Helena; and a 250-acre Chardonnay vineyard,

Jameson Ridge, in southern Napa Valley. In 2007, Raymond sold another three hundred acres of Chardonnay grown in Monterey County to focus on its Napa holdings. In excess of one hundred thousand cases of Cabernet, Chardonnay, Sauvignon Blanc, and Merlot are made across several tiers: the Reserve, Limited Edition, and AVA-specific District, and a lower-priced label called R Collection.

The family sold the winery to Boisset Estates in August, 2009. A new winemaking team headed by Phillippe Melka has been put in place and seems likely to improve wine quality.

REVANA FAMILY VINEYARD 1998		Map 12
www.revanawine.com	707-967-8814	Tasting by Appointment
St. Helena	Napa County	St. Helena AVA

Houston cardiologist Dr. Madaiah Revana bought nine acres of Cabernet Sauvignon, Cabernet Franc, and Petit Verdot grapes in 1998 and proceeded to make Cabernet Sauvignon exclusively. With the talented winemaker Heidi Peterson Barrett and vineyard manager Jim Barbour, Revana makes something in excess of two thousand cases of its Cabernet each vintage year. As a practicing cardiologist, Revana suggests in the winery's publicity that two glasses of wine of an evening may contribute to a healthy heart.

And if you can afford it, the Revana Cabernet Sauvignon, often rated in the 90+-point range, will certainly make your palate feel better as well with its ripe, rich curranty character.

REVERIE ON DIAMOND MOUNTAIN 1993		Map 11
www.reveriewine.com	800-738-3743	Tasting by Appointment
Calistoga	Napa County	Diamond Mountain District AVA

In the early 1990s, Norman Kiken acquired a twenty-seven-acre vineyard on the steep, south-facing slopes of Diamond Mountain, adjacent to Diamond Creek Vineyard, and planted to Cabernet Sauvignon, Cabernet Franc, and Merlot grapes. With consulting winemaker Ted Lemon, Kiken started with 250 cases of Cabernet as his first vintage and has slowly grown to about 2,500 cases of estate-grown Cabernet, a Reserve Cabernet, Cabernet Franc, and a second-label red called A. S. Kiken.

Both the Reverie reds and the A. S. Kiken have, in fact, kicked the backside of the gong in most vintages, with scores in the high 80s and low 90s. These are fairly typical Diamond Mountain reds with deep fruit, rich oak, and tight structures. In lesser vintages, the wines can be quite challenging for anything but long aging.

REYNOLDS FAMILY WINERY 1996		Map 14
www.reynoldsfamilywinery.com	707-258-2558	Tasting by Appointment
Napa	Napa County	Stags Leap District AVA

Steve Reynolds, a former dentist, acquired a chicken ranch in the Stags Leap District and converted it to ten acres of Cabernet Sauvignon vine-yards and a winery. Current production approaches seven thousand cases each year, with Cabernet leading the roster at 35 percent, followed by a red Meritage called Persistence, Chardonnay, and Pinot Noir. On the side, Reynolds partners with three other winemakers in a project to create a Meritage from the grapes of each of the Napa Valley AVAs, currently named Fourteen as that is the current number of subappellations extant. Wine quality has been high but inconsistent over time.

RICHARD PARTRIDGE CELLARS 1998		Map 12
www.richardpartridge.com	562-802-7345	No Tasting
St. Helena	Napa County	St. Helena AVA

Richard Partridge is an electrical engineer who moved from his native Illinois to Southern California, where he sells large commercial generators. Along the way, Richard and his wife, Chris, bought property in the Napa Valley and made their first Cabernet Sauvignon in 1998. Today's produc-tion is under the guidance of winemaker Jeff Fontanella, with most recent experience at Saddleback Cellars. Partridge produces a Cabernet and a Chardonnay, with total production at around 1,100 cases, two-thirds of which is the Cabernet, a blend of grapes from the Hoopes Vineyard in Oakville and Batuello in St. Helena. The Partridge Chardonnay is made from fruit grown on the State Lane Vineyard in Yountville. In '08, the Partridges planted a small, four-acre estate vineyard.

The typical Napa wines of medium-full to full-bodied and attractive fruit have garnered scores in the upper 80s for the most part.

ROBERT BIALE VINEYARDS 1991		Map 14
www.robertbialevineyards.com	707-257-7555	Tasting by Appointment
Napa	Napa County	Oak Knoll District AVA

Northern Italian immigrants, the Biale family grew Zinfandel grapes exclusively as early as the 1930s along with other farm produce. In '91, the Biales brought in several partners, including winemaker Al Perry, to make their own wines. Their product was initially named Aldo's Vineyard after the Biale patriarch. Biale wines started with four hundred cases of Zinfandel from eight acres of vineyards. In '03, a winery was finally built. Today's production approaches the sixteen-thousand-case capacity and is largely Zinfandel, with multiple small batches of vineyard-designated bottlings. Biale also makes Syrahs, Petit Sirah, and Sangiovese, as well as a proprietary blend of Zinfandel, Petit Sirah, and Syrah called Zappa. Vineyard holdings include the estate Aldo's Vineyard and the Black Chicken Vineyard, named after the Prohibition-era code for wine.

Biale has gathered a very enthusiastic following for his big-bodied, tannic, boldly cast wines. To his aficionados, few wines of the type rank higher, and critics who like the style often place his wines in the 90-point and up range, while those who prefer a more balanced approach have been less enthusiastic.

ROBERT CRAIG WINERY 1993		Map 12
www.robertcraigwine.com	707-252-2250	Tasting by Appointment
Napa	Napa County	Howell Mountain AVA

Robert Craig was assistant winemaker for Mount Veeder and general manager in the early days of the Hess Collection before embarking on his own label. He began by making only Cabernet Sauvignon and in 2002 built his own winery to use the eighteen estate acres of Craig vineyards in Coombsville and on Howell Mountain. Production of 8,500 cases is the annual norm, with fully 80 percent of the wines either AVA-designated Cabernet or the top-selling Affinity Cabernet blend. Craig also makes small quantities of Syrah, Zinfandel, and Chardonnay.

Craig's top wine of late has been his Mount Veeder–designated Cabernet Sauvignon, which often scores in the 90s. Affinity and Howell Mountain Cabernet usually top out in the upper 80s, and the other wines have been less consistent. Still, when you see a Craig Cabernet, you can usually count on it to be deep in character, sturdy to the point of slight toughness, and demanding of and capable of improving with time in the cellar.

ROBERT FOLEY VINEYARDS 1998		Map 12
www.robertfoleyvineyards.com	707-965-2669	No Tasting
Angwin	Napa County	Howell Mountain AVA

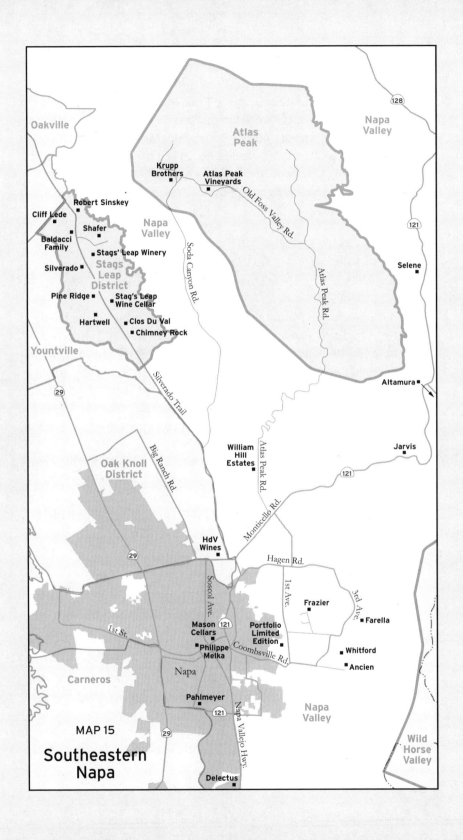

Oakville

Napa Valley

128

Atlas Peak

Krupp Brothers

Atlas Peak Vineyards

Old Foss Valley Rd.

121

Robert Sinskey

Cliff Lede

Napa Valley

Shafer

Baldacci Family

Stags' Leap Winery

Silverado

Stags Leap District

Selene

Soda Canyon Rd.

Pine Ridge

Stag's Leap Wine Cellar

Atlas Peak Rd.

Hartwell

Clos Du Val

Chimney Rock

Yountville

Silverado Trail

Altamura

29

Big Ranch Rd.

Oak Knoll District

William Hill Estates

Atlas Peak Rd.

Jarvis

121

Monticello Rd.

HdV Wines

Hagen Rd.

29

1st Ave.

3rd Ave.

Soscol Ave.

Frazier

Farella

1st St.

Mason Cellars

121

Portfolio Limited Edition

Philippe Melka

Coombsville Rd.

Whitford

Carneros

Napa

Ancien

Pahlmeyer

121

Napa Valley

Napa Vallejo Hwy.

MAP 15

Wild Horse Valley

Southeastern Napa

29

Delectus

Winemaker Bob Foley has been making wine for others since 1977; his experience includes basic training at Heitz, from which he moved on to become founding winemaker at Markham, and to Pride Mountain, where he remains the consulting winemaker. His small mountain vineyard and winery produces on the order of 2,500 cases of Cabernet Sauvignon, Merlot, Petit Sirah, Pinot Blanc, and a flagship Claret (90 percent Cabernet and 10 percent Merlot) along with a cult-inspiring Charbono, the latter made in minuscule quantities.

Foley's bold style has attracted lots of attention, as have scores in the mid-90s for his wines.

ROBERT KEENAN WINERY 1977		Map 11
www.keenanwinery.com	707-963-9178	Tasting by Appointment
St. Helena	Napa County	Spring Mountain District AVA

At 1,700 feet on Spring Mountain in the Mayacamas range lie the Keenan Vineyards. Originally planted to Zinfandel and Syrah in the early 1900s, Prohibition put the vineyards and winery out of action until 1974, when Robert Keenan purchased 180 acres of forest on the site and subsequently planted 50 of those acres to Cabernet Sauvignon, Chardonnay, and Merlot grapes. The small family winery produces ten thousand cases today, including 30 percent Chardonnay, 30 percent Cabernet, 25 percent Merlot, and a smattering of Zinfandel, Cabernet Franc, and Syrah.

Over the three decades of its existence, the winery has seen the high and lows of success, and some of its early Merlots and Chardonnays are still remembered for their top-of-the-charts scores. Although recent results have been less consistent, Keenan still reaches into the 90-point range with the occasional offering from its line of well-structured, medium-depth wines.

ROBERT MONDAVI WINERY 1966		Map 14
www.robertmondaviwinery.com	707-226-1395	Tasting
Oakville	Napa County	Oakville AVA

Robert Mondavi, brother to Peter Mondavi, who is the overseeing power at the Charles Krug Winery, broke from the family over stylistic differences and brotherly competitiveness and founded his own winery. He had a vision for quality wine that went far beyond anything that Krug was producing at the time, and while the separation was anything but amiable, it was Robert and not Peter who was proved right as Krug languished while Robert's eponymous winery flourished. With a string of clean, modern, enticing wines coming from the modern, high-tech, experiment-oriented winery, Mondavi quickly joined the ranks of the top producers of the late '60s and early '70s, eclipsing such legendary names as Martini, Christian Brothers, Krug, Beringer, and Inglenook in short order.

Over the years, expansion followed with vineyards ranging up to one thousand acres, a second winery in Lodi to produce a low-priced string of wines called Robert Mondavi Woodbridge, and eventually yet another line called Robert Mondavi Coastal. The winery and Mr. Mondavi—for that is how he was known in the trade—became legendary in its own time for innovation, for influence, and for forward thinking. In 1993, in order to finance further expansion, the winery went public; and in 2006, with Robert Mondavi in ill health and his sons, Tim and Michael repeating the bizarre sibling rivalry that drove Robert away from his family, the winery was sold to Constellation for a reported $900 million.

Over the now-forty years of its existence, it has almost always rated at or near the top of the rating heap, but the advent of the small, hands-on producers with unlimited funds to spend on wineries, oak barrels, and vineyards, together with the expansion of production, has seen Mondavi slip a little. Nevertheless, its Reserve Cabernet Sauvignon still scores in the middle 90s, and its Sauvignon Blanc, a staple for decades, continues to be well regarded. As for Mr. Mondavi himself, he will always be remembered as the man whose new winery ushered in the wine boom era in California and whose vision and creativity made him the most important person in the premium wine business in the latter parts of the twentieth century.

ROBERT PECOTA WINERY 1978		Map 11
www.robertpecotawinery.com	707-942-6625	No Tasting
Calistoga	Napa County	Calistoga AVA

In 2006, the Pecota winery site was sold to Jess Jackson's Artisan & Estates group to become the home of the high-end Atalon winery. Pecota retains the label and has acquired a nearby twenty-seven-acre estate, twenty-two acres of which have been planted to Cabernet Sauvignon. Robert Pecota and family intend to continue making small quantities of Cabernet, Sauvignon Blanc, Syrah, and Merlot. Pecota had founded the original winery in '78 after working as a coffee buyer for Hills Bros. and MJB and a wine buyer for Beringer. It was while at Beringer that Pecota bought thirty-seven acres and built his winery in northern Calistoga and embarked on his winemaking career.

Pecota's artisan wines are always interesting, occasionally controversial, but rarely boring. He can make ripe wines that occasionally get bigger than life, but, for the most part, the Pecota style has been one of managed power rather than size for size's sake.

ROBERT SINSKEY VINEYARDS 1986		Map 15
www.robertsinskey.com	707-944-9090	Tasting
Napa	Napa County	Stags Leap District AVA

In 1982, eye surgeon Robert Sinskey bought fifteen acres in Carneros and planted it to Pinot Noir. Concurrently, Sinskey was a partner in the Acacia winery, to whom Sinskey sold grapes. When Acacia was purchased by Chalone, in '85, Sinskey started making his own wine. Over the years, the vineyard acreage grew to 160 and wine production to 25,000 cases of estate-bottled wines. In the '90s, with management in the hands of Robert's son, Rob, and with winemaking the purview of Jeff Virnig, the vineyard became an organic farm and continues to specialize in Pinot Noir and vineyard-specific bottlings from Carneros and Stags Leap. Maria Helm Sinskey is a noted chef and brings food pairings to life at the winery and in her writings. The Sinskey Web site is thorough and filled with excellent black-and-white photography.

Sinskey's Pinot Noirs are almost always well received; most rankings for the winery's balanced, well-focused efforts fall in the highly commendable range of high 80s and low 90s.

RUBICON ESTATE 1978		Map 13
www.rubiconestate.com	800-RUBICON	Tasting
Rutherford	Napa County	Rutherford AVA

Much of the history of Napa Valley is reflected in the Inglenook-to-Rubicon Estate saga. Gustave Niebaum made a fortune as a West Coast fur-trading sea captain in the 1860s to 1870s. In 1880, he retired from shipping and bought land in the valley and established the Inglenook Winery. It prospered until Prohibition, when it sold grapes instead of wine. The 1933 Repeal ushered in a resumption of Inglenook's winemaking excellence under a Niebaum descendant, John Daniel Jr. The winery passed into the hands of Heublein in the late 1960s, before Francis Ford Coppola, the famous movie director, bought the Inglenook Estate, including the Niebaum home, in 1975, and renamed the property Niebaum-Coppola Estate Winery.

The year 1978 saw the first harvest for the winery's new Rubicon label, a Bordeaux-style blend, released in '85. In '95, Coppola bought the remaining Inglenook properties and winery, bringing the total estate acreage to over three hundred. In 2002, Coppola purchased the adjacent J. J. Cohn property and returned winemaking to the château, as the Rubicon Winery. In 2006, the name Rubicon Estate replaced Nieman-Coppola. Today, Rubicon produces over twenty thousand cases of some eight wines—most estate grown—ranging from the flagship Rubicon Cabernet Sauvignon blend, to a Cabernet, a white blend, Syrah, Merlot, Cabernet Franc, and Zinfandel. The Web site offers an excellent history of not just the winery but winemaking in the Napa Valley over the past century and a half.

Early bottlings of the Rubicon proprietary red bottling were highly prized by lovers of wines capable of aging for decades, but they were also criticized in some circles as too hard and harsh. By the mid-1990s, the style had moderated, and while Rubicon, the wine, has not become soft and approachable as in its infancy, it is at least more likely to be drinkable with less cellaring than the early bottlings required. Wine scores in the 90s are not uncommon, and the winery Zinfandel, labeled as Edizione Pennino, also gets similar scores more often than not. With great wine, a story line unmatched by any in the Napa Valley, and lots of Coppola influence felt throughout the facility, it has become a prime stop along the wine touring trail. The cost of visiting has risen of late, however, and this is not a place for a casual drop-in but rather one that invites a longer stay and serious attention to the wines being poured.

RUSTRIDGE RANCH & WINERY 1984		Map 14
www.rustridge.com	800-788-0263	Tasting by Appointment
St. Helena	Napa County	Chiles Valley AVA

In 1972, Lu Meyer, a San Francisco real estate broker, found and acquired a 450-acre horse ranch high up in Chiles Valley, in the Vaca Mountains on the northeast side of the Napa Valley. The vineyard grew from scratch to over fifty acres. Stan Meyer built a small winery out of an old barn, and the family brought in their first vintage of a thousand cases of Riesling. Over time, the winery has grown slowly, currently producing over three thousand cases of estate-grown and -bottled wines, principally its Racehorse Red Cabernet Sauvignon–Zinfandel blend, in addition to a Chardonnay-based blend, Cabernet, Zinfandel, and Chardonnay. Now run by Susan Meyer and her husband, Jim Fresquez, with the help of famed vintner

Kent Rosenblum, the ranch remains an active breeding/training facility for horses and has a small B&B on site.

To date, Zinfandel has led the way with its ripe and rich style, mostly earning scores in the mid- to upper-80-point range, and RustRidge-grown Zinfandel has also shown up successfully in the hands of other wineries as well, including Rosenblum Cellars, whose version has rated above 90 points on occasion.

RUTHERFORD HILL WINERY 1976		Map 13
www.rutherfordhill.com	707-963-1871	Tasting
Rutherford	Napa County	Rutherford AVA

Founded in 1976, this Merlot-specialist winery was acquired in 1996 by the Terlato Wine Group, which set about solidifying the quality and consistency of the Rutherford Hill high-volume main street wines. Totaling 150,000 cases produced, fully 75 percent is Merlot, with Chardonnay and Cabernet Sauvignon the other large-volume varieties. Rutherford Hill also produces a group of eight to ten limited-edition varieties, each with five hundred cases. Under the Terlato regime, large caves have been constructed to age over eight thousand barrels. An estate vineyard of sixty acres of Cabernet grapes and several larger contracted vineyards provide the juice for the lines of wines.

Rutherford Hill's glory days are now behind it, yet its Merlot continues to be a staple in the marketplace. The house style has moderated a bit as well, with full-bodied, rich wines giving way to a more moderated style with less bombast but better balance.

SADDLEBACK CELLARS 1983		Map 14
www.saddlebackcellars.com	707-944-1305	Tasting by Appointment
Oakville	Napa County	Oakville AVA

Winemaker and owner Nils Venge is an Angeleno of Danish ancestry whose father was a beverage distributor in Southern California. Nils set out to try his hand at winemaking and gained his experience at Sterling, Villa Mt. Eden, and Groth before establishing his own brand in 1983. While Venge still is a consulting winemaker to a half-dozen Napa Valley wineries, his focus remains on the Saddleback Cellars wines. Grapes are grown on the seventeen-acre estate, in addition to small lots bought from others that go into the small lots of Cabernet Sauvignon, Zinfandel, Merlot, and three to four other varieties. Total production is six thousand cases, of which Cabernet represents fully 30 percent and Zinfandel and Merlot 20 percent each.

No one will ever accuse Saddleback wines of lacking in personality, and because they are high in ripeness and high in rich oakiness, they have strong appeal to those who like the style. Still, the wines have also shown a tendency to vintage variation that is wider than the norm, with great success not always followed by similar results. If this is one winery where it is wisest to taste before committing to large purchases, you will find plenty to like because its best performances can be amazingly handsome, rich wines that score well into the 90-point range.

SAINTSBURY 1981		Map 16
www.saintsbury.com	707-252-0592	Tasting by Appointment
Napa	Napa County	Carneros AVA

David Graves and Richard Ward were friends at UC–Davis who, after working several harvests together, founded Saintsbury in 1981 in the Carneros region of southernmost Napa Valley. Named for George Saintsbury, an Edinburgh don noted for his 1880s tome *Notes on a Cellar Book*, the winery specializes in Carneros Pinot Noir and Chardonnay. Winemaker Jerome Chery uses the grapes from the Estate and Brown Ranch vineyards—totaling about seventy acres—as well as nearby vineyards, to produce over sixty thousand cases, 70 percent of which is Pinot Noir and the remainder Chardonnay.

Saintsbury was among the early leaders in elevating Pinot Noir to exalted status, and the winery's best efforts have reached into the mid-90-point range and have enjoyed near cult status. Brown Ranch Pinot Noir in particular has often topped the charts. The winery has also enjoyed great success, with its light and fruity Pinot Noir labeled as Garnet. Saintsbury Chardonnay has been somewhat less stellar, but it is always balanced, reasonably rich, and consistently enjoyable even if not scoring in the 90s as much as the Pinot Noir.

SAWYER CELLARS 1994		Map 13
www.sawyercellars.com	707-963-1980	Tasting by Appointment
Rutherford	Napa County	Rutherford AVA

The Sawyer Cellars vineyards, in the heart of Rutherford, can be traced as far back as George Yount's first land grant in the 1830s. Charles and

Joanne Sawyer bought forty acres and a Prohibition-era barn in '94. The vineyard has expanded to fifty acres, planted to Cabernet Sauvignon and Merlot, and the barn has morphed into the tasting room. Under the guidance of winemaker Brad Warner, late of Krug and Mondavi, Sawyer produces 4,500 cases of estate-grown and -bottled Cabernet, a Cabernet-based Meritage, Merlot, and Sauvignon Blanc.

With its tasting room located directly on the highway smack in the middle of Rutherford, Sawyer enjoys a choice location from which it dispenses its fairly priced, reliable, midsized Cabernets and Merlot.

SCHRAMSBERG VINEYARDS 1965		Map 11
www.schramsberg.com	800-877-3623	Tasting by Appointment
Calistoga	Napa County	Diamond Mountain District AVA

The Schramsberg Vineyards were originally planted by Jacob Schram in 1862 and at that time were thought to be the first hillside vineyards in the Napa Valley. A century later, after numerous ownership changes, the late Jack and Jamie Davies left careers in industrial management and the arts to purchase the two-hundred-acre estate. Over time, the winery came to be considered the preeminent *méthode champenoise* producer of Sparkling Wines. Today's production of over fifty thousand cases includes the ever-popular Blanc de Blancs and Blanc de Noirs, which represent over half the volume, while smaller batches of the J. Schram and J. Schram Rosé command top dollar. An occasionally produced Crémant Demi-Sec is a less bubbly version based on the rarely seen Flora grape. In '94, the vineyards on Diamond Mountain, formerly planted to Chardonnay and Pinot Noir, were replanted to red Bordeaux varietals, and the grapes sourced for the Sparkling Wines were found in up to eighty sites in cooler climates, including Marin, Sonoma, Mendocino, and Monterey counties. The Cabernet grapes from the estate are now being used in the J. Davies Cabernets, a thousand-case venture honoring Jack Davies. The Schramsberg Web site includes interesting historic perspective as well as thorough wine commentary.

Under the leadership of second-generation Hugh Davies, this venerable winery has reached ever-higher heights for wines whose balance and depth, whose precision and beauty are rarely matched by any in California and have proven time and time again to be able to hold their own with comparable wines from France's Champagne region. The J. Schram bottlings, allowed to age for six years and more as in the many of the world's best bubblies, score in the mid- to upper 90s consistently and have held their own in blind tastings with those world-renowned brands. The very well-made Blanc de Blancs and Blanc de Noirs more often than not score in the lower 90s.

SCOTT HARVEY WINES	2004	Map 12
www.scottharveywines.com	707-968-9575	Tasting
St. Helena	Napa County	Napa Valley AVA

Scott Harvey was first exposed to winemaking as a high school exchange student in the Rhineland. After college, Harvey gained experience at Montevina in Amador County, back in Germany, and at Story and Santino, also in Amador. He headed up Folie à Deux in the Napa Valley before establishing his own label. Focused on Zinfandel, Syrah, Barbera, and Riesling, Scott Harvey Wines produces over twelve thousand cases (35 percent Zinfandel, 30 percent Syrah, and 15 percent Barbera), including several blends with monikers such as One Last Kiss red and white, Cathedral Cabernet Sauvignon blend, and the self-explanatory InZINerator. Grapes are sourced from several Amador County and Napa Valley vineyards.

His second label, Jana, has a Rosé and two Rieslings, one of which is from Michigan and reflects Harvey's continuing affection for the grape that first captured his interest back in his student days. Harvey produces ripe, sometimes fleshy but well-structured Zinfandels whose ratings range from the mid-80s to the lower 90s on occasion.

SCREAMING EAGLE WINERY & VINEYARDS	1986	Map 14
www.screamingeagle.com	707-944-0749	No Tasting
Oakville	Napa County	Oakville AVA

As Napa Valley land became more and more expensive, pushed by the ever-spiraling prices for its best Cabernet Sauvignon-based wines, there came into existence a long list of small, high-powered wineries whose products pushed the envelope in flavor intensity, concentration, and out-and-out opulence. The most recognized of this pack—and the name that comes first to mind when any mention of Napa's cult wineries is on the table—is Screaming Eagle. This limited-production producer saw its expressive, outgoing wines become the darling of the "chase the best and hardest-to-get wines" set. Although the prices for the wine seem to go up every year, the wine, when released, gets turned around on auction sites often at double and triple the prices paid to the winery.

There is now an expanding set of names on this list of "cult producers," including Colgin, Harlan, Bond, Abreu, and Araujo; if they do not all command the stratospheric prices that Screaming Eagle fetches, they are also among the most rare and expensive wines made in the Napa Valley. Needless to say, the critics seem to rate these wines from the mid- to the upper-90-point range, but critics of the critics will often suggest that these wines are too big and blunt for their own good and that they have traded intensity for finesse. Most of us will never know because prices starting in the midhundreds and going up from there are as prohibitive as these wines' low-production levels.

SELENE WINES 1991		Map 15
www.selenewines.com	707-258-8119	No Tasting
Napa	Napa County	Napa Valley AVA

Mia Klein, with experience at Chappellet and Robert Pepi and then as a sought-after consulting winemaker, founded this small winemaking operation in the early 1990s. Selene (a reference to the mother goddess of the full moon in Greek mythology) is made at the Laird Family Estate's custom crush facility in Napa from grapes grown in several Napa Valley vineyards such as the Hyde Vineyard in Carneros and Frediani in Calistoga. Production totals 3,500 cases and runs from 100 to 600 cases per bottling for most wines, with the Sauvignon Blanc topping out at 1,400 cases, or 40 percent of the total. Selene also makes Cabernet Sauvignon, Merlot, and a Cabernet Franc-based proprietary red blend.

Klein's reputation may rest more with her role as winemaker or winemaking consultant for the rightfully famous Dalla Valle, Viader, Araujo, and Palmaz labels, but her own wines have also been spectacular, and if she does not get quite the same broad recognition as a few better-known women winemakers, her success ratio is second to none. Both Merlot and Sauvignon Blanc, mannerly, focused, and age-worthy, have topped out in the mid-90-point area.

SEQUOIA GROVE VINEYARDS 1980		Map 13
www.sequoiagrove.com	800-851-7841	Tasting
Rutherford	Napa County	Rutherford AVA

In 1979, Jim Allen and brother Steve bought an old, pre-Prohibition property in the heart of the Rutherford Bench. The twenty-four-acre vineyard, planted 85 percent to Cabernet Sauvignon, served as the source of the Reserve Cabernet bottlings, with several other well-regarded Napa Valley vineyards satisfying the rest of this medium-sized winery's needs. In 2002, the Allens sold the winery to the Kopf family of New York, owners of several California wineries, Louis Jadot in France, and the Kobrand beverage marketing firm, who installed longtime winemaker Michael Trujillo as the winery's head and infused the winery with capital for much-needed infrastructure improvements. Today, the focus remains on Cabernet, the Reserve Cabernet, and Chardonnay varieties, and a total of forty thousand cases is produced annually, of which fully 80 percent is Cabernet.

Sequoia Grove has had something of a checkered history with many special wines followed by lesser efforts. The attempt to rebuild the brand has a high chance of success given the winery's placement directly in the middle of the best dirt in the Napa Valley. Recent wines have rated in the mid- to upper 80s, nothing higher, thus leaving open all questions about this winery's future results.

SHAFER VINEYARDS 1978		Map 15
www.shafervineyards.com	707-944-2877	Tasting by Appointment
Napa	Napa County	Stags Leap District AVA

In the early 1970s, John Shafer left the publishing business in Chicago for the challenge of making wine. In '72, he bought a fifty-year-old vineyard in the Stags Leap District and immediately replanted. There are now 205 vineyard acres in five locations in the valley, growing principally Cabernet Sauvignon, Chardonnay, and Merlot grapes, all of which go into the estate-grown and -bottled offerings. John's son, Doug, soon took over the winemaking reins; ten years later, they passed to Elias Fernandez, while Doug and John continue to handle overall management of the prestigious winery. Today's production approaches thirty-five thousand cases, including the top-shelf Hillside Select Cabernet Sauvignon, which has topped the $200 mark and has a wide critical following. Other wines include a Chardonnay, Merlot, and Relentless, a Syrah and Petite Sirah blend. The Shafer Web site includes several insightful interview videos with the principals.

Hillside Select Cabernet enjoys near-cult status in the Napa Valley, and it has shown over the years to be one of the most intense, deep, and long-lasting Cabernets. It is perennially near the very top of our ratings, and scores in the 90s, ranging to the mid- to upper 90s, are not uncommon. And like all Shafer wines, it is a wine whose depth and careful crafting comes with a touch of brawniness. Even the Shafer Merlot, another top-of-the-list wine in terms of ratings, is a bold and dramatic effort. It is also one of our favorite choices on restaurant wine lists because its concentration and supple, Merlot underbelly allows it go with the savory meats that so often appear on the menus of California restaurants. Relentless Syrah and Red Shoulder Chardonnay are also made in the winery style and complete a list of exceptional wines from one of California's most accomplished producers. In almost every vintage, the expressive Shafer wines of every stripe have earned ratings of 90 points and up, making Shafer one of the most highly regarded wineries in California.

SIGNORELLO VINEYARDS 1980		Map 14
www.signorellovineyards.com	707-255-5990	Tasting
Napa	Napa County	Napa Valley AVA

The late Ray Signorello Sr. bought a hundred-acre ranch in 1977 on the Silverado Trail, tucked between the Stags Leap and Oak Knoll AVAs. With Ray Jr., who now manages the winery, Signorello initially sold grapes to others, but the '85 crop was large, and they made their own wine with the excess. By the end of the '80s, a winery was built. Most of the grapes are grown on the estate vineyard, now totaling forty-five acres, well over half of which is planted to Cabernet Sauvignon. Signorello also makes three small batches of vineyard-designated Pinot Noirs from the Hudson, Hyde, and Las Amigas vineyards in Carneros. Total production is currently seven thousand cases, of which Cabernet represents over half and another 30 percent is Chardonnay.

With virtually every wine scoring in the 90-point range, the Signorello offerings, high in richness and body, high in oak, and high in concentrated fruit, are widely sought out and hard to get but are well worth the search.

SILVERADO VINEYARDS 1981		Map 15
www.silveradovineyards.com	707-257-1770	Tasting
Napa	Napa County	Stags Leap District AVA

In 1976, Lilian Disney—Mrs. Walt Disney—purchased several vineyards in the valley. One, which later became the Silverado home estate in the

Stags Leap District, had been owned by the Sees candy family. Disney's daughter, Diane, and her husband, Ron Miller—former CEO of Walt Disney Co.—actively developed the vineyards, bought additional land, and built a state-of-the-art winery facility. Silverado now has six vineyards totaling over four hundred acres in Napa and Carneros, including the estate in Stags Leap. Under the leadership of winemaker Jonathan Emmerich, experienced at Conn Creek and Sebastiani, Silverado produces 150,000 cases, principally of Sauvignon Blanc, Chardonnay, and Cabernet Sauvignon.

This lovely winery, set on a hilltop overlooking the Silverado Trail, enjoys one of the best locations in the Napa Valley. It makes a lot of wine, and as one would expect from a high-volume producer in Napa, it has its moments of glory and its moments when it rests within the pack. Its stable of wines is cleanly made, balanced, and reliable, but ratings in the mid-80s are as likely as anything higher—with the exception of the upscale Cabernet Sauvignon labeled Solo, a single-vineyard bottling from the Stags Leap District that regularly reaches the upper 80s and beyond and is full-bodied and ripe in flavor.

SMITH-MADRONE VINEYARDS & WINERY 1971		Map 11
www.smithmadrone.com	707-963-2283	Tasting by Appointment
St. Helena	Napa County	Spring Mountain District AVA

Brothers Stu and Charlie Smith found two hundred acres of forested land high on Spring Mountain in 1971. Indeed, the name Madrone refers not to another partner but, rather, to the abundant type of evergreens that grow on the property. The Smith brothers gradually planted what is now forty-five acres of Cabernet Sauvignon, Chardonnay, and Riesling. Their early emphasis on the Riesling variety remains strong, though its production is outstripped by the more popular, and marketable, Cabernet. The estate-grown grapes are used exclusively in making four thousand to five thousand cases each year of Cabernet (about half), Chardonnay, and Riesling.

The winery style emphasizes balance and restraint in something of an old-fashioned formula. But, with recognition in the marketplace that over-the-top ripeness comes at the expense of varietal character, Smith-Madrone wines are perfectly positioned. The Riesling, one of the few that survived the downturn in that grape's fortunes, is made in a steely, barely off-dry style; like the winery's other offerings, it is going to enjoy increasing attention for its pristine crafting. Prices are reasonable, and if the style suits, the ratings in the upper 80s attest to the overall usefulness of the wines.

SPOTTSWOODE ESTATE VINEYARD & WINERY 1982   Map 12

www.spottswoode.com   707-963-0134   Tasting by Appointment

St. Helena   Napa County   St. Helena AVA

In the early 1970s, San Diego physician Jack Novak and wife Mary purchased 46 acres of 1882 vineyards from the Spotts family. In 1982, five years after Jack's premature death, Mary produced 1,200 cases of Cabernet Sauvignon as the winery's first vintage; she continues to run the winery with the help of her two daughters, Beth and Lindy, winemaker Jennifer Williams, and consulting winemaker Rosemary Cakebread. Forty acres of organically grown estate vineyards are now planted primarily to Cabernet Sauvignon, with small blocks of Cabernet Franc and other blending grapes, and they are the main source of fruit for the wines. Recently, the Sauvignon Blanc has been a blend of fruit from Napa and Sonoma counties. Three wines are made today: two Estate Cabernet Sauvignons—the top of the line labeled as Spottswoode, and the wine made tasty but earlier maturing or less intense lots labeled as Lyndenhurst—and a Sauvignon Blanc. Of the total production of seven thousand cases, 75 percent are the Cabernets. A homemade olive oil is also on offer.

Spottswoode's top Cabernet routinely earns scores in the lower to mid-90s and is one of the Napa Valley's most refined, classically tailored versions of the grape. Lyndenhurst Cabernet Sauvignon scores in the upper 80s to low 90s; and even though styled for earlier drinking, it, too, is a refined bottling. The Spottswoode Sauvignon Blanc resides at the very top of the quality rankings in most vintages, and it also comes with a well-earned reputation for its depth and elegance.

SPRING MOUNTAIN VINEYARD 1968   Map 11

www.springmtn.com   877-769-4637   Tasting by Appointment

St. Helena   Napa County   Spring Mountain District AVA

In the early 1960s, Mike Robbins purchased an old Victorian north of St. Helena and within a few short years was making notable Bordeaux-style wines and a highly regarded Chardonnay. In the late '70s, Robbins traded up to a larger, more impressive Victorian pile that became the memorable set of the TV soap opera *Falcon Crest* and brought hordes of tourists. In the '90s, Robbins sold his interests to a partnership headed by Tom Ferrell, former Inglenook winemaker and president of Sterling. Over time, the group acquired three adjacent vineyards and wineries, so that today the estate includes 850 acres on the eastern slopes of Spring Mountain, with 225 acres planted to Bordeaux varietals in 130 distinct vineyard blocks. Production runs in the range of six thousand to seven thousand cases and features two Cabernet Sauvignons that represent three-quarters of the volume, one of which is a high-ticket blend called Elivette. Spring Mountain also makes a Syrah and Sauvignon Blanc.

The winery is one of the most beautiful in the Napa Valley, and even with its TV-inspired fame no longer driving tourists to its doors, it remains a great place to visit—with an appointment, of course. Its new wine caves are also worth a look. Spring Mountain wines typically earn scores from the mid-80s to the low 90s but can be maddeningly inconsistent at times. Chateau Chevalier, the one-time name of this lovely property, appears as the winery's second label. Recent results for its moderately intense wines have been in the mid-80s to slightly higher.

ST. CLEMENT VINEYARDS 1976		Map 11
www.stclement.com	800-331-8266	Tasting
St. Helena	Napa County	Spring Mountain District AVA

In 1976, San Francisco eye surgeon Bill Casey bought this winery, which at that point had been the site of Mike Robbins's Spring Mountain Vineyards but whose location traces its heritage as far back as an 1841 land grant and initial winemaking in 1878. After building a new winery and substantially increasing production, Casey sold the winery to Sapporo of Japan in 1987, which, in turn, upped the volume to ten thousand cases. In 1991, Sapporo made the first vintage of its top-drawer red Meritage, Oroppas (*Sapporo* backward). Some eight years later Sapporo sold to the Foster's Group. Now under the winemaking leadership of Danielle Cyrot, a descendant of Burgundian vintners with Stag's Leap experience, St. Clement sources fruit from ten vineyards in the valley, ranging from Star Vineyard in Rutherford to Abbott's Vineyard in Carneros. Production stands at twenty-two thousand, of which just under half is Chardonnay and another 40 percent is Cabernet Sauvignon.

Winemaking fortunes have risen and fallen with changes in ownership, and now the winery can be counted on for above-average quality results, with most wines scoring in the upper 80s and Orropas frequently reaching above 90 points. Under the new regime, St. Clement wines have been well made, in a solid but not bombastic style that is about middle-of-the-road for a winery of its ambition.

ST. SUPÉRY VINEYARDS & WINERY 1988		Map 13
www.stsupery.com	800-942-0809	Tasting
Rutherford	Napa County	Rutherford AVA

Robert Skalli, third-generation winemaker and owner of several wineries in the South of France, bought his Napa Valley outpost in 1982 when he purchased a 1,500-acre cattle ranch in the remote Pope Valley area, east of Howell Mountain. There are now three vineyards totaling over five hundred acres planted to Bordeaux varietals and contributing most of the fruit made in the winery. St. Supéry's winemaker Michael Beaulac, late of Murphy Goode and Markham, oversees production of nearly two hundred thousand cases of a wide range of wines, from Cabernet Sauvignon to Sauvignon Blanc to a red and a white Meritage labeled Elu and Virtu, respectively.

As with most wineries of its size, the less expensive, volume end of the line has seen quality flit between average and slightly above average, with Sauvignon Blanc the most likely wine to break out above the norm along with the winery's Meritage bottlings, especially the white Virtu, which blends Sauvignon Blanc and Semillon in nearly equal parts with slight but distinctive vintage variations in the percentages. The St. Supéry visitor center is one of the most interesting and informative in the valley. Both quality and style vary significantly depending on variety and price. Recent Sauvignon Blancs have managed to be both balanced and focused and have earned scores in the upper 80s and low 90s on occasion. The upscale Cabernet Sauvignon varies as well in qualitative ratings and is made in a full-bodied, fleshy, well-oaked style.

STAGLIN FAMILY VINEYARD 1989		Map 13
www.staglinfamily.com	707-944-0477	Tasting by Appointment
Rutherford	Napa County	Rutherford AVA

The Staglin family acquired a fifty-acre vineyard on the Rutherford Bench that had been developed by Beaulieu and provided the grapes for the famous BV Georges de La Tour Private Reserve Cabernet. Continued nurturing of the vineyard by famed vineyardist David Abreu enables Staglin to use principally estate-grown grapes in the seven thousand cases of three varieties made today—Cabernet Sauvignon, Chardonnay, and Sangiovese—while world-renowned consulting winemaker Michel Rolland helps keep the wines on track in the cellar. The Staglins are serious philanthropists, using winery profits and auctions of their wines for charitable causes. The grounds display an excellent modern sculpture collection.

Staglin Cabernets are among the most classic expressions of the West Rutherford terroir and have rightfully earned their continuing scores in the stratospheric mid- to upper-90 range despite some critical concern from purists that ripeness and oak levels have risen a bit of late.

STAG'S LEAP WINE CELLARS 1972		Map 15
www.cask23.com	707-944-2020	Tasting
Napa	Napa County	Stags Leap District AVA

University of Chicago professor Warren Winiarski brought his family to the Napa Valley in the 1960s looking for a more pastoral life than what was afforded in the big city. After spending time learning his trade with some of the leading winemakers in the Napa Valley, he founded his Stag's Leap Wine Cellars in the early 1970s and brought the Stags Leap area and name back into prominence. His immediate success with Cabernet Sauvignon led to his fledgling winery's inclusion in the famous Paris tasting of 1976 in which French and California wines were pitted against each other with French winemakers as the judges. When it turned out that the French had picked Winiarski's 1973 as the best of the best and thought it had been one of their own, *Time* magazine trumpeted the feat as the shot heard round the world. For three decades thereafter, Winiarski and family turned out some of the most famous reds from Napa, including the very expensive and delicious Cask 23 bottling as well as SLV Cabernet and Fay Vineyard Cabernet. The winery also makes Chardonnay, Merlot, and two Sauvignon Blancs and offers a second label, Hawk Crest, for less expensive wines. In 2007, with the Winiarski family happily proclaiming that it had accomplished its goals in life, the winery was sold to a partnership of the Chateau Ste. Michelle interests and the Antinori interests.

Toward the end of his reign, Winiarski set out to make his wines higher in acidity and less forward when young, and the result has been that his regular bottlings have not prospered. But, truth be told, the winery owns some of the finest Cabernet Sauvignon dirt in the Napa Valley, and Cask 23,

SLV, and Fay Vineyard Cabernets still routinely earn ratings in the 90s for the rich, supple, mannerly approach that has marked those wines from their very outset and has kept them in the top tier from beginning to the present.

STAGS' LEAP WINERY	1972	Map 15
www.stagsleapwinery.com	800-395-2441	Tasting by Appointment
Napa	Napa County	Stags Leap District AVA

When Carl Doumani purchased the estate back in the early 1970s, he hardly knew what trouble he had purchased. Not only did the property need restoring, but he also ran into a legal brouhaha with the neighboring Stag's Leap Wine Cellars over whom, if anyone, had rights to the Stags Leap name. It took Doumani over half a decade to get things straightened out, but the winery went ahead with the name and made its mark with bold, heavy-duty reds and ripe, never quite compelling Chardonnay. Eventually, the winery was purchased by the Beringer wine interests and remains part of that conglomerate today.

Under Beringer, the winery has settled into a more predictable pattern and now makes a fairly broad array of wines whose critical ratings range from the mid-80s to the low 90s. Prices reflect both quality and the winery's favored location.

STERLING VINEYARDS	1967	Map 11
www.sterlingvineyards.com	800-726-6136	Tasting
Calistoga	Napa County	Calistoga AVA

When Peter Newton and friends built his modern Moorish castle atop the hill south of Calistoga and right in the middle of the Napa Valley floor, it provided further proof, Robert Mondavi being the first big example, that a boom in the wine industry was fast approaching. And even today, over four decades later, that vision has gifted the valley with one of its iconic architectural treasures. Initially under the leadership of Ric Forman, Sterling made its early reputation for rich reds and ripe but balanced whites, mostly Cabernet Sauvignon, Chardonnay, and Sauvignon Blanc. By 1977, the winery had been acquired by Coca-Cola, and it has since passed through the hands of Seagram's and is now under the corporate control of drinks conglomerate Diageo. Along the way, in the Sterling name, vineyards were acquired on Diamond Mountain, and the highly regarded Three Palms Vineyard in Calistoga and Winery Lake Vineyard in Carneros also came under Sterling's control. Today, the winery sells at price points ranging from upscale for its Reserve and special bottlings to the competitive $10 market. Its advantageous locations, intelligently run tasting facilities, and tram ride up to its aerie-like perch make Sterling one of the valley's most popular visitor stops.

Sterling wines, once among the top wines in the Napa Valley, now rate as good but not exceptional for the location, but the wines are also entirely reliable, and this once-newcomer is now a staple. Sauvignon Blanc is brisk and straightforward, Chardonnay is reliable but rarely earns scores past the mid-80s, and only the big reds occasionally reach to 90 points and beyond.

STEWART CELLARS 2000		Map 13
www.stewartcellars.com	707-963-9160	No Tasting
Rutherford	Napa County	Rutherford AVA

Michael and Anne Stewart of Houston sold off their computer company and bought a majority interest in the Juliana Vineyards in Pope Valley. At the same time, Stewart made the first small batches of Cabernet Sauvignon and Pinot Noir that continue to this day. In recent vintages, winemaker Paul Hobbs made 1,500 cases of Napa Valley Cabernet from grapes grown by the Stagecoach Vineyard and the renowned Beckstoffer Vineyard. An additional five hundred cases of Pinot Noir were made with grapes from the Gibson Vineyard in the Russian River Valley of Sonoma County.

Wine ratings in the lower 90s are the norm for this up-and-coming winery.

STONY HILL VINEYARD 1953		Map 11
www.stonyhillvineyard.com	707-963-2636	Tasting by Appointment
St. Helena	Napa County	Spring Mountain District AVA

Founding pioneers Eleanor and Fred McCrea bought a 160-acre goat ranch on the northeast slope of Spring Mountain in 1943. Planting of Chardonnay grapes began in 1947, and in 1952, the McCreas produced their first Chardonnay vintage. More than fifty years later, wine is made the same way by second-generation vintners Peter and Willinda McCrea and longtime winemaker–vineyard manager Mike Chelini. The estate vineyard, rising 700 to 1,200 feet above the valley floor, consists of 39 planted acres, 25 of which are Chardonnay grapes. Production averages four thousand cases a year, fully 60 percent of which is Chardonnay, with the remainder divided among White Riesling, Gewürztraminer, and Semillon.

One of the ultimate collectibles in the Napa Valley, Stony Hill wines, especially the Chardonnay, tend to be slow-maturing, long-aging, and focused first on fruit that takes on a chalky, stony quality from the limestone-enriched soils in which the grapes are grown.

STORYBOOK MOUNTAIN VINEYARDS 1980		Map 11
www.storybookwines.com	707-942-5310	Tasting by Appointment
Calistoga	Napa County	Calistoga AVA

Former Stanford European history professor Jerry Seps bought ninety acres west of Calistoga on the eastern slope of the Mayacamas range dating back to the Grimm Vineyards of the 1880s. Seps renamed it Storybook Mountain, planted thirty-eight acres of Zinfandel, and rehabbed the caves in time for the 1980 crush. The vineyard has grown slightly to forty-three acres, though the focus remains on Zinfandel, the lion's share of the eight thousand to nine thousand cases produced annually. Seps does make a Cabernet Sauvignon and a Zinfandel-based red blend called Antaeus, a mythological deity who drew his strength from the earth. Look forward to small batches of Viognier in future years.

Today, Zinfandel continues to rule the roost, and Storybook Mountain continues to pull down top ratings from critics and consumers alike for its deep, tightly structured, and age-worthy offerings. The Estate Reserve Zinfandel, with scores consistently in the lower- to mid-90-point range, rates among the very best Zinfandels made in California, and the Eastern Exposures Zinfandel is not far behind. Antaeus also hits the 90-point range and above.

SUMMERS ESTATE WINERY 1987		Map 11
www.summerswinery.com	707-942-5508	Tasting
Calistoga	Napa County	Calistoga AVA

Former bankers Jim and Beth Summers bought a twenty-eight-acre vineyard planted to Merlot in Knights Valley in 1987. Ten years later, they added twenty-two acres in Calistoga next door to the Old Faithful Geyser and planted more Zinfandel, Charbono, and Cabernet Sauvignon grapes. Under winemaker and vineyard manager Ignacio Blancas, Summers produces twenty thousand cases, two-thirds of which is Cabernet, and small lots of Merlot, Zinfandel, and Chardonnay. With about two thousand cases of Charbono, Summers may be the largest single producer of this somewhat exotic wine.

Summers's Villa Andriana Zinfandel has been its most successful wine to date, as vintage after vintage ranks near the top of the rating charts with scores consistently in the low to mid-90s. Other varieties are not far behind and tend to be wholly satisfying with scores that reach into the upper-80-point levels. A recent Cabernet Sauvignon Reserve also reached the 90-point range. Villa Andriana wines tend to be ripe and on the lush but not overdone side.

SUMMIT LAKE VINEYARDS & WINERY 1986		Map 12
www.summitlakevineyards.com	707-965-2488	Tasting by Appointment
Angwin	Napa County	Howell Mountain AVA

In 1971, Bob and Sue Brakesman bought a pre-Prohibition winery and vineyard on Howell Mountain, at 2,300 feet above the valley floor. They set about restoring and replanting the vineyard and building a new winery that uses the grapes grown on their twenty-one acres to make a Zinfandel, Cabernet Sauvignon, and an occasional Port. Production stands at about 2,000 cases, three-quarters of which is Zinfandel; 2,500 cases is the maximum expected.

The Zins of Summit Lake can be maddeningly inconsistent, but they never lack for intensity, and like most wines from Howell Mountain, they also never lack for muscle and age worthiness. As a result, they are the darlings of folks who like a little brawn in their Zins, and in that regard, they never disappoint.

SWANSON VINEYARDS 1985		Map 14
www.swansonvineyards.com	707-967-3500	Tasting by Appointment
Oakville	Napa County	Oakville AVA

Clarke Swanson, heir to the Swanson frozen TV dinner phenomenon, bought eighty acres in the valley in 1985. Two vineyards in Oakville totaling 140 acres provide the grapes for some 27,000 cases of Merlot (over half of the total), Pinot Grigio, and the Cabernet Sauvignon-based Alexis red wine. Small batches of so-called Salon wines include Petite Sirah, Syrah, Chardonnay, and Sangiovese. Winemaker Chris Phelps brings extensive experience at Château Pétrus in Bordeaux, as the founding winemaker at

Dominus Estate, and at Caymus. Tasting is conducted by reservation in an over-the-top Rococo salon in Rutherford.

Alexis is the winery's most consistently high-caliber offering for its ripe, deep, but nicely balanced and fairly rich character; as a result, it has garnered a passel of scores at and above 90 points. Syrah is the next most likely success story for Swanson, followed by Merlot, but we have not found much joy in the ripe but austere Pinot Grigio.

T-VINE CELLARS 1992		Map 11
www.tvinecellars.com	707-942-8685	No Tasting
Calistoga	Napa County	Calistoga AVA

Former banker Greg Brown gave up the pinstripes for winemaking, starting his own winery in 1992 with first releases of Petite Sirah and Rhône-style Grenache. Today's production is about five thousand cases, including several Syrah/Sirahs (about 30 percent of total production), Zinfandel (another 30 percent), Merlot, and a red Meritage called T. Grapes are sourced from the small, twelve-acre Brown Estate and the Frediani Vineyard, also in Calistoga.

Napa Valley Zinfandel does not get enough credit in wine circles, but T-Vine's incredible success with the grape is going a long way toward correcting that wrong-headed impression. Both wines often score in the 90-point range and can show, in best vintages, a nice bit of elegance to go along with their admirable depth. Syrah also scores well, and Rosé drinkers will also be pleased by the deep fruit in the winery's dry but eminently likeable versions.

TERRA VALENTINE 1995		Map 11
www.terravalentine.com	707-967-8340	Tasting by Appointment
St. Helena	Napa County	Spring Mountain District AVA

Angus and Margaret Wurtele sold a large national paint company and retired to two small vineyards on Spring Mountain. The vineyards grew to sixty-five acres in total, planted primarily to Cabernet Sauvignon. With winemaker Sam Baxter, who gained experience in Australia and at Sterling, Terra Valentine now produces over ten thousand cases, half of which are Cabernets and the remainder Pinot Noir and Viognier. *Terra* means "land" and Valentine is Wurtele's father's name.

Terra Valentine has done a good if somewhat inconsistent job with its Cabernet Sauvignons, and it has kept prices at reasonable levels for wines from its highly regarded location on the side of picturesque Spring Mountain.

THE HESS COLLECTION WINERY 1982		Map 14
www.hesscollection.com	707-255-1144	Tasting
Napa	Napa County	Mount Veeder AVA

Founder Donald Hess is the latest in a line of Swiss winemakers, brewers, and hoteliers dating back to 1844. In the late 1970s, Hess was in the valley in pursuit of sources for his successful bottled water business but, instead, bought land on Mount Veeder and jumped into winemaking. Growth saw Hess adding vineyards elsewhere in the valley (now totaling 635 acres) and in Mendocino, Lake, and Monterey counties and the stone winery on Mount Veeder, which had originally been the Christian Brothers Mount La Salle Winery. Winemaker Dave Guffy, at Hess since '99, oversees the production of more than 450,000 cases of all Hess lines. Of that, about fifty thousand cases are made of the Hess Collection and Single Vineyard lines, and four hundred thousand for the Appellation series (formerly Hess Select) Cabernet, Chardonnay, Syrah, and Sauvignon Blanc. The winery contains a thirteen-thousand-square-foot gallery space that is home for Don Hess's eminent contemporary art collection, including the likes of Robert Motherwell, Morris Louis, and Frank Stella. The parent Hess Group includes wineries in Australia, South Africa, and Argentina.

Located high on Mount Veeder, this winery occupies one of Napa's historic sites, and while the winery has an old-fashioned feel on the outside, it is thoroughly modern and incredibly handsome on the inside. It is one of the most favored sites in the Napa Valley for wine touring both for the tasty wines, the best of which score into the 90-point range, and for the beauty of the site and the winery itself.

THE TERRACES AT QUARRY VINEYARDS 1985		Map 13
www.terraceswine.com	707-963-1707	Tasting by Appointment
Rutherford	Napa County	Rutherford AVA

Wayne Hogue originally bought the site on the eastern slopes of Rutherford in the late 1970s and planted Cabernet Sauvignon and Zinfandel vines, making the first wines in 1985 and building a winery in 1991. Timm and Sharon Crull bought the ninety-acre parcel in 1993 and have thirty acres planted. Most fruit is sold to Beringer for its reserve Cabernet and a Quarry Vineyard-designated Cabernet. The rest goes to making just over a thousand cases a year, half of which is Zinfandel and the remainder divided among Cabernet, Chardonnay, and Petite Sirah. The maximum capacity is 2,500 cases. A balsamic vinegar is resting in the caves for the right moment.

In many years, Terrace Zinfandel, made in a ripe but still refined style and reflecting the richness that comes with the best from Napa Valley soils, takes down top honors with scores that have reached high into the 90s.

TITUS VINEYARDS 1967		Map 12
www.titusvineyards.com	707-963-3235	No Tasting
St. Helena	Napa County	St. Helena AVA

The second-generation Titus brothers—vineyard manager Eric and wine-maker Phillip—work a thirty-six-acre vineyard running from the Silverado Trail to the Napa River at the narrowest point on the valley floor. After their parents, Lee and Ruth Titus, acquired the land in 1967, the grapes were sold for many years to Krug, Beaulieu, and several other wineries nearby. Eventually the Titus family started making red wines, principally Cabernet Sauvignon and Zinfandel. Today winemaker Phillip Titus (also the winemaker at Chappellet, where the Titus wines are still produced) makes 9,500 cases, over half of which is Cabernet and another quarter Zinfandel. An olive oil is sometimes available.

Talented winemaker Philip Titus, whose Chappellet offerings are top-drawer, finds time to achieve great things at the family winery as well.

TREFETHEN FAMILY VINEYARDS 1973		Map 14
www.trefethenfamilyvineyards.com	866-895-7696	Tasting
Napa	Napa County	Oak Knoll District AVA

The late head of Kaiser Industries Gene Trefethen and wife Katie bought the ancient Eshcol Winery and Vineyard in 1968. Replanted by legend-ary vineyard manager Tony Baldini, and overall management now with the next generation, John and Janet, Trefethen made its first vintage in '73 but stayed afloat through the '70s by selling grapes to their fledgling neighbor Domaine Chandon. With the vineyards restored over the course of the '80s and '90s, the land under vines now stands at about 550 acres and is considered the largest contiguous vineyard under single ownership in the Napa Valley. Included in the list of varietals is twenty acres on Riesling, also thought to be some sort of record. Winemaker Peter Luthi and vineyard manager Jon Ruel team up to make all Trefethen wines from estate-grown grapes. Production exceeds seventy thousand cases on a roster of some dozen wines, ranging from the top-of-the-line HāLo Cabernet Sauvignon to Pinot Noir, Chardonnay, and Dry Riesling, to a red table wine called Double T.

The Trefethen house style is among the more restrained and polished in the Napa Valley, and even when its ventures into the pricey end of the spectrum with wines like Halo and its Hillside Cabernet Sauvignon, the wines avoid bombast in favor of balance and focused fruit. There are times when this kind of restraint leaves the wines wanting for greater depth and deeper fruit, but there is never a time when Trefethen wines have been other than well knit and incredibly refined.

TRUCHARD VINEYARDS 1989		Map 16
www.truchardvineyards.com 707-253-7153		Tasting by Appointment
Napa	Napa County	Carneros AVA

Tony and Jo Ann Truchard started growing grapes in Carneros in the mid-1970s and started making their own wine in 1989 from grapes grown on their 167 acres. In 1990, Truchard converted a barn into a small winery and soon added ten thousand square feet of caves. Today's vineyard includes 270 planted acres. Eighty percent of the grapes grown are sold to twenty or so valley wineries, and the remaining 20 percent are retained to make the all-estate-grown wines. Winemaker Sal de Ianni, with stints at Hess, Cuvaison, and in Australia, manages the production of more than sixteen thousand cases of a dozen varieties, including three thousand to four thousand cases each of Chardonnay, Pinot Noir, and Syrah.

One of the early leaders in the Carneros District, Truchard wines have ranged in quality from top of the list to average, and that inconsistency continues to this day. Syrah has been the most successful wine in the arsenal.

TURNBULL WINE CELLARS 1979		Map 14
www.turnbullwines.com 800-887-6285		Tasting
Oakville	Napa County	Oakville AVA

Bill Turnbull and Reverdy Johnson, architect and lawyer, respectively, for the Sea Ranch development on the Mendocino coast, purchased twenty acres of vineyard and a farmhouse in 1977 in prime Cabernet Sauvignon territory just north of Oakville. In the early 1990s, phylloxera forced replanting; but the owners sold out in '93 to Patrick O'Dell, who increased the planted vineyards from 20 to 185 acres. Now grown to 205 acres in five vineyards, all in the Oakville area, production has also grown to well over 40,000 cases, of which Cabernet Sauvignon is indeed king, at 55 percent, followed by Merlot (25 percent) and Sauvignon Blanc (15 percent).

Turnbull Cabernet, selling at an attractive price relative to its Napa Valley competition, has always rated well, and its last several vintages have seen the wine scoring in the mid-90s. Sauvignon Blanc has not been far behind, making this artsy-oriented winery a must stop in the middle of the Napa Valley's best growing area.

V. SATTUI WINERY 1975		Map 12
www.vsattui.com	800-799-2337	Tasting
St. Helena	Napa County	St. Helena AVA

Don't expect to savor a V. Sattui wine on your next night out. All sales of Sattui wines are made by mail, at the tasting room, or at the winery. And what a winery it is! A multimillion-dollar castle has been built to provide a new environment for wine tasting, weddings, the visitors center, deli, gift boutique, and events such as Festa Italiano. Daryl Sattui started his winery in 1975 with only modest experience and financial support. Great-grandfather Vittorio Sattui was the inspiration for the winery and its name. Luck had it that the site of the winery would draw legions of tourists to try the wines and enjoy them in the picnic areas, supplemented by provisions provided by the deli/cheese shop/tasting room. On the wine side of the equation, there are 250 planted acres in three valley vineyards growing the grapes for 40,000 cases of a wide variety of wine types.

Sattui wines have been well received, with high marks going to several single-vineyard Cabernet Sauvignons, Zinfandels, and Sauvignon Blanc and to both Dry and Off Dry Riesling.

VIADER VINEYARDS 1986		Map 12
www.viader.com	707-963-3816	Tasting by Appointment
Deer Park	Napa County	Howell Mountain AVA

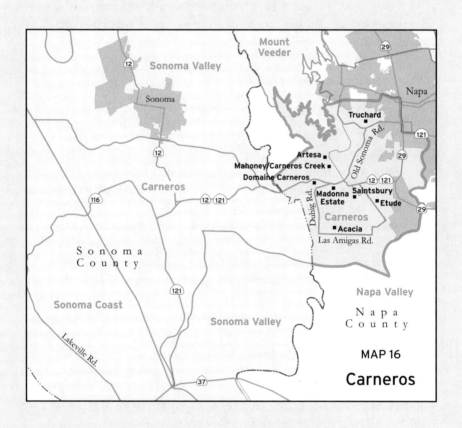

MAP 16

Carneros

Argentinian Delia Viader came to the United States for graduate studies at Cal and stayed to establish her winery and vineyards. Viader manages 30 acres at 1,200 feet above the valley floor on the rocky slopes of Howell Mountain. Of that acreage, half is planted to Cabernet Sauvignon, nine acres to Cabernet Franc, and small blocks of Syrah and Petit Verdot. With winemaker–vineyard manager Alan Viader (Delia's son), six thousand cases are produced, with three-quarters of the total Cabernet or Cabernet blends. For good measure, Viader owns a small vineyard in Tuscany planted to Sangiovese and Merlot.

The Cabernet Sauvignon blend identified simply as Viader is the winery's flagship wine and has earned its continuing plaudits via scores consistently in the 90+ range.

VILLA MT. EDEN WINERY 1974		Map 13
www.villamteden.com	707-963-9100	Tasting
Rutherford	Napa County	Rutherford AVA

Founded in 1974 by Ann and James McWilliams on a winery site from the 1880s, the winery brought in legendary winemaker Nils Venge to run the show. For a decade, Villa Mt. Eden built a reputation based on its Cabernet Sauvignon. In '82, winemaker Mike McGrath, by way of UC–Davis, Argentina, Australia, and the Napa Valley, replaced Venge, and McGrath remains to this day. In '84, the McWilliamses sold the winery to what has become the Ste. Michele Wine Estates group, owners of Chateau Ste. Michelle and Conn Creek, among many others. Under McGrath, Villa Mt. Eden makes several hundred thousand cases of wines in three tiers: the top-flight Signature Series with vineyard-specific bottlings; the midpriced Grand Reserve line, including several wines using grapes from notable vineyards such as Bien Nacido in the Santa Maria Valley; and the entry-level Coastal Collection. In addition to sourcing grapes from throughout the state, Villa Mt. Eden maintains three estate vineyards: 235 acres in Yountville, 200 in Monterey County near Santa Lucia Highlands, and 400 acres in Paso Robles in San Luis Obispo County.

Villa Mt. Eden has changed spots several times and now makes fairly priced, moderately attractive wines that are very good values at their best.

VINE CLIFF WINERY 1990		Map 14
www.vinecliff.com	707-944-2388	Tasting by Appointment
Napa	Napa County	Oakville AVA

Charles Sweeney and family purchased a pre-Prohibition winery and vineyard in the foothills along the east side of the Napa Valley just south of Oakville. Over time, Vine Cliff built its reputation on Cabernet Sauvignon and Chardonnay and is now managed by Charles's son, Robert, and winemaker Rex Smith, a New Zealander by way of Saintsbury, Hess, and Cuvaison wineries. Vineyards in Oakville (twenty-four acres of Cabernet, Merlot, and Zinfandel) and Carneros (twelve acres of Chardonnay) provide most of the grapes for the seven thousand cases made each year, of which fully two-thirds is the notable Cabernet, and the remainder Chardonnay, Merlot, and Cabernet Franc.

From its attractive location, Vine Cliff makes both regular bottlings labeled as Napa Valley and a series of special bottlings that have succeeded in achieving relatively high scores. Sixteen Rows Cabernet Sauvignon and Proprietress Reserve Chardonnay have been the biggest winners, but virtually everything in the Vine Cliff line has been well received.

VOLKER EISELE FAMILY ESTATE 1974		Map 14
www.volkereiselefamilyestate.com	707-965-9485	Tasting by Appointment
St. Helena	Napa County	Chiles Valley AVA

Volker and Liesel Eisele bought a four-hundred-acre estate and ghost winery that goes back to a Joseph Chiles land grant in 1843. After renovating the vineyard and selling grapes to other wineries, the Eiseles started making their own wines with the '91 vintage. Since then the winery has remained stable at about three thousand cases of three varieties: Cabernet Sauvignon, which represents two-thirds of volume; Gemini, a white blend of Semillon and Sauvignon Blanc grapes; and Terzetto, a Cabernet–Cabernet Franc–Merlot blend. All grapes used are organically grown on the sixty planted acres, three-quarters of which is dedicated to Cabernet. Volker is gradually turning over the reins to Alexander in the next generation of the family.

Terzetto, which is nominally composed of one-third each of the three major Bordeaux varieties, is the Eisele flagship offering and its highest-rated wine year in and year out. The Cabernet Sauvignon, while not as consistently top of the field as Terzetto, has also been rated in the 90-point range in the best vintages.

VON STRASSER WINERY 1990		Map 11
www.vonstrasser.com	707-942-0990	Tasting by Appointment
Calistoga	Napa County	Diamond Mountain District AVA

Rudy and Rita Von Strasser bought the eight-acre vineyard and neglected buildings of the former Roddis Estate Winery on the slopes of Diamond Mountain in 1990. Von Strasser brought experience at UC–Davis, a rare internship at Château Lafite Rothschild, and winemaking at Trefethen and Newton wineries. The estate vineyard has grown to fifteen acres, composed largely of Cabernet Sauvignon grapes with small blocks of Petit Verdot and Merlot. An estate Cabernet is made, but most of the vineyard-designated wines are made from grapes bought from nearby vineyards. Cabernet is king, with about 90 percent of the five thousand to six thousand cases produced in total. Von Strasser is experimenting with the Austrian varietal Grüner Veltliner grapes and has planted a third of an acre on his estate vineyard to them, with the expectation of producing five hundred to one thousand cases within a few years. To his knowledge, this is the first planting of the grape in California.

The Von Strasser style of rich, deep, complex, long-aging wines mimics the best of its neighbors in the highly regarded Diamond Mountain District. Single vineyard bottlings from Post and Rainin join the Reserve and the Sori Bricco blend in garnering scores as high as the middle to upper 90s in most years, and this extraordinary success makes Von Strasser one of our highest-rated wineries.

VOSS VINEYARDS 1991		Map 14
www.vossvineyards.com	707-259-0993	No Tasting
Rutherford	Napa County	Rutherford AVA

Australian winemaker Robert Hill Smith began making wine from purchased grapes in 1991. Hill Smith is a fifth-generation winemaker whose family also owns the Yalumba Winery in South Australia's Barossa region and the Nautilus Estate in Marlborough, New Zealand. In '96, Voss Vineyards bought forty-eight acres in Rutherford and planted forty-five of those acres to Sauvignon Blanc, Syrah, Viognier, and Merlot varietals. Most wines have been from estate-grown fruit, made under the supervision of winemaker Michael Lancaster (of Gloria Ferrer and Quail Ridge). Eight thousand cases are made in total, with Syrah leading the way until recently and Viognier, Sauvignon Blanc, and Merlot rounding out the offerings. Today, Voss has decided to concentrate solely on Sauvignon Blanc, its most artistically successful grape, and with scores regularly reaching into the 90-point range, that decision looks like one that will benefit the winery and wine drinkers alike.

Brothers Art Finkelstein and Alan Steen purchased an old vineyard site just south of St. Helena in 1979, ripped out the old planting, and installed twenty-six acres of Chardonnay, Sauvignon Blanc, and Merlot. Winemaking began in '85. Soon, the brothers sold to a Japanese investor who, in turn, resold the property in '93 to current owner Tom Leonardini, a San Francisco businessman and wine retailer. Under Leonardini's watch, the winery has expanded many-fold and now produces upward of forty thousand cases a year, focusing on Cabernet Sauvignon, Sauvignon Blanc, and Merlot; those three wines contribute 90 percent of the total output. Most wine is made from owned vineyards, of which there are six on the valley floor, totaling 110 acres. Art Finklestein, along with wife Bunnie and son Judd, now operates the up-and-coming Judd's Hill winery.

Cabernet Sauvignon Reserve, the winery's top-of-the-line bottling, has regularly earned scores of 90 points and higher, with the rest of the line more often than not coming in with rankings in the still highly commendable upper 80s.

The Whitford property has been owned by the Whitford and Haynes families since 1885. The modern Haynes Vineyard, in the Coombsville area in southeast Napa Valley, was planted in the late 1960s, and winemaking began in '83 under proprietors Dunc and Pat Haynes and winemakers Ken and Teresa Bernards. Today's production is small, with 1,500 cases of estate-grown and -bottled wines. Chardonnay leads the way with over half the output, including a very limited edition Old Vines Chardonnay. A Pinot Noir and Syrah are also on the roster.

With quality high, but production low, one would expect the world to beat a path to the Whitford door, but so far, that has not happened, and Whitford wines, when you can find them, are generally among the better values from the Napa Valley. The Web site is out of date.

WILLIAM HILL ESTATE 1978   Map 15

www.williamhillwinery.com   707-265-3024   Tasting by Appointment

Napa   Napa County   Napa Valley AVA

Sooner William Hill came west for his Stanford MBA and stayed on to develop vineyards in the valley. He made his first vintage wine in 1976 in rented facilities. By the end of the '80s, Hill was making sixty thousand cases of Chardonnay and Cabernet Sauvignon. Today, over one hundred thousand cases are produced, still primarily of Chardonnay and Cabernet, with several Reserve-level wines produced in small batches ranging from 150 to 3,500 cases each. Just east of the Silverado Trail, on the way up Atlas Peak, lies the 140-acre estate Silverado Bench Vineyard, which provides much of the juice, principally Cabernet. The winery is now owned by E & J Gallo.

WILLIAM HARRISON VINEYARDS & WINERY 1993   Map 13

www.whwines.com   707-963-8310   Tasting

St. Helena   Napa County   Rutherford AVA

The vineyards were first established in 1985 by Bill Harrison, descendant of Italian immigrant Antonio Perelli-Minetti, whose winery in the San Joaquin Valley ultimately produced a million cases of table wine. In the early '80s, Bill Harrison moved to the Napa Valley and founded his Rutherford estate just east of the Silverado Trail while also creating a mobile bottling service that still exists. Harrison sold grapes to others for a decade before releasing his first wine in '93. Today, under winemaker Bruce Bradley and consultant Philip Titus (of Chappellet and Titus), Harrison makes about two thousand cases total of Cabernet Sauvignon, a Cabernet blend called Rutherford Red, Chardonnay, and Cabernet Franc. The Cabernet and blend represent two-thirds of total production. The ten-acre Harrison estate vineyard grows all the grapes used in winemaking.

Wine ratings over the years have been primarily in the high 80s, with the occasional wine reaching 90 points.

XTANT 2001   Map 14

www.xtantwines.com   707-224-7844   No Tasting

Napa   Napa County   Napa Valley AVA

Jeffrey O'Neill, a third-generation winemaker and former CEO of the large bulk wine producer Golden State Vintners, hooked up with developer Laurence Vosti to make a single, annual bottling of a proprietary red Cabernet Sauvignon-based blend, Xtant. Winemaker Jeff Gaffner, formerly of Chateau St. Jean, uses grapes sourced from vineyards in Stags Leap, Rutherford, and St. Helena to produce 1,400 cases of this critically acclaimed wine. In its early outings, the wine has garnered highly admirable ratings in the 90-plus range; and while it is not inexpensive, it has outscored many pricier bottlings.

ZAHTILA VINEYARDS	1999	Map 11
www.zahtilavineyards.com	707-942-9251	Tasting
Calistoga	Napa County	Calistoga AVA

Computer marketer Laura Zahtila purchased a small Calistoga estate at the foot of Oat Hill from the Traulsen family and has made her own wines ever since. This modest winery makes about 4,500 cases of Cabernet Sauvignon, Zinfandel, and Chardonnay in fairly equal proportions from Napa and Sonoma valley sources. A single-vineyard Beckstoffer George III Cabernet Sauvignon is made in very small lots, as is the Oak Hill Estate Zinfandel made from the grapes of the two-acre home ranch. Chardonnay is sourced from several small Napa Valley vineyards. An extra virgin olive oil is available at the winery.

Zahtila wines have been well received to date, with most bottlings ranking in the upper 80s and the Beckstoffer George III Cabernet often reaching 90 points.

ZD WINES	1969	Map 13
www.zdwines.com	800-487-7757	Tasting
Napa	Napa County	Rutherford AVA

Aerospace engineers (now deceased) Gino Zepponi and Norman de Leuze founded the winery, first located in the Sonoma Valley. When the partners' production outgrew the facility, they moved to the Napa Valley in 1979 to a site along the Silverado Trail. They planted a six-acre estate winery to Cabernet Sauvignon and, later, a thirty-three-acre vineyard in Carneros to Chardonnay and Pinot Noir. Ownership and management are now solely with the de Leuze family. Production averages over thirty thousand cases, fairly evenly divided among Chardonnay, Pinot Noir, and

Cabernet. Several reserve, Syrah, and Gewürztraminer bottlings are made in much smaller lots. ZD makes a unique "vertical" blend of its Cabernets, called Abacus, made from '92 forward, adding the latest vintage to the brew each year. At the most recent bottling, $400 was asked for each bottle with a two-hundred-case production level.

ZD's Reserve bottlings, of Cabernet Sauvignon, Chardonnay, and Pinot Noir, have each reached into the 90-plus rating level on numerous occasions, while the regular-bottling versions of those grapes have tended to run from the mid- to upper 80s.

San Francisco Bay, Santa Cruz Mountains, and Solano County

People who live in northern California know that the term *Bay Area* includes nine counties in and around San Francisco, the much-loved "City by the Bay." San Francisco Bay has now been adopted as the name under which several grape growing counties (San Francisco, Contra Costa, Alameda, San Mateo and Santa Clara), plus parts of San Benito and Santa Cruz Counties to the east and south of San Francisco have joined together to form the San Francisco Bay American Viticultural Area. Excluded from the AVA are areas to the north, including Marin, Sonoma, Napa and Solano counties. However, for purposes of this chapter, Solano County, and its viticulture, is also discussed here as its grapes are closer to the Bay than the furthest parts of several of the counties included in the AVA. Napa and Sonoma counties may be the major players among Bay Area counties in today's world with their combined acreage count now exceeding one-hundred thousand, but places like Alameda and Santa Clara counties have played significant roles in the 19th century and early to mid-20th century development of the California wine industry and they remain important. The counties in this chapter contain something like ten thousand planted acres of grapes, mostly in Alameda, Santa Clara and Solano counties.

This chapter follows the AVA lines rather than the commonly accepted definition, but it also includes Solano County because that county and its vines are closer to and more directly enjoy the maritime influence of the Bay and its major tributary, the Sacramento River, than do those areas at the southern end of the AVA.

San Francisco Bay AVA

This romantically named appellation conveniently lumps together vines more or less near the San Francisco Bay that have no fancy title to call their own. Its rather broad geography—stretching from the hot, inland sands of Contra Costa County, to the cool bayside hills of San Mateo and Santa Clara counties, and then south to the warmer inland regions of northern San Benito County—present a mix-and-match set of growing conditions having almost nothing to do with one another.

Moreover, if the purpose of appellations is to help consumers understand the places in which the grapes are grown, this appellation gets even more confusing. It is the rare wine that combines grapes from several of its smaller appellations into one bottling. Instead, we are as likely to see the name "San Francisco Bay" listed immediately adjacent to such more clearly identifiable places as Livermore Valley or Contra Costa County. A cynic might even say that the name has more to do with marketing than wine quality. Still, for those whose hearts are left behind, this little slice of the bay might be all they need. The key to understanding the San Francisco Bay appellation is in understanding its disparate parts and then in knowing which of those parts have been the source of the grapes.

Grape acreage in all of the included places is estimated to be five thousand to seven thousand acres depending on who is doing the counting—there being a bit of a dispute as to how much is actually planted in Alameda County but not measured by the voluntary annual grape survey. By almost any measure, the largest concentration of planted acreage does lie in Alameda County within the Livermore Valley AVA. The Santa Cruz Mountains AVA, covering the uplands of San Mateo, Santa Cruz, and the northern part of Santa Clara counties, is also of significance both because of the reputations enjoyed by its top producers and because of the many wineries located there.

Alameda County

It is here, in this county that contains Oakland and Berkeley immediately on the bay and the Livermore Valley inland by no more than a short crow's flight, that the San Francisco Bay AVA finds its roots. The Wente family,

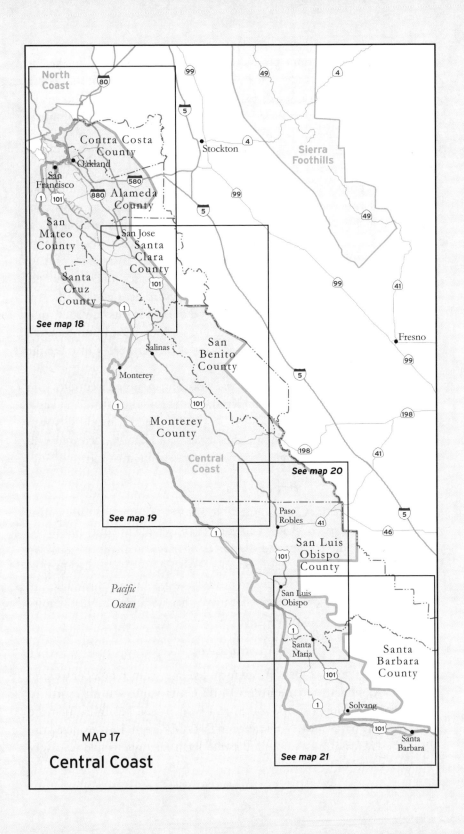

North
Coast

Contra Costa
County
Oakland

Stockton

Sierra
Foothills

San
Francisco

Alameda
County

San
Mateo
County

San Jose
Santa
Clara
County

Santa
Cruz
County

See map 18

Salinas

San
Benito
County

Fresno

Monterey

Monterey
County

Central
Coast

See map 20

See map 19

Paso
Robles

San Luis
Obispo
County

Pacific
Ocean

San Luis
Obispo

Santa
Maria

Santa
Barbara
County

Solvang

MAP 17

Central Coast

Santa
Barbara

See map 21

by far the most important producer in Alameda County and in the San Francisco Bay AVA, is identified with the push for the establishment of the AVA; indeed, every one of its Livermore Valley bottlings also carries the San Francisco Bay identifier. Wente was perhaps the first winery ever established in Alameda County, and it is certainly the oldest in existence today. It makes the most wine and has greatly influenced the resurgence of winegrowing near its Livermore Valley home.

Official reports credit the county with some 2,800 acres of grapes, but the growers association insists that its count is something closer to 5,000. The difference is attributed to the practice of allowing new housing in the wine-friendly areas on twenty-acre lots, with most of the land set aside for agriculture. It turns out that grape growing is often the first choice of these semisuburban newcomers, and while their small plots seemingly do not get counted in the state of California's annual vineyard acreage tally, there is no question that a drive out to the south end of the Livermore Valley finds new vineyards popping up everywhere. For all intents and purposes, the grape acreage totals for the county and for the Livermore Valley are the same no matter who is counting.

Red wine grapes dominate in the warmish climate near Livermore, with Cabernet Sauvignon (eight hundred acres), Merlot (four hundred), and Petite Sirah (three hundred) leading the way. Despite Livermore's long history with Sauvignon Blanc, that variety now claims fewer than a hundred acres, whereas Chardonnay is the white grape leader with some six hundred acres.

Ben Lomond Mountain

To be located in Santa Cruz County is to admit to the fact that few grapes are grown in your AVA. And when you are an isolated uplands area in the western part of the county and the forces of nature make grape growing difficult, you are likely, as has happened to this AVA first created in 1988 by the only winery now standing, to be rarely seen on wine labels. The fact that grape growing goes back over 125 years has not helped Ben Lomond Mountain prosper as an AVA.

Central Coast

All of the San Francisco Bay AVA is included in the much broader Central Coast AVA, which stretches from Contra Costa County in the north to Santa Barbara County in the south, and while it can be argued that the southernmost parts of the San Francisco Bay AVA might be considered the tip of the Central Coast to the folks who live there, one would find very few people in the inner San Francisco Bay who would describe themselves as anything but "Northern Californians." As such, the inclusion of the San Francisco Bay AVA in this larger mass is a convenience to the wineries but is misleading to the rest of the world.

See Central Coast Vineyard Team: www.vineyardteam.org;
Central Coast Winegrowers Association: www.ccwga.org.

Contra Costa County

Far to the east of the bay, along the Sacramento River near Oakley, past the heavily urbanized areas of "West County," lies the residue of a long-established grape-growing industry. Planted in sandy soils, mostly to red grapes that are heat tolerant like Zinfandel and Mourvèdre, but with a fair representation of Chardonnay and Sauvignon Blanc, Contra Costa County has a small but knowledgeable following who flock to the lusty red wines produced from its grapes by people like Neyers and Rosenblum, two of California's leading practitioners of full-bodied reds. Grape plantings add up to 1,500 acres led by Zinfandel and Chardonnay at approximately 400 acres each and Mourvèdre at nearly 200 acres.

Livermore Valley

If not so well-known as their famous neighbors to the north, the grapes of the Livermore Valley have both colorful history and a dynamic future on their side. Over 150 years ago, when Napa was not yet on anyone's wine map, Robert Livermore had planted grapes in "his" valley, but it was not until the latter part of the nineteenth century that wine pioneers Charles Wetmore and James Concannon joined the party and put the Livermore Valley permanently on the wine map. By 1890, grape plantings had grown to a staggering (for the times) total of some six thousand acres, led by Zinfandel and with Pinot Noir and Mourvèdre also prominent. Wine historian Charles Sullivan reports, however, that the white grapes of Sauvignon Blanc and Semillon soon came into prominence and were the leaders in Livermore's growing reputation.

Problems in the vineyards and consolidation of ownership reduced plantings, and by 1920, with the onset of Prohibition, the Livermore acreage had been cut in half. With Repeal in the mid-1930s, Livermore's reputation for white wines was once again on the rise, but acreage was dropping, and the creation of suburban housing in the Livermore Valley hastened the process of vineyard abandonment.

Had it not been for the pioneer families, the Wentes and the Concannons whose wineries are still the most famous in the valley, it is entirely likely that the vinous renaissance filling the southern end of the valley would not have happened. But happening it is, and today it is estimated by the locals that the Livermore Valley is growing grapes on some five thousand acres, led now by Chardonnay and Cabernet Sauvignon.

And with acreage and increased interest has come a slew of new wineries. Many are directly associated with Wente, whose dynamic family leadership continues to be the strong cornerstone of the Livermore Valley wine industry. Concannon is no longer family owned, but the winery's position as the state's leading maker of Petite Sirah and its focus on Rhône varieties keep it a strong number two in the Livermore Valley.

The valley is now home to almost three dozen smaller wineries whose products are very much enjoyed locally, whether by the folks who live in the valley or by the thousands who come to visit its wineries in an endless stream, stopping not just at the well-known producers but filling up the tasting rooms of wineries that spread from Niles Canyon across the southern end of the valley to the hills east of Livermore.

See Livermore Valley Winegrowers Association: www.livermorewine.com.

San Mateo and San Francisco Counties

The inclusion of San Francisco County is an irrelevancy since there are not sufficient grapes grown in the center city to notice, but what would a San Francisco Bay AVA be without its namesake? And although San Mateo County grows less than a hundred acres of grapes, two-thirds of which are Pinot Noir and Chardonnay, it, too, is a statistical small fry. The Thomas Fogarty Winery high in the hills overlooking the bay may not consider its Pinot patch irrelevant, however, as it is not only the largest planting in the county but also its most noteworthy.

Santa Clara County

Old-timers remember the days when this county was filled with orchards and vineyards, and, indeed, some of California's legendary winemakers have made their homes here. Few of us today even know of the contributions to the growth of the California wine industry that were authored by early pioneers like Paul Masson and Charles LeFranc. And, with urbanization and siliconization taking over Santa Clara County, its remaining vines have been pushed out of the area around San Jose. Cabernet Sauvignon,

Chardonnay, and Merlot, all in the 300- to 400-acre range, make up about 80 percent of the county's 1,500 planted acres, almost all of which is now found in the southern, less built-up end of the county.

Santa Clara Valley

With the notable exception of a few isolated vineyards in the hills north of San Jose, most notably belonging to the Ridge and Mount Eden wineries, the grapes of the Santa Clara Valley are, for all intents and purposes, those of Santa Clara County. Where once the valley was the home of a large produce business, there is a small but significant cluster of wineries and vineyards in the Hecker Pass area west of Gilroy and limited planting elsewhere. For every wine lover who knows the name of this AVA, there are hundreds more who think the place is officially called "Silicon Valley."

Santa Cruz Mountains

The uplands of southern San Mateo, northern Santa Clara, and the adjoining parts of Santa Cruz counties make up this multicounty AVA. It is excluded from the San Francisco Bay and Central Coast AVAs, but it is immediately adjacent to both. Its leading wineries—Ridge, Mount Eden, David Bruce, just to mention the three most obvious—have long histories of producing absolutely top-flight wines and enjoy worldwide reputations. Grape plantings are estimated by the local association to be in the range of 1,500 acres, with Chardonnay and Pinot Noir among the leaders. Not to be overlooked, of course, is the fact that both Ridge and Mount Eden have made exceptional Cabernet Sauvignon from their perches on the bay side of the mountaintop. Both Santa Clara and Santa Cruz Mountains have some 45 percent each of the grapes being grown in the appellation; the rest are in San Mateo County. It is an area of small plantings and small wineries, and it is the closest thing to the good old days when it was possible to enter the wine business in a top area yet on a limited budget.

See Santa Cruz Mountains Winegrowers Association: www.scmwa.com.

San Ysidro District

In the low hills east of Gilroy along Highway 152, there are a few hundred acres of vines planted in the foothills. While one rarely sees this AVA on wine labels, it occasionally crops up in someone's limited-production bottling, often to good effect. It is not a place one would normally go on a day trip to taste wine, however, since the area is mostly brush-covered hillside.

Solano County

Located immediately east of Napa County and to the north of Contra Costa County, Solano County may not have much of a following, but its grapes often wind up in wines from its fancier neighbor to the west. Its 3,500 acres of grapes are dwarfed by Napa, yet with few wineries, all of which are limited in production, and with the labeling laws allowing small portions of grapes from places not mentioned on the label, Solano's vineyards are not neglected. Chardonnay with over a thousand acres and Pinot Noir with about seven hundred acres are the two dominant plantings in the county. Both of the county's AVAs, Solano County Green Valley and Suisun Valley, experience moderate warmth, but both are also cooled in the late afternoon by the winds that rush in from the San Francisco Bay and up the Sacramento River.

Solano County Green Valley

Solano's Green Valley gets its extra bit of naming because of the existence of a Green Valley in Sonoma County. It is a small (about a mile or so long) north-south valley tucked next to the southeastern corner of Napa and contains less than a thousand acres of grapes.

Suisun Valley

The Suisun Valley lies just one hill line to the east of Green Valley, abuts Napa County at its northern end, and runs down to the broad, watery, cooling expanse of the Sacramento River at its southern end. It contains the remainder of the county's grapes.

AUGUST WEST WINE	2003	Map 18
www.augustwestwine.com	415-225-2891	No Tasting
San Francisco	San Francisco County	San Francisco Bay AVA

Three partners—noted grower Gary Franscioni of Rosella's Vineyard in the Santa Lucia Highlands AVA in Monterey County, Howard Graham of the Graham Family Vineyard in the Russian River Valley, and winemaker Ed Kurtzman—have ganged up to make small batches of Pinot Noir, Chardonnay, and Syrah from the two vineyards. Fewer than 1,500 cases are made, over half of which are Pinot Noirs. August West recently moved from Sebastopol to a new winery facility in an industrial area of San Francisco, where the capacity will be up to five thousand cases.

At their highest, wine ratings have reached into the stratospheric mid-90s and, based on both exceptional vineyard selection and talented winemaking, have the potential to earn critical acclaim every time out. The Kurtzman hand on the tiller dictates that the wines will be nicely fruited and come with buoyant acidity.

BARGETTO WINERY 1933		Map 18
www.bargetto.com	800-722-7438	Tasting
Soquel	Santa Cruz County	Santa Cruz Mountains AVA

The longest continuously operating winery in the Santa Cruz Mountains was founded by the Bargetto family, the first members of which had emigrated from Italy in the late 1800s. Those earliest Bargettos bought the present site in 1918 and grew apples and produce, with a sideline of wine for their friends and family. After Prohibition ended in 1933, they focused on the winery and sold most of their product in bulk. Over time, the family shifted from producing old-style to contemporary wines. In 1992, now run by third-generation Bargettos, the thirty-six-acre Bargetto Regan Estate Vineyards in the Corralitos area of southern Santa Cruz County were planted to Merlot (40 percent), Chardonnay (30 percent), Pinot Noir (15 percent), and the balance to several Italian varietal grapes. Production of exclusively estate-grown and -bottled wines now exceeds forty thousand cases, of which fully 20 percent is the moderately priced Pinot Grigio. There are two second labels: La Vita, a northern Italian blend, and Chaucer's Cellar with several dessert wines. Bargetto celebrated its seventy-fifth anniversary in 2008.

Quality has been variable, and most of the lower-priced wines with a Central Coast appellation have been about as good as the competition, but Bargetto is also capable of finding real quality in the pricier end of its line. The winery tasting room has been a favorite of ours seemingly forever. With styles that vary by price point, grape variety, and appellation, Bargetto offers something for everyone, but the consumer is required to work hard to find it at times.

BONNY DOON VINEYARD 1981		Map 18
www.bonnydoonvineyard.com	831-425-4518	Tasting
Santa Cruz	Santa Cruz County	Santa Cruz Mountains AVA

The outsized personality of owner-winemaker Randall Grahm may distract from the range of creative wines grown. In 1981, former philosopher Grahm bought land in the remote Santa Cruz Mountains and planted Pinot Noir and Chardonnay grapes. In '84, the first Le Cigare Volant wine appeared (the name is French slang for "flying saucer," a play on the 1950s proclamation banning UFOs from landing in the Châteauneuf du Pape region.). New vineyards totaling 125 acres, near Soledad in the Salinas Valley, were planted to Italian varietals and the resulting wines bottled under the Ca'del Solo name. About two-thirds of the production of thirty-five thousand cases is of the Ca'del Solo line and much of the balance the Cigare wines. Experimentation with dessert wines, such as Eau-de-vie, continues apace. Also notable for many years, and the core of the winery's volume production, was the Big House Red blend (so named because of the proximity of the vineyard to the Soledad state prison), which was recently sold to The Wine Group. Production facilities and the winery tasting room have left their old digs in Bonny Doon and have been consolidated in the town of Santa Cruz, along with the creation of a first-class restaurant, the Cellar Door. The marvelously eccentric Web site reminds one of Monty Python's Flying Circus; be sure to watch the "Vive le Screwcap" video.

Over the years, Bonny Doon wines have been pacesetters and also-rans, depending to some extent on where Grahm's roving attentions have been focused. After helping create the whole Rhône wine craze and being a leader in it, his wines have fallen off the pace as newer plantings and better winemaking has taken over. Still, this is not a winery to be counted out, and everyone who has ever dealt with Grahm knows that his next project, whatever it may be, is likely to influence all who follow him. Bonny Doon wines can be counted on for balance and close attention to varietal expression.

BYINGTON VINEYARD & WINERY 1989		Map 18
www.byington.com	408-354-1111	Tasting
Los Gatos	Santa Clara County	Santa Cruz Mountains AVA

Founded in 1989 by steelmaker William Byington, the château-like winery situated on ninety-five acres high in the Santa Cruz Mountains is now run by the next generation. Pinot Noir was the first variety grown on eight planted acres surrounding the winery and remains the exclusive estate-grown grape today. Over five thousand cases are now produced, largely from grapes purchased from such far-flung vineyards as Cerro Prieto in Paso Robles and Van der Kamp on Sonoma Mountain. Leader in volume at nearly 40 percent is the Alliage Bordeaux-style red blend of Cabernet Sauvignon, Cabernet Franc, and Merlot. The Estate Vineyard Pinot Noir remains the small-volume pride of the fleet of wines, which now ranges from Chardonnay to Cabernet, Merlot, Rosé, and a Port.

If reasonably well-received, Byington wines have been a bit of a hit-or-miss lot, but they are made with high intent and often achieve scores in the upper-80-point range.

CINNABAR VINEYARDS & WINERY 1983		Map 18
www.cinnabarwine.com	408-741-5858	Tasting
Saratoga	Santa Clara County	Santa Cruz Mountains AVA

Stanford engineer Tom Mudd planted an acre of grapes in the mid-1970s on top of the Santa Cruz Mountains. He then moved from engineering to the science of winemaking in '83, gradually adding to the planted acreage comprising the estate; it now stands at thirty acres of Cabernet Sauvignon (about 60 percent of the grapes), Chardonnay (30 percent), and Pinot Noir (10 percent). Under winemaker George Troquato, the program encompasses estate Santa Cruz Mountain Cabernet Sauvignon, Pinot Noir, and Chardonnay; Paso Robles Merlot; Monterey Chardonnay; and a Bordeaux blend of Cabernet, Merlot, Cabernet Franc, and Petite Verdot named Mercury Rising, after the mineral of which cinnabar is a derivative. Eighty percent of Cinnabar's grapes are purchased from vineyards in Paso Robles and Monterey and the remainder elsewhere in the Santa Cruz Mountains. Total production is fifteen thousand cases, with the estate bottlings comprising about three thousand cases. A new tasting facility in Saratoga makes the winery accessible to the public.

From the very beginning, Cinnabar wines have seemed full of promise, but that promise is still waiting to be fully realized. Latest whites, scoring in the upper 80s, have been fully recommendable, but it is still the rare Cinnabar effort that breaks the 90-point barrier. Cinnabar wines can get quite ripe at times, but, for the most part, they tend to favor balance over power.

CLOS LACHANCE WINERY 1992		Map 18
www.closlachance.com	800-ITS-WINE	Tasting
San Martin	Santa Clara County	Santa Clara Valley AVA

Started with a backyard vineyard in Saratoga, Silicon Valley engineer Bill Murphy and wife Brenda were sufficiently successful in their earliest home vintages to inspire a full-time move into winemaking. Buying and planting a vineyard in San Martin, between Morgan Hill and Gilroy, Clos LaChance has expanded to 150 acres of a broad variety of grapes. The winery's current production is forty-five thousand (of a sixty-thousand-case capacity), with the modestly priced line, the Hummingbird Series, leading the way at over 60 percent of the volume. The Estate line of varietals (principally Sauvignon Blanc, Chardonnay, and Pinot Noir) represents another 35 percent of volume. Two vineyard-designated Chardonnays and a Pinot Noir, all from the Santa Cruz Mountains, round out the production. Through a subsidiary, Clos LaChance also manages and sources grapes from small backyard vineyards in the Santa Cruz Mountains and the Central Coast.

Over the last several years, the Hummingbird Series wines have been among the best bargains in California across the entire line of varieties offered. Upscale Chardonnays have also been rated very well, and the best have earned scores in the low 90s. The winery style favors mannerly wines.

CONCANNON VINEYARD 1883		Map 18
www.concannonvineyard.com	925-446-2500	Tasting
Livermore	Alameda County	Livermore Valley AVA

James Concannon emigrated from Ireland and made his first wine in the Livermore Valley in 1883. Now helped by the third Concannon generation, ownership has changed hands several times and now rests with The Wine Group of San Francisco, owner of Glen Ellen and several others. Australian winemaker Adam Richards builds on the legendary Petite Sirah—Concannon was the first in California to introduce this varietal commercially in 1961—with other strong reds including Syrah, Cabernet Sauvignon, and Merlot. The Concannon family of wines includes the Select Vineyards and Limited Release groups with wide distribution, modest price, and Central Coast grapes. A total of three hundred thousand cases is produced annually, most of which is the Limited Release Petite Sirah and the Select Vineyards Cabernet Sauvignon. The Reserve line uses grapes grown on the 200-acre estate, of which 140 acres are dedicated to Petite Sirah grapes, and lovers of this hearty grape owe a great deal to Concannon for its dedication to it.

The winery's Heritage Petite Syrah (note the winery's unique spelling for this high-end bottling) is its top-of-the-line bottling and can be counted on to age famously for a decade or more even though its style is less overtly muscular than most Petite Sirahs on the market today. It has earned scores in the 90s and is among the leaders, especially for folks who seek balance rather than out-and-out brawn in their Petite Sirah.

DASHE CELLARS 1986		Map 18
www.dashecellars.com	510-452-1800	Tasting
Oakland	Alameda County	San Francisco Bay AVA

Michael and Anne Dashe started their artisanal winery over a decade ago in Alameda in space under the same roof as host Rosenblum Cellars, and, by 2005, the Dashes, in conjunction with Jeff Cohn of JC Cellars, found more space in Jack London Square near the Oakland waterfront. The winery's flagship wine is its Dry Creek Valley Zinfandel, which makes up over half of today's current production of 8,500 cases. In addition, the winery produces a line of vineyard-designated wines such as the Todd Brothers Ranch Cabernet Sauvignon from Alexander Valley and an Iron Oak Ranch Merlot from the Potter Valley, as well as a couple of special Zinfandel bottlings. Dashe wines can be tasted both in Oakland at the industrial-looking building they share with JC Cellars (also available for tasting and a nice two-for-one visit) and at the Family Winemakers tasting room in the Dry Creek Valley.

The Dry Creek Zinfandel has been well received from the beginning and has earned ratings in the upper 80s and most recently over 90 points. In addition, the winery's limited-production Dry Riesling from Mendocino County has won great critical acclaim, and it reminds one that Riesling, although not especially popular these days, is a noble grape capable of making beautiful wine in the right hands. The winery's meant-to-be-drunk-young Zin labeled L'Enfant Terrible is brashly brisk and fruity but will surprise those who think the grape should be bold and concentrated.

DAVID BRUCE WINERY 1964		Map 18
www.davidbrucewinery.com	800-397-9972	Tasting
Los Gatos	Santa Clara County	Santa Cruz Mountains AVA

South Bay dermatologist David Bruce went from home winemaking to pioneering numerous now-standard winemaking techniques in the 1960s and 1970s. In '61, Bruce built his winery and planted grapes on twenty-five acres of land in the Santa Cruz Mountains. Experimenting with little-known varietals, he released a White Zinfandel in '64 that preceded the blush wine trend of the '80s. But the Chardonnays of the late '60s and '70s put David Bruce on the map; indeed, the winery was one of twelve California wineries represented at the "Judgment of Paris" that launched the enormous growth of serious winemaking in the state. In the '80s and '90s, Bruce's wines were less experimental but still top-notch; he focused on Pinot Noir, Chardonnay, Cabernet Sauvignon, Zinfandel, and Syrah from his twenty-five-acre estate vineyard and select growers throughout Northern California and the Central Coast. Today, production has topped sixty thousand cases, with Pinot Noir the single largest variety.

Bruce was among the first of the current era to claim that Pinot Noir would reach high levels of quality in California, and his efforts are among those that were most critical in keeping the hope alive. Today, he makes Pinot Noir from all over California in both well-regarded midpriced bottlings and in special, limited-production editions. His wines typically rate in the upper 80s but can drift lower and reach much higher. We have liked his Russian River Pinots of late.

EDMUNDS ST. JOHN 1985		Map 18
www.edmundsstjohn.com	510-981-1510	No Tasting
Berkeley	Alameda County	San Francisco Bay AVA

Steve Edmunds and Cornelia St. John established the winery in 1985 with the then-disfavored intent of making Rhône varietals in California; indeed, Edmunds was one of the original "Rhône Rangers." Previously a wine buyer for retail stores, Edmunds rented space in an old industrial warehouse in west Berkeley, where he still makes small batches of somewhat less-than-mainstream varieties: several red and white blends, Pinot Grigio, Roussanne, Viognier, and Syrah. Vineyards sourced include Pallini in Mendocino, Durell in Carneros, Bassetti in San Luis Obispo, and Rozet in Paso Robles. Total production approaches four thousand cases.

Both respected and occasionally questioned about his wines and their style, Edmunds is nonetheless an iconic figure in the Rhône movement. He deserves—and gets—high marks for his controlled style that emphasizes fruit and balance.

FLEMING JENKINS VINEYARDS 2003		Map 18
www.flemingjenkins.com	408-358-4949	Tasting
Los Gatos	Santa Clara County	Santa Clara Valley AVA

Peggy Fleming (yes, *that* Peggy Fleming) and winemaker-spouse-MD Greg Jenkins planted a one-acre Chardonnay vineyard on their ridge top in the Santa Cruz Mountains foothills in 1999. Their winery was completed in 2003 on the site of the Novitiate Winery, alongside the notable Testarossa Vineyards. There Fleming and Jenkins produce a limited variety of wines, ranging from their estate Chardonnay to a Napa Valley Cabernet Sauvignon blend. The wine portfolio includes a Madden Ranch Syrah, with grapes from John Madden's (yes, *that* John Madden) Livermore Valley vineyard. Production approaches twenty-five hundred cases a year.

Their Syrahs, especially the Madden, but also the Black Ridge bottling have scored at 90 points and above, and the Chardonnay has challenged for those heights and has the potential to get there.

GARRÉ VINEYARD & WINERY 1996		Map 18
www.garrewinery.com	925-371-8200	Tasting
Livermore	Alameda County	Livermore Valley AVA

Italian matriarch Rosa Garré passed on land and a winemaking ethos to grandson Bob Molinaro, whose job is running a nearby garbage collection service but whose hobby is wine. Merlot was the foundation of the winery, which has now expanded into several red varieties, all grown and bottled on the twenty-acre estate. Today, twenty-five hundred cases are produced in small lots, featuring a Bordeaux blend of Cabernet Sauvignon, Cabernet Franc, Merlot, Malbec, and Petite Verdot. It may be that more emphasis is placed on the Garré restaurant, bocce ball courts, and an events center than on the wines.

JC CELLARS 1996		Map 18
www.jccellars.com	510-465-5900	Tasting
Oakland	Alameda County	San Francisco Bay AVA

Jeff Cohn, founder and winemaker, had a background in the food and hospitality industries prior to studying enology at Fresno State and then plunging into winemaking by working for East Bay volume leader Rosenblum Cellars, where Cohn rose to the title of winemaker. Along the way, Cohn established his own brand using Rosenblum as his first home. In 2005, in conjunction with Dashe Cellars, also housed at Rosenblum, Cohn established his own facility near Jack London Square. Known for its top-rated Zinfandels and Syrahs, JC Cellars also produces notable Petite Sirah and Viognier and a white blend of Marsanne and Roussanne known as First Date. The vineyard-designated wines come from outstanding locations both north and south of the San Francisco Bay area, including Fess Parker in Santa Barbara County, Rockpile in Sonoma, and Ventana in Monterey, among others. Currently 4,500 cases are bottled, of which the flagship Zinfandel is over half of the production.

Quality levels, reflecting both Cohn's great skill with full-bodied reds and his time spent at Rosenblum, one of the masters of Zinfandel, has been very high: most wines score from the high 80s to the mid-90s. As a result, Cohn has been widely and justifiably acclaimed as one of the most outstanding new talents on the wine scene. His First Date has regularly earned ratings in the lower to mid-90s making it perhaps the highest-rated white Rhône-type wine made in California.

LA ROCHELLE WINERY 1996		Map 18
www.lrwines.com	925-243-6440	Tasting
Livermore	Alameda County	Livermore Valley AVA

Steven Kent Mirassou, who cut his teeth at the family's winery in San Jose and then moved on and founded the Steven Kent Winery, and son Steven Mirassou have now formed La Rochelle in order to explore their mutual fascination with Pinot Noir. On the same site as Steven Kent, this separate label is offering scads of single-vineyard Pinot Noirs from all over the West Coast. The wines tend to ripeness and richness, and they also tend to be successful, with scores in the upper 80s to low 90s the most frequently seen critical evaluations of their efforts.

MITCHELL KATZ WINERY 1998		Map 18
www.mitchellkatzwinery.com	925-931-0744	Tasting
Pleasanton	Alameda County	Livermore Valley AVA

Starting as a home winemaker with his grandfather, Katz moved to commercial winemaking in 1998. The Mitchell Katz winery now occupies the handsomely rebuilt Ruby Hill winery building, originally constructed in 1887. The focus of the winery is the production—now standing at eight thousand cases annually—of Livermore Valley single-vineyard-designated wines. Vineyards represented include Shadow Hills (the Mitchell Katz Chardonnay), Buttner (Pinot Blanc), Quail Creek (Cabernet Sauvignon), and Ruby Hill (Syrah). Katz also makes Merlot, Sangiovese, Zinfandel, and a Brut Sparkling Wine. The winery is a prime touring target in the

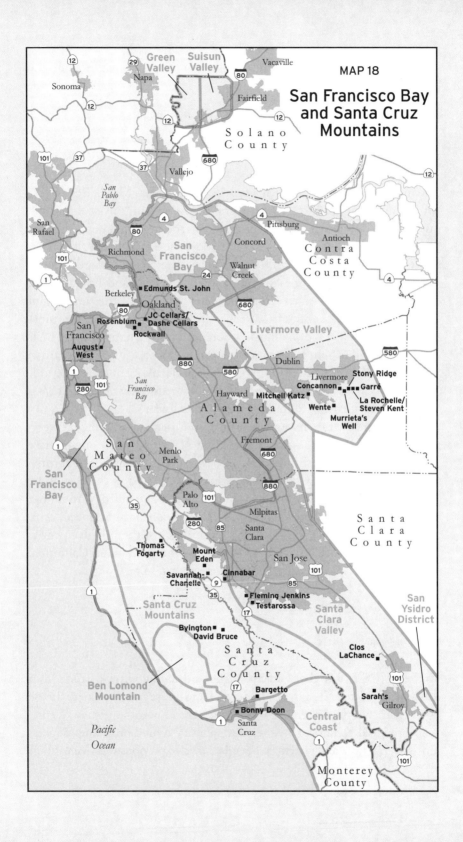

Livermore Valley, and wine prices at the winery can sometimes fall into the bargain range.

MOUNT EDEN VINEYARDS 1972		Map 18
www.mounteden.com	888-865-9463	Tasting by Appointment
Saratoga	Santa Clara County	Santa Cruz Mountains AVA

Originally developed in the early 1940s by the legendary Martin Ray (whose winery operated until 1972 and has nothing to do with the label that still uses his name), at which time the property was split, Mount Eden Vineyards was established on a steep mountainside above the Santa Clara Valley. Since '72, first guided by Dick Graff from Chalone, then Merry Edwards (see the entry for her winery in the Sonoma County chapter), and now for over thirty years under the supervision of winemaker Jeffrey Patterson, Mount Eden has made three wines from grapes grown on its forty-five-acre vineyard: Chardonnay, Pinot Noir, and Cabernet Sauvignon. In addition to its estate bottlings, Mount Eden purchases grapes from the Wolff Vineyard in the Edna Valley of San Luis Obispo County and makes a notable vineyard-designated Chardonnay. Total production exceeds twelve thousand cases annually, of which Chardonnay is the volume leader.

Estate-bottled wines have ranged from near perfection to inconsistent, and while some of California's finest Pinot Noirs and Chardonnays have come from this property, the year-to-year variations have been surprising. The Edna Valley Chardonnay, while not as good as the best estate wines, is far less expensive and has often been recommended, with ratings in the upper 80s. Winemaker Patterson is a proponent of balanced, acid-supported wines and strives to find concentration without high ripeness. When the wines succeed, they are among the most refined in California, but it is also a style that can sell the wines short in some vintages.

MURRIETA'S WELL 1990		Map 18
www.murrietaswell.com	925-456-2390	Tasting
Livermore	Alameda County	Livermore Valley AVA

In the 1880s, Louis Mel of France bought land and imported cuttings from Château Y'Quem and Margaux in Bordeaux to create an early winery. In the 1930s, Mel sold the Livermore Valley vineyards to neighbor Ernest Wente, who produced sacramental wines throughout Prohibition. Philip Wente, Ernest's grandson, and winemaker Sergio Traverso previously at Concannon resuscitated the historic winery in the 1990s and named it after the artesian well where Mexican desperado Joaquín Murrieta watered his horses during the Gold Rush years. Today's estate vineyard of seventy-nine planted acres is home to the grapes used in making several Bordeaux blends, including Red and White Meritage, Zinfandel, and a Zarzuela blend of Spanish and Portuguese grape varieties. Five to eight thousand cases of estate wines are produced annually.

This winery is the crown jewel in the Wente portfolio of Livermore Valley wines, and while quality levels have varied somewhat over the years, the very fine crafting and sophistication of the wines have remained remarkably high.

ROCKWALL 2007		Map 18
www.rockwallwines.com	510-522-5700	Tasting by Appointment
Alameda	Alameda County	San Francisco Bay AVA

With the sale of his thirty-year-old winery, Rosenblum Cellars, to the Diageo interests, Dr. Kent Rosenblum, together with partners from their previous adventure, has now added another star in his firmament with the establishment of Rockwall. It sits on the former navy air base in Alameda, just a stone's throw away from Rosenblum Cellars, and is run on a day-to-day basis by his daughter, Shawna, with the support of consulting winemaker Matt Smith of Blacksmith Cellars. Zinfandel is going to be the focus of Rockwall, and for the near term, production will be limited in volume to five thousand cases.

ROSENBLUM CELLARS 1978		Map 18
www.rosenblumcellars.com	510-865-7007	Tasting
Alameda	Alameda County	San Francisco Bay AVA

Veterinarian Kent and spouse Kathy Rosenblum moved from Minnesota to Alameda in the early 1970s and tinkered with home winemaking, a hobby that turned into a substantial winery operation focusing on Zinfandel and Rhône varietals. When the city of Alameda would not let Rosenblum make his commercial wines in his back yard, he first located in rented digs in nearby Emeryville. With growth, he was able to occupy a former boatbuilding facility directly on the Oakland estuary and to establish a second-floor tasting room with an amazing view across the water to San Francisco. In early 2008, the winery was sold to the Diageo group, with the remarkably friendly and entertaining Dr. Rosenblum staying on until 2010 as guiding light on wine quality and roving ambassador. As of summer 2010, production moved to the Napa Valley.

The original vintage production of 400 cases in 1978 has grown to over 175,000 today. Forty percent of that volume is of the Vintner's Cuvées, particularly the Zinfandel and Syrah. Remaining vineyard-specific bottlings are each in the range of two hundred to one thousand cases. The winery issues approximately twenty separate vineyard-designated Zinfandels each year, making it the clear leader in California in that category, and it offers another seven Syrahs, several Chardonnays, Pinot Noirs, a very good Viognier, and dessert wines. Grapes are sourced from growers throughout California, with close supervision of each vineyard's growing cycle by Rosenblum and staff. The winery also owns its own vineyards in Sonoma County. The tasting room at the Alameda site stays in operation for the time being.

Rosenblum wines, from the beginning, have been among the most popular and highly acclaimed Zinfandels. By selecting vineyards in locations all over the state, Rosenblum is able to offer a variety of styles and tastes, yet there is always the underlying theme of juicy, succulent fruit to the vineyard-designated bottlings. Many of the Rosenblum Zins rate perennially in the 90-point range, and it has not been unusual for Rosenblum to pull down top honors in many Zinfandel tastings. Today, together with Ridge and Ravenswood, the winery is part of the "three Rs" often referred to as Zinfandels' royalty.

Like its Zinfandels, the winery's Syrahs and Petite Sirah tend to be big, fleshy, outgoing wines that enjoy a wide band of admirers, both among collectors and everyday imbibers. And not to be missed is the winery's Viognier, a moderately priced, nicely fruited wine that is almost always among the better values offered in that variety. These latter varieties also score in the high 80s and low 90s range more often than not. Still, it must be noted that under new ownership, the wines have become higher in acidity and less outgoing at times. And at least some of the vineyard-designated wines that made the winery famous will no longer be made under the Rosenblum name. Look to the Rockwall winery, Dr. Rosenblum's latest creation, for some of those limited-edition wines to find a new home.

SARAH'S VINEYARD 1978		Map 18
www.sarahs-vineyard.com	877-44-PINOT	Tasting
Gilroy	Santa Clara County	Santa Clara Valley AVA

Tim Slater, a former Silicon Valley inventor, bought the vineyard and winery from founders Marilyn and John Otterman. Slater lives in the Pacific Northwest but keeps tabs on Sarah's Vineyard through his winemaker Matt Oetinger. Chardonnay grapes were first planted in 1978 on twenty acres of hillside land in the Hecker Pass area of southwest Santa Clara Valley, with more Chardonnay and Pinot Noir grapes following in 1989. Today's 1,200-case production is made principally from estate-grown fruit, and several vineyard-designated wines are made from grapes from other Santa Clara Valley and Santa Cruz Mountains vineyards. About two hundred cases each are made of the principal varieties: Chardonnay, Merlot, Pinot Noir, and Syrah. Despite early successes under the Ottermans, the winery never quite emerged as the quality leader that seemed its destiny, and lately, the wines are less frequently seen in the marketplace. The handsome winery site is a mandatory stop for anyone exploring the Hecker Pass area.

SAVANNAH-CHANELLE VINEYARDS 1996		Map 18
www.savannahchanelle.com	408-741-2934	Tasting
Saratoga	Santa Clara County	Santa Cruz Mountains AVA

Originally established in 1892 by French immigrant Pierre Pourroy, the vines—some planted as early as the 1910s—have survived and flourished on the estate vineyard in the Santa Cruz Mountains above Saratoga. Purchased in the 1990s by Michael Ballard, with the help of winemaker Tony Craig, formerly of David Bruce Winery, the focus here is on small-batch Pinot Noir bottlings from the estate or vineyard-designated wines from grapes grown in the Arroyo Grande Valley, Santa Lucia Highlands, the Sonoma Coast, and the Russian River Valley. Production runs from eight thousand to ten thousand cases, of which fully 80 percent is Pinot Noir, with the remainder spread among Chardonnay, Zinfandel, Cabernet Franc, and the odd Syrah Port.

Quality levels have been average to above average for the price point, with scores often ranging into the upper 80s for wines whose ripeness is high but whose fruit is balanced and can be quite convincing.

STEVEN KENT WINERY 1996		Map 18
www.stevenkent.com	925-243-6440	Tasting
Livermore	Alameda County	Livermore Valley AVA

Steven Kent Mirassou makes two distinct labels at the same Livermore winery. The Steven Kent line includes 3,500 cases of Cabernet Sauvignon (nearly half the output), Chardonnay, Syrah, and a Cabernet Port from the three-acre estate (the "Home Ranch") and vineyards in Mendocino County and the Livermore Valley. Under the La Rochelle label (see that winery's entry earlier in this chapter), the winery makes up to 2,500 cases of Pinot Noir from all over the West Coast as well as limited amounts of Pinot Gris, Riesling, and a Blanc de Blancs Sparkling Wine. Mirassou's son Steven is also part of the venture and represents yet another generation of Mirassous in the wine business, albeit no longer at the old family stand in San Jose, which now belongs to the Gallo empire.

Early results on the winery's Pinot Noirs have been highly encouraging, with several bottlings scoring into the 90-point range and marking La Rochelle as yet another important entrant in the burgeoning ranks of Pinot Noir producers.

STONY RIDGE WINERY 1975		Map 18
www.stonyridgewinery.com	925-449-0458	Tasting
Livermore	Alameda County	Livermore Valley AVA

This small winery has gone through several ownership changes but has recently grown due to its acquisition by Rick Corbett and now includes 180 acres of planted vineyards on site. In addition to its principal line of Chardonnay, Pinot Grigio, Cabernet Sauvignon, Merlot, Syrah, and Zinfandel, Stony Ranch makes several unusual Italian varietals, including an Orobianco blend, Ororosso, several dessert wines, and a sparkler. Production reaches 4,500 cases, of which the Stony Ridge label represents two-thirds. A second label, Crooked Vine, is gradually increasing production of estate-grown wines and will eventually reach 50 percent of overall production. A restaurant named Trio is open occasionally for lunch, dinners, and special events.

TESTAROSSA VINEYARDS 1993		Map 18
www.testarossa.com	408-354-6150	Tasting
Los Gatos	Santa Clara County	Santa Clara Valley AVA

Rob and Diana Jensen—more Silicon Valley refugees—built a modern winery while retaining the character and three-floor gravity-flow design of the 1888 Novitiate winery in downtown Los Gatos. With winemaker

Bill Brosseau, who also manages the family estate of the same name in the Chalone AVA, Testarossa makes several cuvée blends, the Palazzio Pinot Noir, Castello Chardonnay, and Subasio Syrah. More limited are vineyard-designated wines from grapes grown in the Santa Cruz Mountains (Schultze Vineyard), Santa Lucia Highlands (Rosella's, Garys', and Pisoni), the Russian River Valley (Graham and Fritschen), and the Sonoma Coast (La Cruz). Fifteen thousand cases are produced in total, of which 60 percent is Pinot Noir, 25 percent Chardonnay, and 15 percent Syrah.

Testarossa is one of the most successful wineries in California, and although prices range from $30 and up, the continuing and consistently high quality levels of Testarossa wines have placed the winery among a top handful of California producers. It is not unusual for most of the winery's offerings to reach the 90-point level, and the best performers make the list of top wines for the vintage year in and year out. The winery specializes in wines of high concentration and solid balancing acidity, all layered with enriching oak. Yet size is not the driving force for Testarossa, and its wines are deep, tasty and fairly mannerly as well.

THOMAS FOGARTY WINERY 1981		Map 18
www.fogartywinery.com	650-851-6777	Tasting
Woodside	San Mateo County	Santa Cruz Mountains AVA

Physician Thomas Fogarty teaches and practices cardiac surgery at the Stanford Hospital as well as invents medical devices such as the cardiac balloon catheter. Winemaking was first a hobby for Fogarty, but after planting the first grapes on his Woodside land in 1978, the commercial winery began three years later. Now 25 acres of the 325-acre estate are planted in vines, and the top varieties are the Estate bottlings. Totaling fifteen thousand cases, Fogarty focuses on Chardonnay, Pinot Noir, Merlot, and Sangiovese, with Sparkling Wine to boot. Winemaker Michael Martella, who has supervised the growing and winemaking at Fogarty since the earliest days, has his own eponymous label and makes 1,600 cases at the same facility, principally of vineyard-designated Syrahs and Zinfandels made from grapes grown elsewhere in the Santa Cruz Mountains and Mendocino, Fiddletown in the Sierra Foothills, and Lodi. The Fogarty Winery, with its expansive views over the sloping vineyards and out to San Francisco Bay, is a great spot for weddings and other parties. Wine quality has been somewhat variable over the years, with the best bottlings reaching up into the 90-point area. The wines get a little ahead of themselves in ripeness at times.

WENTE VINEYARDS 1883		Map 18
www.wentevineyards.com	925-456-2300	Tasting
Livermore	Alameda County	Livermore Valley AVA

Now run by fourth- and fifth-generation family members, Wente bills itself as "California's Oldest Continuously Family Owned and Operated Winery," and with good reason. Carl Wente came to California from Germany in 1880. After working briefly for Charles Krug, Wente bought the twenty-five-acre Bernard Vineyard in Livermore in 1883. By the turn of the twentieth century, he was making large quantities of bulk wine. After Repeal, his sons Ernest and Herman became leaders of the fledgling California wine industry. In 1936, Wente made the first modern California Chardonnay from Sauternes grapes. By the mid-1970s, the family was producing a wide range of table wines from grapes grown on their eight-hundred-acre Livermore vineyards and three hundred acres in Monterey County. In 1981, Wente bought the old Cresta Blanca winery and made it the Sparkling Wine facility and visitors center. By the 1990s, Wente was leading the Chardonnay charge; 50 percent of its production was of this varietal. Also in the 1990s, Wente became a significant exporter of California wines. Today's production is well over four hundred thousand cases in total, of which the estate bottlings of a wide range of wines represent fully 90 percent. In addition, Wente's Small Lot and The Nth Degree lines are available only to wine club members and on site. Wente has created a substantial second business with its restaurant, golf course, conference center, and summer concert series. An early dinner under the trees followed by an open air concert is a delight that the authors have enjoyed and can recommend with enthusiasm.

The typical Wente wine in the regular bottling line of offerings is light and balanced with an eye toward easy drinkability. The wines may not win the plaudits of highfalutin reviewers, but they are immensely popular and easy on the pocketbook.

Monterey and San Benito Counties

It was not so long ago, certainly within what we now think of as the present day for the wine industry, that these side-by-side counties would be mentioned in one breath—and, more often than not, that breath might well put San Benito first among them. That was in the days when coastal vineyards were transitioning to cool-weather sites and grapes, and jug wine production was leaving Sonoma and Napa for less expensive and far more fertile lands in California's Central Valley. The great expansion of wine interest and the resulting planting boom of the 1970s changed the landscape for good, and with it, Monterey blossomed as a home for massive new plantings, while San Benito County began a slow but inexorable slide into the vinous backwaters where, for the most part, it languishes today. The grapes from both counties also fall within the overall framework of the Central Coast AVA.

MONTEREY COUNTY

There was viticulture in Monterey County before the 1970s wine boom. Just ask the Mirassous, whose interesting whites and too frequently vegetal reds were seen in the years leading up to the great planting explosion nearly four decades ago. But even as late as 1968, there were barely more than a thousand acres planted to grapes, and the leading variety was French Colombard. Cabernet Sauvignon totaled ninety-two acres and Chardonnay just sixty acres.

And then came the early 1970s. In the three-year span of 1972 to 1974, over twenty-five thousand acres of grapes were planted from one end of the Salinas Valley to the other; by 1978, Monterey County's wine plantings had grown from a mere blip on the annual acreage report to the runaway leader among the cooler coastal counties. Only a few inland counties in the hot Central Valley exceeded Monterey's acreage, and their produce was more often than not directed to jug wines. Things have slowed a bit for Monterey since then, but total plantings still reach the 42,300-acre mark.

The reasons that Monterey blew past places like Napa and Sonoma were clear enough. The demand for varietal wines with good pedigrees began to grow like wildfire, and Monterey offered a cool climate, ten of thousands of relatively flat, easily plantable acres already in agricultural use with roads and water in place, and prices that seemed like relative bargains in comparison to the established places north of San Francisco. It is in the boom-and-bust nature of agriculture, however, that not all plantings work out, and as the investors in those newly minted vines soon found out, Monterey County was not necessarily the best place for red grapes. That fact was especially true for vines planted in the deepest, most fertile soils, whose locations not only produced excessive vine vigor at the expense of ripe grapes but whose overall coolness was simply not suited to grapes like Cabernet Sauvignon, Merlot, and Zinfandel. While Cabernet and Merlot both can have an herbal adjunct to their personalities, they simply are unappetizing when they carry full-blooded flavors of lettuce, spinach, zucchini, and broccoli. Today, total Cabernet acreage has been cut by a third overall, and most of today's Cabernet plantings are centered in the very warm, southern end of the county where the ocean's cooling breezes infrequently penetrate.

The most advantageous sites in Monterey County are found in the hills on either side of the Salinas Valley. A few hundred acres of grapes grew in wonderfully picturesque sites on rolling hillsides at the eastern end of the Carmel Valley. On the other side of the Santa Lucia mountains, facing the valley floor, is the Santa Lucia Highlands AVA, and it is now responsible for the greatest number of very successful Monterey County wines. Across the valley is the Chalone AVA, made famous by the Chalone winery, whose incredible success in the early 1970s made it into one of the very first California collectibles.

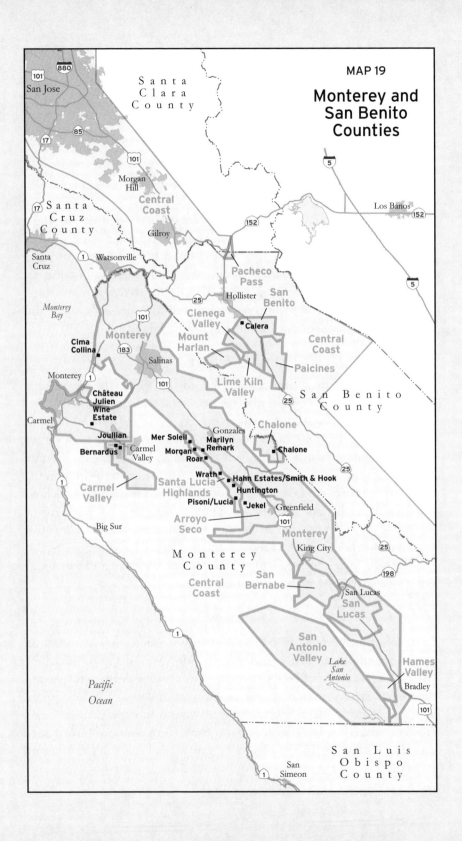

MAP 19

Monterey and San Benito Counties

Santa Clara County

San Jose

San Jose

Morgan Hill

Central Coast

Santa Cruz County

Gilroy

Santa Cruz

Watsonville

Monterey Bay

Pacheco Pass

Hollister

San Benito

Cienega Valley

Calera

Central Coast

Cima Collina

Monterey

Mount Harlan

Paicines

183

Salinas

Lime Kiln Valley

San Benito County

Monterey

Château Julien Wine Estate

Carmel

Chalone

Joullian

Mer Soleil

Gonzales

Chalone

Bernardus

Carmel Valley

Morgan

Marilyn Remark

Chalone

Roar

Carmel Valley

Santa Lucia Highlands

Wrath

Hahn Estates/Smith & Hook

Huntington

Pisoni/Lucia

Jekel

Greenfield

Big Sur

Arroyo Seco

Monterey

Monterey County

King City

Central Coast

San Bernabe

San Lucas

San Lucas

Pacific Ocean

San Antonio Valley

Lake San Antonio

Hames Valley

Bradley

San Simeon

San Luis Obispo County

Today's acreage is led by Chardonnay (16,400), Pinot Noir (8,000), Merlot (4,900), and Cabernet Sauvignon (3,600). Riesling has staged a small comeback in Monterey County, and the 2,200 planted acres there now comprise more than 60 percent of the California total. In the last few years, both Merlot and Cabernet Sauvignon have lost ground.

See Monterey County Vintners & Growers Association: www.montereywines.org.

Arroyo Seco

Sitting at the base of the hill line west of Soledad and Greenfield and abutting the more well-known Santa Lucia Highlands, this growing area has produced interesting Rieslings and Chardonnays but has never won great critical acclaim. Wente, Jekel, Ventana, and J. Lohr are the best-known wineries, using Arroyo Seco grapes as significant players in their lines. Kendall-Jackson also owns a major plot of land that runs right up to and shares some characteristics with the Santa Lucia Highlands.

Carmel Valley

Better known for its luxury resorts than for its wines, the picturesque Carmel Valley boasts a couple of decently known wineries in Joullian and Bernardus and a handful of smaller concerns. The valley itself starts at the oceanfront just south of Carmel town, itself one of California's most handsome and frequently visited, and twists inland following the Carmel River. The vines are up-valley, and most of them are up in the hills on the ocean side of the Santa Lucia Highlands. Aside from small estate-oriented wineries like Heller and Galante, the wineries here look to grapes grown inland for the better part of their output. Overall, there are fewer than five hundred acres under vine and about a dozen wineries. Cabernet Sauvignon produces the most notable Carmel Valley wines, with the occasional success also enjoyed by Sauvignon Blanc.

Chalone

Long before there was a Chalone AVA, there was a Chalone winery located on the limestone-laced hills east of Soledad. Some of California's best Chardonnays and Pinot Noirs were grown there some thirty to forty years ago, albeit in tiny amounts. And long before there was Chalone, there were grapes grown there. Today, the winery is greatly expanded and other growers have come in as well, but success has not always followed success. The Chalone AVA remains well regarded, and it is still the home of

Chardonnay and Pinot Noir for the Chalone winery; for Brosseau and Michaud also located there; and for Testarossa, Loring, and others who source small lots of fruit there. Chalone is often thought to be a cool area, but some summers can be dry and fiercely hot, perhaps accounting for the success recently shown by Syrah grown in the AVA.

Hames Valley

Located at the hot southern end of Monterey County as it abuts the Paso Robles area of San Luis Obispo County, the Hames Valley is home to one winery and thousands of acres of grapes. Other than the Hames Valley Winery, no one has regularly used the Hames Valley appellation on a label despite the fact that the region was granted AVA status almost fifteen years ago. There is a theory that medium-warmth red varieties like the area, but there is no proof yet that the Hames Valley can produce wines that rise above average in quality.

Monterey

For reasons that continue to escape most wine drinkers, there exist in this world AVAs like this one that bear the name of the county in which they are located and encompass virtually every grape grown there. Thus, while little-known AVAs like Hames Valley and San Antonio Valley are excluded, the rest of the county's acreage, over forty thousand, is contained in this almost all-inclusive appellation.

San Antonio Valley

In a hot, dry area west and north of the Hames Valley tucked in between hills on either side, the San Antonio AVA is home to fewer than a thousand acres of vines. Despite the presence of some ten wineries, the San Antonio Valley AVA is as yet unrecognizable to most wine drinkers. Its climate is more suited to reds than whites, but time is needed to know whether this newly minted AVA (2006) will ever receive more than passing recognition.

San Bernabe

Sprawling over twenty square miles of hills and valley, and encompassing everything from very cool, low-lying sites to heated-up hillsides, the San Bernabe AVA is made up of the five-thousand-acre San Bernabe Vineyard belonging to the Indelicato Family, whose far-flung winery operations stretch from the Central Valley to Napa to Monterey. This vineyard is said to be the world's single largest vineyard site. Most of its grapes are sold to a long roster of producers in all parts of California, and while little of the wine bears either AVA or vineyard designation, San Bernabe is an important player in the overall scheme of things. Chardonnay, Merlot, and Syrah lead the list of twenty-one separate varieties planted there, each with something close to five hundred acres.

San Lucas

Yet another limited-visibility, hot-weather appellation at the southern end of Monterey County, San Lucas is also more oriented to full-bodied reds than to whites. About eight thousand acres of vines are located within the AVA, but the Lockwood winery is the only significant local producer. A number of North Coast interests own parcels within the San Lucas AVA, but none use the name on their labels. Most wines from the area appear under broader appellations and are moderately priced.

Santa Lucia Highlands

Despite its relatively recent emergence as a home for significant quantities of grapes, the Santa Lucia Highlands AVA must now be considered the leading appellation in Monterey County and one of the noteworthy places for high-quality Pinot Noir, Chardonnay, and Syrah in California. Pioneering efforts in the area extend back almost three decades, led by Talbott Vineyards and followed by Mer Soleil, belonging to Napa Valley's Caymus Vineyards.

This long, hillside appellation extends more than ten miles along the western edge of the Salinas Valley outside Greenfield and Soledad and enjoys mostly eastern and southeastern exposures for its vineyards at elevations of four hundred to two thousand feet. Morgan's Double L Vineyard joins Talbott and Mer Soleil at the cooler, northern end of the appellation, while important sites like Rosella's Vineyard, Garys' Vineyard, and Pisoni Vineyards stretch increasingly farther to the south and have somewhat warmer and less windy situations. The star-studded roster of highly regarded producers drawing fruit from the area includes Testarossa, Siduri, Miner, Miura, Novy, Roar, August West, Lucia, David Bruce, and Loring—to name just the most obvious. The area's approximately five thousand acres of grapes are devoted primarily to Pinot Noir and Chardonnay, with Syrah now rising as the third important variety.

See Wine Artisans of Santa Lucia Highlands: www.santaluciahighlands.com.

It is an unmistakable fact that San Benito County has become increasingly less relevant to the course of the California wine industry. It matters not that it once was the production home of Almaden Vineyards in the days when that winery was an important player both in producing jug wine and in offering the world a wide array of inexpensive cork-finished bottlings. Today, San Benito has half the acreage of thirty years ago; and, despite the fact that it boasts six separately identified AVAs, it has only one winery of note, Calera. It does have high hopes, however, because a couple of moneyed players in the industry have established beachheads there, and vineyard acreage, once as low as one thousand acres as little as a decade ago, has begun to creep upward.

San Benito's inland location makes it dry and quite warm and gives it a short growing season relative to more coastal locations. It lacks the plantable acreage to be a major factor today in jug wine production, and it lacks vineyard settings and conditions needed to produce an array of world-class wines. Its 2,600 acres of grapes is headed by Chardonnay at nearly 900 acres and recently planted Pinot Noir that has pushed that grape over 500 acres. Cabernet Sauvignon and Merlot make up the greater portion of the rest.

See San Benito County Winegrowers' Association: www.sbcwinegrowers.org.

Cienega Valley

The former home of Almaden, the Cienega Valley is now limited to two wineries, DeRose and Pietra Santa. Neither has distinguished itself as yet, but both are trying, and while there is much to be seen as these efforts go forward, it would seem so far that full-bodied reds may show better than anything else. Pietra Santa, long in the olive oil business, is highly regarded for that product.

Lime Kiln

This small corner of the Cienaga Valley is limited to one winery, Enz, and a handful of grapes, of which Zinfandel has been the most prominent.

Mount Harlan

Yet another one-winery AVA, Mount Harlan is nonetheless world famous because its one winery is Calera, and Calera's Pinot Noirs, coming from four separate patches high on the mountain, have been fabulously successful and incredibly age-worthy. Small amounts of Viognier and Chardonnay also subsist on the stressed soils of Mount Harlan. While it lies on the other side of the hill from the Chalone AVA, it shares that area's predisposition to limestone soils as well as its fondness for Pinot Noir.

Pacheco Pass

One might think that decent wine can come from this area where Highway 152 passes through a draw and links the cooler Santa Clara Valley with the Central Coast, but the truth is that we really do not have proof enough to make a definitive conclusion. Of course, the pass itself is in Santa Clara County, and the AVA, though drawing its name from the pass, lies in San Benito County.

Paicines

Warm and welcoming, the Paicines AVA is trying hard to find a path to glory, but it is in the nature of the California wine industry that good intentions rarely overcome Mother Nature, and the rolling hills and acres of both red and white grapes are struggling to find their full voice. The Donati Family winery and the Vista Verde Vineyard are the area's leading landmarks, although visitors will also enjoy the Paicines General Store, the center of activity in this farming community of some two hundred residents.

San Benito

Like every other California AVA that takes a county name for its own, this title covers almost all the grapes grown in its named county. Those on Mount Harlan, the highest quality grown in San Benito County, are excluded.

Central Coast

The entirety of both Monterey and San Benito counties is included in this catchall AVA that stretches from Contra Costa County in the north to Santa Barbara County in the south.

BERNARDUS VINEYARDS 1992		Map 19
www.bernardus.com	800-223-2533	Tasting
Carmel Valley	Monterey County	Carmel Valley AVA

Dutchman Bernardus (Ben) Pon drove race cars for Porsche, represented Holland in skeet shooting in the 1972 Olympics, and ran the family wine distributorship before buying land and building a winery in the southern end of the Carmel Valley with 220 total acres and 50 planted to Bordeaux varietals on two estate vineyards, Marinus and Featherbow Ranch. Estate selections include Cabernet Sauvignon, Merlot, and the Marinus blend; vineyard-designated wines from other top vineyards include Pinot Noir from Bien Nacido in Santa Ynez and from Rosella's in the Santa Lucia Highlands, and Sauvignon Blanc from the Griva Vineyard in Arroyo Seco. Total production stands at over fifty thousand cases, of which 50 percent is Chardonnay and another 30 percent is Sauvignon Blanc. Ben has recently built the tony Bernardus Lodge, restaurant, and obligatory spa, also in Carmel Valley.

The Sauvignon Blanc has led the way in ratings, with most vintages in our recommended range above 86 points; the regular bottling is a bright, fresh zesty wine that is very often a Good Value, and the special-bottling Sauvignon Blanc labeled as Griva reaches into the low 90s in many vintages. We have liked both bottlings of Pinot Noir second best among Bernadus offerings, with scores ranging up to 90 points, while Chardonnay has been less consistent until the most recent vintages that have rung up commendable 87-point ratings. So far, the Merv Griffin (yes, *that* Merv Griffin) Sauvignon Blanc has not impressed.

CALERA WINE COMPANY 1975		Map 19
www.calerawine.com	831-637-9170	Tasting
Hollister	San Benito County	Mount Harlan AVA

After Yale and Oxford, Josh Jensen was instructed by his Burgundian winemaker mentor that limestone-rich soils were essential to making great Pinot Noir and Chardonnay. In 1974, he found a site on Mount Harlan in the Gabilan range of western San Benito County with such limestone soils as well as a disused lime kiln (a *calera* in Spanish; it's pictured on the label) dating from the nineteenth century. The 2,200-foot elevation Calera is the only producing vineyard in the Mount Harlan AVA. In 1975, Jensen planted twenty-four acres of Pinot Noir grapes in three separate vineyards: Selleck, Reed, and Jensen, producing his first wine in '78. Several years later what is thought to be the first Viognier planted in California took root. Eventually Jensen added another two Pinot vineyards, Mills and Ryan, and others nearby to bring total planted acreage on Mount Harlan to seventy-five. While Calera sells no grapes to others, it does buy Chardonnay grapes from the Central Coast for its midpriced version of the varietal. Total production is over thirty thousand cases, with Pinot Noir leading the way with 55 percent of the volume. The thorough Web site is well worth a browse.

Wine quality at Calera has been above average to brilliant in best years, but the harsh, dry site does not always allow the winemaker's hand to shine through. At their best, the various Pinot Noirs, all made in a refined, firm style that ages exceptionally well, have reached beyond 90 points and have made Calera into one of the California's early Pinot successes. Calera's Viognier also has excelled at times, achieving scores as high as 90 points, and is among those responsible for creating the high level of interest now shown in this once almost obscure grape. All Calera wines are ripe and full of balancing acidity.

CHALONE VINEYARD 1960		Map 19
www.chalonevineyard.com	831-678-1717	Tasting by Appointment
Soledad	Monterey County	Chalone AVA

Just east of Soledad in the rugged Gabilan Range, at 1,800 feet, Chalone Vineyards bumps up against the dramatic Pinnacles National Monument. The first vines were planted as far back as 1919; in 1946, the vineyard expanded and sold grapes to Wente and Beaulieu. The Chalone label was established in 1960, and Dick Graff came along four years later to make top-drawer Burgundian-styled Chardonnay. His '66 vintage became a landmark in the history of California Chardonnay. The largest vineyards in the Chalone AVA, the holdings total one thousand acres, of which three hundred are planted. The winery's focus remains on Chardonnay and Pinot Noir, with excursions into Pinot Blanc, Chenin Blanc, and Syrah. All wine is grown and bottled on site. Chalone was purchased in 2005 by the international drinks business Diageo (brands range from Tanqueray to Guinness to Beaulieu to Sterling).

Three decades ago, when the California wine boom was still in its infancy, Chalone Pinot Noir and Chardonnay were among the best and scarcest wines made in the state. The Pinots, excellent for their layered complexity, also demonstrated great longevity in the bottle. Even today, with Chalone having become a total corporate entity complete with a range of inexpensive bottlings not grown in its fabled limestone soils, the mystique of the Chalone name remains. However, where once Chardonnay and Pinot Noir both earned 90- to 98-point scores on a regular basis, now it is the rare Chalone wine that graces the upper rating levels, landing instead in the 85 to 88 range, and it is as likely to be its limited-production Syrah rather than Chardonnay or Pinot that leads the hit parade.

CHÂTEAU JULIEN WINE ESTATE 1982		Map 19
www.chateaujulien.com	831-624-2600	Tasting
Carmel	Monterey County	Carmel Valley AVA

Founded by Bob and Patty Brower and winemaker Bill Anderson, first releases were the 1982 Merlot and Chardonnay. The winery is styled and named after the châteaux of the St. Julien district of Bordeaux. Located five miles into the Carmel Valley, the estate includes a 5-acre vineyard, supplemented in '96 with a 246-acre vineyard in the Lockwood Valley in southern Monterey County. All wines use the winery's own grapes; depending on the harvest, some grapes may be sold to other bottlers. Production of the Château Julien Private Reserve, Estate, and Barrel Select labels totals forty-five thousand cases, 65 percent of which is Merlot, with the balance Cabernet Sauvignon and Chardonnay. Second labels are Emerald Bay and Garland Ranch, with another fifty thousand total cases annually.

Quality has rarely risen about average, and very little "collectible cachet" attaches to the winery name.

CIMA COLLINA 2004		Map 19
www.cimacollina.com	831-384-7806	Tasting by Appointment
Marina	Monterey County	Monterey AVA

In 2004, Richard Lumpkin established this small winery using grapes from a variety of vineyards in the county. With winemaker Annette Hoff, fresh from apprenticeships in Monterey and New Zealand, Cima Collina ("hilltop" in Italian) has quickly established a reputation for top Pinot Noir, Chardonnay, and Bordeaux-style blends. Its own Hilltop Ranch Vineyard in Carmel Valley, of only three acres, and somewhat larger Monterey vineyards of others, including Chula Vina (on the northeastern side of the Salinas Valley in the foothills of the Gabilan Mountains) and Newell (in the San Antonio Valley of southern Monterey County), produce the grapes for its wines. Production approaches five thousand cases, fairly evenly distributed among Pinot Noir, Chardonnay, and Bordeaux blends.

Early vintages from Cima Collina have focused on Pinot Noir and Chardonnay, with good to excellent results that have seen both varieties scoring in the 90-point and higher range at times. Clearly, the promise here is very high for wines that, at their best, possess both depth and structural firmness.

HAHN ESTATES/SMITH & HOOK 1979   Map 19

www.hahnestates.com   831-678-2132   Tasting

Soledad   Monterey County   Santa Lucia Highlands AVA

The Nicolaus Hahn family—Nicolaus was at the time a Swiss businessman living in London—bought the Smith & Hook winery in the southern end of the Santa Lucia Highlands in 1980. Smith's land had originally been a horse ranch, and Hook had raised cattle—each for generations. Optimal growing conditions encouraged conversion to vineyards, and the first Smith & Hook Cabernet Sauvignon was released in '79. In 1991, the Hahns created Hahn Estates as a label for moderately priced varietals while reserving Smith & Hook for their smaller-production estate wine, the Grand Reserve Cabernet. The vineyards now run to more than one thousand acres in both the Santa Lucia Highlands and Arroyo Seco AVAs, and grapes are also bought from other Monterey vineyards. Production of Hahn Estates wines stands at 180,000 cases, with Smith & Hook another 8,000. Their mass-distribution label, Cycles Gladiator, of the Central Coast, runs to another 400,000 cases annually.

In the last couple of years, the Hahn Estates bottlings, almost across the board, have earned scores in the mid- to upper 80s and have been recommended as Good Values. The lower-priced Cycles Gladiator wines have been less consistent, but we have liked Syrah, and we applaud the handsome packaging that gives the line a distinct upscale feel. A new line of midpriced wines labeled Hahn SLH has been very successful within its price niche, often earning Good Value status for wines that rate at 90 points and higher. The wines are fairly full-bodied but not bold, yet they have depth and richness. If future vintages uphold both price and quality, this new venture will earn a big following.

HUNTINGTON WINE CELLARS 1989   Map 19

www.huntingtonwine.com   707-433-5215   Tasting

Soledad   Monterey County   Santa Lucia Highlands AVA

Huntington makes a range of moderately priced wines, including Merlot, Cabernet Sauvignon, Petite Sirah, Chardonnay, and Sauvignon Blanc, from grapes from growers in Sonoma and Monterey counties. Founder and partner William Leigon and tandem winemakers Barry Gnekow (for the reds) and Kerry Damskey (the whites) make a total of some twenty-five thousand cases annually. Huntington is now owned by Hahn Family Wines, owners of, among others, the Hahn Estates and Smith & Hook labels from Monterey County. The wines are produced at the Hahn facility in Soledad.

A move to upscale wines, with an impressive new package, has so far not seen results rise accordingly, but with a first-class winemaking team in tow, there is reason to expect better things in the future.

JEKEL VINEYARDS 1972		Map 19
www.jekel.com	831-674-5522	No Tasting
Greenfield	Monterey County	Arroyo Seco AVA

Monterey County pioneering winery Jekel was founded by twins Bill and Gus Jekel when they planted vineyards near Greenfield in 1972. Now run by Bill and his wife Pat, and owned since 1992 by drinks conglomerate Brown-Forman (Jack Daniels, Korbel, and many others), Jekel released its first vintage in 1978, prehistoric time for the Monterey wine industry. The Riesling, Chardonnay, Pinot Noir, and Bordeaux blends remain consistently strong and modestly priced. The Arroyo Seco Sanctuary Red stands out as a limited-edition blend of Merlot and Cabernet Sauvignon. The Gravelstone and Sanctuary Estate vineyards total 325 acres and account for about half the grapes used by Jekel to produce over 100,000 cases annually, of which their signature Rieslings represent fully 40 percent.

It is not surprising that wonderfully fruity, perfectly balanced off-dry Riesling, a variety that struggles at times for popularity, has been a good seller for Jekel as it seems always to rate in the upper to mid-80s and to earn full recommendation. Everything else in the winery line, save for the occasionally successful bottling of Sanctuary Red, has been scoring in the 84- to 86-point range.

JOULLIAN VINEYARDS 1982		Map 19
www.joullian.com	866-659-8100	Tasting
Carmel Valley	Monterey County	Carmel Valley AVA

In 1982, the Joullian and Sias families of Oklahoma bought 655 acres at 1,400 feet high in the Carmel Valley, on which they planted 40 acres to Bordeaux varietals. The leading varieties were and remain Chardonnay, Sauvignon

Blanc, Cabernet Sauvignon, and Zinfandel. Under the tutelage of winemaker Ridge Watson (brother of golfer Tom Watson), Joullian expanded, built a new winery in the early 1990s, and added a second label, Cepage, for small-batch wines. Production approaches ten thousand cases, of which Chardonnay and Cabernet Sauvignon comprise 75 percent of the total.

Both Chardonnay and Sauvignon Blanc have earned commendation in more vintages than not, with some Chardonnay bottlings scoring up to 89 points. The reds have been less successful, and the Sias Cuvée Zinfandel has never impressed us in our tastings.

LUCIA VINEYARDS 1979		Map 19
www.luciavineyards.com	800-946-3130	No Tasting
Santa Rosa (winery site)	Sonoma County	Santa Lucia Highlands AVA

In 1979, Eddie and Jane Pisoni purchased land in the Santa Lucia Highlands that would become Pisoni Vineyards (see that entry). The Pisoni label is used for wines that are from the family's own vineyard. Other wines made from nearby patches, including the now-famous Garys' Vineyard (for Gary Pisoni and Gary Franscioni), appear under the Lucia Vineyards label. Their son, the effervescent Gary Pisoni, ostensibly oversees all growing and winemaking, but with Lucia and Pisoni wines both made in Santa Rosa, it is Gary's winemaking son Jeff Pisoni who is the person in charge of daily operations, while Gary's other son Mark manages the Pisoni Vineyard as well as the jointly owned Garys' Vineyard. Lucia—the label is named for the region—makes small batches of vineyard-designated Syrah, Chardonnay, and Rosé, from Pisoni, Garys', and Susan's Hill vineyards' grapes. Production of Lucia wines exceeds three thousand cases. Lately, moniker variants such as Lucy for Rosé and Luli for Chardonnay have appeared.

Wine quality varies rather more widely than one might expect given the cachet attached to the Pisoni name these days (based on the success that several wineries have had with Pisoni Vineyard Pinot Noir) and can range from the mid-80s to the mid-90s for the always-rich, lush home-grown Pinot.

MARILYN REMARK WINERY 2004		Map 19
www.remarkwines.com	831-455-9310	Tasting
Salinas	Monterey County	Santa Lucia Highlands

Marilyn Remark and Joel Burnstein settled in the Santa Lucia Highlands after Joel moved on from a career on the Pacific Stock Exchange. Earning his winemaking spurs at Jekel and San Saba, Joel joined with social worker Marilyn to build the winery. Enamored of French Rhône-style wines, they now produce two thousand cases annually of Rhône varietals from notable Monterey vineyards including Marsanne (from Loma Pacific vineyard), Roussanne (Lockwood Valley), Rose de Saignée, Grenache (Wild Horse Road), Syrah (Arroyo Loma), and Petite Sirah (from Road's End Vineyard).

The reds tend to be very full and tannic in style and have at times seen big success, but the overall record is spotty at best.

MER SOLEIL WINERY 1988		Map 19
www.mersoleilvineyard.com	831-675-7919	No tasting
Gonzales	Monterey County	Santa Lucia Highlands AVA

Charlie Wagner II, whose grandfather established Caymus Vineyards in the Napa Valley, oversees the production of Mer Soleil wines at the facility in the more northerly of the Mer Soleil vineyards in the Santa Lucia Highlands. The winery was originally established by the senior Wagner and his son, Chuck (father of Charlie II), for the production of Chardonnay. Now, with two vineyards totaling 320 acres and located at opposite ends of the Santa Lucia Highlands AVA, the Wagner clan has expanded its Monterey operations to produce not only Chardonnays but also Viognier and a late-harvest Viognier named, appropriately, Late.

Chardonnay, still the dominant grape under Mer Soleil, is made in a very ripe and rich style with lots of oak seasoning. It can vary a bit in quality from year to year, but when all the pieces come together, Mer Soleil Chardonnay will rate in the lower to mid-90s and challenge for highest honors among California offerings.

MORGAN WINERY 1982		Map 19
www.morganwinery.com	831-751-7777	Tasting
Salinas	Monterey County	Santa Lucia Highlands AVA

After UC–Davis, Daniel Morgan Lee moved to Monterey County, where he learned to make wine at Jekel and Durney vineyards. With banker Donna Lee, they started their own winery on the side in 1982, while Daniel was still at Durney, and went full-time two years later with the construction of a winery. The Lees bought the Double L Ranch in the northern Santa Lucia Highlands in '96 and planted it to Pinot Noir, Chardonnay, and most recently an acre of Syrah. Now fifty-five acres strong, the certified-organic Double L Vineyard is supplemented by grapes from Garys' and Rosella's vineyards, renowned Monterey County growers, for several vineyard-designated vintages. Annual production of forty-five thousand cases is about 55 percent Chardonnay; 35 percent Pinot Noir; and the remainder Syrah, Pinot Gris, and Sauvignon Blanc.

Over the years, the winery has proven to be one of California's leading producers of both Pinot Noir and Chardonnay. Under Lee's guiding hand, Morgan has adopted a rich but balanced style of winemaking that steers clear of full-bore intensity and seeks a more refined finished product. His Rosella's Vineyard Pinot Noir has consistently scored in the mid-90s, and his other vineyard-designated bottlings have more often than not scored above 90 points as well. Lately, his Tierra Mar Syrah has also reached 90 points. We have been less enamored of his Sauvignon Blanc and an unoaked Chardonnay nicknamed Metallico that can range from the mid-80s when shrill and narrow to the upper 80s when its fruit is more accessible. Still, Dan Lee and Morgan are resident members of California's vinous pantheon.

PISONI VINEYARDS & WINERY 1982		Map 19
www.pisonivineyards.com	800-270-2525	No Tasting
Santa Rosa (winery site)	Sonoma County	Santa Lucia Highlands AVA

Gary Pisoni of the Pisoni family (see the entries for Lucia Vineyards and Roar Wines) planted five acres of Pinot Noir grapes in the southern end of Santa Lucia Highlands in 1982 on land purchased by his family, highly regarded Salinas Valley vegetable growers. Since then, Gary has also become renowned for his joint venture with Gary Franscioni (of Roar) that became Garys' Vineyard. Today the Pisoni Vineyards include forty-five acres of small blocks, each with slightly different soils and climates. Much of the vineyards' production is sold to other regional wineries and a dozen or more produce vineyard-designated wines. As for their own wine production, Pinot Noir is king, with the Pisoni Estate Pinot Noir leading the way.

Not surprisingly, the Pisoni Pinot Noir, under the winery's own label, has cult standing and sells out very quickly. It has rated above 90 points in most vintages but has often been exceeded in score by the wines from others' estate vineyards.

ROAR WINES 1996   Map 19

www.roarwines.com   831-675-1681   No Tasting

Soledad   Monterey County   Santa Lucia Highlands AVA

Gary and Rosella Franscioni were raised in Monterey, where their families farmed row crops for over a century. In 1996, they planted the fifty-acre Rosella's Vineyard to Pinot Noir; just over an acre is used for Roar wines, while most is sold to other vintners. There are similarly small blocks of vines grown for Roar in the Pisoni Vineyard nearby and in Garys' Vineyard, owned and managed by Gary Franscioni and Gary Pisoni. The Roar production—actually made at the Siduri winery in Sonoma County—consists of Pinots and two Syrahs. Availability is very limited.

Wine quality has varied widely. Most bottlings have been recommendable year in and year out, and the Pinots have hit scores above 90 points on occasion yet have dropped into the mid-80s as well. Syrah has not fared especially well as yet, but this producer has some of California's best vineyards in its arsenal and is likely to impress more often than not.

WRATH VINEYARDS 1981   Map 19

www.wrathwines.com   800-998-7222   Tasting

Soledad   Monterey County   Santa Lucia Highlands AVA

Retired Texas physician Mark Lemmon and wife Barbara planted sixty-eight acres west of Soledad and made their first wines, sold under the San Saba label, in 1981, with a new winery constructed in 2004. Substantial growth followed, and now the four-thousand-case San Saba label's production is almost evenly split among Chardonnay, Merlot, Sauvignon, and an up-and-coming Pinot Noir. A second, lower-priced label, Bocage, accounts for another seven thousand cases, 60 percent of which is Chardonnay and most of the remainder Merlot. Both labels contain only estate-grown fruit. The winery recently changed ownership, and its new wines are all bottled under the Wrath moniker.

With more wines rating in the low to mid-80s and only the occasional bottle making it as high as 87, San Saba was something of an underperformer. Still, the winery is located on prime grape-growing land, and the first Wrath wines look far more promising.

San Luis Obispo County

San Luis Obispo County has become home to almost every variety of grape grown in California—and for good reason. Its arrays of microclimates from very cool to very warm support varieties that are to be made into Sparkling Wine in locations that receive a fair degree of coastal influence and those that want a fair bit of heat, like Syrah and the other Rhône varieties and also Zinfandel. It is not a stretch to suggest that San Luis Obispo County presents the broadest array of climatic conditions of any major wine county. Somewhere between the extremes, the county also finds places for Cabernet Sauvignon, and that variety leads all other in plantings. The county's 30,300 acres of grapes place it seventh among all counties in California, and with 24,500 of those acres devoted to red wine varieties, it ranks fourth in red wine grape acreage. Cabernet Sauvignon (9,300), Merlot (4,100), and Chardonnay (3,100) are the acreage leaders; the county's 2,800 acres of Syrah place it tops in California with that variety.

See San Luis Obispo Vintners & Growers Association: www.slowine.com.

Arroyo Grande Valley

It might not feel like wine country when you are driving down Highway 101 south of the city of San Luis Obispo, but as you pass the exit to the picturesque town of Arroyo Grande, you are entering the AVA that bears its name. One could argue that the name ought to be applied only to the valley that starts at Arroyo Grande and twists east across agricultural lands and up into the foothills, but the grapes that one passes on Highway 101 are also included in the appellation and do bear a reasonable resemblance to fruit that is found in the valley proper. The Edna Valley AVA is immediately to the north, and it is not unknown for wineries in both valleys to source fruit from the other valley.

It is perhaps best to think of this AVA as having three distinct parts. The vines west of Arroyo Grande near the highway live in fog a good part of the year, and they are most useful as Sparkling Wine stock and as the source, from certain hillside patches, of very rich and fruity Pinot Noir in the hands of the Laetitia winery. Heading inland past Arroyo Grande, one is in a patchwork of low hills and agricultural plots. The vines are mostly dedicated to Pinot Noir and Chardonnay, and they produce some of California's finest wines. Talley is the major winery in the heart of the Arroyo Grande Valley, but other Central Coast wineries also get fruit from here. As one gets into the hills at the eastern end of the valley, the temperatures soar, and it is Zinfandel that sets the pace in this higher, warmer growing area.

Edna Valley

Grape growing in this north-south valley just inland from San Luis Obispo city started with emphasis on Chardonnay and Pinot Noir, and those two grapes remain the chief points of focus today. Of late, Syrah has been planted in hospitable microclimates, especially those at least partially hidden from the cooling fog and breezes blowing in from the nearby Pacific Ocean. Paragon Vineyards was the pioneer in the area, and its joint venture with Chalone resulting in Edna Valley Vineyards was the springboard on which further plantings were based. Also found here is Alban Vineyards, one of the early leaders in the Rhône wine movement in California.

Paso Robles

The rather broad reach of this AVA stretches from the coastal Santa Lucia Mountains eastward across the rolling plains of the inland valley that are protected for the most part from the coolest ocean breezes that barely penetrate along the western edge. Thus, this area is both dry and warm all the way to the larger chain of mountains that separate the coastal counties from the overheated Central Valley. The Paso Robles AVA practically has something to offer to everyone.

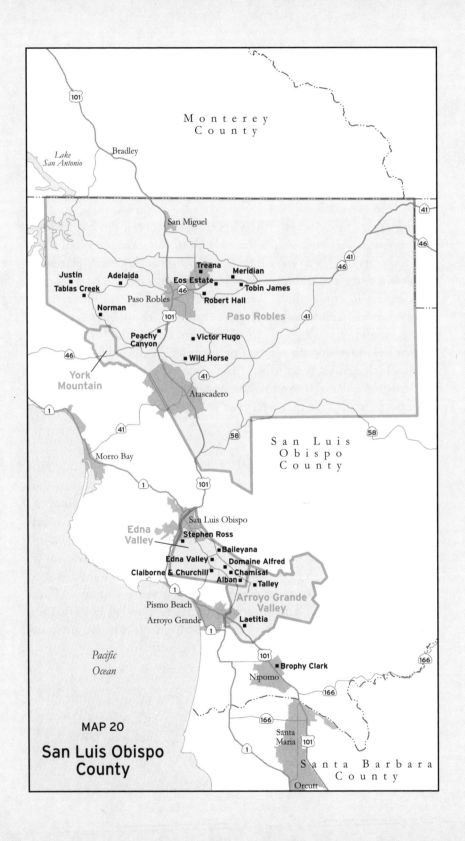

MAP 20

San Luis Obispo County

High in the hills near the coast, in limestone soils, Pinot Noir has been grown successfully for decades. But thinking about Paso Robles as anything other than a warm weather area is misleading. Far more acreage is devoted to Zinfandel, Syrah, and Cabernet Sauvignon than to cool-climate varieties. Of San Luis Obispo County's 30,300 acres of grapes, some 18,000 and counting are grown in the Paso Robles AVA. Excluding the extensive plantings of Chardonnay and Pinot Noir grown elsewhere in the county, it is Cabernet Sauvignon that turns out to be nearly half of all the acreage in the AVA.

To be sure, many noteworthy Cabernets do come from Paso Robles such as Justin, Adelaida, and Robert Hall, but the most successful wines over the years have been the Zinfandels and Syrahs. Almost 15 percent of all Syrah acreage in California stands in Paso Robles alone, and it tends to make big, rich, mouth-filling wines whose size and potency make them very popular. Zinfandel follows the same model, with wineries like Peachy Canyon leading the way, and most Cabernets are full and broad in character as well. Overripeness can be a problem with Paso Robles grapes, but with an increased focus on balance and livelier fruit and acidity, many of the big wines of Paso Robles have become better balanced and more useful as mealtime mates than they were even half a decade ago.

See Paso Robles Wine Country Alliance: www.pasowine.com.

York Mountain

Wine grapes have been grown in this AVA for more than 125 years, but it remains one of the smaller, least intense growing regions in California. Only a handful of vineyards totaling about fifty acres and less than a handful of wineries exist in this AVA, set on the eastern side of the mountains that separate the Pacific Ocean from the inner parts of the county. With vineyards set high in the hills at elevations of 1,175 to 1,900 feet, and because of the proximity to the ocean, this cool growing area favors Pinot Noir and Chardonnay. The history of the appellation has been tied up, part and parcel, with the history of the York Mountain Winery, and it was disappointing to see that winery close after 127 years.

ADELAIDA CELLARS 1981		Map 20
www.adelaida.com	800-676-1232	Tasting
Paso Robles	San Luis Obispo County	Paso Robles AVA

Founder John Munch brought experience from Estrella to his own winery and became partners in 1990 with the Van Steenwyk family. In 1994, they purchased the sixty-acre Hoffman Mountain Ranch in the limestone hill west of Paso Robles. Today, the HMR Estate Vineyard has thirty-two acres of Pinot Noir grapes planted; a second, the Viking Estate Vineyard, has an additional thirty-two acres of Cabernet Sauvignon in vine. Under the guidance of winemaker Terry Culton, Adelaida produces fifteen thousand cases of Cabernet Sauvignon, Chardonnay, Pinot Noir, Syrah, and smatterings of less well-known Rhône varieties under four labels: top-drawer Reserve and Adelaida, and more modestly priced and larger-volume SLO and Schoolhouse. All wines are made from estate-grown grapes or bought from other Paso Robles vineyards. The Adelaida Web site is very thorough and worth a read.

Adelaida wines are typically full-bodied and sturdy, and they can be a little bit brusque at times, but the best versions are age-worthy and earn up to 90 points in many vintages. Adelaida is one of our favorite stops in the Paso Robles area.

ALBAN VINEYARDS 1991		Map 20
www.albanvineyards.com	805-546-0305	No Tasting
Arroyo Grande	San Luis Obispo County	Edna Valley AVA

John Alban, an early Rhône Ranger, started his vineyard in 1989 as likely the first California vineyard and winery devoted solely to Rhône-style grapes, planting 50 acres to Viognier, Roussanne, and Syrah, with another 30 acres plantable on a 250-acre ranch. Alban built his winery in 1992 and now makes five thousand cases of these varieties. Access to Alban wines, particularly the estate Syrah Reva, is difficult at best, with a substantial portion sold through the mailing list.

Alban's early entry to the Rhône varietal sector has both inspired and instructed those who have followed. Although much Syrah grown in California has its origins in clones brought here from Australia, Alban has imported its Syrah and other Rhône varieties from France and has become a major supplier of plant material to the industry. The "Alban clone" is now a widely seen reference when wineries describe their Syrah plantings.

Alban wines, ripe-leading reds and whites that run from full-bodied to austere depending on the bottling, have often led the way in ratings for Rhône varieties, but there have also been the occasional clinker. On the whole, both Syrah and Viognier are considered among the very best, often scoring in the 90s.

BAILEYANA WINERY 1986		Map 20
www.baileyana.com	805-597-8200	Tasting
San Luis Obispo	San Luis Obispo County	Edna Valley AVA

Founded by Catherine Niven and now run by subsequent Niven generations, the vineyard began as 3+ acres planted on the family horse ranch, now known as Firepeak Vineyard and grown to 190 planted acres. It lies at the foot of Islay Mountain, the last of a chain of extinct volcanoes called the Seven Sisters. French winemaker Christian Roguenant brought experience as chief oenologist for Champagne Deutz and its successor, Laetitia, and helped design the Baileyana winery. There are two lines of wines: estate Chardonnay, Pinot Noir, Sauvignon Blanc, and Syrah; and the top-of-the-line Grand Firepeak offerings of Pinot Noir, Chardonnay, and Syrah. A second label, Tangent, makes modestly priced whites. Total production runs to twenty-five thousand cases, but the winery has an ultimate capacity of ten times that, allowing the current use of excess space to offer custom crush capability to other labels. Tasting is available in a restored 1909 one-room schoolhouse.

Quality has been mixed to date. The Firepeak Pinot Noir scores higher, occasionally into the 90-point range, and more consistently than most other wines offered. Baileyana wines reflect the mannerly sensibilities brought to their making by Frenchman Roguenant.

BROPHY CLARK CELLARS 1996		Map 20
www.brophyclarkcellars.com	805-929-4830	No Tasting
Nipomo	San Luis Obispo County	Santa Ynez Valley AVA

Winemaker John Clark and wife Kelley Brophy Clark founded the winery in 1996, focused on making small batches of vineyard-designated Pinot Noir, Sauvignon Blanc, Syrah, and Zinfandel from a select few nearby vineyards. Production is in the 2,500-case vicinity, with half devoted to Pinot Noir. Vineyard sources include Ashley's and Rodney's vineyards. Quality has been somewhat inconsistent, but the wines, made in a balanced style, can earn scores in the upper 80s. Most wines have come from Santa Barbara County sources and are made at the winery just north of the county line.

CHAMISAL VINEYARDS 1994   Map 20

  www.domainealfred.com   805-541-WINE   Tasting

  San Luis Obispo   San Luis Obispo County   Edna Valley AVA

The Chamisal Vineyard was the first planted in the Edna Valley, in 1972. Terry Speizer purchased and revived the dormant vineyard in 1994 when he planted Pinot Noir grapes on thirty acres and Chardonnay on another thirty. Under Speizer, the wines carried the Domaine Alfred moniker, debuting with the 1998 vintage. Eventually, the vineyards grew to over eighty planted acres, fairly evenly divided between Pinot Noir and Chardonnay. Production has reached eleven thousand cases, a third of which is Chamisal Vineyard Pinot Noir, and another quarter of which is estate Chardonnay. The remaining products are a Pinot Noir–Syrah–Grenache blend called DA Red, as well as very small lots of Syrah, Pinot Gris, and Grenache. Califa is the proprietary name attached to the reserve-level wines.

Quality has been high since the outset, with almost everything labeled Califa earning in the high-80- to mid-90-point range and those labeled only as Chamisal coming close behind. With consistent critical success has come a bit of price escalation, but Domaine Alfred wines remained competitively priced, and the less expensive bottlings delivered more for the money than their market niche peers in top vintages.

As of 2008, the winery passed into the ownership of the Crimson Wine Group, and the wines are now bottled with the Chamisal name as their prime identification. *Domaine Alfred* now appears in small letters to make sure that we do not forget, and for the moment, at least, the Web site address has not changed.

CLAIBORNE & CHURCHILL VINTNERS 1983   Map 20

  www.claibornechurchill.com   805-544-4066   Tasting

  San Luis Obispo   San Luis Obispo County   Edna Valley AVA

Claiborne Thompson and Fredericka Churchill gave up teaching at the University of Michigan (Clay taught Old Norse languages and literature, making him one of a very few winemakers with this particular résumé) for winemaking, focusing on Alsatian-styled varietals, particularly Gewürztraminer and Dry Riesling. These varieties represent two-thirds of the ten-thousand-case production, with the occasional Pinot Gris, Chardonnay, and Pinot Noir making up the balance. There have also been experiments with dessert wines—Muscat and Port—and a Sparkling Brut Rosé. Grapes are sourced from the Edna Valley and other Central Coast vineyards, and Monterey County.

Fans of old-fashioned, bone-dry, and bitingly crisp Gewürztraminer are now more likely to find it from this winery than they are in the recent crop of offerings from the grape's Alsatian homeland. Recent Rieslings have had light but evident residual sugar, but even then, the winery penchant for bracing acidity drove right on through.

DOMAINE ALFRED 1994		Map 20
www.domainealfred.com	805-541-WINE	Tasting
San Luis Obispo	San Luis Obispo County	Edna Valley AVA

With an ownership change in 2008, the Domaine Alfred name, so prominent in wine quality considerations for the past decade, has now morphed into Chamisal Vineyards (see that earlier entry).

EDNA VALLEY VINEYARD 1980		Map 20
www.ednavalleyvineyard.com	805-554-4585	Tasting
San Luis Obispo	San Luis Obispo County	Edna Valley AVA

The Niven family planted their Paragon Vineyard southeast of San Luis Obispo in the early 1970s, well before the creation of the AVA. In 1980, the Chalone Wine Group joined the family in a partnership and created Edna Valley Vineyard and Winery. In 2005, Diageo Chateau & Estate Wines (Beaulieu, Sterling, and others) purchased Chalone and Edna Valley. The 1,100-acre vineyard is planted to Chardonnay (63 percent of the grapes), Pinot Noir (18 percent), and Syrah (9 percent), with smaller blocks of Sauvignon Blanc and Pinot Gris grapes. Winemaker Mark Cave was brought to Edna Valley from Washington state wineries and now focuses on estate-grown Chardonnay, though the winery also makes Pinot Noir, Roussanne, Mourvèdre, and Viognier. Production is growing rapidly, reflecting the capital and marketing muscle of Diageo, and currently reaches beyond four hundred thousand cases annually. Chardonnay leads the way (at 70 percent or more of the total output), and significant volumes of Pinot Noir are also made.

One of the better bargains in the past, the wines have not maintained a high level of consistency of late and no longer register brightly on our radar screen. However, the last year has seen the release of Reserve label wines, and they are much more promising than the high-volume, price-conscious regular bottlings.

EOS ESTATE WINERY 1993		Map 20
www.eosvintage.com	805-239-2562	Tasting
Paso Robles	San Luis Obispo County	Paso Robles AVA

Winemaker Leslie Melendez's propensity to harvest estate grapes early in the day to keep them cool led to the name EOS, the goddess of dawn in Greek mythology. Built as a partnership led by the Arciero family, EOS produces a wide variety of wines from its seven hundred acres of grapes, including Petite Sirah, Zinfandel, Cabernet Sauvignon, and Chardonnay in both estate and reserve versions. The Cupa Grandis limited-reserve bottlings top the line. Financial problems became public in May, 2010. Total production approaches two hundred thousand cases.

The EOS and EOS Cupis Grandis wines tend toward fullness of body and outgoing personalities. Although quality has been somewhat inconsistent, the winery has also earned its share of scores in the mid- to upper 80s, with the occasional 90-plus effort showing up from time to time.

JUSTIN VINEYARDS & WINERY 1981		Map 20
www.justinwine.com	805-238-6932	Tasting
Paso Robles	San Luis Obispo County	Paso Robles AVA

Bankers Justin and Deborah Baldwin founded the west Paso Robles winery in 1981 and gradually planted 82 of their 160 acres in the remote Adelaide Valley to Cabernet Sauvignon (nearly 75 percent of the grapes), Cabernet Franc, and Merlot. Focusing on Bordeaux varietals, Justin has made estate and select single-vineyard wines from Laura's Vineyard, MacGillivray Vineyard, and Halter Ranch, among others, primarily in the Paso Robles AVA. Successful bottlings include Syrah, Zinfandel, Cabernet Sauvignon, and a well-received Meritage blend of Cabernet Sauvignon, Cabernet Franc, and Merlot called Isosceles. Up to fifty thousand cases are made each year in the new winery facility, nearly 50 percent of which is Cabernet Sauvignon. The family also operates a restaurant and a B&B, the JUST Inn.

At times, quality has been superlative, especially in Syrah, but at others, ripeness and toughness have run rampant. Still, this winery always makes a fine stab at producing stylish wines, and their popularity remains high.

When not running to excessive ripeness, the Cabernet Sauvignon and the Isosceles blend are rich, deep, and enormously satisfying.

LAETITIA VINEYARD & WINERY 1997		Map 20
www.laetitiawine.com	888-809-WINE	Tasting
Arroyo Grande	San Luis Obispo County	Arroyo Grande Valley AVA

Maison Deutz, the U.S. outpost of Champagne Deutz, was founded in 1982 and made Sparkling Wines using the *méthode champenoise* until 1997, when the winery and vineyards were purchased by French winemaker Jean-Claude Tardivat, who renamed the winery after his daughter. Moving the focus toward still varietals, the winery emphasized Burgundy-style wines including its Pinot Noir, Chardonnay, Pinot Gris, and Pinot Blanc, while still making several Sparkling Wines. With over 450 acres planted to Pinot Noir (three-quarters of all grapes) and the remainder principally Chardonnay and Pinot Blanc, most of the 20,000-case annual bottlings are from estate-grown grapes. Purchased in 1998 by financier Selim Zilkha and daughter Nadia, and overseen by winemaker—and Maison Deutz holdover—Eric Hickey, Laetitia is the parent of Barnwood, Santa Barbara County, and second label Avila.

Single-block bottlings of Pinot Noir labeled Les Galets and La Colline are superb in most vintages; with scores ranging into the mid-90s, these rich, deep, and impeccably polished wines are justifiably held in the highest regard. Sparkling Wines, both vintage and nonvintage, are also successful, ranking in the upper 80s with the occasional 90-pointer.

MERIDIAN VINEYARDS 1991		Map 20
www.meridianvineyards.com	805-226-7133	Tasting
Paso Robles	San Luis Obispo County	Paso Robles AVA

Chuck Ortman learned his trade at Heitz Cellars and Spring Mountain Winery and owned the brand before selling it to Nestlé and staying on as winemaker. Now held by Foster's Group, the Aussie drinks conglomerate (Chateau St. Jean, Stag's Leap, Beringer), Meridian wines offer curb appeal at modest prices in the Classic line, ranging from Sauvignon Blanc to Chardonnay to Pinot Noir. Production of over eight hundred thousand cases guarantees easy access to this line. The Limited Release range, made in lots of four hundred to five hundred cases, is still moderately priced and made in even broader variety, though available only at the winery or through the wine club. All wine is made of grapes sourced throughout the Central Coast.

NORMAN VINEYARDS 1992		Map 20
www.normanvineyards.com	805-237-0138	Tasting
Paso Robles	San Luis Obispo County	Paso Robles AVA

The late Art Norman and wife Lei bought land west of Paso Robles in the Adelaida Hills in 1971. While still in aerospace engineering in Southern California, Art and Lei planted forty acres of red varietals, including Zinfandel, Merlot, Cabernet Sauvignon, and Barbera. In 1992, their first vintages were made with winemaker Steve Felton on board. Norman now makes over twenty-four thousand cases, the vast majority of which is red wine and in particular several Zinfandel choices—including the Classic and The Monster, which together represent over 25 percent of total production. Most wine is made from estate-grown grapes, though some are purchased from other growers in Paso Robles as well as from Cucamonga and Edna valleys. Robust styling has made the wines popular with fans of the style.

PEACHY CANYON WINERY 1982		Map 20
www.peachycanyon.com	805-315-7908	Tasting
Paso Robles	San Luis Obispo County	Paso Robles AVA

Founders Doug and Nancy Beckett, along with son and winemaker Josh Beckett, have created a vineyard and winery focused on red wine varieties. Nearly one hundred acres have been planted to Zinfandel, Cabernet Sauvignon, and Petite Sirah in four vineyards: Mustang Springs, Old School House, Snow, and Mustard Creek, all just northwest of Paso Robles. Production tops eighty-five thousand cases, of which the vast majority is Zinfandel, both vineyard designated and blends. Production ranges from the limited-production estate bottlings, made in 250- to 500-case lots (and available only at the winery or through the wine club), to the widely distributed Incredible Red Zinfandel (thirty thousand cases) and Cirque du Vin blend of Cabernet, Petite Sirah, Merlot, and Syrah (ten thousand cases). Peachy Canyon boasts a very thorough Web site.

The winery style of over-the-top ripeness has been somewhat refined in recent vintages, resulting in wines that are now more easily suited to the dining table. Scores fall in the mid- to upper 80s for most efforts, with the occasional sortie making it to 90 points and higher. Incredible Red rates as a Good Value more often than not. But do not expect Peachy Canyon wines to lose their lusty character—the winery DNA would prevent that from happening.

ROBERT HALL WINERY 1995		Map 20
www.roberthallwinery.com	805-239-1616	Tasting
Paso Robles	San Luis Obispo County	Paso Robles AVA

Minnesota entrepreneur Robert Hall came west to create a winery. Three hundred acres and a new winery with nineteen thousand square feet of caves later, Robert Hall Winery, with winemaker Don Brady, makes thirty thousand cases of some seventeen wines, including Syrah, Cabernet Sauvignon, Chardonnay, and a Brut Rosé sparkler, virtually all with estate-grown grapes from three vineyards: the Home Ranch, Terrace, and Bench vineyards.

To date, reds have fared better than whites, with Syrah Reserve leading the way with scores into the low 90s and Cabernet Sauvignon just a tad behind. Still, the whites are generally quite pleasant, and the winery's Chardonnay often earns Good Value status for its enjoyable fruit and balance combined with its inviting price. The house style, well suited to the winery's location, favors wines of considerable ripeness.

STEPHEN ROSS WINE CELLARS 1994		Map 20
www.stephenrosswine.com	805-594-1318	Tasting by Appointment
San Luis Obispo	San Luis Obispo County	Edna Valley AVA

Stephen Ross Dooley set out to make his own wines in 1994 after itinerant apprenticeships at Louis Martini, Edna Valley Vineyard, and wineries in Australia and South Africa. Initially producing only vineyard-designated wines from San Luis Obispo County, Dooley planted nine acres of Pinot Noir on the Stone Corral Vineyard, a joint venture with Talley Vineyards in the southeast corner of Edna Valley. Now approaching four thousand cases, 50 percent is Pinot Noir—from Dooley's estate, Bien Nacido, Edna Valley, and Aubaine vineyards—40 percent Chardonnay, and the remainder a Petite Sirah and Zinfandel bottling.

Given Dooley's background and his choices of vineyards, one would expect great things from him, but results to date would have to rate as promising rather than exceptional, with very many recommended wines but very few reaching into the 90-point stratosphere.

This partnership of the Perrins of Château de Beaucastel in Châteauneuf du Pape and American importer Robert Haas of Vineyard Brands remains true to its French roots by focusing on a wide range of Rhône varietals, planted on the 100+ -acre estate west of Paso Robles near Adelaida in San Luis Obispo County, felt by the partners to replicate the conditions of their French vineyards. The gradual evolution of the organic vineyards, a wine nursery to nurture the French clones, and the winery has resulted in nearly twenty red and white varieties produced each year, with the estate Esprit de Beaucastel red blend and Esprit de Beaucastel Blanc leading the pack with two to three thousand cases each. About fifteen thousand cases are produced in total, equally distributed between white and red bottlings. The Tablas Creek Web site is unusually informative and includes good information about Rhône varietals.

The array of Rhône-influenced bottlings, more blends than varietally focused, is stunning. Although some of the winery's pricier efforts have also been stunning, Tablas Creek deserves as much credit for its moderately priced offerings, especially its Côtes de Tablas and Côtes de Tablas Blanc, early drinking wines based on Grenache and Viognier, respectively. Especially noteworthy among pricier wines is the Esprit de Beaucastel, a Roussanne-based blend whose depth and structure are pace setting for California versions and rates often in the mid-90s.

The Arroyo Grande Valley has been home to the Talley family since 1948 when Oliver Talley began raising produce. A test vineyard plot was planted in 1982. Subsequently, 190 acres of vines were planted in three separate vineyards in the Arroyo Grande Valley (Rincon, Rosemary's, and Monte Sereno vineyards) and two in the Edna Valley (Oliver's and Stone Corral vineyards, the latter a twenty-eight-acre joint venture with Stephen Ross Wine Cellars), and another 40-acre vineyard (Hazel Talley Vineyard) in the Templeton Gap near Paso Robles. Talley is now devoted to notable estate-grown and

-bottled Chardonnay and Pinot Noirs; of eighteen thousand cases, 65 percent are Chardonnay bottlings and the remainder a half-dozen separate Pinot Noir bottlings. A second label, Bishop's Peak, is a modestly priced line of varieties made from grapes of other San Luis Obispo growers.

Talley ranks among the superstars for top-end Chardonnay and Pinot Noir. Its Rosemary's Vineyard, Rincon Vineyard, and Stone Corral Vineyard Pinot Noirs have scored in the mid- to high 90s on numerous occasions and are almost always among the best-defined, deepest, and richest versions of the grape. Talley's Rincon Chardonnay is not far behind, with ratings in the low to mid-90s more often than not.

TOBIN JAMES CELLARS 1994		Map 20
www.tobinjames.com	805-239-2204	Tasting
Paso Robles	San Luis Obispo County	Paso Robles AVA

Starting as a home winemaker, Tobin James borrowed the facilities of other wineries before apprenticeships at Eberle, Estrella River, and Peachy Canyon. In 1994, James built his own winery just east of Paso Robles in partnership with Lance and Claire Silver. Production stands at thirty thousand cases of moderately priced Zinfandel, Merlot, Cabernet, Syrah, and Chardonnay. Each year, James makes up to thirty separate bottlings, including ten small-batch Zinfandels. A forty-acre vineyard on a seventy-acre site is planted to Zinfandel, Cabernet, and Syrah. Wines are made in a high-ripeness, concentrated style that pleases fans of the winery and sometimes earns high ratings, sometimes not.

TREANA WINERY 1996		Map 20
www.treana.com	805-238-6979	No Tasting
Paso Robles	San Luis Obispo County	Paso Robles AVA

The Hope family started planting grapes in 1978 on their farm lands in western Paso Robles and for years used the Hope Family label. Beginning in 1990, they became the fruit source for Liberty School Cabernet and ultimately bought what would become the second label to Treana. Now under the management of third-generation winemaker Austin Hope, Treana is noted for its red blend of Cabernet Sauvignon, Merlot, and Syrah made from its own grapes, and a white blend of Marsanne and Viognier grapes grown by the Mer Soleil Vineyard in the Santa Lucia Highlands of Monterey County. Production exceeds sixteen thousand cases, of which the red blend comes in at ten thousand. Second label Liberty School makes moderately priced Cabernet Sauvignon, Chardonnay, and Syrah to the tune of two hundred thousand cases a year. Treana wines have been acceptable and enjoyable, and they have earned a bit of praise but have not quite garnered raves.

VICTOR HUGO VINEYARDS & WINERY 1985   Map 20

www.victorhugowinery.com	805-434-1128	Tasting by Appointment
Templeton	San Luis Obispo County	Paso Robles AVA

Victor Hugo Roberts (no literary reference intended, except for naming a Merlot-Syrah blend The Hunchback) owns the winery and makes a limited number of small-batch varietal bottlings, principally from grapes grown on the seventy-eight-acre estate, the Templeton Hills Vineyard, just south of Paso Robles. Roberts makes small batches of some dozen wines, including the aforementioned blend and a Cabernet Sauvignon, Petite Sirah, Zinfandel, Viognier, and Merlot. Quantities range from two hundred to eight hundred cases per vintage bottling for a total production of about five thousand. Quality has ranged from average to slightly above, but this winery is more concerned with value than ratings, and its price range, mostly $20 and under, makes its wines worth pursuing.

WILD HORSE WINERY & VINEYARDS 1981   Map 20

www.wildhorsewinery.com	805-434-2541	Tasting
Templeton	San Luis Obispo County	Paso Robles AVA

Founder Ken Volk first established a winery in 1981 and planted a thirty-three-acre estate vineyard a year later. He quickly built a strong reputation by virtue of making exceptional vineyard-designated wines in small batches. The winery grew apace, sourcing most of its grapes from other Paso Robles and Central Coast vineyards. Volk sold the business to Peak Wines International (Geyser Peak and Canyon Road) in 2003. Wild Horse now bottles about two hundred thousand cases, including about fifty thousand each of Chardonnay, Pinot Noir, and Merlot. In December 2007, Wild Horse was sold, along with the entire Beam Estates portfolio of wineries, to Constellation Brands, the largest conglomeration of winegrowers and producers in the country.

A reserve line called Cheval Sauvage includes a pricey Pinot Noir made in batches of three hundred to five hundred cases. It is the winery's top wine, with scores reaching the upper 80s. Other wines score from 85 to 87 points and, with prices that hover around $20, often rate as Good Values.

Santa Barbara
and Ventura Counties

COASTAL WINEMAKING WITH A TWIST

The wines being produced in these counties are very much influenced by
the placement of their vineyards that are near the Pacific Ocean. Even
with the recent emergence of grape growing in areas back from the coast
in the Santa Barbara County enclaves of Happy Canyon and the Cuyama
Valley, it is grapes like Pinot Noir and Chardonnay that are the prime
focus of the wineries here. Syrah is making strong inroads because of
that grape's ability to grow in cool climates as well as in more moderate
climes, but one has to get away from the coast to find successful patches
of Cabernet Sauvignon. The limited grape growing in Ventura County
is of little significance since the majority of wine produced there is made
with grapes from Santa Barbara County and places farther north.

SANTA BARBARA COUNTY

Winegrowing in Santa Barbara County is very much a product of the 1970s
wine boom. Up until that time, the plantings were barely countable and
did not show up in the California annual census of grape acreage. Then the

wine boom came along, and Santa Barbara County went from fewer than a hundred acres at the start of the decade to almost ten thousand acres by 1980. Today, that total stands at 17,600, split into 9,500 for white grapes and 8,100 acres of red. The leading varieties are Chardonnay (6,800), Pinot Noir (4,500), and Syrah (1,400).

The predominance of cool-loving varieties reflects that ocean-influenced climate in most of the vineyard areas, but there are also warmer pockets where Syrah has shown exceptionally well and rates with the best in California. Cabernet Sauvignon was planted extensively early on but proved unreliable, and it is only now with warmer locations set back from the coast that Cabernet seems again on the rise—buttressed by successes of new wineries like Star Lane. Still, Santa Barbara County's most famous AVAs are all considered cool-climate areas.

See Santa Barbara County Vintners Association: www.sbcountywines.com.

Cuyama Valley

The Cuyama Valley straddles Highway 166 as it weaves inland from Highway 1 near Santa Maria and opens up as it intersects with Highway 33 near the Kern County border. Some 750 acres of grapes are grown in this moderately warm to very warm region, with the best-known wines coming from the Barnwood winery owned by Laetitia. The labels on Barnwood may read Santa Barbara County, but this area is much warmer than any other grape-growing region in the county and sooner or later should get its own AVA designation.

Happy Canyon

Occupying the very eastern end of the Santa Ynez Valley AVA is the newly designated territory with the Happy Canyon AVA moniker. The vineyards there lie east of Santa Ynez town on the mountain side of Highway 154, snug up against and into the foothills of the Los Padres range. It is a warmer area and has been horse country for years and is now becoming vineyard land as well. Three wineries plus several independent vineyard operations presently occupy the area, the best known of which are Star Lane and Vogelzang. The vineyards grow upward from valley floor to the very hilltops and allow wineries to grow both whites like Sauvignon Blanc and lusty reds, with the warmer climate of the region particularly encouraging varieties like Cabernet Sauvignon and Merlot, Syrah, and a smattering of Sangiovese. The designated AVA contains over twenty thousand

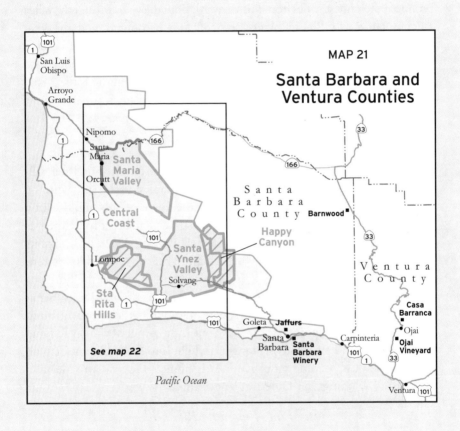

MAP 21

Santa Barbara and Ventura Counties

San Luis Obispo

Arroyo Grande

Nipomo

Santa Maria

Santa Maria Valley

Orcutt

Central Coast

Lompoc

Santa Ynez Valley

Solvang

Sta Rita Hills

See map 22

Santa Barbara County

Barnwood

Happy Canyon

Ventura County

Goleta · Jaffurs

Santa Barbara · Santa Barbara Winery

Carpinteria

Casa Barranca

Ojai

Ojai Vineyard

Ventura

Pacific Ocean

acres of land but something closer to five hundred acres of grapes, about half of which belong to Star Lane.

Santa Maria Valley

The first of the Santa Barbara County grape-growing areas to develop with the advent of the wine boom, it is home to almost three dozen wineries and several well-regarded vineyards. Perhaps the most important of all is the Bien Nacido Vineyard that supplies grapes to over a dozen wineries, many of which have produced their finest wines from this vineyard. Both the vineyard and the valley are most famous for Pinot Noir and secondly for Chardonnay, with the occasional Syrah coming from protected sites that allow the fruit to ripen. Because of its east-west orientation, it is cooled by ocean winds and fog. Although the Sta. Rita Hills AVA is cooler yet, the slight extra warmth in the Santa Maria Valley contributes to a slightly smoother and longer palate impression for its best wines. About 7,500 of the county's grapes are grown here.

Santa Ynez Valley

Lying to the south of the Santa Maria Valley and east of the Sta. Rita Hills AVA, which lies at the western end of and overlaps substantially with the Santa Ynez Valley AVA, and encompassing the towns of Solvang, Buellton and Los Olivos, the Santa Ynez Valley is somewhat broadly defined as opposed to the tighter definitions for its neighboring AVAs. It is, like its immediate neighbors, a cool-growing region, especially toward its western end, but does have warmer pockets, both to the east and in the Purisima Mountains at its northern border, that are particularly inviting to Syrah and even to Cabernet Sauvignon. It is primarily Chardonnay and Pinot Noir territory at this point. At the very southeast corner of the AVA, lying inland and upland and enjoying longer daylight hours, the Happy Canyon area, having just become its own AVA, is home to several wineries and vineyards, including Star Lane and Vogelzang.

Sta. Rita Hills/Santa Rita Hills

This cold and windy AVA very near the ocean started life under the Santa Rita Hills moniker, but, because the Santa Rita wine interests in Chile objected, its name has been truncated to Sta. Rita Hills; as of the 2005 vintage, all wines from the area are required to bear the new handle. Wineries and vineyards have existed in this region, which stretches west toward the ocean from Buellton to Lompoc, for well over three decades; but it has only been in the last ten years, as the grape acreage has increased, that the area was awarded its own title. It lies almost entirely within the Santa Ynez Valley AVA, which stretches much farther to the east. Chardonnay and Pinot Noir are the leading varieties grown in the Sta. Rita Hills AVA, and they tend to be high in acidity and reach fairly high levels of ripeness in order to achieve physiological maturity.

VENTURA COUNTY

With fewer than a dozen wineries and only fifty acres of grapes, Ventura County is not exactly buzzing with wine activity, but it does have recognizable names operating there, mostly with grapes from the counties immediately to the north. Its proximity to Los Angeles makes some of those wineries attractive for day trips.

See Ventura County Wine Trail: www.venturacountywinetrail.com.

ANDREW MURRAY VINEYARDS	1994	Map 22
www.andrewmurrayvineyards.com	805-686-9604	Tasting
Los Olivos	Santa Barbara County	Santa Ynez Valley AVA

The Murray family (Andrew is the son of the founders) planted thirty-four acres of Rhône varietal grapes in the early 1990s. After Cal and Davis, Andrew traveled to France and Australia and became the winemaker for the family estate winery. In 2006, looking to retire, Andrew's parents sold the winery and vineyards, located on the same upland territory as Zaca Mesa, but passed the winery name to Andrew who, still devoted to Rhônes, remains focused on vineyard-designated wines from growers in Santa Barbara and San Luis Obispo counties, including Great Oaks Ranch, Oak Savanna, and Calzada Ridge vineyards. He makes a range of blended cuvées such as his Enchanteé, a Roussanne-Marsanne blend, and Esperance, a Grenache-Syrah-Mourvèdre blend, as well as several Syrahs. The production goal for the new winery is 7,500 cases.

Quality levels to date have varied widely; while there has been the occasional grand success, most wines have scored in the low to mid-80s.

AU BON CLIMAT	1982	Map 21
www.aubonclimat.com	805-937-9801	No Tasting
Los Olivos	Santa Barbara County	Santa Maria Valley AVA

Zaca Mesa Winery alums Adam Tolmach and Jim Clendenen set out to produce small-batch Chardonnay and Pinot Noir. The winery has been located on the grounds of the Bien Nacido Vineyards since 1989; today Clendenen is the sole proprietor and winemaker, while Tolmach went on to the Ojai Vineyard in Ventura County. Au Bon Climat puts out over thirty thousand cases annually, of which fully 75 percent is Chardonnay, with Pinot Noir, Pinot Blanc, and Pinot Gris rounding out the offerings. A second label, Clendenen Family Vineyards, makes very limited quantities of principally Italian varieties. Grapes are sourced from the estate vineyard and Bien Nacido, Sanford & Benedict, Los Alamos, and Talley vineyards.

There has never been any question that Clendenen is his own man, and the wines, in both nomenclature and personality, have reflected his willingness to try the unique. Still, the winery style is far more mannerly than some, and even if there is an eclectic bent to everything that comes forth, there is also a strong sense of direction. At times, quality has been exceptional; at other times, it has lagged the field. Still, that is the price one pays for the Au Bon Climat penchant for the unique.

BABCOCK WINERY & VINEYARDS 1984		Map 22
www.babcockwinery.com	805-736-1455	Tasting
Lompoc	Santa Barbara County	Sta. Rita Hills AVA

Founded by Walt and Mona Babcock of Southern California (the pater-familias was a dentist and restaurateur), 25 acres were planted on a 110-acre ranch in the late 1970s to Chardonnay, Riesling, Gewürztraminer, Sauvignon Blanc, and Pinot Noir. Their son, Bryan Babcock, having just graduated from Davis, became winemaker at the time of the first vintage in 1984. Now, a total of eighty acres has been planted to more contemporary grape varietals, including Chardonnay, Pinot Noir, Pinot Grigio, Syrah, and Sauvignon Blanc. Yet more acreage is being planted each year to yield more than the current twenty thousand cases a year (Chardonnay leads the list of wines, with two-thirds of production, and the Rita's Earth Cuvée Chardonnay comes in at over ten thousand cases). The majority of wines are made with estate-grown grapes, although some are purchased from other Santa Barbara County growers.

The winery's quality record has been a trifle inconsistent as the line has expanded, but almost everything has received recommended ratings of the mid- to upper 80s at times. Several special bottlings, led more often than not by the Black Label Cuvée Syrah, have garnered scores in the 90s.

Selim Zilkha, and daughter Nadia, of Laetitia Vineyard & Winery (see the entry later in the previous chapter), bought Barnwood and its acreage on the eastern slope of the Sierra Madre mountains, in the Cuyama Valley, the driest and hottest vineyards in Santa Barbara County. Plantings are mostly on the flat valley floor and in sloping foothills, but one very spectacular vineyard sits on top of a 3,200-foot-high mesa overlooking the valley. Fifteen thousand cases of estate-grown and -bottled wines include a Cabernet Sauvignon (nine thousand cases) and Sauvignon Blanc (three thousand) and several other red blends, including Trio that combines Cabernet, Merlot, and Syrah grapes. The winery building, an updated barn, is delightfully rustic, and the wines themselves have a rustic rather than a polished quality. Prices are moderate, and ratings have been consistent with pricing.

BECKMEN VINEYARDS 1994   Map 22

www.beckmenvineyards.com   805-688-8664   Tasting

Los Olivos   Santa Barbara County   Santa Ynez Valley AVA

Tom and winemaker son Steve Beckmen acquired the former Houtz Winery and its twenty-three-acre Los Olivos vineyard in 1994. Two years later, they purchased a 365-acre ranch higher up in the valley at about 1,250 feet. This became the Purisima Mountain Vineyard, which will include two hundred acres of Rhône varietal grapes when planting is complete. Nine thousand to ten thousand cases of the Beckmen Estate line (Cabernet Sauvignon, Syrah, Cuvée Le Bec) is in addition to the somewhat smaller production of four thousand to five thousand cases of similar varieties under the Purisima Mountain Vineyard label. Virtually every Syrah made to date, typically in ripe to very ripe yet still sturdy styles, has earned high commendation, with scores in the high 80s and low 90s. Cuvée Le Bec is the winery's well-regarded, moderately priced Grenache-dominated blend, and it's a bargain.

BREWER-CLIFTON 1990   Map 22

www.brewerclifton.com   805-735-9184   No Tasting

Lompoc   Santa Barbara County   Sta. Rita Hills AVA

Greg Brewer and Steve Clifton had each worked in various Santa Barbara County wineries and in the early 1990s established their Lompoc winery to make vineyard-designated Chardonnay and Pinot Noir from the juice of a handful of Santa Rita Hills growers, including Rio Vista, Melville (where Brewer is also winemaker), Clos Pepe, and Ashley's vineyards. Maximum production is about five thousand cases, with Pinot Noir representing nearly 75 percent. Each vintage is made in small batches from two hundred to seven hundred cases each. Brewer-Clifton wines have adopted an extended ripeness style that makes them too hot and ponderous to many wine drinkers, but that style also has earned them great critical acclaim in some circles and has made them the darling of those who want dense, weighty wines as the first order of business. Needless to say, critical ratings have been inconsistent, but winery fans are so in tune with the house style that ratings have little influence on their enthusiasm.

BRIDLEWOOD ESTATE WINERY 1987		Map 22
www.bridlewoodwinery.com	800-467-4100	Tasting
Santa Ynez	Santa Barbara County	Santa Ynez Valley AVA

Once a thoroughbred breeding and training facility, the property, now owned by Gallo, still includes a working horse ranch as well as a winery and seven-acre estate vineyard. Winemaker David Hopkins uses grapes grown on the estate as well as those of several dozen other Central Coast vineyards to produce his range of Rhône-style wines, with particular focus on Syrah and Viognier. Up to twenty thousand cases are produced annually; Viognier leads the way in quantity and consistency, but Syrah dominates the number of different bottlings and shows promise from time to time. The ripe, rich Central Coast style predominates, with wines occasionally reaching overripe status.

BUTTONWOOD FARM WINERY 1983		Map 22
www.buttonwoodwinery.com	800-715-1404	Tasting
Solvang	Santa Barbara County	Santa Ynez Valley AVA

Matriarch Betty Williams bought a hundred acres of land just south of Los Olivos in 1968 and developed a race horse breeding facility. Betty, along with son-in-law Bret Davenport, planted a forty-acre vineyard on the property in 1983 and began a small winery using estate-grown fruit. Today, under the auspices of winemaker Karen Steinwachs, late of Foley

Estates, eight thousand cases are produced, nearly half of which is the estate Sauvignon Blanc. Other notable varieties, all produced in the range of two hundred to eight hundred cases, include Merlot, Syrah, Cabernet Sauvignon, and several blends. The reasonably priced Sauvignon Blanc, tasting of melon and citrus more than of weeds and grasses, has been the quality leader to date with scores in the mid- to upper 80s.

BYRON VINEYARD & WINERY 1984		Map 21
www.byronwines.com	805-934-4770	Tasting by Appointment
Santa Maria	Santa Barbara County	Santa Maria Valley AVA

Byron Ken Brown, known as Ken, had been the founding winemaker at nearby Zaca Mesa when he established Byron and became one of the earliest proponents of Rhône-style varieties in the region. In 1990, the Byron Winery was sold to Robert Mondavi, which in turn sold the winery to Constellation Brands, which in turn resold Byron to Kendall-Jackson, which has retained the identity of the Byron brand under the guidance of winemaker Jonathan Nagy, also the winemaker of second label IO. In the early 1990s, a new gravity-flow winery was built, designed by architect R. Scott Johnson (of Opus One and San Francisco's Transamerica pyramid). Chardonnay, Pinot Noir, and Pinot Blanc are produced from grapes grown on over two hundred estate acres plus Nielson and Sierra Madre vineyards. On an experimental vineyard, plantings are made to a density— commonly used in France—of over three times the California norm. The jury's still out on the results. Production tops twenty-five thousand cases, with Pinot Noir accounting for nearly 70 percent.

Once one of the darlings of Santa Barbara County wine aficionados, the winery has lost its standing with a series of average results, and even the IO brand, often tops among local Syrahs, has suffered of late.

CAMBRIA WINERY & VINEYARDS 1987		Map 21
www.cambriawine.com	888-339-9463	Tasting
Santa Maria	Santa Barbara County	Santa Maria Valley AVA

In the 1980s, Jess Jackson (of Kendall-Jackson) bought Chardonnay grapes from numerous vineyards in the area to satisfy the growing demand for that variety. Among them was the Tepusquet Vineyard, near the famous Bien Nacido Vineyard in the Santa Maria Valley. In 1986, Jackson and wife Barbara Banke bought three-quarters of Tepusquet and built a winery,

Cambria, on the property. Now the estate vineyard land comprises 1,400 acres planted to Chardonnay (80 percent of the grapes), Pinot Noir, and Syrah, with vineyard names Katherine's, Julia's, Bench Break, and the original Tepusquet that grace the Cambria labels. Production is heading toward the winery's capacity of one hundred thousand cases. Most wines are reasonably priced and score in the mid- to upper-80-point range, making them especially good values more often than not.

CASA BARRANCA WINE 1909		Map 21
www.casabarranca.com	805-640-1334	Tasting
Ojai	Ventura County	Central Coast AVA

This small winery in Ojai makes its wines from grapes sourced from Central Coast vineyards and declares itself an organic winery. The stunning landmark craftsman estate was designed by the renowned architects Greene & Greene. Under the watch of winemaker Bill Moses, Casa Barranca makes upward of five thousand cases of principally red varieties, including Cabernet Sauvignon, Grenache, Pinot Noir, Syrah, and Viognier. Not unlike many new and small wineries, the wines are handled gently and bottled with as much purity as can be mustered. Under such circumstances, the results can be quite varied, but Casa Barranca seems to be succeeding across its line of offering. Still, first focus here is on the winery's efforts with Rhône varieties.

COLD HEAVEN CELLARS 1996		Map 22
www.coldheavencellars.com	805-937-9801	No Tasting
Buellton	Santa Barbara County	Santa Maria Valley AVA

Owner-winemaker Morgan Clendenen specializes in Viognier. Her 2,500 annual output is made at Au Bon Climat (see earlier entry on page 349), and one of the handful of Cold Heaven vineyard-designated Viogniers is sourced from the family-owned Le Bon Climat Vineyard. One of the most interesting Viognier experiments is the Deux C wine, with 50 percent Santa Barbara County grapes and 50 percent grapes from widely admired winemaker Yves Cuilleron in the northern Rhône Valley appellation of Condrieu. Production now includes both Pinot Noir and Syrah.

Early vintages of the firm, lean Viognier proved problematic, but there has been noticeable improvement in recent years as scores have edged up to 90 points.

CURRAN 1997		Map 22
www.curranwines.com	805-736-5761	No Tasting
Lompoc	Santa Barbara County	Sta. Rita Hills AVA

Winemaker-owner and Santa Ynez Valley native Kris Curran brought experience at nearby Cambria and Koehler wineries to her own venture in 1997. Two years later, after dabbling in making Pinot Noir, she decided to focus on Syrah, Sangiovese, and Grenache Blanc. Curran makes limited quantities—about 1,200 cases in total—of these three blends, each sourced from a different vineyard in the Santa Ynez Valley, mostly from vineyards away from the ocean. In 2000, Curran also became the winemaker at Sea Smoke (described later), where she was able to use the output of its vineyards to produce a Pinot Noir. Quality has ranged broadly, but the best have scored above 90 points. Not surprisingly, most of the wines reflect a ripe, rich, concentrated style that belongs to grapes grown in the eastern (less bracingly cold) vineyards of the Santa Ynez Valley. In 2009, Curran moved on to become winemaker for Foley.

CURTIS WINERY 1995		Map 22
www.curtiswinery.com	805-686-8999	Tasting
Los Olivos	Santa Barbara County	Santa Ynez Valley AVA

Started by the Firestone family in a building adjacent to their main property until it was sold recently, the former modern art gallery has been transformed into a gorgeous winemaking facility devoted mainly to the production of Rhône varieties. Fruit comes mainly from the family's Ambassador and Crossroads vineyards, and output from the winery stands close to six thousand cases. In recent times, 40 percent has been devoted to Syrah, 30 percent to Viognier, and 30 percent to Rhône-style blends.

Quality has been variable, with ratings falling more into the average category of the mid-80s and only a few wines reaching the recommended levels of the upper 80s.

DIERBERG 2004		Map 22
www.dierbergvineyard.com	(805) 736-0757	Tasting
Santa Ynez	Santa Barbara County	Santa Ynez Valley AVA

Jim and Mary Dierberg are bankers by trade, wine lovers by heart, and winegrowers and producers by choice. They selected Santa Barbara County over a decade ago and now make wine in its four AVAs—Santa Maria Valley, Santa Ynez Valley, Happy Canyon, and Sta. Rita Hills. Their front-line Pinot Noir and Chardonnay come from the cooler areas in the western part of the county, while their Cabernet Sauvignon, bottled under the Star Lane moniker, comes from the Happy Canyon area. Initial results have been favorable for both Dierberg and Star Lane. A second-tier label, Three Saints, is a midpriced effort.

The winery is located on the Dierbergs' Star Lane estate at the eastern extremities of the Santa Maria Valley in the Happy Canyon AVA. Early results have been quite promising, with point scores rising into the 90-plus range for top wines. Star Lane wines have been well received in both Cabernet Sauvignon, including the reserve-level Astral, and Sauvignon Blanc; both are ripe, rich, supple, and full of tasty fruit. Dierberg Pinots and Chardonnays, both made in the rich house style, have often reached the 90-point range, and Three Saints has scored well at times with its lusty versions of Cabernet Sauvignon rating as high as the upper 80s.

FESS PARKER WINERY 1989		Map 22
www.fessparker.com	800-841-1104	Tasting
Los Olivos	Santa Barbara County	Santa Ynez Valley AVA

After his career playing Davy Crockett and Daniel Boone on the small screen, Fess Parker left Hollywood for the Santa Ynez Valley, where he bought a ranch of more than seven hundred acres in the Foxen Canyon, just north of Los Olivos, and set about planting a vineyard. Initially, Fess and son Eli planted five acres of White Riesling; this has grown to more than three hundred acres planted today in two separate vineyards (Rodney's and Camp 4). Wines totaling fifty thousand cases range from the vineyard-specific Pinot Noir to Syrah to Chardonnay, plus moderately priced second labels Epiphany, Frontier Red, and Parker Station. In addition to the wines and vines, Parker is big in the region's hospitality industry, with an inn/spa/restaurant in downtown Los Olivos and two beachfront hotels in posh Santa Barbara.

Early quality was high, then expansion seemed to dull the brand's reputation, but recent bottlings have fared better. The winery is a fun stop along the wine trail. More often than not, the wines are ripe and somewhat fleshy, but some of the cooler-area wines will be more tightly structured.

FIRESTONE VINEYARD 1972		Map 22
www.firestonewine.com	805-688-3940	Tasting
Los Olivos	Santa Barbara County	Santa Ynez Valley AVA

The history of Firestone dates to the early 1970s when Harvey Firestone's son, Leonard, scion of the rubber baron, bought land in the Santa Ynez Valley and with his son, Brooks, built what may have been the first true estate winery in Santa Barbara County. On several hundred acres of land, the next generation, Adam and Andrew, built up a substantial winemaking operation with a wide variety of wines produced. In 2007, a second winery was completed in Paso Robles, focused on small lots of Bordeaux varietals from local vineyards. As of 2007, the Firestone brand, both wineries, and 380 planted acres were purchased by nearby Foley Estates (see next profile). The Firestone family retained some 215 planted acres in Santa Ynez Valley, the next-door Curtis Winery (described earlier), and a microbrewing venture, the Firestone Walker Brewery.

Early indications are that the new Firestone wines are going to be price-conscious.

FOLEY ESTATES VINEYARD & WINERY 1998		Map 22
www.foleywines.com	805-737-6222	Tasting
Lompoc	Santa Barbara County	Sta. Rita Hills AVA

In 1998, Bill Foley found a 460-acre former thoroughbred horse ranch in the Santa Rita Hills called Rancho Santa Rosa, on which was planted 230 acres to Pinot Noir, Chardonnay, and Syrah. The stables became the winery. Foley also created a second label, Lincourt Vineyards, using grapes grown on a thirty-acre Solvang vineyard. Foley makes Chardonnay, Pinot Gris, Pinot Noir, and Syrah, largely from its Rancho Santa Rosa vineyard. Production exceeds nine thousand cases, 60 percent of which are Pinot Noirs and Syrahs. In 2007, Foley Estates purchased the nearby Firestone Vineyard (see preceding entry), including its Santa Ynez Valley and Paso Robles wineries and 380 planted acres. The more than six hundred acres now owned should substantially increase Foley's production and presence in the county.

Foley Pinot Noirs, especially the vineyard block and clonal selection bottlings, have been ripe and rich, and they have scored in the 90-point range more often than not, with the occasional effort reaching as high as 95.

If Chardonnay has been slightly lower in critical evaluation, it is not all that much lower. After years under the oversight of winemaker Alan Philips, Foley has now come under the practiced hand of Kris Curran, she of her own wines, plus great experience at Cambria and having been in charge at Sea Smoke.

FOXEN WINERY & VINEYARD 1985		Map 22
www.foxenvineyard.com	805-937-4251	Tasting
Santa Maria	Santa Barbara County	Santa Maria Valley AVA

Bill Wathen and Dick Doré (the "Foxen Boys" to much of the wine community) founded Foxen in 1985 at the historic Rancho Tinaquaic in northern Santa Barbara County. Doré's great-great-grandfather, William Foxen, was an English sea captain who purchased the rancho in 1837; it's still in the family. Foxen now produces small batches of vineyard-designated wines from the best vineyards in the area (Bien Nacido, Julia's, Sea Smoke, and Vogelzang, among others). Over 40 percent of the nine-thousand-case production is of white varietals and another 35 percent of Pinot Noir, with the remainder composed of small quantities of Syrah, Cabernet Franc, Sangiovese, and Port. A ten-acre estate vineyard, Tinaquaic, provides juice for Foxen's estate bottlings.

Over the years, Foxen has received much praise for Pinots that regularly score in the high 80s, with the occasional foray into the 90-point range. Lately, Foxen Syrah has also reached the same critically acclaimed heights. In a sea of overwrought bottlings, Foxen wines stand out for restrained power and balance.

GAINEY VINEYARD 1984		Map 22
www.gaineyvineyard.com	888-424-6398	Tasting
Santa Ynez	Santa Barbara County	Santa Ynez Valley AVA

In 1962, the Gainey family bought an 1,800-acre ranch, with 1,000 acres for cattle, 600 farmland, 100 for Arabian horses, and 100 for vineyards. Today, the Home Vineyard in Santa Ynez Valley has eighty-five acres planted; another vineyard, Evan's Ranch, purchased in the 1990s, in the Santa Rita Hills, has thirty-five planted acres. Between the output of the 120 total acres and grapes bought from other county vineyards, 18,000 cases of Riesling, Sauvignon Blanc, Chardonnay, Pinot Noir, and Syrah are being produced. The Limited Selection line commands the most attention and highest price.

Much of Gainey's production is sold directly at the winery or through its wine clubs.

Gainey Limited Selection Pinot Noir has been rated in the high 80s to lower and mid-90s more often than not. Limited Selection Sauvignon Blanc has garnered similarly high plaudits, making it among the best of the breed in California for its keenly focused varietal fruit, its richness, and its energy.

HARTLEY OSTINI HITCHING POST WINERY 1984		Map 22
www.hitchingpost2.com	805-688-0676	No Tasting
Buellton	Santa Barbara County	Santa Ynez Valley AVA

The 2005 hit movie *Sideways* focused klieg lights on the region and on Pinot Noir, and particular attention on the Hitching Post II restaurant in Buellton, where much of the film was shot. The restaurant's chef, Frank Ostini, and former commercial fisherman Gary Hartley were home wine-makers in the late '70s. In '84, they made their first commercial wines and for years since have made vineyard-designated Pinot Noir, Syrah, and a Cabernet Franc blend from vineyards in Santa Barbara County. Production of five thousand cases includes mostly Pinot from vineyards including Bien Nacido, Julia's, Sanford & Benedict, and Fiddlestix. Highliner, a Pinot Noir from several sources, and a Syrah round out the wines made here.

Pinot Noir quality has always been fairly high, scoring consistently in the mid- to upper 80s with the occasionally 90-point winner, and the recent addition of a Syrah has met with immediate success. The wines, while not quite as famous as the restaurant has become because of the movie, have always enjoyed a following for their ripe, somewhat lusty style.

JAFFURS WINE CELLARS 1994		Map 21
www.jaffurswine.com	805-962-7003	Tasting
Santa Barbara	Santa Barbara County	Central Coast AVA

Former aerospace industry worker and aspiring Rhône Ranger Craig Jaffurs learned the business from Bruce McGuire of Santa Barbara Winery (described later). He established a winery in downtown Santa Barbara to focus on Rhône varietals made in small batches from the best grapes available in the county. Four thousand to 5,000 cases are made in 150- to 900-case lots of Viognier, Roussanne, and Syrah. Vineyards sourced include Thompson, Bien Nacido, Larner, and Melville. Syrah, the leading variety, has generally earned high ratings, often at and into the 90-point range. Jaffurs wines can be over-the-top in ripeness, but the best of them prove that ripeness by itself is no sin.

LAFOND WINERY 2000		Map 22
www.lafondwinery.com	877-708-9463	Tasting
Buellton	Santa Barbara County	Sta. Rita Hills AVA

Santa Barbara County pioneer Pierre Lafond started his first winery, the Santa Barbara Winery, in 1962. Years later, after expanding his vineyard holdings several times, he then built the Lafond Winery, a separate facility under the same management as the Santa Barbara Winery. Lafond is now the upscale label of the two and makes about ten thousand cases annually.

LANE TANNER WINERY 1989		Map 22
www.lanetanner.com	805-929-1826	No Tasting
Santa Maria	Santa Barbara County	Santa Maria Valley AVA

A chemist by trade, Lane Tanner fell into the wine industry by virtue of her scientific talents that naturally led to employment at Konocti, Zaca Mesa, and Firestone wineries. Early on, Tanner made private-label Pinot Noir for the Hitching Post restaurant of Hartley-Ostini and *Sideways* notoriety. In 1989, she went solo, making small batches of single-vineyard Pinot Noir from vineyards including Bien Nacido, Julia's, and Melville. Production is currently under 2,000 cases, with each of her three Pinot Noirs made in 450- to 550-case lots and the single Syrah coming in at under 400 cases.

Her preference has always been to apply a lighter, balanced hand to her wines, which has led occasionally to thin and underfilled efforts. Still, her stylish, well-focused, fruit-centered wines can trump the big boys from time to time, and whether scoring in the 80s or the 90s, they are distinctly her wines.

LUCAS & LEWELLEN VINEYARDS 1996		Map 22
www.llwine.com	888-777-6663	Tasting
Solvang	Santa Barbara County	Santa Ynez Valley AVA

Retired judge Royce Lewellen and grape grower Louis Lucas started a partnership with two vineyards in the county. Working with winemaker Daniel Gehrs, a veteran of Paul Masson, Congress Springs, and Zaca Mesa,

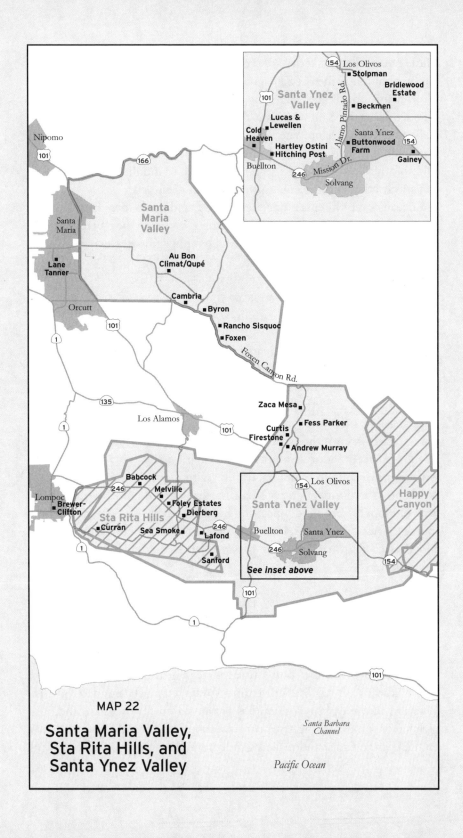

MAP 22

Santa Maria Valley, Sta Rita Hills, and Santa Ynez Valley

Lucas & Lewellen makes 150,000 cases of a wide variety of Bordeaux-style wines, including Cabernet Sauvignon, Cabernet Franc, Merlot, Syrah, Pinot Noir, Sauvignon Blanc, and Viognier. L & L now owns three vineyards: Goodchild in the Santa Maria Valley, Los Alamos Valley Vineyard, and Valley View in the Santa Ynez Valley. Planted acreage totals more than four hundred, with two dozen grape varieties; half of the grape production is sold to other local wineries. Second labels are Mandolina, specializing in Italian varieties, and the lower-priced Queen of Hearts.

Virtually everything is moderately priced, and while there have been no runaway winners to date, with most offerings scoring in the low to mid-80s, the best of the lot offer good value for the money nonetheless.

MELVILLE VINEYARDS & WINERY 1996		Map 22
www.melvillevineyards.com	805-735-7030	Tasting
Lompoc	Santa Barbara County	Sta. Rita Hills AVA

Founded in 1989 by former financier Ron Melville in Sonoma County's Knights Valley, Melville Vineyards grew Chardonnay, Merlot, and Cabernet Sauvignon grapes for sale to local wineries. In 1996, Melville relocated to Santa Rita Hills in Santa Barbara County to grow Burgundian grapes and to establish its own winery operation. Production of Melville estate wines now exceeds twenty thousand cases, of which Pinot Noir bottlings represent 65 percent; another 30 percent is Chardonnay. There are now two vineyards, Melville in Santa Rita Hills (with eighty-three acres of Pinot Noir and Chardonnay) and Verna's north of Los Alamos (with fifty-six acres of Pinot Noir, Chardonnay, and Syrah). Melville is a popular vineyard source for nearby wineries, including Ojai, Jaffurs, LaFond, Lane Tanner, and Brewer-Clifton. The latter is part-owned by Melville's winemaker, Greg Brewer.

OJAI VINEYARD 1983		Map 21
www.ojaivineyard.com	805-649-1674	No Tasting
Oakview	Ventura County	Central Coast AVA

A part owner of the Au Bon Climat winery in the Santa Maria Valley before heading off on his own venture, Adam Tolmach founded the Ojai Vineyard in the early 1980s and has prospered on his own. He and wife Helen buy grapes on long-term contract from a dozen and more vineyards on the Central Coast and make a goodly number of both appellation- and vineyard-designated wines. Their noteworthy six-thousand-case production features twelve to fifteen bottlings each year, including Pinot Noir, Syrah, Sauvignon Blanc, and Chardonnay, and the vineyard designates include such renowned growers as Bien Nacido, Roll Ranch, Pisoni, and Clos Pepe.

Roll Ranch Syrah and White Hawk Vineyard Syrah, along with the Sauvignon Blanc, have been garnering scores in the 90s on a regular basis and have often been at the very top of the rating lists

QUPÉ WINE CELLARS 1982		Map 22
www.qupe.com	805-937-9801	No Tasting
Los Olivos	Santa Barbara County	Santa Maria Valley AVA

Bob Lindquist, with experience primarily at Zaca Mesa, built a winery on the Bien Nacido Vineyard property in collaboration with Jim Clendenen of Au Bon Climat (see earlier entry), bringing badly needed excitement to the Santa Barbara County wine scene. Focusing on Rhône varietals and Chardonnay, Qupé (a Native American word for "poppy") makes thirty-five thousand cases, of which two-thirds are red—virtually all Syrah—from notable vineyards in the area, including Bien Nacido, Stolpman, Vogelzang, and French Camp. Lindquist is planting his own eighty-acre vineyard in the Edna Valley.

Wine ratings have not been Qupé's strong suit, but the winery's style is among the more refined in California, and its wines deserve consideration by that standard as well. Of late, the winery's Bien Nacido Vineyard Chardonnays have been its quality leaders. Expect ratings in the mid- to upper 80s, with the occasional foray into the 90s, and also expect the wines to have a bias toward balance rather than power.

RANCHO SISQUOC WINERY 1977		Map 22
www.ranchosisquoc.com	805-934-4332	Tasting
Santa Maria	Santa Barbara County	Santa Maria Valley AVA

In 1952, James Flood bought a cattle ranch of thirty-eight thousand acres southeast of Santa Maria on the Sisquoc River, which morphed into both grazing land and crops. In 1968, nine acres of Riesling and four of Chardonnay were planted, creating one of the first vineyards in the county; the winery was established in 1977. Today over three hundred acres are planted to vines, a small percentage of which produce Rancho's estate line of bottlings and the remainder sold to other wineries in the region. Production of ten thousand cases ranges from Sauvignon Blanc to Chardonnay to Syrah and Pinot Noir.

Its lovely setting and staying power notwithstanding, Rancho Sisquoc has lagged in wine quality and has missed more often than most of its competitors.

SANFORD WINERY 1971		Map 22
www.sanfordwinery.com	800-426-9463	Tasting
Lompoc	Santa Barbara County	Sta. Rita Hills AVA

The Sanford family first planted Pinot Noir in 1971 in its Sanford & Benedict Vineyard, west of Buellton in what is now the Sta. Rita Hills AVA, becoming one of the earliest Pinot Noir enthusiasts on the Central Coast. After years of gradual growth in both its vineyards and winemaking, Sanford was bought out by its controlling partner, the Terlato Wine Group (Cuvaison, Chimney Rock, Rutherford Hill, and Alderbrook, among a total of thirteen brands in California alone). The split was not unexpected after years of disagreement over everything from wine quality to farming methods.

The winery remains in business, but, after almost three decades, there is no longer a Sanford in charge. Production today stands at fifty-thousand cases; 55 percent is Chardonnay, 25 percent Pinot Noir, and the remainder Sauvignon Blanc and a Pinot Vin Gris. Two estate vineyards produce the bulk of the fruit used in winemaking: Rancho La Rinconada with 130 acres planted (60 Pinot Noir and 70 Chardonnay), and Sanford & Benedict with an additional 135 acres planted (68 Pinot Noir, 52 Chardonnay, and 15 other varietals). A new "green" winemaking/visitors center has recently opened, but the winery, while now following sustainable agricultural practices, has backed away from Richard Sanford's dedication to more rigorous, costly, and somewhat controversial vineyard management practices. The use of cool-area grapes and the orientation of Terlato's head wine practitioner, Doug Fletcher, dictate that Sanford will continue its long tradition of balanced wines.

SANTA BARBARA WINERY 1962		Map 21
www.sbwinery.com	800-225-3633	Tasting
Santa Barbara	Santa Barbara County	Sta Rita Hills AVA

Pierre Lafond, formerly a Santa Barbara wine and cheese merchant, opened the first winery in the town of Santa Barbara since Prohibition in 1962.

Ten years later, Lafond planted his eponymous sixty-five-acre vineyard in the Santa Rita Hills, west of Buellton, and another thirty-five acres in 1997. Half of the needed juice is grown on these two sites, with the remainder bought from area growers. Winemaker Bruce McGuire has been with the winery since 1981 and can truly be called a pioneer of Pinot Noir and Syrah on the Central Coast. Another forty-four thousand cases of red and white varietals (60 percent whites, principally Chardonnay) are produced at the Santa Barbara Winery and sold at moderate prices. Tasting rooms are located at both the downtown and Lafond Winery locations.

The Lafond Chardonnay from the home vineyard is the winery's most consistent bottling in general distribution. Limited-edition Pinot Noirs and Grenache have also been well received of late. Most wines have received ratings in the upper 80s for their fairly rich, well-fruited styles.

The Lafond label consists of ten thousand cases of Pinot Noir and Syrah, made at the Lafond Winery facility.

SEA SMOKE CELLARS 1999		Map 22
www.seasmokecellars.com	866-PINOT NOIR	No Tasting
Lompoc	Santa Barbara County	Sta. Rita Hills AVA

Bob Davids, owner of Sea Smoke, brought Kris Curran of Curran (described earlier) aboard in 2000 to become winemaker for this all-Pinot Noir producer. Now that Curran has moved on to Foley, assistant winemaker Don Schroeder has taken over. Three Pinot Noir bottlings (Sea Smoke Ten, Southing, and Botella Pinot Noirs) are produced from different parts of the hundred-acre vineyard in the Santa Rita Hills (up which blows the evening fog affectionately named "Sea Smoke").

These are limited, estate-only bottlings—with Ten being both the most limited and the wine that fetches top dollar for its big, rich, deep character. The least expensive of the lot, although not carrying a day-to-day-drinking price tag, is Botella, and while it may score a few points lower than its pricey mates, it is often the best value. All of the Sea Smoke wines can approach overripeness, but when that pitfall is avoided, they can also earn ratings at the top of the 80-point scale and into the 90-point area.

STOLPMAN VINEYARDS 1992		Map 22
www.stolpmanvineyards.com	805-688-0400	Tasting
Solvang	Santa Barbara County	Santa Ynez Valley AVA

Tom and Marilyn Stolpman, along with winemaker Sashi Moorman—veteran of the Ojai Vineyard—initially put Stolpman on the vinous map of the Central Coastal with their grapes, first sold to other top wine producers. More recently, their limited-production bottlings—totaling four thousand cases a year—of an estate Syrah, Sangiovese, and a Cabernet blend called Poetry in Red have caught the attention of those who could find the wines. The 220-acre Stolpman vineyard is being developed in Ballard Canyon, between Solvang and Los Olivos. So far, about 150 acres are planted to Syrah (80 acres), Sangiovese (17), Viognier (10), Roussanne (10), and smaller blocks of Grenache, Nebbiolo, Merlot, and Petite Sirah.

Syrah is the star of the show, both in the upscale Angeli bottling and in various "estate" wines. All are pricey; all are deep, ripe, and expressive; and all have earned ratings ranging from the high 80s to low 90s, making Stolpman a name to remember for bold Syrahs.

ZACA MESA WINERY 1972		Map 22
www.zacamesa.com	805-688-9339	Tasting
Los Olivos	Santa Barbara County	Santa Ynez Valley AVA

One of the first wineries in Santa Barbara County, Zaca Mesa was initially bought and planted by an investor group; the Cushman family is the sole remaining member of that group and owns the winery today. Zaca Mesa has evolved into an exclusively estate-grown and -bottled facility specializing in Rhône varietals. The vineyards are up to 240 acres, of which about 60 percent is planted to Syrah and another 20 percent to Chardonnay, with several other Rhônes making up the balance. Production approaches thirty thousand cases, with 50 percent Syrahs and 25 percent Chardonnay. Current winemaker Clay Brock presides over what has become renowned as a hothouse for aspiring winemakers, including alumni such as Ken Brown (who later started Byron), Jim Clendenen (Au Bon Climat), Bob Lindquist (Qupé), and Lane Tanner (of Lane Tanner).

Zaca Mesa quality has jumped all over the map in its nearly forty-year existence, and, happily, its wines are doing quite well today; Syrah and Viognier lead the way with scores in the high 80s and low 90s. The winery's flagship bottling, Black Bear Syrah, is one of the leading examples of the variety made in California. The wines tend toward richness, with more flesh and suppleness than outright power.

Sierra Foothills

It is almost impossible to live in California and not be in love with the Sierra Foothills. It is the most relaxed, scenic, accessible pathway to California's rustic, romantic past, and whether one goes up out of the flat-lands to swim and hike or to visit the home of the Gold Rush or to forage in the endless supply of antiques shops in small towns that look like they have not changed since the gaslight era, the Sierra Foothills is a place of endless allure and, not insignificantly, boasts a small but important supply of good, hearty wine and some hundred wineries.

While there are wineries that will occasionally offer a lighter white, mostly of Sauvignon Blanc or Riesling, truth be told, this is the land of the rich, tasty, full-bodied red wine. For years that red wine was Zinfandel, and, in substantial part, the century-old vines of Amador County were the basis and backbone of the wines that helped make Zinfandel into the popular varietal it has become today.

Sierra Foothills

Listed first because it is the "Godfather" of this chapter, the Sierra Foothills AVA is a most unusual creature. It extends for almost two hundred miles across the lower Sierras at elevations ranging from one thousand to three thousand feet. It takes in parts of eight counties from Calaveras County in the southern end to Yuba County at its northern extremity, and includes both the heavily graped areas of Amador and El Dorado counties and the far less intensely involved plantings in Nevada, Tuolumne, Placer, and Mariposa counties.

As early as Gold Rush days, there seem to have been vines planted in these areas. By some accounts, at the peak of the good times in the nineteenth century, up to ten thousand acres of vines were devoted to slaking the thirst of a hardworking miner population. The twentieth-century expansion of wine grapes in the lower flatlands, especially in the coastal counties, was not replicated in the foothills, however, and as the mines played out, so did the vines. By 1970, only about a thousand acres of grapes remained. Today that number is back up to about 6,600 acres, and it is still Zinfandel that leads the way with its 2,600 acres. Syrah and Cabernet Sauvignon come next at seven hundred acres apiece, and Chardonnay and Merlot account for some three hundred acres each.

Amador County

With half the planted acreage found within the Sierra Foothills AVA, Amador County is the big daddy both in terms of tonnage and also in the quality of wines produced. Its Shenandoah AVA, located at its north end immediately adjacent to El Dorado County, has been recognized for decades as the home of deep, prodigious Zinfandels, and now, with the coming to popularity of Syrah, that variety is also proving to be a stellar performer. Fiddletown, located in a small valley adjoining the Shenandoah Valley, is important and would have gained more fame if it contained a greater quantity of grapes. All told, Amador County can claim 3,300 acres of grapes, 90 percent of which is in red grapes, up from 600 as of 1970. Zinfandel grabs the lion's share at 2,100 acres, up from 450 as of 1970. Syrah chimes in at 200 acres, and no other variety adds up to more than 100 acres to the overall county total. The bulk of Amador County's acreage lies within the Shenandoah Valley.

See Amador Vintners Association: www.amadorwine.com.

Apple Hill

Of the two major growing areas in El Dorado County, the Apple Hill area northeast of Placerville and within a stone's throw of the highway is perhaps the better known and enjoys a steady stream of visitors to its mountainside wineries and fruit orchards. Significant producers located

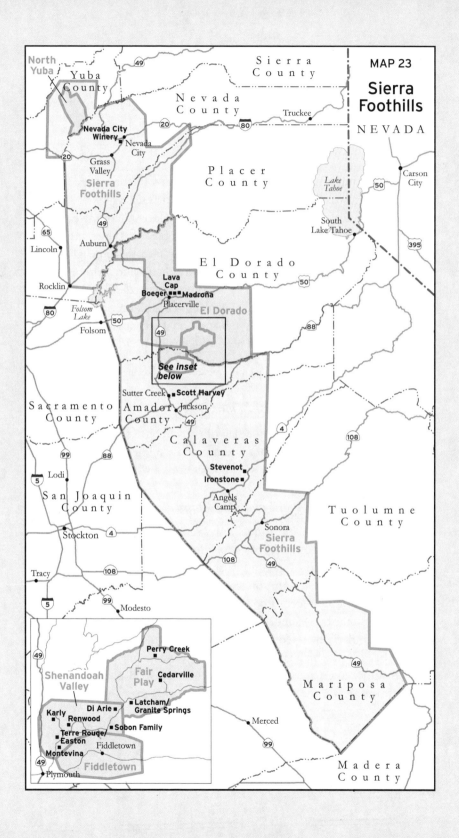

MAP 23

**Sierra
Foothills**

here are Lava Cap, Madroña, and Boeger. Although not a recognized AVA, Apple Hill is its own distinct area and, by virtue of both its wineries and its plantings, deserves to be recognized for its status as a winegrowing region.

Calaveras County

With but five hundred acres of vines, spread across the broad spectrum of varieties that grow in California, and with most wines selling in the $15 to $25 range, the question remains: is the potential of Calaveras County ever to be seen again? As the center of the Gold Rush, it had plenty of vines, but despite that heritage, very few Calaveras wines make it into the limelight today. Only a handful of wineries out of the area try their hands with Calaveras grapes, and only one so far, Prospect 772, located in Oakland and helped by the advice of Jeff Cohn of JC Cellars, has caught the highbrow fancy. Grape acreage totals seven hundred with Syrah and Cabernet Sauvignon in the lead at one hundred acres apiece. Syrah heads the quality parade.

See Calaveras Winegrape Alliance: www.calaveraswines.org.

El Dorado

This AVA is nothing more than a flag of convenience. It covers all of the county between the elevations of 1,200 feet and 3,500 feet and contains, for all practical purposes, all of the wine grapes grown within the county.

El Dorado County

An unregistered blip on the vinous radar screen back in 1970 at the start of the current wine boom, regardless of the reported three thousand acres of vines planted there during Gold Rush days, El Dorado County today is less significant for the amount of acreage currently planted there than for the broad array of producers it boasts and its proximity to Highway 50, one of two major links between urban California and Lake Tahoe. With some 1,800 acres under vine—led by Zinfandel, Cabernet Sauvignon, Merlot, and Syrah, each of which falls in the 150- to 300-acre bracket—El Dorado gains its importance by being home to a host of small, modern wineries whose efforts are, on the whole, a little less blustery than those of Amador County, immediately to its south.

See El Dorado Wine Grape Growers Association: www.edwgga.org/index.htm; El Dorado Winery Association: www.eldoradowines.org.

Fair Play

Located south of Placerville by about fifteen miles, almost to the Amador County line and sharing the more rustic style associated with wines from its neighbor, the Fair Play AVA boasts a handful of recently created wineries. The better known are Cedarville and Perry Creek. Its major grapes are Zinfandel and Syrah, but Fair Play is one of the few locations in the broader Sierra Foothills AVA to have produced noticeably good Cabernet Sauvignon on occasion.

Fiddletown

Located immediately adjacent to the Shenandoah Valley AVA, Fiddletown is, as it has been seemingly forever, a lesser cousin to its more famous and intensively farmed neighbor. A few small, relatively unknown wineries exist within the Fiddletown AVA, and thus Fiddletown's limited reputation has been made by wineries outside the area, mostly in the Shenandoah Valley, that have sourced the occasional Zinfandel from the area. Fiddletown's wines tend to be lighter and less fully concentrated than those of the Shenandoah Valley. Successful, well-regarded Fiddletown Zinfandels have been made recently by Easton, Renwood, and Sobon Estate, all producers located in the adjacent valley.

Mariposa, Placer, and Tuolumne Counties

With less than three hundred acres among the three of them combined, these counties are the junior members of the Sierra Foothills AVA.

See Placer County Wine and Grape Association: www.placerwineandgrape.org.

Nevada County

There was a time, about ten years ago, when Nevada County wineries seemed to be making an aggressive push to enter the broader wine markets, but their wines never quite took hold of the public's imagination; and despite reasonable success, Nevada County's winegrowing fortunes have more or less stagnated. All told, there are only four hundred acres of grapes, headed by Syrah at one hundred acres, and a handful of wineries, of which the most significant and widely respected are the Indian Springs winery with its substantial, two-hundred-acre vineyard and the Nevada City winery. The picturesque town of Grass Valley boasts half a dozen small producers and tasting rooms.

North Yuba

With two wineries and one AVA, Yuba County is a minor player in both quantity and quality. The North Yuba AVA is home to Renaissance Vineyards, owned and operated by a religious group that is sometimes described by others as a cult. At times, its wines have won critical acclaim; at others, they have been far too ordinary, perhaps owing to both the winery's sometimes-difficult climatic challenges and the problem of wine being part vocation and part avocation. Still, there are serious people on the winemaking side, and who they are is less important than the notion that their wines have not hit a consistent stride.

Shenandoah Valley of California

The title shown here is, in fact, the governmentally required name despite the fact that the Shenandoah Valley in Virginia has so few grapes and so little grape-growing history that the only people confused by the two are a few folks within the District of Columbia Beltway. But, be that as it may, we in California will continue to know one of our favorite appellations simply as Shenandoah Valley. Its history is integrally combined with that of California and the Gold Rush that brought fame and fortune to the West.

It is also the Shenandoah Valley's significant claim to fame that it played a major role in the establishment of Zinfandel in its place as one of the state's leading grape varieties. Somewhere in the mid- to late 1960s, folks like the winemakers at Harbor Winery in Sacramento began making Zinfandel from Amador County, relying on old vines that had somehow survived the end of the mining era and Prohibition and lingered mostly as contributors to inexpensive generic red wine. Building on the success with Amador Zinfandel at Harbor, the Sutter Home winery in the Napa Valley became persuaded by Darrell Corti, a young wine aficionado in Sacramento, to try its hand with Amador Zinfandel. Soon, the old and neglected vines in Amador were being made into wine by important players in the Zin world like Ridge and the Carneros Creek winery.

Not much has changed up in the Shenandoah Valley except for the increase in vineyard acreage and the two dozen wineries that now call it home. Sutter Home and Ridge no longer make wine from the area, but they have been replaced by successful producers like Easton, Renwood, Sobon Estate, C. G. Di Arie, Montevina, and others. Even Vino Noceto, whose major product is a very good Sangiovese that actually smells and tastes more like its Tuscany-grown cousins than most versions in California, also offers Zinfandel.

BOEGER WINERY 1972   Map 23

    www.boegerwinery.com   800-655-2634   Tasting

    Placerville   El Dorado County   El Dorado AVA

Boeger's Placerville ranchlands harken to the Gold Rush era when gold was discovered some fifteen minutes away. Purchased from the Fossati family by Greg and Sue Boeger in 1972, their first release was two years later. Greg had spent his youth at his grandfather's winery, Nichelini, in hills east of the Napa Valley floor, and the next generation, in the form of winemaker son Justin Boeger, is carrying on the family tradition. Of the total seventy owned acres, forty are producing grapes on the Estate and Fossati vineyards, with an additional fifty acres leased in the area. The winery's limited production is principally Zinfandel, Cabernet Sauvignon, Sauvignon Blanc, and the occasional Meritage. Second label Carson Peak is sold at lower price points.

Boeger wines have been reasonably well priced and have been good reflections of the area's potential at the chosen price points. Moreover, the winery makes an interesting visit for those who would rather poke through the rustic Sierras than partake of the more upscale offerings of the famous lowland wine areas. Best known for ripe, fairly concentrated, slightly gruff Zinfandel, Boeger can hit the gong from time to time with Cabernet as well.

CEDARVILLE VINEYARD 1998   Map 23

    www.cedarvillevineyard.com   530-620-WINE   Tasting by Appointment

    Fair Play   El Dorado County   Fair Play AVA

Jonathan Lachs and Susan Marks worked in the Silicon Valley until they were ready to plunge into winemaking in the late 1990s. Today, all grapes are grown on the fifteen-acre estate in Fair Play, just north of the Shenandoah Valley, and the winery's capacity maxes out at 2,500 cases. Production is principally Zinfandels, Syrah, and Cabernet Sauvignon, with the occasional Grenache, Viognier, and Mourvèdre. Current production stands at about two thousand cases. The limited quantities are available mainly through a mailing list, although one can often find them in specialty wine stores.

The ripe-leaning, consistently well-made wines are unfailingly good to very good and rate, alongside Terre Rouge, as the quality leaders in the

Sierra Foothills. The underground winery is a delight—as are the winery owners—and Cedarville is one of our favorite stops in the area.

DI ARIE WINERY 2002		Map 23
www.cgdiarie.com	209-245-4700	Tasting
Plymouth	Amador County	Shenandoah Valley AVA

Chaim and Elisheva Gur-Arieh built this small winery on a 209-acre estate, purchased in the early 2000s. Chaim, an Israeli food scientist, built and sold several companies before succumbing to the wine bug. On their estate, Chaim and Elisheva have planted some forty acres to vines, with a production maximum of fifteen thousand cases fast approaching. Wines made are largely Zinfandels, with smaller quantities of Barbera, Primitivo, and Sauvignon Blanc. Elisheva is an accomplished artist, and, in addition to the attractions offered by Di Arie wines, there is a well-appointed gallery with her paintings also on the premises. Up to the 2005 vintage, the winery was known as C. G. Di Arie.

Zinfandel, besides being the volume leader, is also the quality leader here, with scores consistently in the upper 80s and the occasional 90-pointer. The various Zins range from ripe and direct to rich and surprisingly complex given the usual straightforward style of the area.

EASTON WINES 1985		Map 23
www.terrerougewines.com	209-245-3117	Tasting
Plymouth	Amador County	Shenandoah Valley AVA

At their estate called Domaine de la Terre Rouge, former Berkeley wine seller Bill Easton (his Solano Cellars, now under new ownership, is still a fine wine store and spot for a light meal) and chef, cookbook author, and wife Jane O'Riordan make wines under this label and under Terre Rouge (discussed later in this chapter). The Terre Rouge brand is used for Rhône varieties, while Easton is used for Zinfandel, Barbera, and Sauvignon Blanc. Easton makes a total of twenty thousand cases of nearly twenty varietals, all with grapes sourced from Placer, El Dorado, Amador, and Calaveras counties growers.

IRONSTONE VINEYARDS 1988		Map 23
www.ironstonevineyards.com	209-728-1251	Tasting
Murphys	Calaveras County	Sierra Foothills AVA

John and Gail Kautz, under their Kautz Family Vineyards brand, own and operate the large Ironstone facility along with several other labels, including the recently seen Christine Andrews title. Ironstone is primarily a modestly priced, large-quantity wine, but several successful reserve bottlings have emerged. Grapes are purchased from throughout the Sierra Foothills. The Ironstone winery has become something of a destination, what with its concert amphitheater, deli, and shops, plus gold panning for the kiddies.

One does not necessarily visit Ironstone for the brilliance of its wines, as they tend to be relatively low in price and adequate as values; but, with a somewhat rustic style and comfortable price niches, Ironstone manages to stay in focus for everyday drinking and for an exceptional destination for touring wine lovers.

KARLY WINES 1978		Map 23
www.karlywines.com	209-245-3922	Tasting
Plymouth	Amador County	Shenandoah Valley AVA

Ex-fighter jock Lawrence "Buck" Cobb started the winery as a hobby in 1978 and named it for his wife, Karly. As an early Amador County boutique winery, it grew over time into a ten-thousand-case producer today. As with most Sierra Foothills wineries, the lion's share of the production is Zinfandel plus a few select Rhône varietals for good measure. Old vines from the Sadie Upton and Massoni vineyards are the sources of most fruit.

Karly Zinfandels reflect the ripe, direct, somewhat rustic style of wine from the area. The limited-production Warrior Fires Zin has been the most successful over the years, with scores that occasionally have reached into the 90-point range.

LATCHAM VINEYARDS/GRANITE SPRINGS WINERY 1981		Map 23
www.latcham.com	800-638-6041	Tasting
Fair Play	El Dorado County	Fair Play AVA

Jon and Margaret Latcham started Latcham Vineyards as a vineyard only, in 1981, near Fair Play. Over time, Latcham started making its own wine and acquired the nearby Granite Springs Winery in 1994. Today, the two labels operate together, using grapes sourced from the twenty-eight-acre Latcham Vineyard. Both make a wide variety of wine types, in small quantities, anchored by Zinfandel. The wines are generally approachable, if a bit gruff, and more often than not earn mid- to upper-80s scores, making them reasonable values relative to price. Limited production can make these wines hard to find at times, but both the location and the wines are reasons to think of Latcham and Granite Springs.

LAVA CAP WINERY 1981		Map 23
www.lavacap.com	530-621-0175	Tasting
Placerville	El Dorado County	El Dorado AVA

University of California–Berkeley professor Thomas Jones founded Lava Cap in 1981, with the initial harvest in 1986. The winery is named for an old miners' term for a hard volcanic rock layer overlying gold-bearing gravel. In time, the rock weathers to a soil well suited for growing grapes. One hundred twenty acres of estate vineyards are among the highest in the Sierra Foothills at 3,300 feet, and most grapes are sourced from the estate or from the Stromberg-Carpenter Vineyard nearby. Lava Cap specializes in red Bordeaux varieties. Two thirds of the total twenty-thousand-case production is red, featuring Zinfandels, Merlot, Cabernet Sauvignon, and Syrah. Son Thomas Jr. now runs the winery.

Located in the Apple Hill area of El Dorado County east of Placerville, Lava Cap is one of the area's more ambitious producers. Its wines tend to be ripe and rounded in style, often with a bit more juicy sweetness than is typical of the area. Point scores in the mid- to upper 80s are not uncommon, and the occasional Zinfandel has rated higher. The tasting deck overlooking the vineyards is a delightful place to sample Lava Cap wines when the weather invites.

MADROÑA VINEYARDS 1973		Map 23
www.madronavineyards.com	530-644-5948	Tasting
Camino	El Dorado County	El Dorado AVA

Dick and Leslie Bush planted thirty-five acres of vineyards in 1973 at three thousand feet of elevation, making this winery one of the highest-altitude producers in California. Named after the huge Madroña tree in the center of the vineyard, Madroña still uses estate-grown grapes for its ten-thousand-case production. Principally a red wine grower, Madroña is known for Syrah, Zinfandel, Cabernet Sauvignon, and Merlot. In recent years the Bush family has added Cabernet Franc, Riesling, and Gewürztraminer to the roster.

Madroña wines may not get the highest scores around, but its regular-bottling Zinfandel is usually well received and tends to be a little more mannerly than the typical Sierra Foothills red. It is a Good Value in top vintages.

MONTEVINA WINERY	1970	Map 23
www.montevina.com	209-245-6942	Tasting
Plymouth	Amador County	Shenandoah Valley AVA

Founded in 1970 by Carey Gott and father-in-law Walter Field, Montevina has grown into the largest winery in the Shenandoah Valley and possibly the Sierra Foothills. Montevina was acquired by the Trinchero Family Estates (of Sutter Home fame and numerous other labels) in '88 to provide Trinchero access to smaller premium and specialty wines. Today, however, with Zinfandel and Italian varietals—particularly Barbera and Sangiovese—as Montevina's forte and with total production ranging north of one hundred and twenty-five thousand cases, a huge volume for this region, the label is now mostly associated with inexpensive wines of moderate interest to selective consumers. A four-hundred-acre estate supplies some of the grapes for Montevina as well as a second, upscale label called Terra d'Oro.

NEVADA CITY WINERY	1980	Map 23
www.ncwinery.com	800-203-9463	Tasting
Nevada City	Nevada County	Sierra Foothills AVA

One of a very small handful of wineries in Nevada County, the Nevada City Winery was started by Allan Haley—a Nevada County native with European wine experience—as a garage winery in 1980. Two years later it moved to yet a larger garage in downtown Nevada City. Today's winemaking is guided both by Haley and winemaker Mark Foster, experienced at Chalone and Madroña. Some ten thousand cases are bottled, largely from fruit grown on the three-hundred-acre estate. The vast majority of the numerous varieties are red, led by Zinfandel, Merlot, Cabernet Sauvignon, and Syrah.

Wine ratings have generally been in the mid-80s, with a few excursions higher. At the typical Sierra Foothills moderate price levels, they are decent values in better vintages, making the winery well worth a stop when you are in the area.

PERRY CREEK VINEYARDS 1991		Map 23
www.perrycreek.com	800-880-4026	Tasting
Fair Play	El Dorado County	Fair Play AVA

In 2006, owners Michele Wilms and Dieter Jurgens, who already owned the Fair Play Farms estate vineyard, acquired Perry Creek from founder Michael Chazen. Winemaker Nancy Steel continues in her role of overseer of the wine menu that focuses heavily on Zinfandel and Rhône varietals. The forty-acre estate vineyard is about half planted to Syrah and Zinfandel, with the remainder in Cabernet Sauvignon, Petite Sirah, and smaller batches of numerous varietals. The long-popular—and popularly priced—ZinMan Zinfandel will continue to hold a central spot on the roster. Perry Creek's mid-density wines are reasonably priced, and if not knocking down big scores, they are typically attractive at the prices asked.

The winery is an architectural gem both visually and in the way that its spaces work together. Perry Creek is a must stop for visitors to the area. The winery Web site describes many events and attractions.

RENWOOD WINERY 1993		Map 23
www.renwood.com	800-348-VINO	Tasting
Plymouth	Amador County	Shenandoah Valley AVA

Boston native Robert Smerling and partners established this well-known Zinfandel producer in 1993. In a matter of years, Renwood grew from a 2,500-case producer to one bottling well over 100,000 cases—considered the largest independent Zinfandel producer in the state. Production includes about a dozen separate Zinfandels, with the Grandpère Zinfandel the most sought after, as well as numerous other varieties including Barbera and Syrah. Over 350 acres of vines on four owned vineyards nearby provide over two-thirds of the fruit for each vintage; the remaining grapes are purchased from local growers. Renwood also produces a large quantity of modestly priced Red Label wines.

Quality has been varied, but the limited-production Grandpère and the Grandmère bottlings, both of which are ripe, full-bodied, and firmly structured, have led the way. The Jack Rabbit Flat Zinfandel is also usually well received, and the low-priced Sierra Series Zin has occasionally earned Good Value status.

Shirley and Leon Sobon founded Shenandoah Vineyards in Plymouth in 1977 after Leon left Lockheed in the Silicon Valley. In 1989, the Sobons purchased the former D'Agostini winery—one of the oldest in California—and renamed it Sobon. Now under the watch of second-generation winemaker Paul Sobon, the family's 125-acre vineyard produces the fruit for their 40,000-case production wineries. Nearly 80 percent of the wine made in the wineries is red, and virtually all of that is Zinfandel in its many estate, vineyard-designated, and reserve shapes and sizes. Several Rhône varietals and dessert wines round out the offerings.

Fairly typical Amador County wines—ripe, rustic, direct—appear under both the Sobon Family and Shenandoah Vineyards labels and range in price from entry level to medium-priced with their varietal categories. Sobon Rocky Top Zinfandel is often our favorite, and the occasional ReZerve (their spelling) and Fiddletown bottlings also can rise above the mid-80 range and have, at least a few times, achieved 90-point scores and higher.

The Stevenot family first came to the Sierras in the mid-1800s Gold Rush. Fifth-generation Barden Stevenot founded the modern winery in 1978 after purchasing the hundred-year-old Shaw Ranch in the 1960s and gradually planting vines on the property. More recently—in 2006—Stevenot was acquired by the Munari family. Winemaker Kate MacDonald keeps close watch on the production of a wide variety of wines, ranging from the Argentine varietal Torrontes to the Portuguese Verdelho to Zinfandel and Merlot. Production stands at upward of twenty-five thousand cases. Stevenot has recently added Red Rover, a second, modestly priced label. Most wines are made from grapes grown on the estate's developed seventy-seven acres.

Prices have tended to be inviting over the years, and while ratings have rarely been high, they are not out of line relative to the cost of the wine.

TERRE ROUGE WINES 1985		Map 23
www.terrerougewines.com	209-245-3117	Tasting
Plymouth	Amador County	Shenandoah Valley AVA

Bill Easton and wife Jane O'Riordan left the flatlands behind for the hills of Amador County and have not looked back. Their Terre Rouge brand is used for Rhône varieties, while Easton (see that entry in this chapter) is used for Zinfandel, Barbera, and Sauvignon Blanc. Easton makes a total of twenty thousand cases of nearly twenty varietals, all with grapes sourced from Placer, El Dorado, Amador, and Calaveras counties growers.

The Terre Rouge Ascent Syrah has been an industry pacesetter from its inception and was named the Connoisseurs' Guide Wine of the Year within recent history. It remains a spectacular wine with critical evaluations in the lower to mid-90s. Other Terre Rouge offerings have also been well received, as have the Easton Zinfandel, all with scores that typically range from the upper 80s to the lower 90s. Even the lower-priced entry-level wines have often rated as Good Values.

The Rest of California

California wine is most often associated with the famous coastal counties and their revered valleys, and to a lesser extent with the foothills of the Sierra Madre Mountains. However, there is enormous wine acreage and the greater portion of all grapes crushed found in the less well-known places that spread up and down the state's Central Valley and in important if isolated pockets near and also south and east of Los Angeles. By itself, the Central Valley, with grapes stretching from Bakersfield to Redding and beyond, contains 50 percent of all the grapevines in California; and this valley grows, because of higher tonnages, some 75 percent of the total tonnage crushed in most years. The greatest portion of that production goes directly into inexpensive wines for everyday table use, but there are places from one end of the Central Valley to the other that try for better and succeed.

This chapter is divided into two sections, each of which deserves to be considered on its own. Because the Central Valley is not simply a monolithic breeding ground for inexpensive wines, it has seen choice pockets of land develop into unique growing areas, each of which is appreciated for the differences it can bring to wines. That few of these locations challenge the more coastal counties for "collectibility" status does not mean that they are unimportant. Indeed, whether Lodi or Clarksburg, Madera or the Dunnigan Hills, these are places that produce lots of very good, moderately priced wine for everyday drinking.

Also included in this chapter are small AVAs that exist at the margins of the Central Valley. Some wander off into the hills of the far north, and others find shelter in the rising foothills on either side of the valley floor. The existence of alluvial soils, better air movement with elevation, and greater range of temperature from day to night help many of these regions deliver wines of interest.

The second section of the chapter is devoted to a different world entirely. Here are described the AVAs and wineries in the large South Coast AVA that covers five counties. Most of the world would describe the area as Southern California and immediately think of Los Angeles and San Diego as the centers of interest. And although there are vineyards and wineries in quite close proximity to both cities, it is the Cucamonga Valley and the Temecula Valley, both removed from the central cities by almost a hundred miles, that contain the largest portions of the three thousand acres of grapes in the area. The Cucamonga area has a very long grape-growing heritage, but it has slowly and inexorably lost its standing over the last ninety years. Temecula, in contrast, is rapidly becoming a hotbed of winemaking activity, in large part because it offers both attractive growing conditions and an easy day trip from both of the large cities in the area.

CENTRAL VALLEY

Alta Mesa

To the east of the cool (by Lodi standards) Cosumnes River AVA and just upland of it—thus warmer and containing less silt in its soils, which are more of clay loam—this intermediate area lying mostly in Sacramento County boasts more than four thousand acres of grapes, mostly red, but some whites as well. The Sloughhouse AVA abuts to the east.

Borden Ranch

Located in the northeastern quadrant of the Lodi AVA, above Clements Hills but below Alta Mesa, this region features rolling hills that rise from seventy-five up to five hundred feet. For the most part, this area is the home of big wineries: Delicato, Woodbridge, and Sutter Home all have substantial acreage here. Delicato's Clay Station brand is sourced from its holdings here, and those wines have often shown more fruit and less overripeness than their neighbors in the flatlands to the west even though the AVA is generally

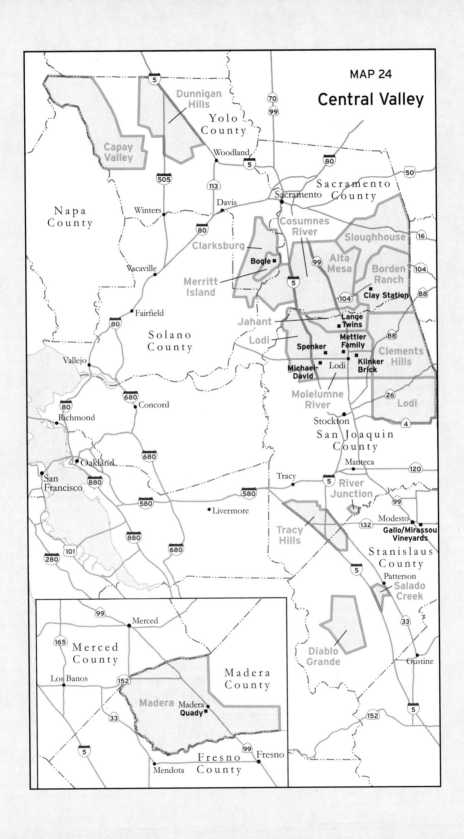

MAP 24

Central Valley

warmer and wetter than the lowlands nearer the delta. Approximately twelve thousand acres of grapes are planted in the Borden Ranch AVA.

Capay Valley

This secluded little valley just to the west of the Dunnigan Hills AVA in Yolo County is home to one winery and several vineyards. It is a picturesque slice of heaven, but it is now far better known for its Indian-run gaming casino than it is for its bucolic lifestyle and gentleman farmers whose organic produce is well-regarded.

Clarksburg

Less often seen on labels than its influence in California would dictate, Clarksburg lies smack in the Sacramento River Delta as it snuggles up to the higher ground of the Lodi AVA. Its rich soils and large diurnal temperature swings allow Clarksburg to specialize in grapes like Chenin Blanc and Petite Sirah in particular, but also to be able to grow almost anything else save for the most cold-loving varieties like Pinot Noir and Riesling. Bogle Vineyards is the largest producer in the AVA, but the handful of other wineries is relatively small and unheard of. As a result, most Clarksburg grapes go elsewhere. The very well-received Dry Creek Vineyard Chenin Blanc comes with a Clarksburg appellation, and there are lots of other wines made from Clarksburg grapes that do not have the name but nevertheless make the area an important growing region. Over sixteen thousand acres of grapes are grown on the islands and adjoining lands of this sixteen-mile-long, eight-mile-wide AVA. The Merritt Island AVA is a one-island site entirely within the larger Clarksburg AVA.

See Clarksburg Winegrowers Association: www.clarksburgwinegrowers.com.

Clements Hills

East of Lodi running up into the low foothills, this AVA offers a variety of soil types and some of the more interesting plantings in the greater Lodi AVA. With varieties like Albarino and Tempranillo joining the more likely candidates in the rolling hills, the Clements Hills area may be the first of the Lodi AVAs to earn its own standing. It has twenty thousand acres of grapes—some belong to the Gallos, and others, especially small plantings of Spanish varieties, are in the hands of Markus Bokisch. Bokisch's energy and vision led to the establishment of Lodi's overlay of smaller AVAs based on science, not on tradition or grower envy of the type that has made some very famous coastal AVAs into less than well-defined places.

Cosumnes River

Lying at the northwest corner of the Lodi AVA, mostly in Sacramento County, the three thousand acres of this AVA exist in the coolest climate within the greater Lodi limits. It is greatly influenced by its relative proximity to the Sacramento River Delta and the foggy breezes that whip through the area. More than any other in the larger Lodi AVA, Cosumnes River is more likely to support white varieties like Pinot Gris, Sauvignon Blanc, and Chardonnay than red grapes.

Diablo Grande

This one-winery AVA in the western hills of Stanislaus County, to the west of Patterson, has fewer than fifty acres of grapes surrounded by golf courses and a resort community. Its elevation of approximately 1,100 feet and east-facing location allows the grapes to avoid some of the scorching Central Valley heat. Like other Central Valley west-side AVAs, it is not far by direct line to the cooler coastal areas but is quite different in character because of its Central Valley situation.

Dunnigan Hills

In the rolling hills north of Sacramento, in Yolo County, along the west side of the Central Valley but close enough to the delta to be cooled by the evening breezes that rush in from San Francisco Bay, this AVA has always seemed more promising than its results to date. Its mix of grapes favors Syrah, with Chardonnay a close second. Total plantings exceed 1,600 acres of the 90,000 acres within the AVA boundaries. One winery, R. H. Phillips, with its inexpensive Night Harvest label, dominates the area with holdings of some 1,300 acres. The area may be only thirty miles removed from the Napa Valley, if you are a crow, but it is light-years away in growing conditions.

Jahant

The Mokelumne River slices through the Lodi AVA from east to west and separates the rich, deep alluvial fan on the south side of the river from slightly higher but less deep soils that show up in the Jahant AVA to the north of the river. The climate may not be different, but the change in soils and the less extensive presence of century-old vines means that Jahant can create its own narrative over time. The Lange Twins Winery located in Jahant turns out wines for a long roster of clients. There are about thirty thousand acres of vines in the Jahant AVA, making it the second-most planted area within the greater Lodi AVA.

Lodi

Lodi town is a pleasant little burg sitting in the middle of prime agricultural land between Stockton and Sacramento. It's likable enough, with its cute downtown and its fruit stands and homespun restaurants. It is also the center of a densely packed grape-growing region that encompasses some hundred thousand acres of grapes and a rapidly increasing population of wineries, now numbering more than seventy-five, most of which are new and grower owned and operated. Lodi's grape-growing history stretches back to the 1860s, and while there are acres and acres of the gnarliest old vines in California, some with unusual pruning systems that look more like trees than vines, the oldest standings seem to be no more than 120 years old.

When the AVA system was put in place, Lodi, the town, and its surrounding towns banded together and formed an area that stretches far beyond city boundaries. The Lodi AVA encompasses almost all of the agricultural land north of Stockton up to and then east of Sacramento's urban sprawl—and then some, a distance of about thirty miles north to south and from the lowlands near Interstate 5 some ten miles and more east up into the low foothills of the Sierras. It also includes seven smaller AVAs within its borders; and while those names rarely make their way onto wine labels at present, the grower-winery owners are likely to some day add those names to their products. Eighty percent of the Lodi AVA is situated in San Joaquin County, and the other 20 percent is in Sacramento County. The grapes of the AVA dominate the crops of both counties and account for 80 to 85 percent of the annual tonnage in each of those counties.

The temptation to call Lodi a hot place is not without cause, but the truth is that it is somewhat cooler than many sites in the Central Valley, especially in its westernmost lands that sit near the delta and benefit from cooling breezes that moderate the heat late in the day. The eastern uplands are warmer but with less deep and less fertile soils. As a result, Lodi wines, now substantially from grapes grown surrounding Lodi town in deep, rich soils, are not as uniform as one might think looking at the area. And with the rapid expansion in plantings that has propelled the Lodi AVA to the top of the charts in volume, the numbers are truly staggering and make Lodi far more important in the California industry than just the numbers of labels bearing its name.

Zinfandel and Tokay were the backbone of the Lodi grape-growing community for decades. During Prohibition, when other areas were running into hard times, Lodi suffered less first because it had few wineries to shut down and, importantly, because it became the center for the shipment of grapes all over the United States. Today, old-vine Zinfandel is still a staple of the industry, but it is joined by tens of thousands of acres of grapes that have been planted in just the last thirty years. With one hundred thousand acres of grapes, most producing at higher tonnages per acre than cooler coastal locations, the Lodi AVA now accounts for 36 percent of the California Zinfandel crush, 41 percent of the Petite Sirah crush, 25 percent of the Cabernet Sauvignon and Merlot crushes, and 21 percent of the Chardonnay crush.

The area's seventy-five wineries use up a fair percentage of those grapes for their own bottlings under labels that focus first on large-production wineries like the fifty-five-grower Oak Ridge Winery, Woodbridge by Robert Mondavi, and Turner Road, with its inexpensive but often tasty Talus wines. But specialty labels use Lodi grapes, too—from Michael and David Phillips and Klinker Brick, to wines bearing the Lodi AVA title that show up under the nameplates of wineries as diverse as Laurel Glen on Sonoma Mountain and Eola Hills up in Oregon. And while they are unknown today, Lodi has a roster of rising stars whose products are likely to become far better known.

Within the Lodi AVA are seven smaller AVAs, all carved out by the Lodi group as a way of differentiating the significant differences that exist in soils and, to a lesser extent, in climate within the fairly broad geographic turf of the AVA. Each is profiled in this section under its own entry. They are Mokelumne River surrounded by Lodi town center and running east to Interstate 5; Clements Hills directly to the east and occupying the low foothills; Jahant directly north of the Mokelumne River AVA and just on the other side of the river on slightly higher ground; Borden Ranch occupying the high ground north of the Clements Hills district; Sloughhouse, also in the hills at the northeast corner of the Lodi AVA and running up to and past Highway 50 in the north and to the El Dorado and Amador county boundaries at its eastern extremities; Alta Mesa to the north of Jahant; and Cosumnes River at the northwest corner.

See Lodi Winegrape Commission: www.lodiwine.com.

Madera

This large AVA covering parts of both Madera and Fresno counties is in the very heart of the Central Valley and is among the valley's hotter areas.

It has long been a place for the growing of jug wines and for the production of fortified wines. For years, Ficklin made the best Port in California, and lately Quady Vineyards has gained great fame for a wide variety of sweet and fortified wines as well as for the production of its incredibly fragrant Vya Vermouth. Napa's Miner Family Vineyards makes an exceptional Viognier from the Simpson Vineyard in Madera.

See Madera Vintners Association: www.maderavintners.com.

Merritt Island

On the east side of the larger Clarksburg AVA sits Merritt Island, completely surrounded by water and the source of grapes for large wineries like Bogle and several smaller wineries, including wineries outside the area. Its name is rarely seen on wine labels.

Mokelumne River

The Mokelumne River has been a key feature of Lodi area geography from the time the area was settled over 150 years ago. As it comes out of the hills and follows the contours eastward, the river has tended to flood to the south, filling up the central Lodi area with deep, rich soils and encouraging intensive agricultural development. As one exits Interstate 5 and heads east into the Lodi AVA toward the small but attractive downtown area, it is clear that this is grape country. If the land is not covered with twisted old vines, it is all but smothered with new plantings as far as the eye can see. It is in this AVA that Lodi got its early reputation for heavy Zinfandels and dessert wines made from Tokay. New wineries like Michael-David and Jessie's Grove may be making modern, oak-aged wines in the old, fleshy, ripe style, but they are also changing the face of Lodi and its reputation in the bargain. With fifty thousand acres in vines, and with its old-vine heritage, it is the Mokelumne River AVA that is still the most likely to define what the world thinks of the name Lodi.

River Junction

Set between the Stanislaus and San Joaquin rivers south of Modesto near the town of Ripon and filled with fine, sandy loam soil, this one-winery (McManis) AVA grows some two thousand acres of grapes, mostly Chardonnay. The influence of the rivers keeps the area cooler than surrounding areas in the Central Valley, but this is still a warm place to grow grapes.

Salado Creek

With forty acres of vines in an area near Patterson, the Salado Creek AVA has yet to make much of a mark on the world. Like Diablo Grande, this AVA draws small benefit from its west-side location; but unlike Diablo Grande, Salada Creek is flatter and mostly devoted to agriculture, including pistachios and other tree crops.

Seiad Valley

Way up in the northern end of California in Siskiyou County, beyond even the Central Valley and tucked away in the hills fifteen miles from the Oregon border and east of Interstate 5, sits the quaint little town of Seiad Valley with its 350 residents and its one significant restaurant. It also once had a winery, but it is no more. The most recent wine acreage listings show eleven acres of grapes.

Sloughhouse

Originally proposed as Deer Creek Hills but approved as Sloughhouse, this area is higher and hotter than its partners in the Lodi AVA. Situated totally within Sacramento County, it contains rolling hills that see more winter rain than the other areas but also less cooling fog in summer. Its approximately five thousand acres of grapes are dominated by red varieties. Although some of its lower portions are not dissimilar in condition to what is found in the neighboring Borden Ranch AVA, its uplands begin to take on the shorter, hotter growing characteristics of Amador County, which forms its eastern border.

Tracy Hills

Located on Mount Oso in the middle of an otherwise-flat area of the Central Valley near Tracy town, this relatively unheralded AVA shows up in the wines of Tulip Hill Winery and Cleavage Creek wines, both owned by Budge Brown, who also owns the vineyard in the AVA.

Trinity Lakes

Way up north in Trinity County in an area of steep mountains and alpine-like hills and lakes, this tiny AVA is home to some thirty-two acres of grapes, three-quarters of which are crushed by the appropriately named Alpen Cellars. The Trinity Lake moderates the summer temperatures to a balmy mid-90s, but it also helps keep the temperature in the 70s deep into the fall, thereby extending the growing season. Reds, Merlot, and Syrah are grown at high elevations of approximately 1,800 feet, while Riesling, Gewürztraminer, and Pinot Noir grow at higher elevations of 2,700 feet. Chardonnay grows everywhere.

Willow Creek

One of the earlier AVAs established, back in the mid-1980s, the Willow Creek AVA remains fairly unchanged. Its isolated location about fifty miles east of Eureka, in a fold of the mountains that follows the Trinity River between the towns of Willow Creek and Salyer, seems unlikely to encourage vigorous vineyard expansion unless one of the handful of tiny wineries there somehow makes a breakout wine. Even then, the entire area encompasses but six thousand acres, much of it hard to plant; but with a growing season that brings temperatures similar to Napa and Bordeaux, there is potential in those hills.

BOGLE VINEYARDS 1968		Map 24
www.boglewinery.com	916-744-1139	Tasting
Clarksburg	Yolo County	Merritt Island AVA

The Bogle family farmed in the Sacramento River Delta from the mid-1800s forward. In 1968, father and son team Warren Bogle Sr. and Chris Bogle planted their first twenty acres of grapes on the ranch, near the Elk Slough. Now at 1,200 acres, with a winery built in 1978, the vineyards and winery are run by Patty Bogle, wife of the late Chris Bogle. The mega-winery produces hundreds of thousands of cases of wines targeted at the budget-minded supermarket wine buyer. Winemaker Christopher Smith, with history at Jordan and Kendall-Jackson, brings in a moderately priced Petite Sirah with a production of eighty thousand cases alone, in addition to Chardonnay and an Old Vine Zinfandel.

With most prices barely reaching double digits, Bogle can be among the most price-worthy wines available from California wineries—with medium/full-bodied Zinfandel and Sauvignon Blanc reaching Good Value status more often than not.

CLAY STATION WINES 1995		Map 24
www.claystationwine.com	209-824-3600	Tasting
Manteca	San Joaquin County	Borden Ranch AVA

In the mid-1990s, the Indelicato family—of Delicato Family Vineyards—acquired the 1,600-acre former Borden Ranch in foothills east of Lodi town and renamed it after a stagecoach stop used during the Gold Rush. Clay Station has since become a label in the Delicato stable of moderately priced varieties. The Clay Station range includes Viognier, Old Vine Zinfandel, Petite Sirah, and Pinot Gris, all totaling about twenty thousand cases.

Zinfandel has been the quality leader, but all of the Clay Station wines have succeeded from time to time and at reasonable prices. The wines are made, and the tasting room located, at the Delicato facility in Manteca.

KLINKER BRICK WINERY 2000		Map 24
www.klinkerbrickwinery.com	866-333-1845	Tasting
Lodi	San Joaquin County	Mokelumne River AVA

Owners Steve and Lori Felten are fifth-generation Lodi-area growers. From their sixteen blocks of grapes, ranging in age from 35 to 110 years old, most in the Mokelumne River AVA west of Lodi town but also in the Clements Hills east of town (all of which are also within the larger Lodi AVA), the Feltons produce some five thousand cases of Zinfandel and Syrah. The upscale Zin called Old Ghost is among the top wines produced in the Lodi area, and it is fully reflective of the highly ripened, lush, lusty, chocolaty style that is so often seen in the wines of the region. It has regularly earned scores up to 90 points. The winery name is derived from a type of brick made in the area during the early twentieth century. The bricks were dense, large, and made a distinctive "clink" when banged together.

LANGE TWINS WINERY & VINEYARDS 2003		Map 24
www.langetwins.com	209-334-9780	Tasting by Appointment
Acampo	San Joaquin County	Jahant AVA

This five-generation family farm was founded by German immigrants in the 1870s. After many years of grape growing, twins Randall and Brad Lange cofounded the winery in 2003. With winemaker David Akiyoshi (of UC–Davis and extensive experience at Robert Mondavi, as well as being the owner of the very well-regarded School Street Bistro in downtown Lodi), the Langes built an expandable winery, now producing a modest seven thousand cases of Sauvignon Blanc, Chardonnay,

Merlot, and Cabernet Sauvignon varieties. The vineyard includes over 900 acres of vines on an 1,800-acre estate. The family also has a substantial vineyard management service, with over seven thousand acres under management in the region. The winery is new, modern, and energy efficient; it is home to many Lodi-grown Zinfandels under famous North Coast labels.

METTLER FAMILY VINEYARDS 1999		Map 24
www.mettlerwine.com	888-509-5969	No Tasting
Lodi	San Joaquin County	Mokelumne River AVA

Now in the fifth generation, the Mettler family has grown grapes on the east side of Lodi since 1899, with another three generations before that in Alsace. It was only in 1999 that the family embarked on winemaking. The winery has grown to produce ten thousand cases of Cabernet Sauvignon, Petite Sirah, and an Old-Vine Zinfandel.

Mettler wines are ripe and rich with chocolaty overtones. If not classic by North Coast standards, they can be fine representatives of the Lodi style, and their mid- to upper-80-point rankings, particularly for the rugged Petite Sirah, earn the winery a respectable following.

MICHAEL-DAVID WINERY 1984		Map 24
www.lodivineyards.com	888-707-WINE	Tasting
Lodi	San Joaquin County	Mokelumne River AVA

Michael and David Phillips's great-great-grandparents homesteaded 160 acres in Lodi after the Civil War. The family originally farmed vegetables and other fruits in the region as well as grapes. Michael and David established their five-hundred-acre vineyards in the early 1980s and now grow some fifteen grape varietals. The winery produces over two hundred thousand cases of modestly priced wines with catchy monikers, including 7 Deadly Zins, 7 Heavenly Chards, 6th Sense Syrah, Earthquake Cab, Incognito Viognier, Don's Lodi Red, and a bubbly named Sparkling Duet. In recent years, the Phillipses have introduced several very expensive Lodi standards—Zinfandels with names like Lust, Greed, and Envy and a Cabernet Sauvignon labeled as Rapture, all with price tags nearing $60 and proving, in the process, that there is a growing, enthusiastic market for the rich, voluptuous style they offer in those upscale reds. Noteworthy also is Petite Petit, a surprisingly tasty blend of Petite Sirah and Petit Verdot, two grapes that have rarely met but somehow make upper-80-point magic at a fair price.

There is no doubt that the Phillips brothers have stepped out in front of their Lodi competition by both artistic and market acceptance measures. Their tasting room on Highway 12, just off Interstate 5, is a popular spot for tastings, local produce, and down-home lunches.

MIRASSOU VINEYARDS 1966		Map 24
www.mirassou.com	888-MIRASSOU	No Tasting
Modesto	Stanislaus County	California

Pierre Pellier emigrated from France in 1854 and settled in the Santa Clara Valley, planting the grape cuttings he had brought along. His daughter married neighboring winemaker Pierre Mirassou, the second of six generations of the family business continuing today. Surviving Prohibition, Mirassou made bulk wines for many years until, in 1966, it moved into the bottled wine era. Now owned by Gallo and making wines in Gallo's own plants but no longer at the historic winery in the Santa Clara Valley, Mirassou produces modestly priced Chardonnay, Pinot Noir, Cabernet, Merlot, Sauvignon Blanc, and Riesling from Monterey, Santa Clara, and the North and Central coasts. Two hundred acres in Santa Clara County and six hundred in Monterey provide much of the fruit. There are several small-production labels recently introduced, including Showcase, Harvest Reserve, Coastal Selections, and vineyard-designated lines that have garnered more critical acclaim than the higher-volume standbys. The Monterey County Riesling, made in a slightly sweet style, is an incredibly price-worthy choice for summertime sipping.

QUADY WINERY 1975		Map 24
www.quadywinery.com	800-733-8068	Tasting
Madera	Madera County	Madera AVA

Andrew and Laurel Quady, after leaving Southern California jobs in pyrotechnics and merchandising for the allure of winemaking in central California, established a winery focused exclusively on dessert and aperitif wines. Under winemaker Michael Blaylock's supervision, Quady bottles some forty thousand cases with names such as Essensia, Elysium, Electra, and Red Electra, made from Muscat grapes. They also make a Port-type wine (named Starboard, of course), highly aromatic red and white vermouths named Vya, and a sherry named Palomino Fino. Quady rightfully reigns as California's leading exponent of dessert wines and deliciously perfumed martinis and Manhattans.

SPENKER WINERY 1902		Map 24
No Web site	209-367-0467	Tasting
Lodi	San Joaquin County	Mokelumne River AVA

Fritz Spenker established the winery in 1902. Today, grandson Chuck Spenker and his wife, Betty Ann, produce a single Estate Zinfandel from the same old vines. Spenker grows grapes on the sixty-acre vineyard for its own wines and sells grapes to others, with several wineries making vineyard-designated bottlings featuring Spenker grapes. Look to Spenker Zinfandels to find a blending of the ripe richness so typical of most Lodi Zins, with a tighter structure that reminds one of coastally grown offerings.

THE SOUTH COAST

Cucamonga Valley

If you knew only two facts about this AVA, it would be these: This area, east of Los Angeles by almost one hundred miles, was once home to an amazing expanse of grapes measuring in the tens of thousands and twice the total in Napa and Sonoma counties combined. Today, its acreage has dropped into the one-thousand-acre range. And its grapes, mostly old vines, favor Zinfandel more than anything else and tend to make high-alcohol, jammy, raisiny wines.

At present, there are no more than a handful of surviving wineries, but the old-vine grapes draw attention both from makers in other Southern California locations as well as Zinfandel specialists from the north such as Paso Robles' Norman Vineyards and Sonoma's Carol Shelton, whose Monga Zin has occasionally bested many of its more famous competitors.

Leona Valley

Not unlike the Cucamonga area, the Leona Valley, some fifty miles northeast of Los Angeles in the Lancaster/Palmdale area, has a long history as a grape-growing, winemaking location, although that history belongs to the pre-Prohibition era. Today there are fewer than one hundred acres of grapes growing in the area and one winery of note—the appropriately named Leona Valley Winery.

MAP 25

South Coast

Ventura
County

Leona
Valley

138 Lancaster

Palmdale

395

15

Saddle
Rock-
Malibu

101

14

138

San Bernardino
County

Ventura

Los
Angeles
County

210

Cucamonga
Valley

1

101

Los
Angeles

10

210

San Bernardino

Malibu-
Newton
Canyon

Rosenthal-
The Malibu
Estate

60

10

405

5

215

Long Beach

Orange
County

15

Temecula
Valley

Pacific
Ocean

1

See inset below Riverside
County

5

5

San Pasqual
Valley

79

San Diego
County

215

79

Mount
Palomar

Callaway
Hart

South Coast

Leonesse

Thornton

Keyways

Orfila

15

78

Temecula

15

Ramona
Valley

79

8

Temecula
Valley

San Diego

5

8

Malibu–Newton Canyon

Hidden up a canyon four miles inland from the beach made famous by Hollywood, this one-winery AVA is home to Rosenthal, which has twenty-five acres of grapes and whose Cabernet Sauvignon and related wines can occasionally reach highly recommended levels. Despite not having the same range of temperatures of northern coastal locations, this AVA does benefit both from its 1,500-foot elevation and the cooling influence of winds off the Pacific Ocean.

Ramona Valley

Located in the northeastern corner of San Diego County at approximately 1,400-feet elevation, the Ramona Valley AVA is centered on a broad, flat stretch of land surrounded by mountains. The locals point out that they are almost equidistant from the Pacific Ocean and its cooling influences and the inland desert and its dry heat. With fewer than a dozen wineries and fewer than one hundred acres of vines, the area has yet to hit the big time, but the enthusiasm of the growers and wineries at least gives Ramona Valley a chance.

See Ramona Vineyard Association: www.ramonavalleyvineyards.org; San Diego County Vintners Association: www.sandiegowineries.org.

Saddle Rock–Malibu

Located in the Santa Monica Mountains west of Los Angeles, this small AVA covers approximately 2,000 acres of land at elevations ranging up to 1,900 feet. It is home to a few acres of vines and not enough wine to notice, even for most hometown folks.

San Pasqual Valley

In this tiny AVA east of San Diego and just around the corner from the Ramona Valley, a small coterie of wineries makes limited-edition bottlings that only occasionally find their way far from home. The Orfila Winery is the most prominent.

South Coast

Covering all of the AVAs in the area below the Tehachapi Mountains (meaning Southern California), this catchall AVA is the southland's equivalent of North Coast, Central Coast, San Francisco Bay, and any other oversized AVA in existence. It covers all kinds of regions and growing conditions, but its primary focus in terms of acreage is on the burgeoning Temecula Valley and the slowly less important but historically significant Cucamonga Valley. With something like three thousand acres planted in the entire area, it is certainly not high on the volume charts; and, to date, there is no variety that predominates the plantings of the area. Cabernet Sauvignon, Chardonnay, Syrah, and Merlot each have about 10 to 15 percent of the area total; Zinfandel, Sangiovese, and Pinot Noir also have enough acreage to notice. But it is the catchall category of "Other Varieties" that comes in with a third of all grapes grown in the southland. One way to look at this diversity is to conclude that the South Coast, with its vineyards that stand as near to the coast as a few miles and as far away as a good drive on a light traffic day, has not yet found its métier. But there is a better and more accurate view, and that is the notion that the experiments here with Rhône and Italian varieties are part of the creative spirit that has always seemed to propel California winemaking forward.

Temecula Valley

The 1,500 acres of vines in the Temecula Valley may not seem like much in comparison to places like Napa, Sonoma, and Santa Barbara counties, but the two dozen wineries are being joined by another dozen now getting ready to release wine and yet another dozen already in the planning and planting phases. Of the thirty-three thousand acres within the AVA boundaries, it is estimated that some five thousand acres are plantable—and given the area's advantages, there is every likelihood that the growth within the AVA will continue. The proven attractiveness of the red wines from Temecula attracts hordes of Angelenos and San Diegans to the Temecula Valley to taste the wine and to take advantage of the vacation-like atmosphere that exists there. Estimates of some one million visitors per year is supported by the existence of a very healthy hospitality industry in the area. Early vineyard and winery development began with folks like Cilurzo and Callaway and continued with Hart and Keyways, among others.

The area is inland and thus can be quite warm, typically in the 90s, but it is able to grow quality grapes both because it gets cooling late-afternoon breezes from the Pacific Ocean just twenty miles away, and also because the surrounding mountains drop cooler air into the valley at night. The result is a fairly wide diurnal range of temperatures of the type that allows other inland areas to keep enough acidity in the grapes to maintain decent quality. Still, this is a warm area and is not suited for the production of cold-loving varieties. For the moment, the valley seems to grow most popular and many less popular varieties, with no single variety taking charge. Prices for Temecula wines are high in comparison to most other isolated, small-area appellations—mostly because the Temecula Valley is really not all that isolated for the day-trippers among the fifteen million people who live within an easily reachable distance.

See Temecula Valley Winegrowers Association: www.temeculawines.org.

CALLAWAY VINEYARD & WINERY 1969		Map 25
www.callawaywinery.com	800-472-2377	Tasting
Temecula	Riverside County	Temecula Valley AVA

Founded by Ely Callaway, who would later go on to develop the Callaway golf equipment company, this was the first vineyard in the Temecula Valley. Callaway planted what would become 750 acres of vineyards, the source of most grapes for the brand. In 2005, the Lin family of San Diego purchased Callaway from Allied Domecq. Overseen by winemaker Craig Larson, with extensive winemaking experience in Washington state, Callaway produces some twenty-five thousand cases of a fairly rich selection of red and white varieties, including Chardonnays, Merlots, Syrahs, and Viogniers.

What was once a full-volume label with hopes of achieving world-class status has retreated to a more manageable size and more consistent results. Callaway's first emphasis on red wines increasingly turned to Chardonnay but is now more balanced. A dozen or more different bottlings appear in the line, ranging from a sparkling Chardonnay called Bella Blanc, to an award-winning dryish Rosé, to a fruit-bomb white called Winemaker's Reserve Quartet. At this point, Callaway wines are sold only at the winery and online. Like so many of its neighboring wineries in the Temecula Valley, Callaway is very well set up to receive visitors with its complimentary tours, extensive arrays of tastings, and visitor and meetings facilities.

HART WINERY 1980		Map 25
www.thehartfamilywinery.com	909-676-6300	Tasting
Temecula	Riverside County	Temecula Valley AVA

Joe and Nancy Hart bought land in the Temecula Valley in the early 1970s, planted their first of ten vineyard acres in 1974, and made their first wines in 1980. The small, family-run winery produces five thousand cases annually of varieties including Merlot, Viognier, Syrah, Sangiovese, Zinfandel, and Cabernet Sauvignon. Located at 1,500-feet elevation and looking like a modern version of an old, familiar farmhouse, Hart is worth the search.

KEYWAYS VINEYARD & WINERY 1989		Map 25
www.keywayswine.com	877-KEYWAYS	Tasting
Temecula	Riverside County	Temecula Valley AVA

With vines originally planted in the 1960s, Orange County investor Carl Key went on to establish a winery in 1989 and later sold it to the current owner, Terri Pebley, in 2004. The modest thirteen-acre vineyard produces a portion of the grapes for the ten thousand cases made annually. Cabernet Sauvignon, Syrah, Barbera, Petite Sirah, Merlot, and Zinfandel lead the list of offerings. The recently introduced Krystal Ice dessert wine is made from frozen Chenin Blanc grapes. Keyways is yet another lovely place to stop in the Temecula area.

LEONESSE CELLARS 2003		Map 25
www.leonessecellars.com	951-302-7601	Tasting
Temecula	Riverside County	Temecula Valley AVA

Founders Mike Rennie and Gary Winder were longtime growers in the Temecula Valley when they chose to establish their own winery. Their wines are made from grapes grown on their twenty-acre vineyard and sourced from other nearby growers. Winemaker Tim Kramer oversees the production of nearly fifteen thousand cases of a variety of wines, starring Syrah, Merlot, Pinot Gris, and Riesling. A seasonal restaurant, Block 5, is on the premises.

Wine quality at Leonesse has been quite high, and though the winery is an insider's secret among wine collectors, the locals have made it a favorite stop. Look for Merlot and an exceptional Cabernet Sauvignon–Merlot blend, each of which have scored 90+ points and have bested pricier wines from more expensive regions in blind tastings. Leonesse wines are highly sought after for their inviting combination of deep fruit, richness, and lush yet balanced textures.

MOUNT PALOMAR WINERY 1969		Map 25
www.mountpalomar.com	800-854-5177	Tasting
Temecula	Riverside County	Temecula Valley AVA

Founder and radio-television pioneer John Poole acquired land and developed vineyards in 1969, followed by winemaking in 1975. The 150 vineyard acres grow grapes for the eleven-thousand-case production overseen by winemaker Craig Boyd, experienced in the Sierra Foothills and New York state. Production focuses on Bordeaux varieties, made under the Mount Palomar label, and Italian varieties under the Castelletto label. A Port and cream Sherry round out the offerings.

ORFILA VINEYARDS & WINERY 1994		Map 25
www.orfila.com	760-738-6500	Tasting
Escondido	San Diego County	San Pasqual Valley AVA

In 1994, Alejandro Orfila purchased the boutique Thomas Yeager winery in the San Pasqual Valley. Orfila had been the Argentine ambassador to the United States and Japan as well as the secretary-general of the Organization of American States. Orfila, with the hands-on supervision of the late winemaker–general manager Leon Santoro, expanded production to some thirteen thousand cases of Rhône varieties, with much of the juice produced on their own seventy-acre estate. Fully 75 percent of wine sales are through the tasting room.

If not always ranking with the best of its peers, Orfila is nonetheless among the quality leaders among wineries south of Los Angeles. Its Gold Rush Zinfandel and its Ambassador's Reserve Merlot have led the way among its many offerings.

ROSENTHAL—THE MALIBU ESTATE 1987		Map 25
www.rosenthalestatewines.com	800-814-0733	Tasting
Malibu	Los Angeles County	Malibu-Newton Canyon AVA

Los Angeles developer and hotelier George Rosenthal spotted the Newton Canyon, 1,500 feet and 4 miles above the Malibu beach, as a potential growing area and planted his 25-acre vineyard in 1987. Rosenthal subsequently secured an AVA designation for the valley. French winemaker Christian Roguenant, whose résumé includes stops at Maison Deutz/Laetitia and extends now to Baileyana, has also worked with Rosenthal since '96, making the final product on the Central Coast. Today's production exceeds four thousand cases, with Cabernet Sauvignon representing over half the output, and Merlot and Chardonnay rounding out the principal offerings—all made from estate-grown fruit.

We somehow love the idea of Los Angeles County wines, especially from Malibu, but quality has been inconsistent, and ratings have drifted from the mid-80s to the lower 90s almost randomly. Yet, we keep trying the wines and insist that we are not starstruck. The wines are fairly classic in style, with decently focused fruit buttressed by supportive oak—all of which is not surprising given the way the inestimable Christian Roguenant has been making wines for years now at his various stops.

SOUTH COAST WINERY 2003		Map 25
www.wineresort.com	866-9WI-NERY	Tasting
Temecula	Riverside County	Temecula Valley AVA

The formal name of the facility is the South Coast Winery Resort & Spa, so it's unclear just which tail is wagging the dog. James Carter bought four hundred acres of land in 1981. In the 1990s, son Jim Carter developed nearly forty acres of vineyards. A winery was added in 2003, and wine production now hovers around thirty thousand cases. Winemakers Jon McPherson and Javier Flores make numerous varieties in four quality levels. A restaurant, spa, and villas are the nonvinous features—and important features at that—but make no mistake: these folks take their wines seriously as well.

THORNTON WINERY 1988		Map 25
www.thorntonwine.com	909-699-0099	Tasting
Temecula	Riverside County	Temecula Valley AVA

Initially known as Culbertson but changed to Thornton when partner John Thornton, a successful electronics entrepreneur, and his wife, Sally, took over, the winery was established with twenty vineyard acres in 1988. Initially a *méthode champenoise* specialty winery, it added still varietals to the repertoire in 1993. Today's production approaches fifty thousand cases of Sparkling, white, and red wines, made under the supervision of winemaker Don Reha (of Fetzer, Cline, and Renwood wineries). Tastings and a restaurant are included in the faux-château winery.

If quality has not always been consistent, so, too, has it had its high moments. Thornton rates as one of the significant and not-to-be-ignored places in the Temecula Valley.

THE READING LIST

AT SOME POINT, each of us has made the transition from everyday wine drinker to devoted fan of fermented grape juice. The journey can be casual and lengthy, as was ours from collegiate consumers of Gallo Hearty Burgundy when we started, to inexpensive Beaujolais by the time we graduated and then made our ways to the West for additional education. We had no idea that leaving New England and ending up in California four days later in our beat-up VW would also set us on the path to vinous edification.

During our decade-long descent into the inescapable grip of Bacchus, we were lucky to be able to visit wineries from Livermore and San Jose to the Napa Valley and up into Sonoma and Mendocino and to try a wide range of offerings in their tasting rooms. Tasting was without charge in those happy days, and more often than not, one would find a winery family member doing the pouring. Things are different today, but tasting wine in the company of folks who know more than you do is still a great way to learn—even when it costs a few dollars for the privilege at today's wineries.

The written word is also a wonderful way to enhance your information base and to find pathways to even greater knowledge and more interesting tasting experiences. The list of recommended titles and sources here is long and goes off in many directions. For that reason, each of the referenced works comes with a discussion of its contents, its use, and its place in the development of knowledge about California wine. Many are not limited to California in focus, and that is a good thing. Wine is not unique to California, and it is just one source of fine wine. Moreover, we are somewhat late to the game. We may have had wine here in California for hundreds of years, but the fine wine industry grew with fits and starts and stops from the mid-1800s until the great wine boom of the 1970s. Thus, all that we now know about California wine had its origins at some point somewhere else.

GENERAL REFERENCE TEXTS

The Oxford Companion to Wine, 3rd ed.
Jancis Robinson (New York: Oxford University Press, 2006)

Every wine library needs a good encyclopedia and a good atlas, and there is none better in the first category than this comprehensive work by the "ubiquitous Ms. Robinson," who must now be regarded as the leading writer of wine books in the world. *Oz Clarke's New Encyclopedia of Wine* is more opinionated and perhaps somewhat more likely to raise an eyebrow, and Tom Stevenson's *Sotheby's Encyclopedia* has better maps than its competition and more information on wines and wineries, but neither is as comprehensive as Robinson's book.

The World Atlas of Wine, 5th rev. ed.
Hugh Johnson and Jancis Robinson (London: Mitchell Beazley, 2001)

First published in 1971 by Hugh Johnson, who owned the title of top wine writer for decades, this latest edition has become the province of Jancis Robinson, and with that, the passing of the crown. The maps in this book have been guiding our vinous journeys for decades; and whether you are trying to separate La Tâche from La Turque or Sonoma Mountain from Sonoma Valley, this is the first place to look. *Oz Clarke's New Wine Atlas* uses photography rather than outright cartography to explain wine geography. Although we would recommend a second atlas before a second encyclopedia, and typically we consult both the Johnson/Robinson work and the Clarke edition for our geography lessons, and although we continue to enjoy Clarke's open, irreverent take on the world, it is the Johnson/Robinson atlas that comes first for us.

Oz Clarke's Grapes and Wines: The Definitive Guide to the World's Great Grapes and the Wines They Make
Oz Clarke and Margaret Rand (Orlando, FL: Harcourt, 2007)

The study of fine wine begins with the notion of place, and that is why an atlas is recommended as more important than a discussion of grapes. But one cannot ignore the grape, either. It is true, of course, that most discussions of place, including those in this book, will discuss the grapes that grow in the various locales. But, when one wants to go further, when one wants to explore how Chardonnay, for instance, performs in the many places it appears all around the world or why Grenache, admittedly not a grape that has been widely successful in California, is so important in Spain, France, and Australia, it is a book about grapes that will provide the answers. Until a couple of decades ago, such books were dry analyses of what varieties looked like and how they grew. Not much mention of wine there. Then, in 1986, the "ubiquitous Ms. Robinson" penned *Vines, Grapes and Wines: The Wine Drinker's Guide to Grape Varieties,* a marvelous book whose pages we have worn thin. She followed that book with a shorter version in 1996, *Jancis Robinson's Guide to Wine Grapes.* Ah, but here Oz Clarke has done her one better by delivering the only up-to-date assessment of the fortunes of the world's leading wine grapes.

The Science of Wine: From Vine to Glass
Jamie Goode (Berkeley: University of California Press, 2005)

At some point, and at some level, wine lovers need to know about how wine is made and why it tastes the way it does. No book does that better than Jamie Goode's sometimes academic but detailed tome. It is the kind of book to which one returns time and time again, and its explanations of why things turn out as they do will be drunk up eagerly by everyone with a thirst for the topic.

Perfect Pairings: A Master Sommelier's Practical Advice
for Partnering Wine with Food
Evan Goldstein, with recipes by Joyce Goldstein (Berkeley: University of California Press, 2006)

Evan Goldstein was brought up right. His mother, Joyce, is a renowned chef whose stove time at Berkeley's fabled Chez Panisse led to the creation of her own fabulous restaurant, Square One in San Francisco, and he obviously earned his food chops at a young age. As an adult, he became one of the youngest master sommeliers on record and has gone on to guide wineries and countless students in the ways of fine wine. In this book, he combines both knowledge sets with the help of his mother and provides us with the single-most insightful and instructive wine and food book in existence. No mere recipe book this: it is an exploration into the whys and wherefores of food pairings.

Wine and Philosophy: A Symposium on Thinking and Drinking
Fritz Allhof, editor (Oxford: Wiley-Blackwell, 2007)

We are tempted to describe this book as "serious reading for serious wine lovers," but that would suggest a somewhat dense, impenetrable set of long essays by writers who may have a lot to say but do not know how to say it. In fact, this is a book filled with thoughtful, highly penetrable essays by writers who know exactly how to take serious topics and make them accessible. It may be "cold winter's night" reading that asks you to pay attention, but this book belongs in the library of anyone who, like us, has been captured by Bacchus and cannot escape.

The 30 Second Wine Advisor: Learn about Wine in 30-Second Tastes—Quick, Easy and Fun
Robin Garr (Louisville, KY: CreateSpace, 2007)

Robin Garr is the creative force behind the exceptionally successful Wine Lovers Discussion Group, the single-most widely followed wine discussion forum on the Internet. He is also a Pulitzer Prize-winning reporter, and he knows a thing or two about how to express himself. Over the years, he has penned numerous short essays on almost every vinous topic known to mankind, and now, a broad-ranging selection of his light, breezy, and insightful treatises have been gathered together in one place. Unlike Fritz Allhof's *Wine and Philosophy* (also mentioned here), which consists of deep thinking, this book is a collection of simple but quickly digested thoughts that make great reading under a shady tree on a lazy weekend afternoon.

BOOKS ABOUT CALIFORNIA WINE

A Companion to California Wine
Charles L. Sullivan (Berkeley: University of California Press, 1998)

Charles Sullivan, a highly regarded wine historian, is best when he is writing about the people and places that have influenced the development of the wine industry, especially over the last seventy-five years. This book is part encyclopedia, part chronicle of events laid out in an alphabetical series of entries. It is a required text in any California wine library.

Zinfandel
Charles L. Sullivan (Berkeley: University of California Press, 2003)

For too long, the story of Zinfandel's heritage and its arrival in California where it has achieved a uniquely high level of importance has been the stuff of fable and failed guesswork, not rigorous investigation. In this book, Sullivan has unlocked the mystery of what has become known as the "California's grape." It is a story well told and a must for all who admire Zinfandel's lusty, ripe-berry charms.

The Oxford Companion to the Wines of North America
Bruce Cass, editor (New York: Oxford University Press, 2000)

Bruce Cass has created the closest thing to an encyclopedia of the wines, wineries, and places where wine grows in North America. We use it often, especially for details outside California because those places have received very little organized attention in print over the years. If not a must-have, this book is a valuable addition to any extended library of California wines.

Pacific Pinot Noir
John Winthrop Haeger (Berkeley: University of California Press, 2008)

It has taken many decades for Pinot Noir to find its voice here in California. Now, with the grape's expanding popularity, John Haeger has given us a book of unparalleled depth in its discussion of the whos and wheres of Pinot Noir in the West.

New Classic Winemakers of California
Steve Heimoff (Berkeley: University of California Press, 2007)

Steve Heimoff, he of *The Wine Enthusiast* magazine and his eponymously named blog, somehow finds time to also write interesting books. This inspired effort builds on an earlier work from the 1970s by Robert Benson in which the boom and expansion of California wine is chronicled midstream by the folks who were making that era's history. In Heimoff's version, we get to meet the people who are at the heart of a much more mature wine industry but also an industry that still has new worlds of wine to explore and new mountains to climb. The vivacious Genevieve Janssens, head of winemaking at Robert Mondavi and also master of her own little world at her Portfolio winery, are joined with the likes of John Alban, whose family winery is pushing the envelope with Rhône varieties. This is an important read for all fans of California wineries, especially those who want to look inside the minds of those who are making today's and tomorrow's news.

The Wines of America, 4th ed.
Leon D. Adams, with Bridgett Novak (New York: McGraw-Hill, 1990)

The great Leon Adams was known for years as the dean of American wine writers. His visits to the producers of his day are captured in this book, first penned in the 1970s. Even this fourth edition may be out of date and suitable more for nostalgia buffs at this point, but its commentary takes us back to an earlier day and makes a great read for anyone who wants to get a feel for the folks who were there when the wine boom took off.

California Wine Country
Peter Fish and Sara Schneider (Menlo Park, CA: Sunset Books, 2007)

Sunset magazine has long had its finger on the pulse of California comforts, from design to gardens to cuisine and wine. In this small, easy-to-pack book, the Sunset staff, under the organizational eye of Peter Fish and Sarah Schneider, has compiled a very helpful look at wineries to visit and things to do along the way. Pick out a few favorites and consult the winery Web sites to confirm opening times and special tastings and events.

A History of Wine in America, Volume 1: From the Beginnings to Prohibition
Thomas Pinney (Berkeley: University of California Press, 2007)

A History of Wine in America, Volume 2: From Prohibition to the Present
Thomas Pinney (Berkeley: University of California Press, 2005)

If Charles Sullivan is the leading chronicler of the people and places behind the development of the wine industry in California, his good friend Thomas Pinney is the chronicler of the whys. His discussion of the establishment and subsequent dismemberment of Prohibition is worth the read by itself.

Wines and Wineries of California's Central Coast
William Ausmus (Berkeley: University of California Press, 2008)

By limiting his focus to wineries of the Central Coast, William Ausmus is able to reach further into their history and their souls to bring us close looks at the people behind the wineries, their backgrounds, and their expectations. The commentary about individual wines is less important because so much of it relies on winery judgments and relates to wines now long off the market. But wine criticism is not the reason to own this book. Its insights into the area and the producers make it worthwhile.

A Moveable Thirst: Tales and Tastes from a Season in Napa Wine Country
Rick Kushman and Hank Beal (New York: Wiley, 2007)

When a couple of buddies set out to drink their way through the Napa Valley's tasting rooms, the results could have been less than pretty. But Rick Kushman, whose day job is television reviewer for the *Sacramento Times*, knows how to spin a yarn, and anyone who would spend time in the Napa Valley will be well served by this easy-to-read, at times downright hilarious tome.

Back Lane Wineries of Sonoma
Tilar Mazzeo (New York: Wiley, 2009)

Tilar Mazzeo teaches English at Colby College in Maine for part of the year and writes about travel and wine the rest of the time. Her little, four-color introduction to Sonoma County bypasses the usual suspects and takes you into smaller, less well-known producers. She also tells you where to eat and what to do on your visits to Sonoma County. It was not created as a guidebook so much as a paean to the intimate little places in her West Coast second home.

California Wine for Dummies
Ed McCarthy and Mary Ewing-Mulligan (Hoboken, NJ: Wiley, 2009)

This vital wine couple also penned the *Wine for Dummies* book, and while they have never been in wine-writing backwaters, they are now among the most widely read authors anywhere. The "Dummies" methodology may not be your cup of tea, but this book is not really for dummies so much as it is for those who would want a jump start on their California wine education.

Wine Grape Varieties in California
University of California, Agriculture and Natural Resources (Berkeley: Author, 2003)

The title and source say it all. This book discusses the grapes that grow in California. It is more concerned with their technical aspect than with the wines they produce. Yet, we use this book often as an important reference. Only those whose lives are now integrally and inescapably tied to wine and vineyards need apply.

Matt Kramer's New California Wine: Making Sense of Napa Valley, Sonoma, Mendocino, and Beyond
Matt Kramer (Philadelphia: Running Press, 2004)

Wine Spectator columnist Matt Kramer provides a very valuable take on the whys and wherefores of California wine. He is a good reporter and brings his subject to life in ways that make it more human. And while this book is neither guidebook nor classic reference text, it does provide plenty of detail about the evolution of California wine from the 1980s until the date of publication.

Judgment of Paris
George M. Taber (New York: Scribner's, 2006)

In 1976, driven in part by the increasing quality of California wine, Parisian wine merchant Steven Spurrier sponsored a blind tasting of comparable California and French products in honor of the American bicentennial. At that tasting, a panel of French wine professionals chose Stag's Leap Wine Cellars Cabernet Sauvignon and Chateau Montelena Chardonnay over their much more famous French peers. The results, reported in *Time* magazine, greatly enhanced the reputation of California wines in Europe but, more important, in the United States, and the tasting stands as a seminal event in the history of California wine. The *Time* reporter, George Taber, has now done further research into the tasting itself and has written a book that tells the whole tale.

PRINT PERIODICALS

There is no question that books are among the best ways to develop a broad background of wine information. However, books are typically out-of-date guides to wine-buying advice. Even this book, with its multitude of ratings information, is backward looking and provides only general guidance when it comes to current vintages on the market. That niche is filled by magazines and newsletters. The four newsletters are listed first because they take no advertising, do not sell label placements, are sold by subscription only, and generally taste all wine blind. The two magazines listed here offer broad coverage, including lifestyle-oriented information, take advertising, and typically have a wide variety of palates and scoring methodologies.

Connoisseurs' Guide to California Wine
www.cgcw.com

Connoisseurs' Guide is a monthly, subscriber-only newsletter that provides in-depth evaluations of California and West Coast wines and comments on trends and market forces affecting the wine consumer. In existence for three decades, and with our book in print for most of that time, the *Guide* has become recognized as the authoritative voice of the California wine consumer. The authors invite you to examine a sample copy of *Connoisseurs' Guide* at www.cgcw.com and also to visit www.cgcw.com/book, for periodic updates to the book. Please register with the password Guidebook.

California Grapevine
www.calgrapevine.com

The *Grapevine* newsletter, published every other month, reviews significant numbers of California wines and provides lengthy editorial content through the comments of Dan Berger and book reviews by Bob Foster. At half the price of *Connoisseurs' Guide*, it provides half the content and is a great place for folks to get advice about California wine. Its Web site is inactive except for providing subscription and contact information.

Stephen Tanzer's International Wine Cellar
www.wineaccess.com/tanzer

Reviewing mostly wines from outside the United States but covering California periodically, Steve Tanzer and associates review thousands of wines annually. Those not in the thrall of Robert Parker are well served by Tanzer's more scholarly approach. The Web site offers subscriber-only information. It is attractive and easy to read.

The Wine Advocate
www.eRobertParker.com

The most widely read of the newsletters, it covers the same ground as Tanzer's *International Wine Cellar* and has gained its large and loyal following based on the insightful writing provided by its founder, Robert Parker. Lately, however, responsibility for reviews has been assigned to a series of individual reviewers of varying competence. Parker remains our favorite sources for comments on the wines of Bordeaux, and his associate, David Schildknecht, is a brilliant analyst of German wines. The electronic edition of the newsletter is filled with subscription information and also has a very active and occasionally controversial discussion group.

Wine Spectator
www.winespectator.com

If there is a big dog in the wine publishing business, it is the *Spectator*. With more readers than all the rest of the publications on our list combined, the *Spectator* casts a wide net across wine, upscale lifestyle issues, and even food and places to stay. Its large-format magazine is handsomely laid out and easy to read. There are those who criticize some of its wine coverage, but no publication cuts a wider swath. Still, any of the newsletters present more precise reviewers, in our opinion.

Wine Enthusiast
www.wineenthusiast.com

Number two to *Wine Spectator* and trying hard, this slick paper magazine gets our nod for its California coverage written by Steve Heimoff, a gifted writer. The commercial aspects of the *Enthusiast* occasionally raise the eyebrows of wine aficionados, yet we sense no taint in the judgment calls of its writers.

Decanter, www.decanter.com
This English publication is our favorite source for well-written information about wines from around the world. Its California coverage is admittedly a bit spotty and uneven, but one does not read the opinions of a bunch of Englishmen to learn about California wine. Rather, one reads *Decanter* to stay abreast of events and wine from the rest of the world.

WINE BLOGS

There was a time when writing about wine was confined to books and the occasional newspaper column or wine magazine. With the explosion of wine consumption, the volume of wine verbiage also exploded. Now, we are in the Internet era, and the face of wine writing is changing again. A tectonic shift is underway, but it is so new that no one quite knows where it is going. The Internet allows anyone with a computer and belief in his or her own opinion to become an instant journalist. The existing media have, of course, migrated also to the Internet with their own for-pay subscription sites and a fair amount of free content as well.

Here is a listing of public writings on the Internet. Some are done by wine professionals, and some are offered by enthusiastic amateurs. By some accounts, there are as many as one thousand wine blogs, most of which are periodic offerings of enthusiastic bibbers and do not make it into this list. But they are out there covering any and every corner of the wine world.

1WineDude
Joe Roberts, www.1winedude.com

Hip, occasionally irreverent, friendly, and easily digestible wine commentary and recommendations are the forte of young Joe Roberts, whose infectious enthusiasm virtually bubbles off the screen when you visit his site. He is rapidly being recognized as one of the voices most likely to go from unpaid writer of blogs to important member of the wine-writing profession.

The Connoisseurs' Blog
Charles Olken, www.cgcw.com

Pardon our immodesty, but we cannot avoid plugging our own efforts on the Internet. This daily compendium of wine information, rants and rumblings, comments on the wine news of the day, restaurant and winery reviews, and almost all things vinous is more than a series of editorials and thus diverges from the normal wine blog fare. There are even those who argue that it is no blog at all but rather an online daily magazine.

Diner's Journal/The Pour
Eric Asimov, www.dinersjournal.blogs.nytimes.com

No American-based wine-writing newspaper columnist is as important as Eric Asimov. That goes with the territory when you are "The Guy" at the *New York Times*. His columns are smart, artful, and serious. His blog is a more personal discussion of his wine scene, but it does not ever get mired in the muck of "See what wonderful things I have done today with the beautiful persons of the wine world." He does not post every day, and some of his writings look a little like his columns at times, but he did not come by his day job without being very good—and so is his blog. The Asimov blog is part of a combined Diner's Journal on the *Times* site, so be sure to click on the "Drinking" button when you get there.

Dr. Vino
Tyler Coleman, www.drvino.com

Tyler Coleman has quickly established himself as one of the most admired and well-read wine bloggers. He stays away from wine recommendations and instead focuses on editorials, personal travels in the wine world, and examination of hot topics. It is one of our mandatory daily reads. And he deserves a great deal of credit for being willing to expose the foibles of others in the writing community when they do not live up to a reasonable set of ethical standards.

Fermentation: The Daily Wine Blog
Tom Wark, www.fermentation.typepad.com

Tom Wark is a public relations professional with a sense of humor, a keen eye for inconsistency and hypocrisy, and a writing style that can be acerbic when necessary, investigative as called for, and tender at times. He speaks with authority.

Good Grape: A Wine Manifesto
Jeff Lefevere, www.goodgrape.com

Jeff Lefevere describes himself as "an analyst, activist, and cultural observer," and that pretty much sums up our thinking about his work as well. Despite his occasional bursts of whimsy, Lefevere is a serious and thoughtful observer whose writings ask that we think about the world of wine. Whether he is introducing us to a winemaker or talking about wine glasses that he likes or does not like, Lefevere makes us listen and learn, and that is a very special skill.

Hosemaster of Wine
Ron Washam, www.hosemasterofwine.blogspot.com

Ron Washam, former sommelier, is easily the most bitingly funny blogger–wine writer that we have ever come across. He is an equal opportunity crusader who pillories big wineries and amateur bloggers alike, as well as everything and everyone in between. His writing will never be described as refined or elegant. Indeed, if it ever became that, he would likely hoist himself on his own petard. One needs a sense of humor and a tolerance for earthiness to enjoy reading *The Hosemaster*. We must have both because this guy deserves a wider audience, in our humble opinion. Be aware, however, that he is known to take an occasional sabbatical when the muse is not with him.

Reign of Terroir
Ken Payton, www.reignofterroir.com

Ken Payton is new to blogging, and his blog is an earnest endeavor indeed. He is its main contributor, but there are occasional articles from other places around the world. Some of his writing is practically winery insider stuff; some of it is commentary on the events and controversies of the day. He is one of the less excitable, even-handed voices in the new media.

Samantha Sans Dosage
Samantha Duggan, www.sansdosage.blogspot.com

Wine writing is rarely about the drama of life. Not so *Samantha Sans Dosage*. Wine merchant Samantha Duggan makes choosing a wine to go with a piece of cheese into a cross between a short story and a passion play. And that was one of her "quiet" pieces. She regularly moves her readers to tears, to laughter, to outrage with her ability to turn everyday events, in her life or in her store, into moving, charming stories. Her followers are simply addicted to her honesty and her passion. And we are among them.

Steve Heimoff
Steve Heimoff, www.steveheimoff.com

The California beat writer for *Wine Enthusiast* magazine, Steve Heimoff is a keen observer of the wine scene, and his blog, which exists independently of his day job, sees him covering the waterfront from wine writer ethics, to long and thoughtful commentaries on controversial subjects, to some of the funniest writing about wine that has come along in some time. His blog has rapidly grown in popularity, and if not the most widely read, it has come very close in the fairly short time of its existence.

Vinography
Alder Yarrow, www.vinography.com

Voted America's favorite blog several years in a row, *Vinography* and its creator, Alder Yarrow, will rake the muck now and again, but its favorite focuses are on new wine and winery discoveries, wine art, and significant wine-tasting events that Yarrow has attended or will be attending. He blasts through loads of wine when he tastes and offers ratings but no tasting notes. Although there is something less than professional about that approach, it is helpful to remember that he is not a wine writer by profession but a high-powered graphic artist who brings a fresh approach to the blogosphere—and therein lies a reason he is a top-rated blogger. Another of our must-reads.

THE LANGUAGE OF WINE

THE LANGUAGE OF WINE IS RICH AND VARIED, abstruse and inbred, sometimes accessible only to the few who know the secret handshake. Whole publications are devoted to the thousands of words that might be used to describe wine, but, in this book, we are willing to let you work out for yourself what words like *mild, big, appley, herbaceous, simple,* and their easily understood relatives say about wine.

When writers compile wine jargon lists by the hundreds, they tend to do so in brief squibs of ten to twenty-five words. You will find a few of those here as well, but you will also find much longer and informative essays about words that have a certain technical bent or an important descriptive component. In those instances, we are providing explanations, not just short definitions. For the rest, there is always the Internet—which, by the way, has the ability to overwhelm you with definitions and explanations when you set out to do further research.

ACETIC   All wines contain a certain amount of acetic acid—vinegar. Usually the amount is so small that we do not notice a sweet/sour/vinegary component in the aromas and flavors, but it is there and helps the wine express its aromas because it is volatile. Indeed, volatile acidity (known in the trade as "VA") is the measurement of acetic aspects in wine. The legal limit for VA in wine is 0.12 percent, and most tasters will begin to notice its presence at about half that level, or 0.06 percent. Ethyl acetate, a related compound, contributes the characteristic smell of acetic acid.

ACID/ACIDITY/ACIDULATION   All wines contain a mix of acids, and it is these acids, in combination, that are part of a wine's balance. Depending on the wine, acidity in a given wine will generally range from 0.5 percent to 1.0 percent. Most dry table wines tend to fall in the range of 0.5 to 0.7 percent, while sweeter wines and sparkling wines will have higher levels of acidity, often greater than 1.0 percent. In winemaking terms, the level of the combined acids in wine is usually referred to as "total acidity," or TA. In California and some other parts of the world, especially those with warm climates, winemakers are allowed to add acid to the must and to the wine in order to bring it into balance. The process of acid adjustment is *acidulation*.

ACIDIC   Wines whose total acidity is so high that they taste tart or sour and have a sharp feel in the mouth are referred to as acidic. Often such wines are thought to be out of balance, but very dry wines with high acid levels can very often be perfect mates to seafood and shellfish, and certain reds with pert flavors are thought to be good accompaniment to foods with red sauces. In this instance, it is the food choice that brings the entire wine and food experience into balance.

AFTERTASTE   The taste left in the mouth after the wine is swallowed. *Finish* is a related term. A long and pleasant aftertaste is typically considered a virtue.

ALCOHOL BY VOLUME   Wineries are required by United States regulation to state the alcohol level on their labels, generally expressed as a numerical percentage of the volume. Wine labeling regulations also allow the use of the term *Table Wine* in place of a more specific number, but, in that case, the wine must be between 11 and 14 percent alcohol by volume (also called ABV). California table wines will more often than not fall in the range of 12 to 15 percent with a few lower, mainly aromatic whites, and some that stretch the envelope and go higher than 15 percent, mostly full-bodied reds like Zinfandel and Syrah. Alcohol levels are a factor of grape ripeness, and some winemakers believe that highly ripened grapes have more character. Others argue that wines at the high end of the alcohol scale are too hot, are out of balance, and have lost some of their varietal character. Although plenty of evidence suggests that these disadvantages can happen at high alcohol levels, there are also examples of wines that succeed at those levels. The key, then, is not so much in the numbers as in the wine's overall balance of fruitiness, acidity, richness, and retention of varietal character.

AMERICAN VITICULTURAL AREA   Wine labels have historically been required to show a place of origin for the grapes in the bottle. This designation is called the wine's appellation, and prior to 1980, when the American Viticultural Area (AVA) system came into existence, the designations were limited to the names of counties and states or as American. With the AVA system, specific growing areas can be recognized that do not conform to county boundaries, and upon petition to the federal regulators of wine and wine labels, a delineated area can become accepted as an AVA if it can show cause for its uniqueness based on climate, soil, elevation, history, or definable boundaries. Thus, it is possible today to label a wine with the prior appellation system (Sonoma County, Mendocino County, Santa Barbara County, etc., or as California or as American), but it is also allowed to use the AVA name, which can cover an area as limited as the one-vineyard Cole Valley and as large as the North Coast, Central Coast, San Francisco Bay, and other multicounty delineations.

The result of this new and improved system is a patchwork of place names, some of which are precise in meaning, others that are historic in their use such as Napa Valley, and some that have grown over the years to take in adjoining areas that want to share in the value of the place name (Russian River Valley). Unlike in parts of Europe where the use of a place name can come with specific rules about which varieties can be grown, how much can be produced, how the vineyards can be tended, and whether the finished wine meets qualitative criteria for the use of that place name, AVAs in this country are simply places, and the only rule applying to them is that the use of those AVA names must mean that 85 percent of the grapes in the bottle came from the delineated area. By comparison, if a wine is designated by a state name or as American, 100 percent of the grapes must be grown in the area covered by the name used. Wines bearing county appellations are required to have only 75 percent of the product grown in the designated area.

ANGULAR   The palate feel of wines is important to our enjoyment of them. A combination of hard, often tart characteristics, especially in many young, dry wines, can give the wine an angular tactile impression. The underlying causes can be high acidity, low pH, and limited fruit depth and richness. If angular wines can age or can be paired with food liking their edginess (fresh-shucked oysters come to mind), then angularity is not a disqualifying characteristic.

AROMA   A wise person once wrote, "I like to smell wine, but I would rather drink it." The smells of a wine, often described as its "nose." are an important part of the way in which we enjoy a given wine. Indeed, more of what we experience of the wine is aroma than taste. And we acquire a wine's aroma both through our own nose as well as through the mouth because the wine's character comes up through our nasal passages to our smell receptors.

ASTRINGENCY   Many reds and a few whites have a rough, harsh, puckery feel in the mouth, usually from tannin. The tannins in wine come from several sources, primarily from the grape skins when the grapes are pressed but also from the seeds in the grapes if the pressing is hard and from oak barrels that impart richness to the wine but can also contribute a "toothpicky" astringency. It is also possible for winemakers to add tannin to a wine, typically to give it a sturdier, harder texture, through the use of tannin powder. Wines with high levels of astringency can often find balance when young if served with sturdy or savory foods, but astringency is also a signal that a wine might well benefit from long aging.

AUSTERE   Wines that are low in fruit and firm, sometimes hard, in texture are referred to as austere. Sparkling Wine is meant to be austere, in the sense that fruit is intentionally kept in the background so that the wine can showcase the richness it has acquired through the winemaking process. Indeed, it is that richness, plus the small amount of sugar that is added at the end of the aging process, that brings the wine into balance. Some table wines, mostly whites, are also austere; and if they are in balance in other ways, they can be fine accompaniments to tangy or briny shellfish dishes.

BALANCE   A wine is balanced when its elements are harmonious and no one part dominates. And because wine is complex, balance results from the interplay of fruitiness; aromatic and flavor intensity; sweetness and acidity levels; the amounts of oak, astringency, and bitterness in the wine; and even the way a wine is used with food. "Balance" can be a difficult concept to describe, but we know it when we taste it.

BARREL-FERMENTED   Most wine is fermented in large containers that can range in size from a few hundred gallons to tens of thousands. But wine can also be fermented in small casks—typically fifty-five-gallon oak barrels—rather than in large tanks. The procedure is more typical of dry whites than other wines and is used to enhance the integration of oak characteristics in the wine as well as to achieve higher levels of richness without otherwise changing the balance of the wine.

BIODYNAMIC   The movement to earth-friendly grape growing has several levels of effort, and none of them is more a product of faith in the unknown than biodynamic farming. To be sure, there are great benefits to be had, but many of those benefits are also seen with organic farming and with what is called sustainable agriculture. Biodynamics are the most aggressive of the lot and involve the use of soil preparations prescribed through the teaching of Rudolph Steiner in 1924—including inserting cow manure into the soil with cow horns, applying minerals and herbs in water that is stirred to excite its ions, and planting and picking according to the phases of the moon. Those wineries that practice biodynamic farming and winemaking are wholly and irrevocably convinced that these practices allow their wines to be the purest expressions of the land where they are grown. Others look at biodynamics and see witchcraft and some form of new religion. For our part, we have tasted biodynamic wines that are beautiful in their own right and biodynamic wines that are not.

BITTER   One of the four basic tastes (along with sour, salty, and sweet). Bitterness may be caused by phenols that derive primarily from tannin but can occasionally have its origins in certain compounds formed during fermentation. A small level of bitterness can be useful in some wines and in uses with some foods by contributing positively to the overall balance of the experience, but when bitterness interferes with enjoyment, it then becomes a problem.

BLANC DE BLANCS   Literally meaning "white of whites," this designation is used typically with Sparkling Wines made from white grapes only instead of the more traditional blend of white and red grapes. In Champagne, the allowed varieties are Chardonnay, from which Blanc de Blancs are made there, plus Pinot Noir and Pinot Meunier. In California, there are no limits on the grapes that can be used for Sparkling Wine, but Chardonnay dominates in most whites priced about entry level.

BLANC DE NOIRS   Meaning "white of blacks," this term is used with light-colored wines, mostly Sparkling Wines, made primarily from red wine grapes (called "black" by the growers because the skins are very deeply colored). As in France, most Sparkling Wines made here and called Blanc de Noirs are focused first on Pinot Noir and Pinot Meunier, although it is not unusual for a small amount of white wine to find its way into Blanc de Noirs.

BODY   The tactile impression of weight or fullness on the palate. While full-bodied wines are not unusual in California, there is nothing about fullness of body by itself that connotes a measure of quality. Viscosity is a related characteristic but is not always synonymous with full-bodied.

BOTRYTIS CINEREA   Botrytis is mold or fungus that attacks grapes under certain climatic conditions, in particular high humidity and/or some moisture. When it occurs just before maturity, it causes the grapes to shrivel, concentrating both sugar and acid. It is beneficial for many white grapes and is the deus ex machina that allows the creation of many luscious late-harvest wines. Botrytis can also occur at early times in the growing season, and it is then a problem as it harms the proper development of the grapes. The term *noble rot* also refers to Botrytis.

BOTTLED BY   One of the requirements of wine labels is that the bottler must state how much of the process was controlled by itself. A series of almost identical terms is used in this regard, and all include the language "Bottled by." The highest order of control is expressed as "Estate Bottled," which means that the producer grew, crushed, fermented, and controlled the wine from start to finish. "Produced and Bottled by" means that at least 75 percent of the wine was crushed, fermented, and bottled by the maker in one specific winemaking facility. When the wine is bottled with an AVA designation, the phrase means that 85 percent of the wine was entirely under the control of the winery from crush to bottling. Other variations of these phrases come with considerably lower standards. For example, the misleading phrase "Made and Bottled by" means that only 10 percent of the wine was held in the producer's winery from start to finish. All other phrases, including the frequently seen "Vinted and Bottled by," have no legal meaning whatsoever other than that the wine was bottled under the maker's name somewhere.

BOUQUET   A wine's smell is made up of many things, from the grapes that went into it, to the yeast used to ferment it, to the vessel in which it was aged prior to bottling. The part of a wine's smell that develops after bottling is its bouquet, and it usually comes with years of cellar aging. A less frequently heard term with an identical meaning is *bottle bouquet*.

BRIGHT   Wines with fresh, zesty, fruity qualities are said to be bright. It is a quality more often seen in younger wines, especially whites and Rosés, but can also be a characteristic of lighter red wines. Bright wines typically have noticeable acidity and equally noticeable fruit. You will also see related descriptive terms including *energetic*, *pert*, and *spry*. Wines at the elevated acidity end of the brightness scale are occasionally referred to as brisk or crisp.

BRIX   At harvest time, both grape growers and winemakers need to measure the amount of sugar in the grapes and then in the must (the grape juice in the tank after crush but before fermentation). Sugar levels in unharvested grapes help the winery determine when the grapes are ready for picking. Through the use of a refractometer, they are able determine the specific gravity of the juice in degrees Brix and get a measurement that closely approximates the sugar as a percentage of the juice. Because sugar converts to alcohol at a ratio of 1 degree Brix to 0.55 percent alcohol, grapes that average 20 degrees Brix at harvest would be expected to yield a dry wine (a wine in which all the sugar has been converted to alcohol) of 11 percent alcohol.

BRUT   Although lacking legal definition, the term *Brut* is typically used to denote Sparkling Wines that are relatively dry in overall flavor profile. Except for producers who make a wine labeled as "Natural," "Natur," or some other suggestion of limited or no sweetness, Brut wines are typically the driest wine made by the producer. And since virtually all Sparkling Wines and Champagnes have a small amount of residual sugar in order to balance the typically high acids of such wines, the perceived sweetness of wines labeled as Brut can vary significantly, but it is not especially high in any but the least expensive bulk bottlings.

CARBONIC MACERATION   A process in which grapes are placed whole into a fermenter. Their weight breaks the skins, beginning an intracellular fermentation. The resulting wines—typically reds—are intensely fruity, light-bodied, and meant for early consumption. Wineries will sometimes blend carbonic maceration wine with conventionally fermented wine to bring added fruitiness and freshness into the finished product.

CLONE   Almost all grape varieties experience small mutational changes over time that result in unique variations in the character of the wines they produce. Those changes are natural and do not result in the creation of a new variety, yet the differences are of such magnitude that wineries go out of their way to choose clones that will give them the style of wine they prefer to make. In both Sauvignon Blanc and Chardonnay, for instance, there are clones referred to as "Musque" that produce wine with much more flowery aspects than the majority of clones of their varieties. Some varieties, of which Pinot Noir is the most obvious, are more given to the development of separate clones than others.

CLOSED-IN   Wines that are low in intensity but high in concentrated, correct character and that are expected to develop greater interest and intensity with age are described as closed-in. *Dumb* and *backward* are related terms, and, like *closed-in*, they are used when a wine taster senses that there is more to a young wine than it is showing in its first few years.

COMPLEX   Primarily used in a positive manner, this term is most often applied to wines of beauty and balance harmoniously combining many aroma and flavor elements. As such, complexity is an integral component of very good to exceptional wines, and the term is strongly positive unless modified by other words.

COOPERAGE   A barrel builder is a *cooper*. In today's wine industry, *cooperage* refers, somewhat confusingly, to any container for holding or aging wine, from oak barrels to stainless steel tanks.

CORKS AND ALTERNATIVE CLOSURES   As the result of studies that revealed the presence of TCA in some corks (see the next entry), the cork industry has been under enormous pressure on all fronts. Where once virtually every wine more significant than the cheapest jug wine bottlings were closed with natural corks, now a variety of closures is in use, and the cork manufacturers have finally begun to fight back. It may be too late, however. A very high percentage of wines meant to be drunk young are now closed with materials other than cork. One of the most popular is the old screw cap that we associate with those jug wines—only now it is known that these types of closures are basically inert and seal a bottle of wine more completely than cork. Screw caps also have the problem that the wines they close do not breathe and do not develop as naturally as wines with good corks. There have also been instances in which bottles with screw caps have caused the sulfur dioxide added to wine in small amounts at bottling to keep it from oxidizing to stay in the wine rather than reduce over time. There are two kinds of plastic closures, and they have their own problems. While attractive to wineries because they are cheaper than cork and do not cause corkiness, the solid form of plastic cork never forms a perfect seal and allows wines to oxidize over time. The extruded form of plastic corks forms a better seal but can occasionally add an unusual perfumed character to wine with extended usage. A new form of closure, a glass plug lined with silicone, is very attractive visually, but it remains limited in use. And all of these alternatives have arisen because the cork industry failed in its duty to provide good corks. Chances are that the alternatives are here to stay and that some or all of them will improve their performance over time.

CORKED/CORKY   We expect corks to do their jobs and protect the wine from going bad in the bottle. Some corks, however, impart their own flaws to wine because they are carriers of a chemical compound known as TCA (2,4,6-trichloroanisole). The aroma of a corked wine is unmistakable in its aggressively moldy, sometimes old oyster shell pungency, and it can totally overwhelm any wine. Less intense levels of corkiness may not totally destroy the wine but will knock down its desirability. It was long thought that corked wines occurred in something like 2 percent of all bottles, but studies in the last decade or so have suggested that TCA could be affecting as much as 5 percent or more of wines under cork. As a result, a number of alternative closures have come into use, including plastic corks, corks that are ground into tiny pieces and chemically treated to eliminate TCA and then glued back into shape and returned to bottles with screw caps. It is worth noting that TCA can occur in wines for reasons other than cork taint and also that other compounds with related off-putting characteristics can also occur in wine. The cork industry, hurt by its failure to do anything about the problem even though it has been a known concern for decades, has finally changed the way it processes corks and has reduced the incidences of corkiness to somewhere closer to 1 percent.

CRISP   A tactile sensation somewhat akin to hardness but less imposing, crispness is generally the result of high levels of acidity relative to other balancing aspects. Wines that are low in measured pH can also be crisp; and, in general, the lower the pH, the higher the acidity. But one cannot rely on measurements to determine "crispness" because it is something experienced while tasting.

CUVÉE   In its various uses, *cuvée* is a term referring to an individual batch of wine. One sees the term on wine labels usually with a further designation, typically to identify that there is something special about the wine in the bottle. The term has no legal definition, however, and because it refers to a batch or lot of wine, it is simply a term with proprietary uses. In France, some vats are called *cuves*, but there is no similar usage in California. The term has also been used as a substitute for a vintage date, but even in that usage, it has no legal meaning.

DECANTING   The process by which wine is poured slowly and deliberately from the bottle into another container before serving. Most often, the process is carried out with older wines that throw a sediment in the bottom of the bottle during aging and must be decanted in order to leave the sediment in the original bottle. There is a decades-old debate in wine circles about the wisdom of also decanting young wines for the purpose of letting them breathe in the expectation that aeration will allow them to open up. Recent studies suggest the practice yields no change in the wine, but the belief persists nonetheless that decanting young wines does make a difference.

DESSERT WINE   Not surprisingly, such wines are generally meant to be consumed postprandially. As a legal definition, the term applies to wines whose alcohol content is 17 to 24 percent by volume and whose alcohol was, in part, obtained by adding either brandy or neutral spirits to lower-alcohol wine. In wine parlance, dessert wines can mean anything sweet, often late harvest, but also produced through techniques like drying on mats in the vineyard or in other hot places. For such wines, typically no alcohol is added, and the wines can range in alcohol from 7 to 17 percent or above.

DRY   An old expression in the wine business is "Think dry and drink sweet." It generally refers to the notion that consumers always claim to prefer dry wines but in actuality will invariably prefer a wine with a bit of sweetness to one that is totally dry. As a result, we see a continuing debate over the use of terminology to describe sweetness in wines with the result that wineries, lacking any legal restraint, are known to call wines dry when they are not. Dry, in absolute terms, means that the wine has been fermented to the point at which it no longer carries any fermentable sugars. In fact, wines of that total dryness usually measure 0.1 percent sugar. Most trained wine tasters begin to perceive residual sugar (the sugar in the wine after fermentation) at about 0.5 percent, although that level varies from taster to taster and from wine to wine. The majority of table wines, both red and white, are essentially dry. It is not unknown, however, for some wines to wind up with very low but intentionally less than totally dry levels of sugar. Wines in the range of 0.3 to 0.5 percent residual sugar may not taste sweet, but they can and usually do taste fruitier than if they were totally dry. Lately, the makers of Riesling, a grape that seems often to benefit by being made with sweetness, have struggled with definitions of sweetness that can be put on labels. They have come up with a complex formula involving both sugar and acid levels, and a set of definitions that includes the term *medium dry*, which means slightly sweet.

EARTHY   This term covers a lot of ground and can mean anything from a pleasant, rich earthiness of loamy topsoil to the unpleasant, rotting-grass earthiness of the compost heap, to the funky, burnt smells associated with several unwanted sulfur compounds. Context is everything in understanding its meaning.

EN TIRAGE Sparkling Wines are aged in the bottle during the secondary fermentation stage. This time spent *en tirage* (the French term means "in drawing" and refers to the removal of wine from the barrel) keeps the wine in contact with the dead yeast cells and adds a rich, toasty, sometimes-creamy aspect to the best sparklers. Depending on the wine, and often reflected in its price, Sparkling Wines can be kept on the yeast from twelve to eighteen months for everyday brands and to eight to ten years for very fancy bottlings.

ESTATE BOTTLED Once meaning that the wine in the bottle was grown and vinified at the estate, this term now means that the grapes were grown anywhere within the designated appellation under the control of the winery and were turned into wine at the winery.

FERMENTATION Fermentation, the complex chemical reaction in which sugar is turned into alcohol through the work of yeasts and enzymes, is what turns grape juice into wine. It is typically carried out in a closed container that can be as small as a glass jug or as big as a tank holding tens of thousands of gallons of grape juice. The process generates heat, so most winemakers control the temperature by circulating cooling agents within the jackets of their stainless steel fermentation tanks or by placing the fermentation barrels in a cold room. It is also possible to remove the wine from the tank and to pass it through a heat exchanger to lower its temperature. The choices of fermentation vessel, yeast strain, and fermentation temperature all have significant impacts on the quality of the wine. The cooler and longer fermentations are typically intended to produce lighter, fruitier, fresher wines with lively aromas. Hotter fermentations are more often reserved for fuller-bodied reds and are intended to extract flavor and complexity. See also a more extended discussion of fermentation in the chapter "How Wine Is Made."

FIELD BLEND Though now a somewhat infrequent practice in California, it was not unusual a century ago to plant vineyards to several varieties of grapes thought to be complementary to one another. These field blends were harvested, fermented, and bottled together, producing a single generic wine. Some of the old field blends still stand today, and those that do remain are often oriented substantially to varieties like Zinfandel or Petite Sirah.

FILTRATION A process of removing yeast cells and other particles from wine after fermentation by passing the wine through a screen of sorts meant to remove suspended matter.

FINING A technique of clarifying wine by introducing various agents that precipitate to the bottom of the tank or barrel, carrying suspended particles with them. Both filtering and fining are intended to produce stable, clear wines. And while clarity is still the goal for most wines, it is not unknown for a few Chardonnays and the very occasional Sauvignon Blanc to be bottled with some solids still in suspension and thus having a somewhat hazy appearance. See also "How Wine Is Made" for extended discussion of filtration and fining.

FLORAL   Possessing the aromas of flowers. Typically, white wines such as Riesling, Muscat, and Gewürztraminer have floral characteristics, as do some Viogniers and Roussannes. And there are clones of both Sauvignon Blanc and Chardonnay that are known to have floral characteristics.

FREE-RUN JUICE   The juice that flows out of the wine press when the skins are broken but before the grapes are pressed hard is called *free run*. Typically, this juice is full of fruit and has few harsh components, thus making it more significant for white wines than for reds. Many Rosé wines are also made from free-run juice of red grapes bled off the skins and then removed from skin contact quickly enough to yield a pink tint to the juice. This process, called *saigné*, can also be used to make white wines from red grapes such as Vin Gris and Blanc de Noirs (although it is typical for California Blanc de Noirs to be as pink in color as French Rosé Sparkling Wines.

GENERIC WINE   Any wine whose name is part of a general category or type, such as European place names (Burgundy, Chablis, Chianti, Champagne) or type categories (Blanc de Blancs, Claret, Rosé, Sherry). Many of the old generic names have now gone out of use because they can no longer be used for legal reasons.

GROWN, PRODUCED, AND BOTTLED BY   This term is used by a producer that does indeed grow, produce, and bottle its wine. The rules for "produced and bottled by" apply here as well. "Estate bottled" is a similar term.

HAZY   There was a time when hazy-appearing wines were considered to be flawed. Most of the causes of those then-unwanted hazes were problems of one sort or another, but today's winemaking is so technically advanced that one rarely sees a hazy wine except when the winemaker intentionally leaves some of the grape solids in the wine. Moreover, wineries that intentionally produce wine with noticeable haze will stir the wine in the barrel to keep the solids in suspension. The desire is to produce a wine with more character by keeping fruit solids in contact with the wine. Chardonnay is the variety most likely to have a hazy appearance; the rare but occasional Sauvignon Blanc will also have a hazy appearance. A slight haze in a wine, particularly if it carries the words *unfined* or *unfiltered*, is no cause for alarm, but loss of clarity may be an indication of a flawed wine.

HOT   Wines high in alcohol that tend to burn or prickle the palate and nose are called "hot." Some tasters decry any noticeable amount of heat in their preferred wines, while others are willing to accept a certain amount of noticeable alcohol in exchange for the greater intensity of such wines. The operative theory is that grapes left longer on the vine and harvested at higher sugars produce more intense wines. It is a perfectly fine theory up to a point; for us, that point is reached when the hotness of the alcohol gets in the way of the wine's flavors even when the wine is consumed with complementary foods.

LATE HARVEST   Lacking specific legal definition, wineries are free to call any wine "late harvest." Usually, however, they reserve the term for wines that were picked with unusually high levels of sugar in the grapes and that have been bottled as sweet wines. While it is not unusual for wines dubbed late harvest to carry notations of sugar in the finished wine and even some discussion of the process by which the high picking sugar was attained, there are no requirements that such wines be harvested late by the calendar and no requirement about the levels of sugar at picking or the levels of sugar in the finished wines. Many wines, especially white wines called late harvest, achieve their high levels of sugar through the action of Botrytis (described earlier) on the grapes, but sugar can also be concentrated by simply letting the grapes hang on the vine until dehydration concentrates the sugars.

LEES   After fermentation, there is typically a modest but noticeable amount of particles in suspension, most of which will, over time, drop to the bottom of the fermentation vessel. These leftovers, much of which are dead yeast cells, are easily separated from the wine by moving the wine to another container or from barrel to barrel in a process called *racking*. But there are times, in the making of Sparkling Wine in particular but also for some other wines (Chardonnay is the most notable), when the wine is not removed from the lees and, instead, is allowed to age in contact with them. Some wineries will even stir up the lees to increase the amount of contact with the wine in a process called *battonage*. The reason for aging wine on the lees (you will also see the French name *sur lie* or *sur lies* or some odd combination like *sur lees*) is that the wine will often pick up an extra dimension of character that could be described as toasty or roasted grains from the process, and there is the further expectation that "on the lees" aging can produce a creamier texture in the wine.

MALOLACTIC FERMENTATION   The acidity in wine is composed of many types, one of which is malic acid. In wines from cool to cold growing areas, the level of acidity is often high, and the proportion of malic tends to be an increased proportion of that acidity. It is possible to reduce the overall acid level in wine by allowing or encouraging the malic acid to change into lactic acid by means of a bacteria-based fermentation—separate and apart from the wine's alcoholic fermentation. Not only does malic acid convert into lactic acid, but also the wine gains a softer, smoother texture because lactic acid is rounder and richer. It is not unusual for most high-acid red wines and for dry whites such as Chardonnay to undergo malolactic fermentation. The practice, however, is not universal, and some wineries that prefer the higher-acid approach will not put its wines through malolactic fermentation.

MERITAGE   In the early days of California winemaking, and basically up to the 1970s, wines labeled as Cabernet Sauvignon could contain as little as 51 percent of that variety. This rule affected all varieties, but when the rule was changed to 75 percent at the same time as the introduction of so-called Bordeaux blending grapes (Merlot, Cabernet Franc, Malbec, and Petit Verdot), it became impossible for wines that were intentional blends that were close to the blends of Bordeaux to carry any varietal name. Wineries began making up proprietary names like Phelps Insignia and Cain Five, and then a group of wineries got together and decided that a common name for wines that were blends of traditional Bordeaux varieties was needed. To help bring recognition to their efforts, they staged a naming contest and chose the name Meritage, which is intended to rhyme with *heritage*. But, to use the name, a winery had to join the "Meritage" family, and several producers, including those whose proprietary names for their Bordeaux blends had become well established, never signed on. The term can cover reds using the varieties mentioned and also whites using a combination of Sauvignon Blanc and Semillon.

MÉTHODE CHAMPENOISE   For years, this term has been applied to Sparkling Wines made in the manner of Champagne. Still wine is placed in the bottle together with a small sugary addition to begin its second fermentation, during which time the sugar is converted into alcohol and carbon dioxide. With the wine left in the same bottle to age, the bubbles go into suspension, thus giving Sparkling Wines their sparkle. At the same time, the aging of the wine in the bottle with the dead yeasts adds personality to the wine. There is now a large brouhaha in European trade talks that may prevent California wines from using the term in the future if they are to be imported into Europe. While all this may seem a little silly, it is true that Sparkling Wine made in Europe other than in Champagne long ago gave up the term and now refer to the *méthode traditionelle*.

MINERALITY   One way to describe minerality in wine is to suggest that the wine tastes of stones, chalk, flint, or other hard objects found in the ground. That is a useful approach, and the proponents of minerality as a good thing will argue that minerality is part of the "terroir" of the wine. And so it is for good wines that actually have a minerally terroir contribution, but the term is too often also applied to wines that are lacking fruit and winemaking characteristics and wind up shallow and stiff.

MUST   The unfermented juice produced by crushing or pressing the grapes.

OAK AGING   Wine is often aged in contact with oak (and infrequently with other hardwoods), both to add to its aromas and flavors directly and also to produce a richer, fuller texture. The extent to which the oak changes a wine depends on many factors, the most important of which are the form of the oak used, the length of time spent in contact with the oak, the age of the oak, the source of the oak, and the way in which the oak was treated in preparation for its use. Most oak influences are derived as the result of the aging, and for Chardonnay and a few Pinot Noirs and Sauvignon Blancs, fermentation occurs in oak barrels that are approximately fifty-five to sixty gallons in size. Less expensive wines can gain an oak-aged character by the insertion of oak chips in wine stored in large and typically neutral containers. And it is also possible to derive oak-aged characteristics with the use of long boards (staves) inserted into the larger vessel. Oak made into barrels is heated (mostly with fire) in order to bend the staves into the barrel shape, and thus the wood comes with varying levels of toasty character depending on the extent to which the flames stay in contact with the wood. Regardless of which type of wood structure is used, the longer the wine stays in contact with it, the more it acquires an oak-aged character. Some wineries use very large vats made of oak with the intent to acquire a certain richness but to limit the contribution of oak to the wine's aromas and flavors. The use of older barrels also limits the oak-derived character. Most oak in wine vessels comes from France or the United States, but there are oak, and other wood, barrels produced also in Slovenia, Hungary, and Russia.

OILY   Wines with a round, slippery tactile impression on the palate, typically caused by a combination of high glycerin and low acid, are described as oily. Many of the best Chardonnays and late-harvest wines have this characteristic, and, in and of itself, it is more often a positive than a negative.

OLD VINE   In the 1970s, when wineries realized that wines of special character could be derived from vines that had been long in the ground, this designation was applied almost entirely to wines made from vines planted in the pre-Prohibition era. There is, however, no legal definition for the use of the term, and because vines begin to reduce the crop they grow after twenty years, it is not unusual to see the term applied to wines from what would seem to be relatively young vines. Many wineries specify how old their vines are, and the ones that do almost always have very old vines of fifty to one hundred years in age. Like "Reserve," which also has no legal definition, "old vine" can mean whatever the winery wants it to mean.

ORGANIC   In order to be labeled "organically grown," the most common designation in the organic hierarchy, the grapes must have been grown in a vineyard that is certified to have been free of chemical fertilizers, pesticides, and herbicides for three years as certified by the California Certified Organic Farmers (CCOF). Organic grape growing involves the uses of natural fertilizers, nontoxic weed control, and the introduction of beneficial insects to control unwanted pest populations. It is also possible to produce organic wines, in which the antioxidant sulfur dioxide is not added at bottling or during aging. Such wines typically have shortened life spans, and even the most ardent biodynamic producers use sulfur dioxide to protect their wines. There is an open debate as to whether organic wines have improved taste profiles, but there is little debate that they are earth-friendly.

OXIDIZATION   Wine is a surprisingly fragile commodity. Left to its own devices, it will change character in a hurry, which is why winemakers have for centuries gone to such lengths to protect it from spoiling. Aside from wine's willingness to turn into vinegar (wine is the half-life of vinegar and, left to its own devices, will turn into vinegar over time), table wines easily lose their most positive characteristics with long exposure to air. Oxidation—also sometimes called "sherrification" or "maderization" after two products that achieve much of their character by being allowed to interact with air—results in the loss of fruit, the darkening of color, the increase of volatile acids in the wine, and a change of character into one that is often associated with sherry or sometimes cut apples that have been left out for days. Except for those few vinous products intended to be made with exposure to air and the occasional step in the making of fresh table wines that are helped by a brief exposure to air, oxidation is not beneficial; when a table wine becomes oxidized, it is usually thought to be deficient.

PHYLLOXERA   Tiny aphid-like creatures that will attack the roots of and eventually kill off European grapevines of the family *Vitis vinifera*. Phylloxera became widespread in Europe and the United States in the late nineteenth century, and after much experimentation, it was found that native American grapevines were not susceptible to phylloxera. The result is that most *Vitis vinifera* in the world is grafted onto native American rootstock.

PRODUCED AND BOTTLED   This indication on a wine label means that 75 percent of the wine in the bottle was produced from start to finish in one winery.

RACKING   Racking is the process of moving wine from one container to another during the winemaking and aging cycle. It is done both to change the aging vessel, often from tank to barrel, and typically to remove the wine from the sediments that have formed at the bottom of the container. This labor-intensive process also aids in clarifying the wine and can be augmented by or even replaced by filtration, fining and centrifugation.

RESIDUAL SUGAR   A measure of the unfermented grape sugar in a finished wine, residual sugar is typically expressed as a percentage of volume. While fruit, oak, and glycerin can all contribute to the perception of sweetness in wine, it is residual sugar that is the most significant reason that a wine tastes sweet. See also the definitions here of *dry* and *sweetness* for related discussions.

ROUND   This wine taster's term describes completeness of flavor and smoothness of texture as well as the absence of angularity or other intrusive tactile sensations on the palate.

SOFT   Wines that are low in acid or tannin, and often both, have a comfortable, sometimes low-vitality feel on the palate. *Soft* is not a pejorative term, but it is most likely to be applied to wines that are more appropriate for immediate drinking than for aging. It is also possible for wines to be soft at their hearts but tannic at the same time; while such wines are likely to offer a few years of aging potential, their inner softness argues against long-term age worthiness.

SPRITZY   Wines with modest degrees of pinpoint carbonation are described as spritzy; *petillant* is a related term. Small amounts of bubbles in lighter white wines and Rosés, especially those that contain a touch of sweetness, usually come as added enhancements. Spritz in red wines or full-bodied whites is typically less welcome.

SUR LIE   Wines aged "sur lie" are kept in contact with the dead yeast cells and other sedimentary matter that remain when the fermentation is completed. It is a common practice in making Chardonnay and Sauvignon Blanc.

SUSTAINABLE AGRICULTURE   Absent the kind of rigorous standards and certification processes required of wineries and vineyards that would label themselves as either biodynamic or organic, the term *sustainable agriculture* tends to mean earth-friendly, noninterventionist practices that enable the land to continue to serve and persevere. We like the definition "to take from the earth what it can sustainably provide."

TANNIN   The puckery substance found primarily in red wines and at low levels in a few whites. It is derived primarily from grape skins and also grape seeds and stems, and the barrels in which wine is aged. It also can be added to the wine in the form of tannin powder. Tannin is part of a wine's structure, and it aids in the longevity of red wines by serving as a protector of fruit, although it can also add a bitter edge to the finish. Winemakers often speak of soft tannins, or long-chain tannins, as providing structure with less of the harsh, alum-like character than harder tannins. Ultimately, the best red wines are those in which tannin balances fruit and acid in such a way as to add a sense of spine to the wine yet are not so excessive that they rob the wine of drinkability and last far longer than the wine will age.

TART   Acidity is part of the taste of wine and part of the balance equation that makes wine interesting. It keeps wine fresh and vibrant, but, in excess, it can become excessively sour, with green pineapple and lemony characteristics that take over. We expect tartness in dry whites and in Sparkling Wines, but a wine that tastes overly tart when consumed by itself is often just the ticket with foods that bring it back to balance.

TERROIR   Wherever grapes are grown, they produce unique results based on a variety of factors, not the least of which is the site from which they come. Site-induced character in grapes is called *terroir*, and there is a school of thought that a wine without unique terroir cannot be a great wine no matter what it tastes like or how much you like it. We tend not to belong to that school, but we do recognize the special, differentiable character that shows up in wines from place to place. Indeed, an early attribution of site-induced character in California wines was the concept of "Rutherford Dust" that attaches to the wines of that area. Modern winemaking, with its increased emphasis on ripe fruit and rich oak, can reduce the impact of the land on the finished wine, but it is the rare wine that attains great character without also expressing something of the site where the grapes were grown.

TOASTY   Toasty smells and flavors in wines are derived from the oak barrels in which the wines are aged, and from contact with dead yeast cells and other sedimentary matter following the completion of fermentation. This quality is thought to be attractive in Chardonnay and Sparkling Wines.

TOTAL ACIDITY   Acidity in wine is made up of varying acids of which malic and tartaric are the most prevalent at harvest. The overall measure of a wine's acidity is known as its total acidity (TA). Although a wine's TA is not an indicator of quality in and of itself, it does give us an idea about the wine's character because of acidity's role in providing balance and vitality to wine. In the most general of terms, dry whites can range from 0.5 TA to 0.8 TA, and they thus will range in textures and taste from soft and round to firm and tart. Reds tend toward the lower end of the scale, and they get their balance also from tannin. Sweet wines and Sparkling Wines typically have higher TAs, with some late-harvest bottlings and bubblies ranging up to and beyond 1.0 percent TA. An extensive, somewhat technical, highly instructive discussion of acidity in wine can be found on the Internet at www.wineperspective.com/the_acidity_of_wine.htm.

VARIETAL   Wine names in the United States are primarily focused on the name of the dominant variety in the wine's makeup. For years, such varietal wines needed only 51 percent of the named variety; but in the 1970s, when the wine boom hit and varietal names like Cabernet Sauvignon began to take on great importance to the consumer, the varietal content rules were upgraded to require at least 75 percent of the named variety. If the official name of the wine contains more than one variety, the wine must contain 100 percent of the named varieties. Most wines coming from Europe, especially those of France, Italy, and Spain, have tended to carry geographic names because their growing areas have rules that limit the choices of grapes that can appear under those place names. We have no such rules here, nor are there such rules in Argentina, Chile, Australia, or New Zealand—hence the predominance of grape names on those labels. The adoption of the name Meritage (see that entry) for wines that contain blends similar to those from Bordeaux was a direct response to the need to have an identifier for wines that contain blends of the varieties allowed in Bordeaux. As yet, we have no made-up names for blends that mimic the southern Rhône where over a dozen varieties are authorized.

VARIETAL CHARACTER   As simple as the concept sounds, and as widely used as this term is in wine descriptions, it is widely accepted that the varietal character of most grapes differs from place to place depending on soils and climate. It is said, for example, that Cabernet Sauvignon can be reminiscent of currants, black cherries, herbs, cedar, briar, and other lesser components; and it is true that the grapes, when well grown in France or California or Australia or Argentina, will have a tell-tale similarity. But there are differences, and when those differences become magnified by site as they do for Pinot Noir, for example, there ensure long and earnest debates about whether Pinot Noir must be as close to its French personality as Cabernet Sauvignon can be to its. Still, when wine discussions turn to varietal character, they are referring to some generalized standard around which most wines of the variety cluster.

VINTAGE DATE   A vintage date on a label of a California wine indicates that 95 percent of the wine in the bottle comes from the identified year.

CONNOISSEURS' GUIDE THEN AND NOW

THE NEWSLETTER IS BORN

Earl Singer and I (Charles Olken), a couple of San Francisco area wine lovers and tasting buddies, started the wine newsletter *Connoisseurs' Guide to California Wine* (www.cgcw.com) in 1974 because of the growing role that California wine was taking in our cellars. The wine writing of the day, both in the traditional press and in the growing wine press, was oriented mostly to European wine. Despite the increasing excellence of California wine and the expanding production coming from places like Napa and Sonoma, the established wine publications were way behind the curve. We asked a simple question: "Why isn't there a publication for California wine enthusiasts like us?" Not long thereafter, we accepted our own challenge to create one, and *Connoisseurs' Guide* was born.

It met with immediate critical acclaim and has been in existence ever since serving the needs of California wine enthusiasts for serious, authoritative analysis and evaluation of California wines and the local wine scene. At every step, *Connoisseurs' Guide* adopted policies for honest, bias-free, learned discussions and wine criticism. With visits to most wineries of the time and reviews of their wines, the *Guide* quickly became a staple in the wine press for its knowledge and its valuable guidance and commentary.

THE CONNOISSEURS' HANDBOOK SOON FOLLOWS

We soon realized that we were amassing a significant body of background knowledge as well. For example, our treatise on potential subappellations in the Napa Valley, published in 1976, has been cited numerous times as one of the seminal works that helped shape the existing AVA system now in place in the Napa Valley. With the recognition that there did not exist a complete California wine reference book, and borrowing on the earlier works of William Massee, and Hurst Hannum and Robert Blumberg in California, and of Alexine Lichine on a worldwide basis, we created *The Connoisseurs' Handbook of California Wine*. Working with friend and fellow wine writer Norman Roby, we brought the book into existence in 1979. Through four major revisions and eleven updates, the *Handbook* stayed in print for over twenty years and sold almost four hundred thousand copies. When it exited the scene shortly after the millennium, nothing took its place. Now, almost a decade later, we at *Connoisseurs' Guide to California Wine*, based on the information gathered in our monthly publication, have given birth to a new and more complete California wine book.

While we never set out to become the definitive word on California wine, we did fully intend to be comprehensive and authoritative. To that end, we developed and implemented a tasting and research methodology that we expected to bring accuracy to our written words while eliminating any chance of bias. This methodology was based on several principles that have stood the test of time in the wine-writing field and that have now allowed us to write this latest book with full assurance to our readers that we measure our words passionately and carefully, that we observe strict rules and procedures that guarantee neutrality and open-mindedness to the wines and wineries that cross our paths, and that we listen and think and research before we write.

OUR TASTING AND RESEARCH METHODOLOGY

The *Connoisseurs' Guide* methodology begins first with the notion that there is no one universally superior palate. As a result, from the very beginning, all of our wine evaluations have been done by panels of experts whose knowledge and tasting acumen are widely recognized. Our tastings are private, by invitation only, and include other members of the press, members of the wine distribution trade, and winemakers (who are never allowed to taste their own wines). A panel typically consists of five members, including *Connoisseurs' Guide* staff, and the panel is asked to judge only two flights of eight to ten wines per day. All wines are tasted blind, and the tasters know only the variety being tasted. They never know which wineries are present because the labels are covered and not revealed until the wines have been tasted, the discussion held, and the individual preference rankings collected. Only then are the wines identified. All wines that are to be recommended highly to our readers and all wines with notable flaws are retasted as a matter of policy before we publish. The references to wine evaluations and ratings in this book are drawn directly from our tastings at *Connoisseurs' Guide*.

We adopted this rigorous methodology from the very outset, and it was not all that unique at the time. Now, many publications openly admit to tasting wines at the wineries with the labels showing or in large blocks at sponsored tastings. In our opinion, that procedure leads to grade inflation, and while *Connoisseurs' Guide* is known as the stingiest of all the critics when it comes to awarding our rankings, we take pride in only recommending wines to you that we would purchase for ourselves.

Our research for this book has also followed a rigorous path. While wineries were contacted directly to ascertain insider information about their production levels, acreage, and varietal distribution, and every entry in the book has been written as a compilation of the most important segments of the information gleaned from the wineries, the subsequent descriptions of winery styles and levels of winery success are uniquely our own and are drawn from our independent examinations of the wines as they have shown themselves in our blind tastings.

THE INTERSECTION BETWEEN
BOOK AND NEWSLETTER

Wines vary from vintage to vintage, and in that beautiful, inescapable fact lies the raison d'être for the existence of wine periodicals. A book like this one is like a program at a stage play or even a baseball game. A program tells the readers about the players, the field of play, the rules, the hidden meanings in the author's words. But only the action on the stage or on the field, and the subsequent reporting of it, tells us what we have experienced. A wine book tells us about place, grapes, and producers; discusses alternative strategies; and even lays out the general direction for each of the wineries and their typical levels of success based on past performance. It does not tell us if today's performance or today's result on the field will measure up.

When one tastes wine blind for evaluation, one generally knows only the name of the grape and possibly the vintage and the place from which the grapes came, if that knowledge is intended as a frame for the tasters. For example, at the famous Paris tasting of 1976, the experienced professionals in Paris were told only that they were tasting French and California wines made from the same grapes—Chardonnay in the first group and Cabernet Sauvignon and its Bordelais compatriots in the second. Their background knowledge about grape and place are what brought them to that tasting, and that same mass of background information, focused here on California, is what this book is about.

The individual evaluations of wine—in our case, mostly newly released wines as they come to market—are the business of the newsletter. That is why wine books like this one are published and updated every several years, while *Connoisseurs' Guide* is published every month. It is said that you cannot tell the players without a scorecard, and this book gives you place, grape, and producer. When one then looks at and evaluates individual wines, we start our descriptions with the factual data of grape, place, producer, and vintage. But, when we delve into analysis and ranking, we go beyond the reference material and provide current, firsthand descriptions of the new wines. We could not produce *Connoisseurs' Guide* without the knowledge that is delivered in this book, and we could not have written this book if we had not tasted hundreds of thousands of wines and studied them, their origins, and their journeys from grape to bottle. They are part and parcel of the same continuum, but because each new wine is different from its previous vintage and from the vintage before that and the vintage before that, wine lovers read both books like this one and periodicals like *Connoisseurs' Guide to California Wine*.

AN INVITATION TO SAMPLE *CONNOISSEURS' GUIDE* AND TO STAY IN TOUCH

We intend to publish periodic updates to this book through the newsletter's Web site. Please go to www.cgcw.com/book to register for our added commentary on the world of California wine and to receive your free, complimentary access to *Connoisseurs' Guide to California Wine*. If you are not a subscriber to *Connoisseurs' Guide*, simply register with your functioning e-mail address and the password "guidebook." No purchase, beyond that of this book, is necessary to receive the periodic updates to the book, and no public use of your registration will ever be made or permitted outside of the book and the newsletter. We have never done so in thirty-five years, and we are not going to start now.

WINERY INDEX

GENERAL INDEX

Cycles Gladiator, 322
Cyrot, Danielle, 267

DaKine Vineyard, 135
Dalla Valle, Gustav, 200
Dalla Valle, Naoko, 200
Damskey, Kerry, 108, 323
Daniels, John, 205
Dappen, Duane David, 200
Davenport, Bret, 352
Davids, Bob, 365
Davies, Hugh, 260
Davies, Jack, 260
Davies, Jamie, 260
Davis, Guy, 113
Davis, Jill, 133
de Brye, Alexander, 125
de Ianni, Sal, 277
de Latour, Georges, 8, 182
de Leuze, Norman, 285
De Loach, Cecil, 126, 113
De Loach, Christine, 126
De Loach, Jason, 126
de Villaine, Aubert, 220
Dean & Deluca, 215
Dehlinger, Tom, 114, 121
Deis, Ken, 210
Delicato Family Vineyards, 391
DeLorimier, Dr. Alfred, 114
Demostene, Dave, 154
Dervin, Ludovic, 238
Diageo, 176, 182, 222, 248, 270, 305, 320, 336
DiGiulio, Marco, 215
Disney, Diane, 265
Disney, Lilian, 264
Dizmang, Eva, 211
Dizmang, Larry, 211
Domaine Alfred, 335
Domaine Chandon, 240
Donnelley Creek Vineyard, 73
Doobie Brothers, 102
Doré, Dick, 358
Dorman, Stewart, 98
Doumani, Carl, 270
Doyle, Susan, 136
Drash, Mike, 230
Drew, Jason, 73
Drew, Molly, 73

Drip irrigation, 19
Drummond, John, 130
Dry farming, 19
Duckhorn, Dan, 75, 205
Duckhorn, Margaret, 75
Duncan, Bonny, 81
Duncan, Ray, 81
Dunn, Randy, 243
Durell Vineyard, 129, 137, 300
Dutton Ranch Vineyard, 129, 136
Dutton, Steve, 116
Dyson, John, 164
Dyson, Kathe, 164

E & J Gallo, 136, 148, 230, 284, 352, 393
Easton, Bill, 374, 380
Edna Valley Vineyard, 340
Edwards, Merry, 120
Edwards, Michelle, 194
Edwards, Ted, 214
Eighteenth Amendment, 9
Eisele Vineyard, 178
Eisele, Liesel, 281
Eisele, Volker, 281
Emerald Bay, 321
Emerson, Keith, 123
Emmerich, Jonathan, 265
Endeavour Vineyard, 116
Estrin, Mark, 151

Failla, Anne-Marie, 209
Farrell, Gary, 101, 105
Farrell, Jane, 98
Father Junipero Serra, 4
Felten, Lori, 391
Felten, Steve, 391
Fermentation, 20
Fernandez, Elias, 263
Ferrell, Tom, 267
Ferrington Vineyard, 73
Fess Parker Vineyard, 302
Fetzer, Barney, 74
Fiddlestix Vineyard, 176
Field, Walter, 377
Filtration, 21
Fining, 21
Finkelstein, Art, 283
Firestone, Adam, 357

Novak, Jack, 266
Novak, Mary, 266
Novella, 337
Novitiate Winery, 301

O'Dell, Patrick, 278
O'Neel Vineyard, 135
O'Neill, Jeffrey, 285
O'Riordan, Jane, 374, 380
Oak barrels, 24
Oetinger, Matt, 307
Officer, Mike, 106
Ohio, 4
Ojai Vineyard, 350
Old Hill Vineyard, 150
Olive Hill Estate Vineyard, 102
Oliver, Lily, 207
Oliver, Reg, 207
Olivet Lane Vineyard, 140, 145
Orfila, Alejandro, 400
Organic Viticulture, 15
Ortman, Chuck, 338
Ostini, Frank, 359
Oswald, Hugo, 79

Paicines General Store, 318
Pallini Vineyard, 300
Pällman, Christina, 120
Palomino grape, 3
Papapietro, Ben, 143
Paraboll Vineyard, 80
Paras Vineyard, 248
Parducci, Harry, 161
Paris Tasting of 1976, 192, 195
Paterson, Jeffrey, 304
Paulsen, Pat, 162
Pebley, Terri, 399
Pedroncelli, John Sr., 145
Pellegrini, Robert, 145
Pellegrini's Vineyard, 140
Pellier, Pierre, 393
Penpraze, Jim, 115
Perelli-Minetti, Antonio, 284
Pernod Richard, 238
Perry, Al, 252
Perry, Bruce, 143
Peterson Vineyard, 159
Peterson, Joel, 150

Peterson, Richard, 228
Petit Verdot, 43
Petite Sirah, 43–45
Phelps, Bill, 120
Phelps, Chris, 273
Phelps, Joseph, 120, 224Phillips, David, 392
Phillips, Michael, 392
Phylloxera, 8
Physiological maturity, 19
Pinot Blanc, 45
Pinot Meunier, 46
Pinot Noir, 46–48
Pinto Gris/Pinot Grigio, 45–46
Piper Sonoma, 127
Pisoni Vineyard, 143, 146, 157, 309, 316, 324, 327
Pisoni, Eddie, 324
Pisoni, Gary, 324, 326
Pisoni, Jeff, 324
Pisoni, Mark, 324
Pisoni, Jane, 324
Pocai, Libero, 181
Pochan, Sebastien, 161
Poetry Inn, 194
Pon, Bernardus (Ben), 318
Poole, John, 400
Porter, Bernard, 195
Porter-Bass Vineyard, 103
Pourroy, Pierre, 307
Pressing, 20
Pressler, Elizabeth, 207
Priest, Jon, 208
Primitivo, 48
Pritchard Hill, 190, 196
Prohibition, 9
Purisima Mountain Vineyard, 351

Quail Creek Vineyard, 302

Racke International, 115, 151
Racking, 21
Rafanelli, Mark, 100
Ramal Vineyard, 105
Ramey, David, 133, 148, 153
Ray Teldeschi Ranch, 106
Ray, Martin, 10, 304
Ready, David, 142

Terlato Wine Group, 100, 153, 193, 232, 258
Testarossa Vineyard, 301
The Connoisseurs' Handbook of California Wines, ix
The Narrows Vineyard, 75
The Wine Group, 296, 298
Thompson Vineyard, 359
Thompson, Clarborne, 335
Tina Marie Vineyard, 181
Titus, Philip, 284
Tofanelli Vineyard, 241
Tolmach, Adam, 350, 362
Tolmach, Helen, 362
Torres, Marimar, 137
Touquette, Benoit, 219
Toyon Vineyard, 176
Trader Joe's, 15
Transcontinental railroad, 3
Travers, Bob, 233
Travers, Elinor, 233
Traverso, Sergio, 304
Trefethen, Gene, 276
Trefethen, Janet, 276
Trefethen, John, 276
Trefethen, Katie, 276
Trellises, 18
Trentadue, Leo, 160
T-Rex Vineyard, 78
Trinchero Family Estates, 211, 238, 377
Trio Vineyard, 114
Troquato, George, 297
Truchard Vineyard, 246
Trujillo, Michael, 225, 263
Tubbs, Alfred, 192
Turley, Helen, 146
Two Buck Chuck, 15
Two Sisters Vineyard, 100
Tychson Cellars, 213
Tychson, Josephine Marlin, 213

University of California at Davis, 55
Unti, Mick, 161

Valdez Vineyard, 145
Van der Kamp Vineyard, 103, 296
Van Staaveren, Margo, 109
Van Steenwyk family, 333

Vare, George, 230
Venge, Nils, 258, 280
Ventana Vineyard, 302
Viader, Delia, 280
Vianna, Elizabeth, 194
Vignes, Jean Louis, 4
Vine Hill Ranch Vineyard, 209
Vineburg Vineyard, 155
Vineyard Brands, 341
Vino Farms Vineyard, 142
Vintners Club, 150
Viognier, 56–58
Virnig, Jeff, 256
Vista Verde vineyard, 318
Vivier, Stéphane, 220
Vogelzang Vineyard, 363
Volcano Ridge Vineyard, 72
Volk, Ken, 343
Volstead Act, 9
Vosti, Laurence, 285

Wagner, Charlie II, 325
Wagner, Charlie, 189
Wagner, Chuck, 189
Wagner, Lorna, 189
Wappo Indians, 170
Ward, Richard, 259
Wathen, Bill, 358
Watson, Ridge, 324
Watson, Tom, 324
Weir, Ernie, 218
Wendt, Henry, 147
Wendt, Holly, 147
Wente, Carl, 310
Wente, Karl, 8
Wente, Philip, 304
Wetmore, Charles, 291
Wetzel, Hank, 100
Wetzel, Harry, 100
Wetzel, Maggie, 100
Wildwood Vineyard, 130
Wiley Vineyard, 73
Williams, Betty, 352
Williams, Burt, 163
Williams, Chris, 162
Williams, Jennifer, 266
Williams, John, 214

Production Management: Michael Bass Associates
Text: 11.25 / 13.5 Adobe Garamond
Display: Adobe Garamond and Perpetua
Printer and Binder: Thomson-Shore, Inc.

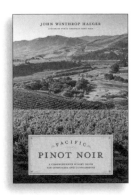

JOHN WINTHROP HAEGER

Pacific Pinot Noir

A Comprehensive Winery
Guide for Consumers and
Connoisseurs

496 pages, 7 x 10", 4 maps
paper 978-0-520-25317-9

STEVE HEIMOFF

A Wine Journey along
the Russian River

296 pages, 6 x 8", 20 b/w photographs,
1 map
paper 978-0-520-26811-1

STEVE HEIMOFF

New Classic Winemakers
of California

Conversations with
Steve Heimoff

292 pages, 6 x 9", 27 b/w photographs,
1 map
paper 978-0-520-26791-6

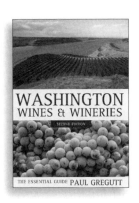

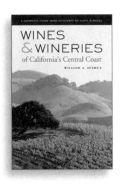

PAUL GREGUTT

Washington Wines
and Wineries

SECOND EDITION

392 pages, 7 x 10", 57 b/w photographs,
7 maps
cloth 978-0-520-26138-9

WILLIAM A. AUSMUS

Wines and Wineries
of California's
Central Coast

A Complete Guide from
Monterey to Santa Barbara

376 pages, 6 x 9", 51 b/w photographs,
6 maps
paper 978-0-520-24437-5

For more UC Press wine titles visit www.ucpress.edu/go/wine